University Planning for Canadians For Dummies

D0744829

Know Your Post-Secondary Options

You can:

- ✔ Decide between universities, colleges, and technical institutes
- ✔ Take a year off
- ✔ Combine your schooling with military service
- ✔ Enrol in a co-op program
- ✔ Enrol in a distance learning program
- ✔ Go abroad to university
- ✔ Do part-time or full-time study
- ✔ Go to school later in life

You may be able to transfer from a college program to a university program, or from one university program to another. But be sure to check out the details about transferring credits before you apply — otherwise, you may lose some of your hard-earned credits.

Five Big Changes in the Canadian Post-Secondary System That You Should Know About

1. **The double cohort:** Two sets of high school students will graduate in Ontario in 2003, resulting in much greater competition for university spaces all across Canada.
2. **Private universities:** These new universities have different standards than publicly funded universities. One of the most notable differences is tuition, which will be much higher at these institutions.
3. **Sports scholarships:** Some Canadian universities now offer them.
4. **Technical institutes:** Many technical institutes are becoming recognized as universities.
5. **Community colleges:** Many community colleges are becoming viable options for higher education, as many of them have significantly raised their standards and become affiliated with nearby universities.

Big Mistakes in University Planning

- ✔ Ignoring your other options
- ✔ Applying to a university that you haven't visited (or haven't thoroughly researched)
- ✔ Ruling out going to university because of lack of money
- ✔ Making up stuff on your application
- ✔ Missing application deadlines
- ✔ Missing (or messing up) parts of your application
- ✔ Considering only the reputations of universities when deciding where you'll apply
- ✔ Putting your parents in charge

How to Pay for University

- ✔ Save your money the family way: RESPs, CESGs, trusts, and investments
- ✔ Find out if you will receive gifts and inheritances
- ✔ Work after school and during the summer
- ✔ Get top marks to earn scholarships
- ✔ Find out if you qualify for grants or bursaries
- ✔ Get a student loan
- ✔ Work part-time while you're in university

...For Dummies: Bestselling Book Series for Beginners

University Planning For Canadians For Dummies®

Cheat Sheet

Ten Good Reasons to Go to University

1. A university degree makes it much easier to get a job afterward.

2. A university degree is required for most executive positions, so you will be able to get a *better* job afterward.

3. University graduates earn more over their lifetime.

4. A university degree opens doors (and makes your parents proud)!

5. You need to go to university to get into professional schools.

6. A university degree gives you greater flexibility if you decide to change careers.

7. A university degree is recognized around the world, making it easier for you to go abroad to work.

8. You will learn how to think critically and question everything. You'll be able to concentrate on the topics that interest you the most, with some of the brightest people around. You'll learn, grow, and discover what you truly love to do.

9. You will have a terrific experience, which will probably be one of the best times in your life. You will meet people who will become — and remain — close friends.

10. You will accomplish something that will make you happier and more satisfied, and that will help you grow as a person.

Ten Not-So-Good Reasons to Go to University

1. To party.

2. To hang out with friends.

3. To meet the man or woman of your dreams.

4. To get away from Mom and Dad without having to pay for your own living expenses.

5. To delay starting to work, or because you couldn't find a job.

6. Because trade schools are too expensive.

7. To milk the university's bandwidth for all it's worth, downloading pirated movies and software.

8. To get credit cards. (For some reason, credit card companies will gladly give cards to university students, but it becomes much harder to qualify for them *after* you start working.)

9. Because your parents told you to.

10. Because you couldn't think of anything else to do.

If these reasons sound familiar, you'd better read this book!

...For Dummies: Bestselling Book Series for Beginners

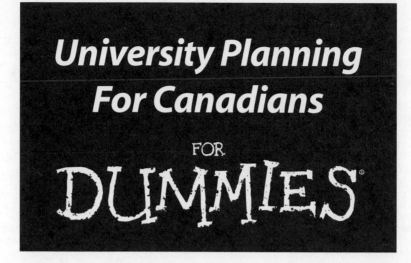

University Planning
For Canadians
FOR DUMMIES®

by Caryn Mladen, David Rosen,
and Pat Ordovensky

CDG
BOOKS
CANADA

Best-Selling Books • Digital Downloads • e-Books • Answer Networks • e-Newsletters • Branded Web Sites • e-Learning

◆ Toronto, ON ◆

University Planning For Canadians For Dummies®

Published by
CDG Books Canada, Inc.
99 Yorkville Avenue
Suite 400
Toronto, ON M5R 3K5
www.cdgbooks.com (CDG Books Canada Web Site)
www.idgbooks.com (IDG Books Worldwide Web Site)
www.dummies.com (Dummies Press Web Site)

National Library of Canada Cataloguing in Publication Data

Mladen, Caryn, 1965–
  University planning for Canadians for dummies

Includes index.
ISBN: 1-894413-31-8

1. Universities and college — Admission. 2. College choice — Canada. 3. Student aid — Canada.
I. Rosen, David, 1961- II. Ordovensky, Pat. III. Title.

LB2350.5.M48 2001   378.1'61'0971   C2001-901545-3

Printed in Canada

1 2 3 4 5 TRI 04 03 02 01

Distributed in Canada by CDG Books Canada, Inc.

For general information on CDG Books, including all IDG Books Worldwide publications, please call our distribution center: HarperCollins Canada at 1-800-387-0117. For reseller information, including discounts and premium sales, please call our Sales department at 1-877-963-8830.

This book is available at special discounts for bulk purchases by your group or organization for resale, premiums, fundraising and seminars. For details, contact CDG Books Canada, Special Sales Department, 99 Yorkville Avenue, Suite 400, Toronto, ON, M5K 3K5; Tel: 416-963-8830; Email: spmarkets@cdgbooks.com.

For press review copies, author interviews, or other publicity information, please contact our Marketing department at 416-963-8830, fax 416-923-4821, or e-mail publicity@cdgbooks.com.

For authorization to photocopy items for corporate, personal, or educational use, please contact Cancopy, The Canadian Copyright Licensing Agency, One Yonge Street, Suite 1900, Toronto, ON, M5E 1E5; Tel: 416-868-1620; Fax: 416-868-1621; www.cancopy.com.

is a trademark under exclusive license to CDG Books Canada, Inc., from Hungry Minds, Inc.

About the Authors

Caryn Mladen and **David Rosen** are business consultants, writers, and educators whose work focuses on the high-tech and financial industries. They teach at the University of Toronto and the Bell Centre for Creative Communications, the high-tech division of Centennial College. They were editors-in-chief of America Online's member magazine, *Multimedia Online*, and continue writing for various publications. They are education editors and columnists at CanadaComputes.com, Canada's largest and most-respected high-technology newspaper. Their previous bestselling books include *Making Money with Multimedia*, which has been used as a textbook at universities and colleges, and *The Canadian Computer Handbook*, soon to be in its third edition. This is their sixth book together as a writing team.

Before devoting her life to consulting, education, and writing, Caryn was a lawyer specializing in technology and intellectual property. She continues to speak at conferences and appear in the media as an expert on intellectual property and the high-tech industry.

David has been teaching at the university, college, and corporate levels for more than 20 years. He is an internationally known expert in high-tech marketing and frequently consults for corporations and government agencies around the world.

The late **Pat Ordovensky** is the author of *College Planning For Dummies*, from which this book is adapted. Pat first became an expert in dealing with college officials and administration during his student days at Ohio University.

One of the highlights of Pat's career came in 1992 when the College Board invited him to a convention of admission officials — from Harvard's Dean Richard Fitzsimmons on down — and asked him to speak at the concluding session about what he learned from the meetings. He always recalled that speech with the words, "You think this book is irreverent?" Beginning in 1992, Pat was a freelance writer based in Sarasota, Florida. During that time he coordinated the annual USA Today hotline and the All-USA Academic Team programs, which honour outstanding college and high-school students. He wrote three other books on getting into college and paying for it: *Opening College Doors* (co-authored with Robert Thornton), *USA Today's Getting Into College*, and *USA Today's Financial Aid for College*.

Dedication

To my parents, Mary and Tom, who constantly help me learn the most important lessons in life. To David, who forced me, kicking and screaming, to become a writer. To Steve, whose furry comfort and demands give me the perspective I need. And to Mark, who researched for me, kept me sane and joyful, and put up with me patiently and lovingly through the writing of this book. Thank you!

— Caryn

To my parents, Mary and Ivor, who made me realize the truth behind Mark Twain's revelation that as he got older, his parents seemed to get smarter. To Marnie, whose nurturing love and understanding are more than any harried writer could ask for. And to Hank Reardon, who continues to show me how to keep climbing mountains, despite my fear of heights. Thanks.

— David

To Cathy, Michael, Ree, John, and Farley.

— Pat

Authors' Acknowledgements

While we're happy to accept all the glory for the writing of this book, any complaints should be directed toward other people, and we wanted to list them all here.

Okay, we're joking. If you have any complaints, they should be directed at us, because we could not have had greater support while writing this book. First, thanks go to our editor, Melanie Rutledge. She is surprisingly positive for someone who has to work with us and we give her great credit for her precision and for her patience. She obviously has some terrific backup at CDG Books — after all, we've worn down scores of people in our time — so thanks to Joan Whitman, Robert Harris, Marnie McCann, and Christiane Coté as well.

Special thanks must go to the officials of the many universities, colleges, and organizations who gave us their time, answers, and insights. There is absolutely no way we could have pulled together the materials in this book if we had not been generously granted access to their extensive knowledge base. There are a few individuals we would like to mention specially. Gregory Marcotte, Executive Director of the Ontario Universities' Application Centre, and Michelle Leblanc, Publications Coordinator at the OUAC, for granting permission to include their application form in the book. We'd also like to thank Victoria Collins, Director, University Relations, Memorial University of Newfoundland, and Ivan Muzychka, at Canada Wide Information System, for generously agreeing to let us include a screenshot from Memorial's Web site. Similarly, permission to use a screenshot from Grant MacEwan College's site was granted by Melanie Busby, Director, Marketing & Communications at Grant MacEwan, and Trevor Beck, Electronic Communications Manager. Finally, Lil Blume, a professor at Mohawk College, in Hamilton, Ontario, reviewed the manuscript for technical accuracy. She did a terrific job.

Finally, we'd like to thank the next generation of university students for making all the work that went into this book worthwhile. All through the researching and writing of this book, we've been thinking about you — our nieces and nephews and cousins, friends and children of friends, and people we don't even know. We've been thinking about how we can make university a more enriching experience for you, knowing that it all starts with going to the right university. It helped to have real people in mind, knowing that what we wrote would have an impact on your lives.

If it does have an impact, please let us know. Give us your ideas for the next edition of this book — praise or criticism, it all helps to make the material better! Let's keep the cycle of information growing, because we are all here to educate each other.

— *Caryn and David*

Special thanks must go to the college officials who allowed me, as an education writer, to visit their offices, talk to their staffs, and listen while they made decisions. They include Lee Stetson at Penn, Cliff Sjogren (then at Michigan), Ted O'Neill at the University of Chicago, Ron Pomona, and others I've probably forgotten. The ever-candid Barry McCarty at Lafayette College has taught me more than anyone else about the nuances of giving away money. And Rob Thornton, a vice president at Teikyo Post University with whom I collaborated on an earlier book, gave me valuable insight into the mind of a college admission officer — which he once was.

And finally I must thank my wife, Mary Ann, for happily forgetting the idea that when we moved to Florida I would work less and play more.

— *Pat*

Publisher's Acknowledgements

We're proud of this book; please send us your comments through our Online Registration Form located at www.hungryminds.com

Some of the people who helped bring this book to market include the following:

Acquisitions, Editorial, and Media Development

Editorial Director: Joan Whitman

Associate Editor: Melanie Rutledge

Copy Editor: Kelli Howey

Production

Director of Production: Donna Brown

Production Editor: Rebecca Conolly

Layout and Graphics: Kim Monteforte, Heidy Lawrance Associates

Proofreader: Pamela Erlichman

Indexers: Caryn Mladen and David Rosen

Special Help: Susan Johnson

General and Administrative

Hungry Minds, Inc.: John Kilcullen, CEO; Bill Barry, President and COO; John Ball, Executive VP, Operations & Administration; John Harris, CFO

Hungry Minds Consumer Reference Group

Business: Kathleen Nebenhaus, Vice President and Publisher; Kevin Thornton, Acquisitions Manager

Cooking/Gardening: Jennifer Feldman, Associate Vice President and Publisher; Anne Ficklen, Executive Editor; Kristi Hart, Managing Editor

Education/Reference: Diane Graves Steele, Vice President and Publisher

Lifestyles: Kathleen Nebenhaus, Vice President and Publisher; Tracy Boggier, Managing Editor

Pets: Kathleen Nebenhaus, Vice President and Publisher; Tracy Boggier, Managing Editor

Travel: Michael Spring, Vice President and Publisher; Brice Gosnell, Publishing Director; Suzanne Jannetta, Editorial Director

Hungry Minds Consumer Editorial Services: Kathleen Nebenhaus, Vice President and Publisher; Kristin A. Cocks, Editorial Director; Cindy Kitchel, Editorial Director

Hungry Minds Consumer Production: Debbie Stailey, Production Director

◆

The publisher would like to give special thanks to Patrick J. McGovern, without whom this book would not have been possible.

◆

Contents at a Glance

Cartoons at a Glance

By Rich Tennant

Fax: 978-546-7747
E-mail: the5wave@tiac.net

Table of Contents

Part IV: Please Report to the Financial Aid Office: Paying for University 175

Chapter 12: Shake Off the Sticker Shock (Remember, It Costs More in the U.S.!) 177

Introduction

Welcome to *University Planning For Canadians For Dummies.*
Getting into university — and finding the money to pay for it — is not
a mystery, although it may seem mysterious as you start looking at all your
options and discover confusing forms and perplexing processes. That's why
we wrote this book — to help you understand exactly what you need to know
to navigate your way into university with confidence. We explain how to:

- Find the university that's the best fit for you;
- Convince the university that *it* wants *you*;
- Pay for it (how could we forget this all-important concern?).

There's no mystery to it. No magic formula. Just the right information and
some good old-fashioned common sense. Ready? Okay, let's go!

About This Book

This book is organized so that you can pick it up and start reading anywhere.
It will make sense no matter where you start. It's a reference book. It has 24
chapters, each of which discusses a specific part of the university planning
process. If you'd like to read about filling out an application or applying for
financial aid, look up the topic in the index, find the page for that chapter, and
start reading. Each chapter covers one part of the process and is loaded with
valuable nuggets of information. The chapter on visiting a university campus
(Chapter 9, if you'd like to flip there now), offers advice on:

- Planning your visit
- Getting details from the admissions office and the financial aid office
- Talking to your future professors
- Getting real information from students
- Getting the feel of the university's town or city
- Finding housing options
- Figuring out what to do when you get home

There's nothing to memorize. Read what you need, mark it for future reference, and get on with your life. Feel free to take notes and to use that yellow highlighter — or whatever colour you like — to identify the most valuable information and make it leap out in the future. This book doesn't mind being marked up. That's why it's here.

You may be undecided about what kind of institution you want to attend after high school. Maybe you were thinking about heading off to Queen's University, where your parents went and where they have hinted they expect you to go. But now you're not so sure. There are so many options. You've always been interested in graphic arts, and you've heard about all sorts of well-respected multimedia and information technology programs at Sheridan College. What do you do?

University isn't for everyone. The post-secondary scene has changed today; there are a number of high-end colleges and technical institutes in Canada, often in the high-tech arena, that are considered on a par with many universities. They offer state-of-the-art education in their particular field, in one- to four-year programs. For some students, these post-secondary institutions are where they belong after high school. Well, this book is for you, too. Virtually all of the information in this book is useful for students considering attending that type of college or technical institute instead of university. There are many more trade schools and career colleges that use the same terminology, but their application procedures, teaching methodologies, standards, and overall positioning in the educational world is quite different from that of universities. This book covers those colleges and institutes that operate in a similar manner to universities.

For the sake of convenience (and to keep our word count at a reasonable level), we use the word *university* throughout this book to refer to both universities and the top-level colleges and institutes — although sometimes you'll realize from the context that we are referring to universities only. Whether you end up going to Queen's or Sheridan, this book is here to help you plan for either experience.

How to Use This Book

A novel, it's not. Just because you (or someone you know) paid good money for this book, don't feel obligated to read it from beginning to end. If you'd like to do it that way, fine. But it's not necessary. Look for the parts that interest you — the areas of university planning where you're confused or concerned.

Check out the table of contents or consult the more detailed index for topics of special interest to you. Once you start reading, you'll realize that planning for university can be a pretty convoluted process. Still, you can figure it out — with the help of this book!

As we said, getting into university is no mystery. It's actually very simple, once you know where to get the right information and understand how the process works. We're here to share our insights with the person who needs it most: you.

Who Are You, Anyway?

The word *you* appears in this book more often than any other word. (Okay, we meant that figuratively, so don't bother using some fancy computer program to count the number of *yous* in the book. There will be no prize awarded for showing us up on that point.) This book is written for you and addressed to you. And when we say "you," we mean the student planning for university.

Of course, people other than students should, and no doubt will, use this book. Some of these people are mentioned in the next section of this introduction. The reason they're reading it, however, is to help you, the student. So we're asking them to remember that you are the person whose future is on the line here — you're the one trying to decide where to spend three or four (or more) valuable years of your life.

Who Should Read This Book?

This book is not just for high school students gearing up to make the big decision. It's for all students, of any age, who may one day go to university. And it's for relatives and friends of such students who may want to help.

Elementary students

Yes, elementary school is the ideal time to start planning for university. You don't believe us? The earlier you start thinking about university and planning for it, the easier it will be when the time comes. Suppose that you're in grade 11 right now. Think about this: If you knew in grade 4 what you know now about, say, how important an *A* in math is, you may have adjusted your attitude toward the subject back then.

Grade 9 students

Grade 9 is essentially a turning point. It's when you start making decisions that show up on your university application and in later life. The university application provides a picture of everything you've done in high school. If you've started planning ahead, you'll have an edge on all your friends and classmates. And every little edge helps!

High school students

High school students will get the most out of this book. It helps guide you on the journey toward finding a university, applying to it, winning an admission, and paying for it.

Mom and Dad

We've heard countless horror stories about parents and kids getting into shouting matches over choosing a university. It can get even worse when it comes to paying for university. These tensions almost always arise because parents and kids don't have the information needed to make the right decisions. Well, we've tried to include the best, most relevant information for Canadian students and their parents, to help make sure all of you are on the same page.

This brings us to the subject of finances. As we discuss later in the book, it's never too early to start saving for a university education. Parents-to-be can set up a university fund to ensure their child's education is looked after. There are investment vehicles that, if made the most of, can pay for your child's university tuition and other costs, regardless of what school your child chooses to attend. We let you know all about your savings options in Chapter 13.

It's important for parents to work with their children from the very start to encourage them to achieve the best they can scholastically. Students with parents who expect positive results tend to achieve higher grades. When parents combine that with a supportive attitude, their children are more likely to be both happy and successful.

If you're a student, make sure that all the adults — parents and others — who try to influence your university decisions take a look at this book. If you're a parent, you might want to try a different approach than just telling your kid what to do. Instead, start off by handing your daughter or son this book, saying, "Read this, then let's talk."

Grandparents

If you're a parent, you've probably wondered why your own parents never spent as much on you as they do on your kids. You're not alone. A department-store clerk in a children's wear section that had a rack full of $200 jackets for two-year-olds was once asked who would spend this much money on a toddler's jacket. She replied quickly, "Grandparents."

Yes, grandparents can be the most generous of human beings. And if they'd like to direct some of that generosity toward their grandchildren's education, this book offers advice on how it can best be done.

Adults thinking about university

If you're past the traditional university age but thinking about entering university anyway, you've got lots of company. The over-25 crowd is the fastest-growing segment of the student population in Canada. There is no reason why you shouldn't plan just like the younger folks. Most of the advice in this book applies to students of all ages. The parts that are specific to mature students (that is, students over the ripe old age of 25) are even marked with a specific icon.

Anyone accepted to university

Congratulations! If a university has accepted you, you've figured out the application process. Or you've at least successfully coped with it. But you're probably wondering what to do next. If so, check out Chapters 19 and 20. But don't forget to give some serious attention to the chapters in Part IV — which focus on paying for university — because every university student has to be concerned about financing their education.

Who Should Not Read This Book

It's not good business for authors to recommend that people *not* read their published advice. But, let's face it, some people out there just don't need this book.

Anyone with a Ph.D.

If you've inhabited a university campus long enough to put Ph.D. after your name, you probably know more about how things are done than the rookies in the admissions office who are doing them. Put this book down and move on to the important stuff, such as accepting that Nobel Prize in physics.

Anyone who works at a university

Admissions officers, financial aid officers, professors, and others don't need to read this book. In fact, some may become offended that we've translated their jargon into English. Of course, the best of them will be pleased that we've streamlined the process for potential students.

How This Book Is Organized

This book has seven parts, each made up of a certain number of chapters. Each chapter covers a particular topic and is split into sections that look at specific issues within the topic. That's how it's organized; how you read it is up to you. Pick a part, a chapter, a section, whatever, and just start reading. Any related information is cross-referenced in the text.

If you're just starting your search through the vast sea of universities and options, and you don't know where to begin, check out Chapters 1 and 2.

If you know where you're applying, but you're in a tizzy about making the best impression at the admissions office, go to Chapters 10 and 11.

If you've heard hair-raising stories from friends about the trauma of applying for financial aid, and you're ready to chuck the entire process because you can't figure it out, this book is here to help. Read Part IV, and you'll realize that your friends are telling those stories because they *didn't* read this book. So there!

Part I: Crack Open the Book: Getting Ready for University

This part explains what you need to know to start planning for university. It outlines some important questions you should ask yourself about whether university is even the right place for you. If it is, Part I then takes you through the process of deciding when and where to apply. It looks at what you can do to become a more attractive university candidate when the time comes. The chapters in this part also help you deal with the massive amounts of information out there, and sort out what you can use from what you can do without.

Part II: Start Taking Notes: Finding the Right Universities

How do you narrow your choice down to three, five, or even a few more universities where you'll thrive as a student — and at which you stand a good chance of getting in? This part takes you through the process during your early and middle high school years and shows you how to collect all the information you need to successfully complete your university application.

Part III: Crunch Time: Getting into University

This part lets you in on what universities want to see from applicants, how to be as presentable as possible, and how universities judge your application. We also walk you through a typical application, so you know what to expect when the time comes.

Part IV: Please Report to the Financial Aid Office: Paying for University

These chapters offer plain, straightforward talk on figuring out how much money you need for university, where to get that money, and how to reduce your debt. We also talk about attending international universities, getting grants, loans, and scholarships, and alternative methods of paying for your education. It's financing made easy!

Part V: Dotting the "i"s and Crossing the "t"s: The Final Details

After you've applied and the universities have made their decisions, there is still work to be done. This part shows you how to do it.

Part VI: The Part of Tens

It's now a tradition in these ...For Dummies books that the last part gives you lists. For some reason, perhaps the David Letterman influence, they're all supposed to be lists of ten. They're important, useful reading that didn't quite fit elsewhere, or that summarizes topics from all over the rest of the book. No extra charge. They're kind of fun, too.

Part VII: Appendixes

What would a book on planning to attend Canadian universities be without a section on the universities themselves? Incomplete, that's what. Alphabetically ordered on bright yellow can't-miss-it paper, our "Directory of Universities and Colleges" gives you key information about tuition costs, class sizes, size of campus, and other important facts. Even if you've figured everything else out, it's a great resource on its own. And after you've pored over the directory, check out the other appendixes in this section on financial aid sources and useful university-related Web sites.

Icons and Conventions Used in This Book

At times in this book, we refer to grade 12 as your final year of high school. This is fine and dandy for students in all provinces and territories except Ontario. To our Ontario readers, we know you'll have no problem just mentally tacking on an extra year whenever this comes up. Of course, if you're graduating after 2003, you won't have to add a thing.

This icon indicates some good advice to remember. Time to reach for your highlighter.

When you see this icon, read the text carefully. It's something that could blow up your application for admission or financial aid or something that could damage your university experience.

More than a "Tip," this icon represents an important concept about university planning. It's information we recommend you tuck away, because you may want to come back to it as you get further along in your own planning process.

If you're past the traditional university age, then make sure that you check out the paragraphs marked with this icon; they contain information especially for you.

This icon highlights information relating to financial matters.

This icon points to key pieces of information to keep in mind as you plan for university. It may also signal a book or Web site we recommend you check out.

Where to Go from Here

Now you're ready to take on the questions, concerns, fears, and hype of getting into university. This book equips you with the right stuff. So turn to the topic that interests you most and, as you read, mark it up to your delight. The more ink you put on these pages, the more successful you'll be. Trust us!

Part I

Crack Open the Book: Getting Ready for University

City School of Interpretive Dance

"Believe me Miss Wilcox, this isn't the type of school you can just waltz into, pick up a degree and waltz out of again."

In this part . . .

*I*f you're ready to begin looking for a university, start reading here. This part assumes you know nothing about universities except that they are schools you can attend after high school. The chapters in this part set the stage to help you make those first important decisions about university. We explain what to think about when considering going to university and how to plan ahead to be the best applicant you can be.

Chapters 3 and 4 explain some of the big changes taking place in Canadian universities today, and give you tips about other schooling options you may not have considered. Your years at university are an important part of your life. We want to help you get there prepared — knowing that you have weighed all the possibilities and chosen the path that is right for you!

Chapter 1

What You Need to Know about University

- -

- -

*Y*ou've probably heard all sorts of crazy stories about getting into university, and you're not sure you're ready to try. Reams of paperwork to fill out; trying to impress someone reading about you at a time when you feel your life is just starting; a multitude of campuses to visit; big decisions to make. Plus, the trauma of baring your soul (not to mention your parents' bank accounts) on a financial aid application.

And, before any of that, somehow you must find a few universities you think you'll like. Where do you look? In those thick, cumbersome directories? On the Internet? In that collection of brochures in your high school counsellor's office? Even if you already know a few universities you may want to attend, how do you know if you can get in? Are you going to be able to afford tuition? Your mind is probably starting to boggle already.

Relax. You *can* avoid the stress. If you take your university search process one step at a time, you'll find it much easier than you first imagined.

Keep in mind that you're the buyer here. You want something — an education and a few years of personal growth — that universities are selling. However, in Canada, more people are applying for places at universities than there are places to be filled. The demand for spaces outweighs the supply. (Okay, there *are* a few spaces in certain universities that sometimes go unfilled. However, this is rare and happens only in programs that interest very few people.) If you want to get into the program of your choice at the university of your choice, competition is likely to be fierce. It's up to you to become the sort of person that any university in Canada would jump at.

The best way to ensure you are one of those that gets accepted is to prepare. And, hey, you're doing that right now. See, you've taken the first step. Feel better? Now remember to breathe normally and we'll take each step slowly. This way, finding your university can even be fun! Okay, maybe not fun, exactly — perhaps "enjoyable" would be a better word. Anyway, let's get started!

What Is a University?

A *university* is a *post-secondary school* (a school you go to after high school) that awards *undergraduate,* and sometimes *post-graduate, degrees*. You take a post-graduate degree when you've completed your undergraduate degree and are so dazzled by a particular subject you learned that you want to learn more. In this book, we talk mostly about undergraduate degrees, the first step. Universities give these degrees to people who successfully complete a prescribed series of courses, seminars, term papers, and other academic stuff and earn high enough marks to satisfy professors that they know what they're talking about. The degrees can be standard three-year degrees or so-called *specialist* or *honours degrees,* which require four years of effort.

We provide a list of Canadian universities in Appendix A, "Directory of Universities and Colleges," at the back of the book. This is a great resource, with contact information and basic facts about each university, that will be useful when researching your choices.

Universities, colleges, and institutes

Post-secondary schools come in all shapes and sizes, with different purposes, philosophies, and capabilities. Here's a basic run-down:

- **Universities:** These are schools where you can get an undergraduate degree. A university may also have a *graduate school* offering post-graduate degrees, while colleges and institutes generally do not. There are 51 Canadian universities listed in our Directory of Universities and Colleges, with at least one located in every province.

- **Colleges:** In the United States, *college* is the generic word for *university,* but it means something different here in Canada. Canadian colleges offer *diplomas* or *certificates* in a given subject. Diplomas typically require a two-year study commitment, while certificates can be achieved in as little as a few weeks. Colleges can be general or specialized. For example, *community colleges* offer a broad range of courses, while so-called *career colleges* tend to focus on a particular field, usually administrative in nature.

✔ **Institutes:** These are schools where you learn a specific skill. It could be technical or clerical in nature, such as word processing or bookkeeping. It could be service-oriented, such as bartending, hairdressing, or computer repair. Students obtain a certificate upon completion of a course, which can take anywhere from a few days to two years to complete. Just like colleges, there is a wide range of options, standards, and quality levels in the hundreds of institutes across Canada.

As recently as a decade ago, people who went to universities might have looked down on people who went to colleges or institutes. But times have changed. The boom in the technology industry has altered the way people think about getting — and valuing — an education.

People who want to work in the technology field often choose the more hands-on learning opportunities and shorter period of study offered by colleges and institutes. Several of these, such as Sheridan College, in Ontario, or the Emily Carr Institute of Art and Design, in British Columbia, have excellent reputations in their respective fields. Indeed, top companies comb these and other colleges and institutes for graduates, and even students still enrolled there, hoping to lure them into immediate employment afterward.

It's not just people in technology who have changed their perceptions of colleges and institutes. Observing the tight job market for university graduates, many students opt to use their post-secondary education to gain the skills they need for a specific career.

The quality of education you get from colleges and institutes varies greatly from school to school. Top colleges and institutes rival universities in such areas as computer design. But there are also fly-by-night operations, so it pays to research your choice extensively before paying for it.

Most companies looking to hire future executives, however, expect to see a university degree on an applicant's résumé. Universities are intended to provide a well-rounded *higher* education. They are intended to teach you how to think, instead of simply how to do a particular thing. If you don't have a university degree when applying for a job you hope will take you far, you'd better be able to show some relevant experience to make up for it.

Public universities and private universities

Public universities are operated and subsidized by the provinces in which they're located. The costs associated with teaching are covered by both the provincial government and tuition fees.

Private universities are a relatively new phenomenon in Canada. They charge higher tuition fees, but may also rely on endowments and fundraising campaigns for money. The Ontario government recently passed legislation to allow organizations to apply to become private universities. We could see the first of these schools up and running as early as 2002. We tell you more about private universities in Chapter 3.

Several other types of private universities exist — and have existed for years. These are degree-granting schools that offer education with a particular slant — for example, religious. These universities comply with the appropriate provincial legislation with respect to the granting of degrees; however, their focus is different from traditional universities. In this book, we focus on secular (or non-religious) universities.

Canadian universities and American colleges

Let's face it: Canadians get a lot of their information from American media sources. From watching American television and news, Canadians often believe that the American justice system, health-care system, and even educational system are all pretty much the same as they are in Canada.

Well, there are a lot of important differences between the Canadian and American educational systems. Other than just the names used (Americans use "college" for pretty much any post-secondary educational facility, while we have universities, colleges, and institutes that are all quite different from each other), entry requirements for universities in the United States are very different from those in Canada.

American students must write the *SAT I*, a standardized three-hour test that attempts to encapsulate all the knowledge of a student into two marks. (*SAT* used to be short for Scholastic Aptitude Test. But the name went through so many permutations over the years, now it's known simply as the SAT.) American students must also submit an essay as part of their application, and interview with the school prior to acceptance. In Canada, you fill out the applications, send them in, and wait to hear from the schools of your choice. A lot easier, isn't it? You can supplement your credentials by choosing to write the SAT I or adding personal information, but it's not required and rarely requested. Nevertheless, sometimes those supplementary submissions can make the difference between a *yes* and a *no* from the university of your choice. See Chapter 11 for more on the application process in Canadian schools.

There are no single-sex universities in Canada, as there are in the United States. Some, such as Mount Saint Vincent University, in Halifax, Nova Scotia, started out as female-only schools and continue to have an extremely high female–male ratio. Others, like the Royal Military College, in Kingston, Ontario, were originally male-only bastions. Today, men and women are given equal opportunity to apply to all universities in Canada.

Open-admission universities

There is no guarantee that you can be granted admission to most universities in Canada. What, you thought this was going to be easy?

However, there are a few schools that offer "open admission" — they accept anyone with a high school diploma or the equivalent. One of these is Athabasca University, in Athabasca, Alberta.

Universities in other countries

Most Canadians who study at universities abroad do so in the United States. If you choose this path, you will likely face tuition fees and costs that are many times what you would pay in Canada. However, especially if you apply to a university that is not considered "Ivy League," you may find it easier to get into and even get financial aid from an American university.

Alternatively, you may wish to venture elsewhere — to the United Kingdom, Australia, or another English-speaking country, or to somewhere more exotic where the language, culture, and attitudes are different from what you find in Canada.

It may sound like an adventure, but there are a few barriers to overcome. Universities in other countries are often just as particular about their admission requirements as are Canadian universities. Even if your grades are not an issue, many international universities will grant admission only to someone who understands and speaks the language of instruction. Still, many international universities bend the rules for those who are in the process of learning their language. We talk more about going to an international university — and how you go about scraping together the money to pay for it — in Chapter 17.

The best source of information on international universities is the *International Handbook of Universities,* published by the Paris-based International Association of Universities. This guide contains descriptions of 4,000 schools in 169 countries, including a brief history, list of majors, and language of instruction. The text is updated every two years. The handbook can be found in the reference section of many libraries, or you can order it from Stockton Press, 15 E. 26th St., New York, NY, 10010.

Is University for You?

In this book, we focus on planning to attend a university. However, we know that part of the planning process is deciding whether or not a university is the right place for you to begin with.

A lot of students planning their university career don't even consider this question, but it's probably the most important thing you can ask yourself. University might be for you — but, then again, it might not. Or maybe it's something you should do after you've worked for a year, or travelled, or volunteered for an aid organization on another continent. Only you (and whoever is writing the cheques for your educational life) can decide.

Maybe you know exactly what you are doing. Perhaps you have your entire future mapped out, from high school through university and on to your intended career, where you'll live, and when you'll retire. Or perhaps you just have an idea of what you want to study.

Think about these issues before you decide whether to attend university:

✔ **Are you going to university just because it seems like the next logical step or because your parents expect you to go?**

Many students don't even consider other alternatives. There's a whole world out there, you know — take a look at your options before you decide. Those who do not know why they are studying tend to be ill-prepared for it. Think long and hard about the choices you are making and do that extra bit of research on every course you plan to take.

✔ **Do you want to go to university just because your friends are going?**

We call this following the path of least resistance. Your friends have already chosen a particular university, maybe one that's nearby, so you just follow the crowd and go there as well. But university is a time for discovering who you truly are — your strengths and weaknesses — warts and all. Think about what *you* really want first, not what your friends want. Trust us on this one: don't follow the crowd.

✔ **Are you going to university to get away from your parents?**

University is a perfect time to experience the initial freedom of adulthood in a relatively safe setting. But remember, there's a lot more to university than just getting away from Mom and Dad. You need to adjust to living with a whole new crowd of people and learn to take care of yourself, while entering a level of scholastic challenge higher than you've ever faced. Yikes! Meanwhile, there are temptations aplenty that could cause you to lose focus on your academics. It takes a clear head and a mature attitude to focus on your university career. So, if you don't have a driving passion for your studies and just want to get out from under your parents' roof, you might be better off working for a year, then hitting the books.

✔ **Do you know what you plan to do after university?**

You may not have much of an idea where your degree will lead. This isn't the end of the world — university should be a process of discovery. But, if you really want to fly airplanes for a living, studying Russian history at university probably won't get you any closer to your goal. You need to choose a course of study that is more in tune with what you want to do.

✔ **Are you going to university to get a degree that will lead to a higher-paying job or to train yourself for a specific career?**

These are perfectly legitimate reasons to go to university. However, you may want to investigate your chosen profession a little before you spend three or four years training for it. Many people form their ideas about certain professions — especially medicine and law — based on how they are depicted in popular media and are cruelly disappointed when they discover how vastly different the professions are in real life.

Your answers to these questions will probably change over time, as you learn more about your intended career and yourself. So think often about why you want to go to university. Your answers will help immensely in your search.

University Is for Me — Now What?

Fantastic! You've made your first big decision. Now that you know you're in for the long haul, here are still more questions to ask yourself:

Can you get in?

More than 80,000 people applied to an Ontario university for admission into first-year studies for the 2000/2001 academic year, while fewer than 50,000 became registered. Does that answer your question? Not by a long shot.

Higher, but not necessarily brighter

While high school averages have risen steadily over the years, the students hitting those high marks aren't necessarily any smarter than those who came before them. High schools recognize that certain university programs have higher entrance standards and have taken to "boosting" their students' marks to help them get in. This makes it more difficult for admissions officers to decide whom to accept.

Universities are now engaging in more sophisticated selection processes to ensure they get the very cream of the crop.

You don't know how many of these 30,000 students who didn't end up registering chose to go elsewhere — to a university in a different province, to an international university, or to a college or institute. Some of them may even have taken a year off. You also don't know how you would do in competition with today's applicants.

You do know (because you've been reading this chapter) that university entrance standards are at an all-time high, and getting steadily higher. The more elite university programs — where demand is highest — expect to see students with high school marks averaging 90 percent or better. For the school year starting in September 2000, you needed a 90 percent average to make it into the commerce program at Queen's University. Computer and electrical engineering programs at the University of Waterloo are filled with students sporting grades in the low 90s or higher.

What does this mean for you? Did we mention that you should start planning in grade 4? You have as good a shot as anyone else at making it in to your top-choice university if you prepare early enough — and this includes working on raising your marks as soon as possible.

It's not the end of the world if you don't get into your chosen university. You'll probably be put on the Waiting List with a bunch of other kids who didn't get in either. But it's not so bad. If enough students decide they don't want to go to that university in the end, you may get your chance to say yes. Or you can reapply next year. Plus, there are other universities that may accept you — what about your second and third choices? Turn to Chapter 19 for more on dealing with a Waiting List if that's where you find yourself.

The best option is to prepare yourself by getting the highest possible marks so that any university will accept you right off the bat.

Can you afford it?

Post-secondary education in Canada costs a base amount of approximately $6,000 per year if you live at home. If you want to go away to school, that number jumps to $12,000, which includes tuition, residence, meals, books, and other university fees. At least, that's what it costs the student. Make a beeline for Chapters 14, 15, and 16 to find out about creative ways to pay for this long list of expenses.

Your jaw may have hit the table after reading those amounts, but it's good to remember that it costs the universities and the provinces a lot more money each year to teach a student. Fortunately, Canadian students (and their parents) don't see all the costs. That's because Canadian universities are still heavily subsidized by the governments of the provinces they operate in. Having an educated population is considered a good thing by Canadian law-makers and by Canadian people. Educated people earn more money on average and pay more taxes over the long haul. Today's university graduates become tomorrow's political leaders.

Subsidized tuition is a good thing for Canadians applying to university. By contrast, one year at Harvard will set you back about $35,000 — and that's in American dollars! So breathe a little sigh of relief that you live in this great country, where education is considered a priority.

Still, $12,000 is not peanuts. For a four-year degree, that's $48,000 — plus inflation, plus other living expenses.

There are a bevy of scholarships, loans, and grants available to students who just can't pony up the dough. We won't kid you, though. Tuition costs are rising and available cash is dwindling. More than ever, it's important to plan ahead to make sure you can afford the investment.

Part IV is designed to help you determine exactly how much your university education will set you back, and how you can afford it.

Which university is for you?

This is a question only you can answer. We're not passing the buck here, and we have every intention of helping you find the best answer to this question. In fact, if you want to start answering this question now, jump ahead to Chapters 8 and 9, which deal with researching online and the all-important campus visit, respectively. Every university is different — sometimes in very obvious ways, sometimes in subtle ways — and only you can judge which is the best for you.

What is university life really like?

Have you seen the movie *Animal House?* How about the TV show *Beverly Hills 90210* — not the early shows, but the seasons after they graduated from high school? You have? Great. Well, university is nothing like that. The university experience is different for each person, but by and large students spend a lot of time reading, writing, going to classes, and doing labs.

There's definitely a social side to university. In fact, for some students there's almost nothing *but* a social side. These students tend to fail out or spend several extra years trying to eke out a degree. You probably don't want to be one of them.

There's a lot of opportunity to expand your horizons at university through student organizations, clubs, and sports teams. You can join a sorority or fraternity if you are so inclined, or form study groups to enrich your learning environment.

Your university experience depends on what you want to make it. Regardless of what you choose to study or pursue, you will probably make at least a few friends who will stay with you for many years — or your whole life. Be on the lookout!

Where to Go First: Information Sources

Okay, where do you start? Information about universities seems to be everywhere: Books, catalogues, brochures, Web sites, magazines — and how could you miss those brightly coloured promotional materials in your high school counsellor's office? How do you make sense of all this?

We start off with the people you should talk to and then move on to all the things you can read and use for research. Don't worry about trying to keep all the information straight in your head immediately. We revisit all of it in Chapter 7, and help you do the research in Chapter 8. For now, just start asking questions and looking around.

Counsellors

These lovely, caring people are often your first source for information about universities. After all, it's part of their job to inform high school students about their options following graduation, and to help those who are interested apply to post-secondary schools.

Good high school counsellors know as much about the university admission process as university admission officers themselves. The good counsellors go to admission officers' conventions, share the gossip, and speak the jargon. When they recommend that three of their students apply to Dalhousie, these counsellors are reasonably sure all three students will be accepted and will do well at this school because they know how Dalhousie operates. Poor high school counsellors know as much about the admission process as you. Maybe less.

Older students whose high school years are in the distant past don't have access to high school counsellors. That could be a blessing, because the older students don't face the risk of being misinformed by a poor counsellor spewing out bad advice. If you are an older student, you should drop in to the admissions office at a local university to chat about the kind of learning environment where you could be most successful. For best results, don't drop in cold — call for an appointment and come prepared with your list of questions.

If you're lucky and you have a good counsellor, rely heavily on her wisdom. This counsellor can accurately steer you to universities that are likely to be a good fit for you. The final decision, of course, is yours.

If you're unlucky, as many high school students are, use your counsellor only for essential tasks. And, hey, you're not all that unlucky. After all, you've got this book.

Teachers

All teachers have been to university. And they talk to other teachers who have been to other universities. They have a pretty good idea of what types of students fit well, academically and socially, and at which schools.

If you're a typical student, you have two or three teachers you highly respect who know you as more than just a kid in a seat. Don't be shy about asking them for advice. Good teachers are wise people. The ones who know you well can point you in some good directions.

Friends and family

You probably already know this advice. Older friends, siblings, cousins, and even parents who have gone through the process you're just beginning can offer first-hand knowledge of how it works from the student's perspective. Ask your siblings or friends who've gone to university to tell you about the real university experience that isn't part of the glossy brochure. If you have friends you trust who are in university, listen to their advice now.

University literature

Don't overlook those shelves in your high school counsellor's office and local library that contain promotional literature sent by universities. You can search through the materials for maps, fees, courses of study, the history of the university, its organizational structure, and much more. Some universities provide guides to the city where they're located, materials about housing, cultural activities, and even nightlife.

These brochures are created to recruit you. The pretty pictures of smiling students on landscaped lawns and good-looking faculty members in well-kept classrooms are designed to lure you in and grab your tuition money. Don't worry too much about the pretty pictures. Most of the literature provided by these universities includes the hard facts and details you need to figure out the costs of attending that particular school. Application requirements and actual application forms are included in the packages, too.

Ontario universities have their own centralized application process, so you won't find any application forms in literature from an Ontario school. We tell you more about applying to Ontario universities in Chapter 11.

Directories

Directories are a serious information source for students looking to attend an American university. But, here in Canada, we do things a mite differently.

Researching and comparing universities in Canada is a much easier task because there aren't nearly as many of them. As well, compiling information is more of a public matter because most Canadian universities and their admissions are administered in association with the governments of the provinces where they are located.

The directory that all the high school counsellors use is compiled by the *Association of Universities and Colleges of Canada (AUCC)*, whose Web site is chock-full of even more important information (www.aucc.ca).

Here is a list of useful directories:

- ✔ *The Directory of Canadian Universities,* from the Association of Universities and Colleges of Canada (AUCC), has everything you need to know about all universities in the country, from application procedures, tuition rates, and financial aid to housing and sports. Available for $39.95 from the AUCC itself, this is the directory used by most high school counsellors.

✔ ***SchoolFinder.com Directory 2001*** contains contact information for more than 600 universities, colleges, and career colleges across Canada, along with more detailed profiles of many of them. The types of schools profiled run the gamut from medical schools to institutes of cosmetology. Edge Interactive Publishing puts out this book, available for $34.95.

✔ ***The Student's Guide to Canadian Universities,*** edited by Christine Ibarra and Blair Trudell, gives the student's perspective on life at 48 universities across Canada. This directory explains a given university's reputation and offers testimonials from students themselves. They generalize about the hard facts such as tuition rates and application procedures, however. Available from Key Porter Books for $19.95.

✔ ***Canadian University Distance Education Directory,*** edited by Rose-Mary Wright, focuses on universities that offer distance learning. (See Chapter 4 for more on this option.) It's published by the Canadian Association for University Continuing Education and available for $29.95.

When you look through these directories, be aware that some information may not be accurate. Nobody's trying to mislead you, but some stuff can be out of date. After all, each directory is only as good as the information submitted by the universities and the information is as current as the last time each university updated its own listing. The directories get their data by asking the universities for information. Sometimes the staff at universities don't know the answers, or they get busy with other things. The result is that sometimes they overlook the request, so old numbers have a way of being repeated.

If you use the directories as a starting point, be sure to double-check the data that are important to you as you get further into your search.

Web sites

Much of the information available in the big directories can also be found through the mouse-and-modem route. Each university in Canada has an extensive Web site where you can find admissions information and details about courses and campus life. In many cases, you can even apply for university online.

There are some online search organizations that claim to be able to find the perfect university for you — for a fee. Don't bother with these guys. A couple of guidelines to follow as you surf the Web for information on universities:

✔ Don't pay any money to anyone claiming to run a search organization.

✔ Don't give anyone associated with one of these organizations your (or your parents') credit card number.

All the information you need to make an informed decision about the best universities for you is available free — electronically and on paper.

There are also organizations operated by the government or by students themselves that provide overviews of all universities across Canada or that focus on a particular university or even a particular part of a university. For the experienced surfer, the Net can be a valuable source of university information. Chat rooms, forums, bulletin boards, newsgroups, and e-mail are fantastic tools that you can use to talk to students, professors, admission officers, recent graduates, and others with first-hand knowledge of specific universities. University newspapers and online magazines are also valuable sources.

We tell you more about Web-based resources — and researching these resources — in Chapter 8. There's a list of them in Appendix C, "Useful Web Sites."

Computer programs

Some of the university directories come with software that offers the same information and works the same way as Web site searches. They instantly access the sites of the universities they profile and screen out universities that don't meet the criteria you've established.

The database and software is contained on a CD-ROM that comes with the directory, but you may also find CD-ROMs available for use at your school or local library. Of course, the computer programs have the same intrinsic drawback as the directories and Web sites: the information they contain is the information universities choose to submit.

What If You're Older?

Don't worry about it! Older students are wanted, too.

Of course, calling them "older" is a bit of a misnomer. At most universities, students applying to first year are considered mature at the tender age of 25. Certainly they are older than the students coming directly from high school — but not by much.

In fact, the traditional university age range of 18 to 24 is rapidly disappearing. More older students are appearing on campuses every year. They bring maturity and stability to the classroom and to campus life.

Chapter 2

Planning 101

When you start to think about university, two questions probably pop into your mind. The first question is, "Where do I want to go to university?" The second question is, "How do I know that the university will want me?" You may also wonder about a third question. That question is, "Can I afford the university of my choice?"

Finding university money has so many ramifications, and the money can be found in so many places, that this book devotes several chapters — in fact, an entire section — to the subject of getting money for university. But this is not one of those chapters. This chapter looks at *you*, the prospective university student, to help you with your first task: finding universities where you can thrive.

No one right university is out there waiting for you. When you start to look seriously, you'll probably find several, maybe dozens that you think could be right for you. Then you'll decide which three, or six, or ten of them to favour with an application.

How do you know that the universities of your choice will think you're a student they would like to have? Well, it's hard to be absolutely sure, but we're here to make the process a lot easier. If you know what universities want (and you will after reading Chapter 10), you can do everything possible to make yourself someone they want.

Like all good planners, you need to look ahead and start the university selection process as early as you can. If you have given some serious thought to finding a university and making yourself attractive to your choices, your application process will be an easy one. The trauma and stress will be for the *other* guys.

Planning may sound boring, but it's the key to succeeding at university.

Read This Book in Grade 4

How many kids in grade 4 buy a book on university planning? Your guess is probably right: zilch. Getting into university is not high on a nine-year-old's priority list, unless you're Doogie Howser M.D. reincarnated.

The most important thing about planning is to start early. You already know that planning is important in other parts of your life. The more time you have to walk somewhere, the more likely you are to get there on time. Grade 4 is a good time to start to plan for university because that's when most people start to think about what's important to them and to make decisions based on those thoughts.

When you get to high school, you'll find that what was important in grade 4 has been mostly forgotten. You have more mature priorities, and getting into university probably ranks right up at the top of your list. You know that a university will look at your entire high school record, from grade 9 on, and you know that you can do nothing to change the record that you've already got.

However, the decisions you made in grade 4 — and since then — have had a big impact on who you are right now. What if you knew in grade 4 what you now know in high school? Think how different things might be.

You'd know, for example, that a university would like you to have high grades in the toughest math and science courses. You'd be prepared to handle the enriched courses, but now you're just not ready for them. You shrugged off math and science years ago because doing other subjects seemed easier or because your teacher made all those numbers and chemical compounds sound b-o-r-i-n-g.

Then there's French. You stopped taking it as soon as you could, figuring everyone you know speaks English. Why waste your time on something you're never going to use? Knowing French would have looked good on your university application, and some universities that you really like happen to be French-speaking, but you know there's no point in applying to them because you couldn't understand a word the professors say. And, you know, you could have been fluent by now. You had a chance to know a whole other language in grade 4, but you missed out. If only you knew then what you know now.

Okay, so your nine-year-old sister doesn't care about reading this book. Be nice and share its advice with her.

If You're Not in Grade 4, Just Read Faster

If grade 4 is only a distant memory for you, don't despair. Regardless of when you start to think about university, at whatever stage of life you want to make yourself an attractive university applicant, a few simple facts can guide your decisions.

A university looks first at your high school record. A university wants your record to show that you took the toughest available courses and that you received top grades, preferably As, in those courses. You need to lay the foundation as soon as you can so that you do well in the tough courses. Challenge yourself. Work hard. Always do more than you have to do.

And, oh yeah — read this book faster.

If You're Out of High School

If your high school diploma has been gathering dust under your bed for years, you still have no reason to fret. Anything you do at this point won't change your high school record, but you can certainly make yourself an attractive university candidate.

Most universities enthusiastically welcome older students for the simple reason that older, mature people often make better students. They have been out in the "real world" and have a compelling reason to study. They are not there just because they didn't know what else to do; they chose to expand their horizons by getting a post-secondary education. They are making a big sacrifice: forgoing a paycheque to attend university. And they are almost always paying their own way.

Many universities consider your *life experience*, the practical education you have acquired from your work experience and other activities, as a supplement, or even an alternative, to your high school record.

About 24 percent of university students in Canada are 25 years of age or older. In the 1999/2000 academic year that was about 140,000 students, so, if you don't apply directly out of high school, chances are excellent that you won't be the only one at your university in the "mature" category.

Beginner Level: What to Do Early On

If you want to think about what's important before it really becomes important, here are a few steps to take as you approach those crucial high school years. Many of these steps are also good advice for high school students as application time nears.

Stay awake in grade 4 math

We know, we know, enough with the emphasis on math. But have we made our point? If you don't take math in your final year of high school, you cut yourself off from a lot of potential majors in university. Math counts not only in pursuit of a science or engineering degree. You also need it for economics and commerce, architecture, criminology, and a bevy of other fields of study.

And it's not good enough just to have barely passed. You want good grades in high school math, and we all know that getting good grades is difficult enough — even if you're well prepared. If you're unprepared for algebra and calculus because you slept through grade 4 fractions, your chances of doing well in these subjects are remote. We hate to repeat ourselves like this, but make sure that you have a thorough grounding in math. If you missed something in grade 4, go back and study it again.

If you slept through grade 4 math and don't turn yourself into an ace student by high school, you can torpedo your chances of getting into certain programs at university — even programs you might not think of as being "math-type" fields of study.

Unplug the TV

If pulling the plug is too hard, just turn your television off. If the rest of the family complains, let them have their way but find a place where you can't hear the TV. You don't need to swear off TV forever. Start off with cutting out just a couple of hours a day.

For those two TV-free hours, do something that actually requires some brainpower. You can do homework, of course. You can read a magazine, visit a Web site, or look up stuff in your CD-ROM encyclopedia that you need for a term paper. You can write something — maybe the term paper, maybe a diary entry. (See the sidebar, "Dear diary . . . ," later in this chapter.)

You can accomplish several good things this way. You can keep your mind from getting rusty. (You need a well-tuned mind for the challenges ahead.) And you can practise skills (reading, writing, thinking) that serve you well in those tough high school courses and in the tests and essays you must endure in university.

You can do all of these activities with the TV on, of course, but the experience isn't the same. TV has a way of quickly numbing all minds within the sound of its speakers. Did you know that your brain is more active when you are *asleep* than when you are watching TV? So just do it. Unplug the TV.

Empower yourself for two hours

We know we just mentioned that you can read a magazine or visit a Web site, but we want to clarify that point. Put down that comic book or computer gaming magazine — that's not what we meant, and you know it.

The point of those two hours is to stimulate your mind. There's so much fascinating stuff in the world, but if you simply look at, read, and do the same old stuff over and over again, your mind starts to get slower. What's worse, you become, well, less than fascinating.

So, grab *Scientific American,* or *Canadian Business* magazine, or the *Globe and Mail.* Search out Web sites that teach you about computer programming or that have a lively forum where people discuss politics. Whatever you do, turn off your Instant Messenger or ICQ. These are wonderful tools of communication but, during your two hours of self-empowerment, you really don't want to be interrupted with gossip from your pals.

Take the toughest courses

Take the toughest courses — the earlier the better. When you're trying to impress a university admissions officer, you want your record to show that you met (and excelled at) every academic challenge you faced. When you have choices earlier in life, choose the road that's hardest to travel. You'll thank yourself later.

Dear diary...

Keeping a diary is silly, you say? Who would ever want to read what you do every day in your dull life? You'll be surprised. You will.

A diary can do several things to ease the stress when university application time comes. Its most basic service is keeping your mind alert. For the time you spend entering each day's report, even if it's just five minutes, your mind is in gear and in less danger of sputtering when you need to work this divine muscle.

Your diary is a record of your life. The time will come when you will thank your diary for being there. Some specialized courses of study require more information from you than your high school transcript. When you apply to university you should send a supplementary letter listing all your relevant activities and the roles you played in them. Your memory will probably overlook a few things, but you won't have to trust your memory alone, because your written record doesn't forget.

For your diary to make its most important contribution, you must help. When you write in your diary, use whole sentences. Make sure that each one has a subject and a verb. Resist the temptation to just scribble stream-of-consciousness thoughts.

By keeping a diary you gain daily practice in writing coherently. That's a skill you need during high school English, history, and other courses, not to mention during high-pressure test situations.

Get a job

Working at a part-time job gets you out in the real world — and there are a lot of benefits to doing that. You learn skills that you won't learn in school. You learn the value of money, something that should be taught in school, but isn't. Depending on the job, you will also probably learn the importance of getting an education beyond high school, so that you can pursue a career instead of going back to your part-time job.

Your part-time job will also teach you about time management. You need to be adept at this throughout your life. It may come in handy sooner than you think, if, for example, you need to work while attending university.

Find something you like doing as early in life as you can. If a particular career interests you, find out if you can get a job where you can see the inner workings of the profession. Perhaps you can do some part-time filing at a law firm or volunteer as a candystriper at a hospital. Don't value your experience only by how much money you will earn. You can obtain valuable guidance through first-hand experience.

Sorry, all you budding Wayne Gretzkys

You know it's important to keep fit. Studies show that healthy, active students are more likely to get higher marks in school. While you *can* get money for scholastic excellence, for leadership activities, and for student involvement, you can count on the fingers of one hand the universities that will give you money for being a star quarterback or hockey centre.

However, this might be changing. It was decided at a recent university conference that universities could begin to offer sports scholarships to incoming students. These would be limited in amount, covering tuition only. Still, it's a step toward a more American approach.

Our advice is to check with each university you apply to about the availability of athletic scholarships.

Making money is an added bonus of working during your pre-university days. Socking away some cash will make the financial commitment less of a burden once you get to university.

Be exceptional

For the most part, you get into a university because of your marks. However, in some cases, students with less than stellar high school transcripts are accepted. Why? Because they are "exceptional."

Students that are in the marginal category for acceptance may be asked to supply supplementary information to show why they should be granted admission. (If you suspect that you may be in the marginal category, you should volunteer this information, as we discuss in Chapter 11.) In these cases, you need to show that you:

- Are a school leader.
- Are outrageously talented in a particular field (did you play the tuba with the local symphony?).
- Are involved in a wide range of extracurricular activities.

Any combination of the above might carry some weight at the admissions office, as long as you make the minimum requirements with your grades!

While everyone wants to be considered exceptional (that's what Mom and Dad have always said you are, right?), it's not worth sacrificing your marks in pursuit of this special status. Having high marks is far more likely to get you where you want to go. They should be your first priority.

Intermediate Level: Decisions You Need to Make

Somewhere around grade 9 or 10, you need to start thinking about university in specifics — about where you may want to go and why. If your sophomore year (that's grade 10, in case you're wondering) is already history, don't worry. Just think faster and act now.

The first thing you need to do is make a list of universities that may be right for you. In Part II, we show you how and where to start the university-finding process. But you can't very well make a list until you know what you want to put on it. And you may be mulling over some of those list items for months ahead of time. Don't worry about it. No decisions are needed yet. Just mull. See which way your feelings make you lean.

Stay or leave home?

Deciding whether you want to leave home is one of the first decisions you need to make. Are you ready to flee the nest and try flying on your own? Do you look forward to university as, among other things, your first experience with independent living, a chance to explore life free from your hovering family?

Or are you not yet ready to make the break? Are you more comfortable entering university from the security of your home? Is dealing with university life challenge enough that you don't need other major disruptions? Do you want to save the expense of room and board by living at home during university?

Think about where you want to live as you begin university and think about some other things as well. If you're ready to leave, how far do you want to go? Do you want to come home every weekend? Do you want to be close enough to stay in touch with friends?

Does travelling across the country appeal to you? Can you get by if you see your family only at major holidays and spring break? Can you handle a climate change? If you now live in Victoria, British Columbia, can you cope with several months of snow in Ottawa?

Mull these questions over every now and then (while you have the TV unplugged). Get a sense of how strongly you feel about each answer. When the time comes to make your decisions, you'll be ready.

Large or small campus?

Dalhousie University is a big, bustling campus with about 13,000 students, while the University of King's College is smaller, quieter, and has only 800 students. The only things they have in common are that they both offer an excellent education, and they're both located in Halifax, Nova Scotia. Each is the right school for some students, but neither is right for *all* students.

Some students thrive in the big sea. They enjoy the wide variety of social, cultural, and other activities that come with a large university. They're willing to sacrifice some individual attention (sometimes they'll just be numbers in huge classes) in exchange for a giant school's opportunities.

Other students have the opposite reaction. They like the small-university atmosphere, where everyone seems to know everyone else, where full professors teach courses and know students' names. These students would probably feel as if they were drowning if they were dropped in an ocean of 15,000 students.

Do you have strong feelings one way or the other? Or is the size of a university not an issue for you? It's something to think about.

Big city or university town?

The size of a university is not necessarily related to the size of its town. You can find tiny schools in major urban areas and relatively large campuses in such remote outposts as Thunder Bay, Ontario (that's Lakehead University, with more than 6,000 students). A university's location is another variable for your list.

Do you want to avoid, or be in, a big city? Do you like the rural life, where a shopping mall is a major journey? Do you lean toward a campus in the suburbs with big-city amenities a short drive away? How about a quaint small town where the university and community live as equal partners? Do you love the hustle and bustle of big-city life? Or do you care? Think about the type of community in which you want your university to be located.

What do you want to major in?

Do you have an idea of what you want to study in university? If not, it's something else for the Mull List (check out Appendix D, where we've put one together). But don't lose any sleep over such decisions. Even if you show up at a university without a major, you'll have lots of company. Most students don't decide how to focus their studies until well after they arrive. And many schools, recognizing this widespread indecision, don't require a choice of major until a student's second or third year — at least, for students in arts or science faculties.

If you have strong leanings toward a certain field of study, think about how strong those feelings are. Will you be ready, when the time comes, to narrow your search to universities with your chosen major? If you're not totally sure, stay flexible. Wait until you're 100-percent certain before nailing down your decision. You can always change your major as you go, although this may require taking more qualifying courses and adding to the total time you spend at university.

Where do you want to live?

Do you feel strongly about being a part of campus life? Are you looking forward to living in residence? If so, are you fussy about a single-sex or coed residence?

Do you want to attend a school where most students live on campus? Or do you care whether most of them commute from home each day? A majority of universities can be classified as either *residential* or *commuter,* with at least two-thirds of their students in one of the two categories. But some universities strike an even balance between on-campus and live-at-home students. Is that important to you? See Chapter 9 for more on housing options at university.

With whom do you want to live?

How about your peers? Are you more comfortable with grungy or are you a neat freak? Is the party scene a big thing for you? Do you crave life in a fraternity or sorority? Do you want to be on a campus where your gender dominates? Or where you're outnumbered by the opposite sex?

Is ethnic diversity important? What about geographic diversity? On some university campuses, you can hear over a hundred different languages being spoken by the students. On others, you'll be hard pressed even to find someone who can converse in French.

Don't worry about finding answers to these questions. All you're doing now is thinking about how you might answer them. These are the kinds of questions that make mulling fun. Simply the act of considering these questions will really help once you start investigating universities. You'll know what supplementary questions to ask, over and above the standard concerns about tuition fees, number of spaces available, and average marks needed to get accepted.

Advanced Level: Life Planning

This is the philosophical part. We could limit this book to the facts of how to fill out a university application form, what kind of marks each university requires, and how much university costs. But, if we did that, we would be doing you a disservice.

The time you spend at university is a big chunk of your formative years. What you do, where you go, and how well you do affect you for the rest of your life.

Life planning is something you do throughout your life, but it is particularly important while planning for university.

- You should think about what kind of person you want to be in the future.
- You should think about your future profession, where you hope to live, and how much you value prestige, money, and personal fulfillment.
- You should think about the possibility of carrying on to graduate school.

Studying what you're good at or what you love

Ah! The eternal question! Best-case scenario: Find something that you are good at that you also love. But sometimes this just isn't possible.

University is the time to explore all the fields of study you're interested in. Even if you don't major in the subject you love, take a few courses that allow you to get a fuller understanding of it. You may end up changing your major to follow your heart, or it may simply end up as a lifelong hobby. Then again, you may find yourself sick of it after a short period of time. Who knows? Only you can figure it out.

What's most important is that you listen to your feelings. What you love may sound completely ridiculous to other people, but that doesn't change the fact that you love it. You may find that the subjects that fascinate you keep coming back to nag you throughout your life. Best to start studying them early.

Investigating your chosen career

Your parents, grandparents, teachers — everyone, it seems — are constantly asking you what you want to be when you grow up. Instead of a shrug or a quick retort, it's easier all around if you have a solid answer. Now, your answer doesn't have to be carved in stone. You can change your dream career as many times as you like. You may be answering just out of a desire to please the adults asking the question — or to induce them to *stop* asking the question. The thing is, lots of high school students claim to have a chosen career, but, when pressed about exactly what it means to work in their chosen field, they usually don't know or are completely misinformed.

We can't say enough about the importance of knowing what you are doing before you do it. Investigating your chosen career is a perfect example.

By now, you've figured out that the professions typically glamourized on TV and in the movies — doctors, lawyers, journalists, police officers — are generally nothing like that in real life. Other professions can be equally misunderstood. For example, you probably know that architects design buildings for a living, but what do they really *do* on a day-to-day basis? How do they get clients to hire them? Do they work directly with the construction teams? Do most of them work independently or as part of a group of architects in a large firm? If you think you want to be an architect, you need to know the answers to these questions, and hundreds of others. If the answers aren't what you imagined, maybe you really don't want to be an architect after all. It's important to know that before you spend several years getting a degree in architecture.

Talk to your parents and friends to find out if someone they know works in a career that interests you. Then join them for a day on the job and ask a million questions. They won't think you're a pest. They'll probably be flattered by your interest. Hey, they may even buy you lunch! Your high school counsellor may also be able to set you up with a mentor in your chosen field. Investigate career fairs.

If you can't find a connection to your career of choice, make your own. Get a part-time job at an accounting firm or offer to volunteer at a local clinic. Whatever it takes to find out is a small effort compared to several years of (potentially) wasted study.

Investigating the job market

Okay, so you're in grade 10: You'll graduate in two years and attend university for four. So, in six years you'll be in the job market. Welcome to the real world.

You know how much has happened over the last six years, right? The Internet went from being a plaything used by only a small percentage of the population to a global communication medium that has become indispensable to most of us. People have cracked and tracked the code of the human body in the Human Genome Project. The face of popular media has changed a few times and market trends are in constant flux.

And we're telling you to plan ahead. How can you possibly be prepared for the job market of the future? What skills will be in demand? How can you figure this out?

Relax, we don't expect you to be psychic. We just want you to be as prepared as you can be. Here are a few ideas:

- ✔ **Read the newspaper:** You can stay informed about what's happening all over the world by looking through the newspaper each day, or at least on a consistent basis. Columnists give their opinions about all sorts of things, and there are also reports by *futurists*, people who predict the future based on present trends.

- ✔ **Read magazines:** We're not talking about fashion magazines or comic books. *Time* magazine includes snapshot reports of worldwide events at the beginning of the magazine. *The Economist* provides a distinctly unbiased (and non-American) view on the world and is favoured by people dealing with international issues. Along with general newsy publications, you should read magazines specific to your area of interest. That can be *PC Gamer,* if you want to design computer games, or *Architectural Digest,* if you want to be an architect.

- ✔ **Visit Web sites:** There are thousands of Web sites devoted to every topic imaginable. Find the ones that interest you most and bookmark them.

- ✔ **Express yourself:** You have a right to your opinions. If you plan to be a lawyer, or a politician, or an activist, start practising your trade by debating issues. Seek out people in your chosen profession and ask them where they see the industry going. Express your ideas and find out what they say.

- ✔ **Get started now:** Alan Kay, an Apple Master at Apple Computer and an Imagineer for Disney, once said, "The best way to predict the future is to invent it." You have ideas. You have a brain. Start working on your chosen career immediately. If you want to study computer engineering, start programming now. Find and fix holes in some existing software and let the company that designed the software (and others in the online community) know about it. If comparative literature is your field, write reviews and offer them to literary magazines. Maybe they'll reject your submissions — but maybe they won't! You'll never know until you try. Even if you don't get paid for your efforts, you'll be learning a lot and doing the work you love.

Looking forward to graduate school

Some people who attend university decide that four years just isn't enough — so they go back for more. You may think they're insane, but the rest of the world calls these people *graduate students.* Some get a second degree to become professionally qualified in fields such as medicine, law, or teaching.

Become fluent in a second language

We've said it before but it bears repeating: Unless you're absolutely, positively, 100-percent sure you will *never* need a second language — either for professional or personal reasons — you should consider taking (and doing well at) another language in high school. There's little doubt that English has become the world's "universal language" over the past few decades. That said, you might be surprised at how often other languages crop up.

David studied French, Latin, and Greek in high school. Caryn studied French, Italian, and Latin. And, while neither of them got translating jobs at the United Nations, they both can hold their own in a business meeting in Montreal, figure out if their parents' prescriptions are correct using high school Latin, and strike up a conversation in Greek or Italian restaurants. Considering Canada's increasingly multicultural population, speaking another language besides English is increasingly important.

Knowing a second or even third language helps you arrange your thoughts clearly and better understand how the English language works. These are important skills for anyone involved in communicating (both in writing and orally) — vital skills in today's white collar workforce. Looking down the road, speaking another language may make you more valuable as an employee, and even get you paid more.

Many large companies look more favourably on bilingual (or even trilingual) staff than they do on those who can speak only one language. Air Canada pays its staff a bit more money if they speak both official languages (English and French) — and gives preference for coveted international routes such as Rome, Paris, Tel Aviv, and Tokyo to those flight attendants who speak languages native to those regions.

Changing careers during your life

This is more than just an option — it's positively a trend! Careers are far more fluid than they once were. What was once a linear path from university to retirement is now filled with tempting detours. Fifty years ago, you were expected to have the same career for life. If you were trained as a physician, you were a physician for the next 25 or 30 years of your life, until you retired. If you went to law school, you practised law, and perhaps served as a judge, until you retired. If you went to school or apprenticed to be an auto mechanic, you fixed cars until you were too old to fix cars. You get the idea.

Nowadays, changing careers is pretty commonplace. We're not talking about just changing *jobs* here; we're talking about changing your life's work — the work that you commit to for reasons other than your regular paycheque. Executive search consultants, also known as headhunters, tell us that some people will have five (or more) careers in their working life.

For example, you can now train to be a lawyer, practise law for a few years, then go into politics.

Once you've had your fill of politics, you can write a few tell-all books about your experiences. Maybe then you can become a speaker on the lecture circuit. Who knows, maybe you'll then become a TV personality! If you think about it, you can probably name a few people who have done just that.

How do you prepare for all these changes? Keep your options open. Do well in your courses, especially those *gateway courses* such as math, science, and English. Keep your eyes open to change and excel at what you do.

Talk to people already doing what you want to do. Go to career fairs — held periodically especially in big cities, this is usually a day-long event where companies set up booths and encourage prospective employees to approach them about careers. Talk to your parents, talk to your friends' parents (okay, we know it's not cool to do this so do it while your friends aren't around), and, in general, keep asking questions.

You may find your particular field of study so fascinating that you want to study it in more detail, earning a master's degree along the way. It can be whatever you studied in your undergraduate degree — French history, women's studies, astrophysics — or another subject altogether.

Some *professional* programs (such as medicine or law) require only one, two, or three years of undergraduate study before they let you in. We talk more about graduate and professional programs in Chapter 11.

Don't Sweat It

We've probably been scaring you. We tell you tales of extremely high admission requirements and the numbers of students who don't get accepted into university, and then we only whisper about the money. It's disconcerting, we're sure.

You should know that we don't do it to be mean. We do it because we know it's better for you to concentrate on one thing at a time. Start off by figuring out what you really want to do, then find the right universities, and finally, raise your marks to make sure you can get into the schools and programs you want. You'll be better equipped to deal with these issues if you take them seriously early on.

While planning for university, you get to do a lot more than fret about serious stuff. That's another reason we wrote this book — to remind you of the amazing experiences that lie ahead. For example, you get to visit university campuses and experience your first taste of post-secondary life. You get to mull over what you might do at some of these schools with your friends. Once you get accepted and go to university, you get to experience all the enlightenment, stimulation, and interaction of university life. Imagine, a place where smart people get together to get smarter, experiment, and explore their favourite interests. Sounds good to us.

Money Is Not Important — Yet

Okay. Here it is. The nasty word. Money.

In that long list of things to think about, we didn't mention money. That's because you don't need to think about money. Not yet. At least not while you're mulling over the decisions you'll have to make soon.

The cost of a university, of course, is a key factor in determining where you go. You won't enrol in a university if you can't pay its bills. But money is not something to think about when you compare universities. After all, most Canadian universities have pretty much similar tuition fees. Besides, you really don't know how much each university will cost because you have no idea — yet — how much your price will be reduced by financial aid.

Students from low-income families aren't the only ones who qualify for financial aid. Some aid flows to students whose families earn six-figure incomes. And no one bends the rules to get this money. You can get an estimate of your financial-aid eligibility by reading Chapter 14. But that's just an estimate. Financial aid is, well, flexible — if not negotiable. Still, you need to spend money to go to university, you just don't know how much. So your concern right now should not be how expensive University *X* is compared to University *Y*. Wait until you have some real numbers for comparison. Your financial concern, as you move through high school, should be finding the money to spend no matter where you decide to go.

Early Steps to Get More University Money

As you set the stage to become an attractive university applicant, you can do several things to set the stage for paying the bills. If you plan with care, you'll ensure not only that you maximize your own resources, but also that you'll be eligible for all the money the rules say you deserve when the time comes to distribute financial aid.

We talk a lot more about financial planning in Part IV, but we wanted to let you know about a few things in advance.

What you can do

We already mentioned the part-time job. Come summer, that should become a full-time job. The problem is, with a job comes money. And with money comes the possibility of spending that money. So here's another option.

Believe it or not, there are people out there willing to pay you good money without asking you for even a few minutes' worth of work. They go by lots of different names, but quite a few call themselves bankers. These people want to borrow your money for a while, and they pay you to let them have it. They'll take $1 a week if that's all you can afford. But you can probably afford more.

This profitable activity, lending money to bankers, is usually called *saving*. It doesn't sound terribly exciting — and that's probably why most people don't save. We admit it — saving is not much fun. But, then again, neither is coming out of university with $60,000 worth of debt. There are many students who do just that every year.

So, we're not suggesting you save money. We're encouraging you to find a new, work-free source of income. How does that sound? Lend some money to a banker every week, every month, or whatever suits your budget. When the banker pays you for using your money, let him hold onto that money, too. Then he'll pay you not only for using your money, but also for using the money that he paid you earlier. This is the magic of compounding. *Compounding* allows you to get even richer — just by lending money to bankers.

What your parents can do

If your parents don't have a *Registered Education Savings Plan (RESP)*, encourage them to start one for you — fast. A Registered Education Savings Plan is a Canadian government initiative that provides incentives for people to save for education purposes. The income from any investment made in a

RESP will be shielded from taxation as long as it remains in a fund that will be used for a child's education. People (usually parents) set up a RESP in the name of the child who will eventually be the recipient of the money. When the child eventually withdraws the money — and all the interest it has earned — to go to university, income tax is then payable *by the recipient*. Since the child generally has no or very little other income while going to university, the tax rate is negligible.

So, not only is a RESP a work-free income source, but also you save taxes on the income from the money you put into it. And, as an added bonus, RESPs make you eligible for more financial aid. The government provides a grant of 20 percent of your RESP contribution (to a maximum of $400 per year) just for saving! There's more on RESPs and other ways parents can save money to send you to university in Chapter 13. Get them to read it.

What everyone else can do

You may have heard about tax shelters. Tax shelters are where some people put their money because, through loopholes in the law, they legitimately can avoid paying taxes on it. Anyone thinking about going to university should be aware of the provision in the financial-aid rules that we'll call the Grandma Shelter.

The shelter is available to any friend or relative who is not in your immediate family. Grandma is used here because she's handy and she's often very generous with her grandkids.

When you apply for financial aid in the form of a student loan or bursary, you'll be asked to bare your financial soul. If you're a dependent of your parents, they must do the same. Every dollar of your and your parents' income and assets must be reported — then the numbers are crunched and a computer decides how much you should pay for university. That's the starting point to figure out your financial aid.

Nobody will ask about Grandma's money. She could be holding your university nest egg, and it wouldn't be counted in determining how much aid you need. Now we're not suggesting that your parents transfer all their mutual funds into Grandma's name so that you can get more financial aid. Not only would that be illegal, it's also bad karma.

However, let's say Grandma — or Uncle John, or Aunt Kathy — decides that your birthday present every year will be a $100 contribution toward your university education. Tell Grandma the money will be worth more if she keeps the money in her name until the time comes to pay tuition.

Chapter 3

Big Changes in Canadian Schools

There are more people applying to Canadian universities than ever before. The bottom line is that you're going to face some stiff competition when applying to university. The faces of many of these universities are also changing — sometimes drastically. According to Statistics Canada (the folks at the government who keep track of these things), more than 500,000 high school students were heading to university for full-time studies in the 2001/2002 academic year. Our job (that's both you and us) is to ensure you're one of them — if not this year, then in one of these coming years. But before you hit the books, read a little further in this one. The increased competition for spots in universities gives you some new options for your post-secondary education. We talk about a few of these options in this chapter, and we outline more in Chapter 4.

More Competition for Spaces

If you're going to graduate from high school or plan to go to university anytime before 2010, there are three factors you need to be aware of that are going to radically increase competition for spots at universities across Canada:

✔ Ontario's *double cohort,* the class of 2003 that will include both the final OAC class and the grade 12 graduating class;

✔ Population increases across Canada;

✔ Increasing numbers of mature students going to university because of changing workplace expectations.

What does this mean? There will be more students of all ages — up to 40 percent more in some provinces — competing for virtually the same number of spots at Canadian universities (although the province of Ontario is undertaking several construction projects to accommodate the glut).

Ontario's double cohort

In the spring of 2003, one group of Ontario high school students will complete their *OACs (Ontario Academic Credits* — what your parents may remember fondly as grade 13) and bid high school farewell. At the same time, another group of Ontario high school students will graduate after completing grade 12 — the result of Ontario's new four-year high school program. The Ontario government believes this giant one-time graduation "bubble" will result in some 33,500 additional students applying to Canadian universities for the 2003/2004 academic year. This phenomenon has been coined the *double cohort* — a very official-sounding name that gives you no clue as to its meaning. That's why we're explaining it. This massive influx of students into the university system will cause a fair bit of disruption for everyone concerned.

Even though the joining of the graduations will happen in that one year of 2003, the effect will be felt both before that time and for a few years to come. Some students that would normally graduate in 2003 have looked ahead and realized they don't want to compete with twice the graduating class. They have worked ahead to graduate a year early, making the 2002 year more competitive as well. Others will not get into a university in 2003, so they will reapply the next year or the year after that, making 2004 and 2005 more competitive, too.

If you're going to graduate from high school or if you plan to go to university anytime before 2010 anywhere across Canada, you'll be affected by what's going on in Ontario. Here's the ugly truth about the double cohort: You will not only be competing for university spots with students from your own province, you will likely also be competing with students from that double graduating class in Ontario who are applying to universities in other provinces. You didn't think they would all apply to universities in Ontario, did you?

Population growth across Canada

Canada's population is growing, especially in the key 18- to 24-year-old group that comprises the majority of university students. As an example, by the year 2010 there will be approximately 100,000 more 18- to 24-year-olds living in British Columbia, and almost 180,000 more 18- to 24-year-olds living in Ontario. And more people in this age group are enrolling in university.

Why get rid of Ontario's OAC?

There has been a lot of talk about educational reform across Canada in the last few decades. The argument over whether a four- or five-year high school curriculum is better preparation for students has been fought particularly long and hard. With the notable exception of Ontario, all high schools across this fair land felt that the shorter system was best for them. In fact, for students in Alberta, Quebec, New Brunswick, and the other six provinces, grades 9, 10, 11, and 12 were the *only* high school they ever knew. Only Ontario had an "extra" grade. With the inception of the new four-year high school system — and the resulting, one-time double cohort — the province of Ontario now moves into sync with the rest of Canada.

More mature students

At the same time, demand for university education from other groups is up as well. More students are entering university from the workplace, either to upgrade their work skills or to change career directions. These mid-career applicants know that continuing education is the cornerstone to professional advancement and career development. For many members in this group, their workplace foots the bill for their university education so there's even less of a barrier for them to return to school.

Are you as prepared as you can be?

Here's the super-secret method that universities use to decide who gets offered admission and who doesn't: marks, and that's it. Almost had you fooled, right? Are your marks higher than the cut-off level for this year? If they are, you get in. If not, you don't.

Okay, perhaps your marks aren't the *only* way a particular university decides on admission, but marks are by far the most important way universities have to evaluate prospective students. While our American counterparts rely on the results of standardized national tests such as the *PSAT* or the *SAT I,* Canadian universities rely mostly (or entirely, in some cases) on your marks in high school. We tell you more about the SAT I in Chapter 7, and we discuss other things universities may choose to consider in Chapter 10.

They say a picture's worth a thousand words. Well, Figure 3-1 shows you the average admission marks for universities in Ontario from 1983 to 1999. Look at that rising tide! Table 3-1 zeroes in on one university, the University of British Columbia, and shows you the average marks required to get into several programs for the 2000/2001 academic year. Looking at these numbers, you can clearly see that it's tough to make it into university.

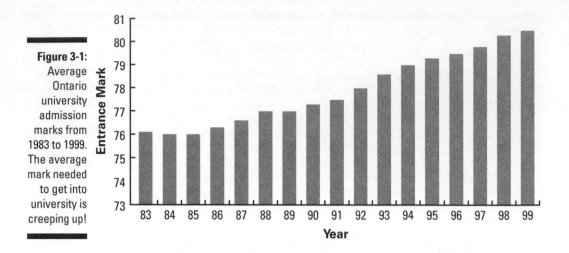

Figure 3-1:
Average
Ontario
university
admission
marks from
1983 to 1999.
The average
mark needed
to get into
university is
creeping up!

As you can see in Table 3-1, if you want to get into programs such as science, engineering, and human kinetics at UBC, you need *A*s. And, if you want to be *sure* about getting into the program of your choice, you need marks *higher* than Table 3-1 illustrates. This is because the marks you see are just *average marks*. The universities admit that some students score higher and some score lower than those averages, but it's better to be safe than sorry.

Knowing there is so much competition for university admission, some students (and often, the *parents* of these students) start preparing for university early, some as early as primary school. They enrol in extra classes to learn more and, consequently, get a step up over other students at the same level. If they're having trouble with a subject or two, they get a tutor to help them understand the particular subject.

Table 3-1 Average Entrance Marks Required at the University of British Columbia for the 2000/2001 Academic Year

Program	Average Mark Required
Agricultural sciences	76%
Applied science (engineering)	82%
Arts	78%
Home economics	74%
Human kinetics	81%
Music (audition required)	67%

Table 3-1	Average Entrance Marks Required at the University of British Columbia for the 2000/2001 Academic Year
Program	**Average Mark Required**
Nursing	76%
Science	83%

Others have their first big jolt of reality at the beginning of grade 9, when they have to pick courses that will pretty much dictate what they do for the rest of their life, how much money they make, and what kind of life they'll lead (but no pressure, right?). Don't worry — there's still time to hit the books!

Some Technical Schools Are Becoming Universities

While it's true that new universities are built from time to time, the majority of growth happening now is because community colleges and technical institutes are becoming full-fledged universities, granting students the same accreditation — and recognition — they get from traditional universities. Other growth is coming from the private sector. We talk about that a bit later in this chapter.

Technology is becoming an increasingly important part of many industries, and companies are looking to hire people with these specialized, highly marketable skills. These are exactly the kinds of skills taught at technical schools. A few years ago, however, employers wouldn't look at people with a diploma from a technical school in the same way as they would those with a degree from a university. Today, that attitude has changed — at least somewhat. Many technical institutes are now fully accredited, degree-granting institutions — virtually the same as traditional universities.

Ryerson Polytechnic University, located in downtown Toronto, is a case in point. Until 1989, Ryerson was known as Ryerson Polytechnical Institute. Students who studied at RPI, as it was called, got a diploma instead of a university degree, though they took similar courses to their peers in university. Ryerson became an accredited university in 1989. Now, Ryerson students graduate with a university degree that is recognized by potential employers and society in general.

The quality of instruction in some of the less specialized courses at technical institutes used to be fairly poor. It has improved dramatically, however, and you can get an excellent education at any of the schools listed below and several others.

You may want to consider applying to a technical institute if you are interested in studying in a high-tech or specialized area.

Here are a few well-known and respected Canadian institutes:

- British Columbia Institute of Technology (BCIT), in Vancouver, British Columbia (www.bcit.ca);
- Canadian Film Centre, in Toronto, Ontario (www.cdnfilmcentre.com);
- Emily Carr Institute of Art and Design, in Vancouver, British Columbia (www.eciad.bc.ca);
- Northern Alberta Institute of Technology, in Edmonton, Alberta (www.nait.ab.ca);
- Southern Alberta Institute of Technology, in Calgary, Alberta (www.sait.ab.ca).

Community Colleges Are Becoming Mainstream

If you think of community colleges as small schools designed to teach vocational skills to those students who can't get into university, you've got another think coming. Today's community colleges are far more mainstream and are graduating students into far more cool jobs than they were a decade or two ago. Drop by a community college and check out the differences.

Today's community colleges have courses in multimedia sales, CD-ROM and DVD-ROM production, Web design, Internet marketing, and many, many more topics that aren't available at universities. If you fancy yourself as the next Bill Gates or Steve Jobs, you may be able to find relevant training in computers and other technical subjects that surpasses that of a university.

Sure, there are still courses (and diplomas) for aspiring nurses, ambulance paramedics, car mechanics, and other traditional college vocations. But there are also many professional development courses taught through community colleges in areas such as purchasing, engineering, real estate, sales, marketing, and dozens of other practical subjects. If you think you'll never see the inside of a community college just because you have your fancy university degree, you may be in for a big surprise.

Community college is often a much less expensive alternative to university. According to Statistics Canada, most community colleges charge about one-half to two-thirds what universities charge for tuition. However, the most competitive programs in the top colleges *are* comparable to university tuition levels — some are even more expensive. A popular 16-week 3-D animation program at Seneca College, in Toronto, costs nearly $10,000!

Even if tuition is high in some programs, most college diplomas take only two years (and, sometimes, much less time) to complete, instead of the three or four years required at university. This means you spend less time slaving in school and more time making money in the real world. Of course, university students love to tell you that people with university degrees make a lot more money than people with college diplomas. This may be true overall, but it isn't always true in every case anymore, especially for people who studied those in-demand technical skills in college.

A few of the best-known and respected colleges in their particular disciplines are:

✔ Banff Centre for the Arts, in Banff, Alberta (`www.banffcentre.ab.ca`);

✔ Centennial College, in Toronto, Ontario (`www.centennialcollege.ca`);

✔ Seneca College of Applied Arts and Technology, in Toronto, Ontario (`www.senecac.on.ca`);

✔ Sheridan College, in Oakville, Ontario (`www.sheridanc.on.ca`);

✔ Vancouver Film School, in Vancouver, British Columbia (`www.multimedia.edu`).

Blending a Degree with a Diploma or a Certificate

Many students with general bachelor of arts degrees (B.A.), and even some students with predominantly theoretical bachelor of science degrees (B.Sc.), face a difficult transition when entering the real-world job market after graduation. While their degree is useful, they may lack the practical knowledge and training that makes them especially attractive to employers.

"I learned a lot at university, but is any of it directly useful to an employer?" is often the first thing out of these students' mouths once the thrill of graduating has worn off and they begin to wake up to what may lie ahead of them.

Doing a one-year certificate or diploma program (some take less time) at a college or technical institute after you've graduated from university is one way to ease this transition and increase your marketability. You get the best of both worlds: a high-end general knowledge base coupled with more specific application-based training, which will, with some luck, help you land that job sooner. If you do a three-year B.A. or B.Sc., the whole thing is a mere four-year investment.

Private Universities: Coming Soon to an Application Near You

Provincial governments have cut funding to universities over the last few years. Consequently, tuition fees have risen, sometimes dramatically so. Many students and student unions have protested the cuts, but governments seem bent on cutting even further.

Unlike our American neighbours, there are currently no private general universities in Canada — they haven't been popular in this country, mainly because many Canadians believe education should be available to everyone and this availability should be safeguarded through government funding of universities. But this is about to change.

Some provinces are considering passing legislation to allow *private universities* to set up shop; others have already done so. Ontario's Progressive Conservative government recently passed such a bill. These private universities could be up and running as early as January 2002! Private universities would be similar to their publicly funded counterparts with one notable difference: money, and where they get it from. Instead of relying on the government, the new private universities will turn to two main sources: private individuals and corporations, and tuition fees paid by students.

What does this mean to you, the soon-to-be-graduating high school student? On the one hand, private universities could ease some of the load caused by the ever-increasing competitiveness to get into public universities (we talk about the causes of this earlier in this chapter). On the other hand, private universities may lead the way to a two-tier education system, with admissions decided not on marks but rather on who can afford to attend.

Chapter 4

Big Options for You

*I*s going to a Canadian university right after high school the only option available to you? Not by a long shot! It may be the most popular option among students who intend to go to university, but there are lots of other things you can do.

You might want to get some life experience before hitting the books again. Many people find they have more incentive to do well in university after they find out what the real world is like. On the other hand, you may be eager to start studying but interested in a change of pace. Perhaps you want to study in French at one of the French-language universities in Canada. Then again, perhaps heading to a whole new country is what you need to expand your horizons.

Whatever interests you, there are lots of options available. Make sure you consider them all before blindly making the easiest choice.

Taking a Year off Before University

Just because lots of people go directly from high school to university doesn't mean you have to be one of them. Taking a year off is increasingly common these days. Here's what some of our friends ended up doing:

- Travelling around Europe.
- Working on a fishing trawler in the South China Sea.
- Starting a company (yes, some of our friends actually chose to work).
- Saving more money for university (oh yeah, how can we forget that one?).

Taking a year off could in fact turn out to be one of the most educational experiences of your life, making you better equipped to handle the pressures of university. It also tends to make you more motivated once you get to university. After all, you've seen the reality of the world and you know how hard it can be to compete.

You do, however, need to plan. You need to treat your year off as a pre-university year, not just a goof-off period. You didn't work hard in high school just to waste an entire year not doing anything of value, right?

Deferring Your Acceptance

The trick to taking a year off is to work your hardest during high school, research your top-choice universities, apply to those universities, and, once accepted, *defer your acceptance.* A deferral delays the date you start university. It is granted on the understanding that it is for a specified amount of time — usually a year.

You need to officially defer your university acceptance before you begin your year off, or your wonderful school may give your place to some other lucky kid. Ask more than one official at each of your university choices to get the straight story on admission deferrals. Get names and titles of the people who you speak with in case people change their jobs. Whenever possible, get everything on paper. Check university calendars — they usually have a section that explains specific regulations concerning deferrals. Your counsellor will likely be a good source of information as well. Ask questions and keep asking until you get answers.

Some universities don't offer the deferral option at all. Make sure you check this out — right at the beginning of the application process. (We take you through the application process step-by-step in Chapter 11.)

Going Abroad: International Universities

Okay, we admit we're biased. We think that Canadian universities offer some of the best education and research opportunities in the world. Many life-saving and life-enhancing inventions and discoveries have originated right here in Canada.

Frederick Banting and Charles Best discovered how insulin can control diabetes, thus saving millions of lives around the world. Dr. Wilbur Franks developed the "anti-black-out suit." Credited with saving thousands of Allied

Parlez-vous français?

You probably assume you're going to go to a university whose language of instruction is English. But you have another option. You can attend a French-speaking university, where the students use French as their primary language, classes are held in French, and papers and exams are written in French.

Here are two great reasons to attend a French-speaking university:

✔ **You'll become a more interesting person:** Let's say you've lived your whole life in Calgary. If you choose to attend the Université du Québec en Abitibi-Témiscamingue, instead of playing it safe and going to the University of Calgary, you may emerge from university with an understanding and appreciation of Quebec — and probably a newfound respect for the term "French Canadian."

✔ **You'll get a leg up in the job market:** It's truly amazing how many people cannot hold a conversation in both of Canada's official languages. Bosses value this ability. If you can speak French well, you've just increased your chances of being called back for that second interview. And who said anything about staying in Canada? Ever thought about working in Paris? Now you can.

You may think you know French. You may have scored high marks in high school French class (see Chapter 2, where we tell you how important it is to learn that second language — why not French?). You may even listen once in a while to French TV or radio. But these experiences don't hold a candle to really immersing yourself in French culture and language at university. Going to school in French may add a lot of fun to your school life.

Of course, speaking French is not for everyone. If you're not pretty much bilingual by the time grade 12 rolls around, you probably shouldn't consider the francophone university option. After all, university is difficult enough without having a language barrier between you and your coursework. It's difficult to learn when you don't understand what the instructor is saying.

fighter pilots during the Second World War, this invention has since been worn by every air-force pilot in the world and was developed into the space suit now worn by today's astronauts. Even Pablum, the baby formula that revolutionized infant feeding and nutrition, was invented here in Canada. You don't have to travel far to get a great education and even do some important research!

What's more, post-secondary education at a university in Canada comes relatively inexpensively, especially when you compare it to what our American friends spend. Despite the ongoing tuition increases caused by provincial governments spending less and less on education, Canadian universities are a fantastic value for the money. Even American state colleges are at least *twice* the price when compared with their Canadian equivalents — and that's not even considering the hefty out-of-state surcharges that most state colleges charge to non-residents.

When you compare the costs to what you would pay for a degree at a private American university, such as Harvard, Yale, or Stanford, you really see the advantage of staying north of the border for your post-secondary education. First year tuition at these Ivy League schools is well over $50,000 CAN. Graduate programs are even more expensive. In 2001, Harvard said tuition for its renowned M.B.A. sets students back about $52,000 US annually — that's almost $80,000 in Canadian dollars! And don't forget you'll be paying for any "extras" with more expensive U.S. dollars, too.

Going American

Still, there are numerous reasons why you might consider going to an American university. Reasons like:

- Prestige;
- Educational rigour;
- And, of course, connections.

Prestige is certainly one reason to go to some American universities. There's no doubt that a Harvard degree is worth more than its Canadian equivalent, at least in terms of prestige. An average employer would likely pay a better starting salary and other benefits to someone who holds a degree from Harvard than to another person with the same degree from a Canadian university. Even though both students learned the same material, there's certainly a cachet to attending a so-called Ivy League university such as Harvard.

It's difficult to assess the educational rigour of a given university, so it's hard to say whether American schools are tougher — or better — than Canadian ones academically. Do more expensive American universities really offer a better education than less expensive schools?

While there's practically no evidence to suggest that students learn a particular subject at one university better than at another, a lot of people perceive that this is *exactly* the case. And sometimes, perception is more important than reality. This goes a long way toward explaining the myths that flourish about receiving a vastly superior education at Ivy League universities.

Great connections are the currency of prestigious American universities. The thinking is that if you put smart and rich people together, odds are you'll get more smart and rich people. Students attending Harvard, Princeton, Yale, Stanford, and many other private universities make friendships and form bonds with other students that help in their subsequent careers. For many, going to an exclusive university is much like joining an exclusive country club.

Corporate recruiters who visit different campuses assess a job applicant not just on his marks, but on the university itself. Some employers assume it's more difficult to get an *A* at Yale than it is at Florida State, for example. So they will likely offer the Yale grad a higher starting salary than the Florida State grad, and be more likely to offer the Yale grad a job at all. This may not be fair, but it's reality. If you want to work as a bond trader in a Wall Street brokerage firm, your future boss will probably offer you a higher salary if you sport a degree from Harvard, Wharton, or M.I.T. (Massachusetts Institute of Technology) instead of one from a Canadian university.

Going farther away

We cover the subject of international universities more extensively in Chapter 17. For now, though, you can add the possibility of going to an international university to your growing list of things to ponder. See, this is why we keep saying it's a good idea to start thinking about your university plans as early as you can.

Attending a university in Britain, France, Germany, Italy, Russia, China, or more than a dozen additional countries is a dream for some Canadian students. Every year, thousands of them live that dream. Although it's an expensive alternative to Canadian universities — after all, you'll be a foreign student in another country and subject to significantly higher *foreign-student fees* — attending school abroad will definitely give more of an international flavour to your post-secondary education.

Not all universities in foreign countries use foreign languages. Obviously, universities in English-speaking countries conduct classes in English, but many other countries have excellent English-speaking universities as well. From Jakarta to Cairo to Paris, there are English-speaking universities in all sorts of exotic lands. You will probably have to learn the local language to get along in everyday life — but it will make it easier to do well in classes if you can use your native language.

In turn, your international education may make you more desirable to future employers, widen your personal horizons, and even be a lot of fun.

Perhaps you can live with a distant relative in Madrid while you study European art at the city's Saint Louis University. Maybe you can learn architecture at the University of Prague and board with a classmate. Your choices depend on your personal opportunities. But studying at an international university does mean you'll have to be more organized and more motivated than if you were to stay in Canada. There are hundreds of details involved in studying abroad, from ensuring you know the language, to paying for accommodation, to securing student visas, to setting up a bank account. Studying at an international university involves some important decisions:

✔ **Can you afford the international costs?** Ignore for the moment the actual cost of an international education (which can easily cost two or three times the equivalent Canadian university tuition). Overall, prices in Canada look cheap when you compare them to many other countries. Accommodation, food, transit, entertainment, and clothing are all much more expensive in large European and Asian cities than they are in Canadian ones.

✔ **Where are you going to live while abroad?** In a residence on campus is the obvious answer, but you may find that this produces too much culture shock. After all, you'll be surrounded by the new culture at school. Maybe you'll want to balance this out with your own place off-campus. Most cities in Europe and Asia have large English-speaking communities. Taking an apartment near one of these enclaves may provide the balance you need between easing into the culture at your own pace and feeling totally overwhelmed.

✔ **Can you handle being away from your friends and family?** Let's face it: when you leave home, you get lonely. Remember when you were a kid and you had your first few nights at summer camp? Well, going to another country for a few years can be a lot lonelier. With no friends, an unfamiliar country, and a strange culture, you may feel cut off from a big part of *you*. And, if you're thinking about a university in a country whose native language is not English, you may feel even more isolated. Do some soul searching. Can you make friends easily? Do you like time to yourself? Do you see taking classes in a foreign country as an exciting adventure? If so, then perhaps an international university is for you.

If you think you might enjoy the international experience but are somewhat skittish about committing your entire university career to living abroad, take heart. Many Canadian universities offer programs that send you abroad for just a portion of your university career.

✔ *Foreign-exchange programs,* or *Study-elsewhere programs,* let you study for a term (or a year) at an overseas university and then return to the familiar surroundings of the Canadian school. As you might imagine, these are very popular programs and competition to get into them can be very tough. That's just another reason to keep your marks up, even once you get into university! Not all Canadian universities offer foreign-exchange programs, so if you're considering studying abroad add this point to the Mull List you're making for each school. More on that important list in Chapter 6.

✔ A *Professional Experience Year* (or *PEY*) gives you the opportunity to gain experience in fields directly related to your university program of study. A close relative of the more regimented *co-op work program*, a PEY is sometimes available in second or third year and usually involves a twelve- or sixteen-month work period. We talk more about co-op work programs in Chapter 16 and going to an international university in Chapter 17.

If you are considering an international university, you have to deal with a completely different set of application and admission procedures. If you're applying to an American university, you should expect to write the PSAT and the SAT I and SAT II exams. There are other exams you may choose to write, such as the _American College Test_ (usually just shortened to _ACT_). And that's just for American schools. The rules for universities in other parts of the world are as diverse as the cultures themselves.

Developed by an organization called the American College Testing Program, the ACT is often considered a substitute for the SAT because that's how the test is used. Some American colleges, mostly in the Midwest and South, prefer an ACT score. SAT scores are in demand by colleges mainly on the East and West coasts. In these enlightened times, however, almost every college accepts either test. If a school says it prefers the ACT, it doesn't mean an SAT score makes you ineligible. There are, of course, rare exceptions, so find out which score the school prefers well in advance.

Coming to Canada: Canadian Universities for International Students

Each year, thousands of international students come to Canada to study. If you are planning to be one of these students (or if you know someone — like your friend in England, maybe — who is), there's some documentation you must have before you crack the Canadian books:

- ✔ **You need written confirmation from the university you will be attending, also known as an _offer of admission_, stating that you have been admitted there as a student:** This is usually supplied in the form of a bureaucratic-sounding letter.

- ✔ **You need a document called a _student authorization_, also known as a _student visa_, which gives you formal permission to study in Canada:** Prospective students should contact the nearest Canadian embassy, high commission, or consulate as soon as they receive the offer of admission from their university. (American students wishing to study in Canada can typically get their student authorization at point of Canadian entry, such as an airport or border crossing.) See the sidebar, "Authorization granted," for more on obtaining your student authorization.

- ✔ **You need an _entry visa_:** This document allows you to cross the border into Canada, and is normally issued along with your student authorization. Depending on which country you're from, you may not need to get an entry visa. Check with the Canadian consulate or embassy in your home country for more information.

> ✔ **You need a good score on the *TOEFL (Test of English as a Foreign Language):*** If your first language isn't English, you must take this test (or a comparable test) if you want to attend an English-speaking university. We provide more details on these tests in Chapter 11.

GOOD TO KNOW

Authorization granted

As a rule, all non-Canadians who wish to study in Canada must have a *student authorization* (often called a *student visa* or, more simply, just a *visa*). Applying for a student visa to study at a Canadian university can be a complicated and lengthy process, so it is essential you start early!

In general, the farther away you live from Canada, the more stringent are the rules and regulations you must follow to study here. As an example, for the vast majority of American students wishing to study in Canada the student authorization is pretty much a formality (although one that can't be ignored).

For students coming to Canada from more distant countries, however, the process is more complex, takes more time, and generally involves more hassle. Once you have been offered admission to a Canadian university, you can get your student authorization from any Canadian embassy or consulate abroad.

When you apply for your student authorization, be sure to bring the following documentation:

> ✔ The offer of admission from the particular university you plan to attend, as well as the length of the program you're enrolling in (three or four years).

> ✔ Evidence that you have adequate funds to meet your needs without having to get a job in Canada. Tuition costs are much higher for visa students. You should budget at least $10,000 per year for tuition and supplementary fees alone.

> **Note:** While having this much money in your bank account may be sufficient for the

Canadian government to grant you your student authorization, you will need more, especially if you're going to school in a high-cost city such as Toronto, Vancouver, Calgary, or Montréal.

Warning: If you ignore your visa restrictions and work in Canada during your studies, recognize that Canadian immigration authorities take a very dim view of this. They are likely to have you deported, which quickly ends your stay in Canada — and your Canadian university education. Don't do it!

> ✔ A return plane ticket, or proof you have enough money to buy one.

> ✔ Evidence that you've recently undergone a health exam. Depending on your country of residence, you may be required to undergo a health exam here in Canada. Canadian immigration officials may issue a form for medical clearance that must be completed and returned before a visa can be issued. (Prospective American students are usually exempt from this regulation.) We may seem a little vague on this subject because, as with most things relating to Canadian immigration policy, many of the requirements are discretionary. Canadian immigration officials could require an American student to obtain a medical clearance, but most don't. It's the same thing with students from Australia, Great Britain, and other industrialized countries such as Japan, Germany, Switzerland, France, and others. This said, if you come from a country where there is a known health warning in effect (due to a communicable disease such as cholera,

malaria, or yellow fever, for example) you will *definitely* be required to obtain a medical clearance, probably from a Canadian physician.

When you enter Canada, show your university acceptance letter to the immigration officer. When all the necessary documents have been processed, Canadian immigration authorities will issue you a student authorization (or *visa*, as it is sometimes called). In most cases, your student authorization will be valid for the entire duration of your time studying in Canada. Don't forget to apply early. As a general rule, the farther away you live from Canada the earlier you should prepare. Obtaining a student authorization can be very time-consuming, particularly if you need a medical clearance, official translations, or a medical examination. Apply for it as soon as you receive your offer of admission from the university.

Going Back to School: What Mature Students Need to Know

In case you're wondering, a mature student isn't someone who dresses in high-rise white pants and sits on a deck chair studying shuffleboard scores.

Mature student is a phrase with special meaning in most universities. Definitions vary from school to school, but you likely qualify as a mature student if you've reached the age of 21 (some universities push it to 23 or even 25) but do not have what university folks call an "academic basis of admission." This means you probably haven't been in full-time attendance at a university or college in the last four years.

What else do you need on your side besides age? Well, you need to show evidence that you're a good student (or at least could be again). Most universities require incoming mature students to show a *C* average on previous academic work. This tells the folks who make the admissions decisions that you've got the right stuff.

In some universities, mature students are considered only for part-time admission during their first year. This means you can take a maximum of three full courses during the traditional September-to-April academic year — not the usual five or six that full-time students can study. Presumably, this is to ease you back into the harsh academic world.

As a mature student, the university may ask you to submit a letter telling it why you think you'll be successful there and what you wish to gain from the experience. Your letter should include information relevant to your academic goals, career ambitions or plans, and any relevant work experience you have.

All this seems as if it's a great deal of work, right? So why bother? Well, there are likely as many reasons to become a mature student as there are mature students themselves — but they boil down to professional reasons and personal ones.

Professional reasons for becoming a mature student

Maybe you had to drop out of school to work and support your family. Perhaps you had to leave home to escape a bad situation. Whatever the reason for not taking the traditional high-school-to-university route, you now feel constrained by your high school education. Maybe your boss has dropped a few hints that you need a degree to keep up with others at work.

Or maybe you've been in the workforce for a few years and realize you don't want to be doing the same thing for the rest of your life. Maybe you find yourself longing for an intellectual challenge. Sure, putting up with your high school teachers was a real chore, but you now realize that digging ditches for the rest of your life would be much, much worse.

Personal reasons for becoming a mature student

Perhaps you've just split up from a long-time partner and want to get back into the workforce. Maybe the kids are in school and you need something to keep you busy. Hey, it's possible you've just won the lottery and you always promised yourself you'd go back to school if you only had the chance. (Congratulations, by the way — you can thank us for all this great advice by buying some more copies of this book and giving them to your friends and family.)

Whatever their reasons, mature students often do better at university than do traditional students. Although there is little scientific data to explain this phenomenon, it might be that mature students know how to avoid distractions and take school a bit more seriously than do the younger set. After all, they've already sown their wild oats years ago!

Easing back into it

Of course, mature students have their challenges too. Many have forgotten what the cosine of a tangent is, for example. More significantly, mature students sometimes find it difficult to juggle real-life responsibilities — such as mortgage payments, kids, and taking the car in for service — with the responsibilities of school life, such as finding time to get to the library, meeting with other students to exchange notes, and so on.

Many universities offer *transitional-year programs* for mature students entering the university world. These programs are specifically designed to ease mature students into the rigours of academic life. They also usually let students brush up on their math, science, and English skills — skills that are crucial to many university programs. Not incidentally, as far as universities are concerned these transitional-year programs also provide a tidy revenue stream to the school.

So how do you find out if the universities you're interested in offer transitional-year programs? It's simple! Just call each school directly or fire up your computer and check out each school's Web site on the Internet. We've got the phone numbers and Internet addresses of all the Canadian universities in Appendix A, "Directory of Universities and Colleges." Have a look now, if you like. Just come back here when you're done.

Distance learning

Distance learning is the term used to describe a situation where the instructor is physically separate from his or her students. Distance learning can encompass a wide variety of educational options including correspondence courses, taped video lectures sent to students through the mail, live lectures beamed over satellite TV, or even courseware sent over the Internet in the form of QuickTime files. In short, almost anything that can be used to transmit information can be used for distance learning.

Distance learning is not a sneaky way to get a university degree easily. In fact, distance learning may be more difficult for the average student. This is because it's harder to gain the sense of community that fosters great learning if you're not physically present in a big lecture hall or discussing the day's classes with your friends over a coffee. Distance learning requires students to be very motivated, to be adept at time-management, and to be able to apply themselves to the task at hand.

Certain universities specialize in distance learning. Athabasca University (Athabasca, Alberta) and British Columbia Open University (Burnaby, British Columbia) are two open-admission universities that welcome all students who wish to study at a distance.

Distance learning is well suited to students who have been out of the academic world for a long time and may lack the grades to get into a traditional university. Tuition is a fair bit cheaper, too. And it can be a very effective way for mature students to get back into the academic swing of things. Many mature students can't take time off during the week to attend classes or meet with study groups. Mature students can also be responsible for real-life challenges such as taking care of the kids, cooking for the family, cleaning the house, or working at a second job. Distance learning may be a great way to earn a university degree without many of the challenges (and distractions) involved in campus life.

Part II
Start Taking Notes: Finding the Right Universities

The 5th Wave

By Rich Tennant

"Here's a good one. 'Located next to an old cemetery, Misery University offers a brooding environment in which students can explore their darker side.'"

In this part . . .

Let the search begin! There are three main issues to address when planning for university: Figuring out which universities you want to attend, figuring out how to get into those universities, and figuring out how to pay for it.

In this part, we take you through what you need to know to conquer the first two issues: finding the best schools for you, and getting into them. (We focus more on the nuts and bolts of filling out your applications in Part III — so turn there if you're ready for this more technical stage.) In this part, Chapters 5, 8, and 9 help you gather all the information you need about universities across Canada, and show you how to organize this wealth of material into a format you can really use. Chapters 6 and 7 get you in the application groove early in high school (yes, that's as early as grades 9, 10, and 11) with tips on how to prepare for the big crunch time in grade 12. In the end, you should have the resources to apply and put your best foot forward to any university on your list.

The third issue — paying for university — is so important that we devote an entire section to it. You and your parents can check out the chapters in Part IV to find smart and creative ways to finance your post-secondary education.

Chapter 5

What You're Doing (and Not Doing)

● ●

In This Chapter

▶ Looking for the right universities

▶ Comparing personalities — yours and the university's

▶ Identifying reasons *not* to choose a university

▶ Putting magazine rankings in their proper place

● ●

Without a doubt, grade 10 is the time to start your serious search for a university. Conditions are ideal if you're reading this book as a grade 10 student or earlier. But not everyone's conditions are ideal all of the time. If only it were that easy! Even if you're starting your search in grade 12, you can still conduct a serious search for a university and do it right. It just means you have to crunch more work into less time.

You want to find the universities that best fit your educational needs and your personality. This book offers sound advice for making those choices. But the choices must be yours. You and your best friend may follow the same advice and reach totally different conclusions, because you are two different people. Go figure, eh?

Nobody else can make the decision for you because nobody else *is* you. Other people will have advice for you — some of it good, some of it not so good. Accept all advice graciously, digest it, sort it out, and then decide where you want to spend three, or four, or more years of your life.

If you conduct your university search the right way, you can be a very happy student. You can get a great education at a school that's suited to your academic goals, your personal interests, and your lifestyle. Best of all, you won't have to transfer somewhere else after your first year — unlike some of your friends who didn't plan right the first time.

You're Looking for Places Where You Can Thrive

If you haven't yet asked yourself the all-important question, ask it now: *"Why do I want to go to university?"* If you answer truthfully, you'll likely find a long list of reasons. Some will be education-related (to learn more than you already know). Some will be linked to your future (to get a job in your chosen field). Some may be connected to your personal life (to learn to live away from home).

To help you answer these all-important questions, here are some preliminary things to think about. Nobody else needs to know your answers, so make sure that you tell yourself the truth.

Do I want to go to university because:

✔ My friends are going?

✔ My parents expect me to go?

✔ I can make more money with a university degree?

✔ I'm ready to live on my own?

✔ I want to learn how to be a doctor, teacher, engineer, or other professional?

✔ I haven't learned as much as I think I should know?

✔ I'm not sure what I want to do, and I think university can help me find out?

✔ I can't think of anything better to do?

Mull your answers around for a while in your head. If you're a typical student, you have more than one reason for going to university. When you search for the "right" universities, you want to look for places where all those needs — educational, career-oriented, personal — can be fully satisfied. You want to look for places where you can thrive, academically and socially, as a student *and* as a person.

Your chosen universities are places where you will thrive, not just survive!

Let's say you want to become a chemist. One of the things you want to look for in your university of choice, then, is a top-notch science faculty and chemistry department. But you'd be wrong to base your choice on academics alone. You may find an outstanding chemistry curriculum, but at a school whose *personality,* or culture, clashes with yours. You might learn a lot of chemistry, but you won't be happy while you're learning it. You won't thrive. Universities have personalities, much like people. We tackle this issue later in this chapter, in the section, "You're Checking Personalities."

You're looking for universities where everything comes together for you. Trust us, these universities are out there. Finding these schools takes a little work, but when you find them you'll be happy you invested the time.

You're Making Lists

Lists are a big part of your search process, so get ready for them. You don't have to be too formal. You can write them on a pad of paper. (Don't worry, only you have to read them.) You can make them look pretty on a word processor. You can print them from a Web site. If you're lucky enough to have the right software at your school or library, you can have a computer compile some of them for you. So many options. Isn't technology great? It doesn't matter how you do it, as long as you get it done.

The first list is already made for you. It's a list of the 51 universities across the country that award degrees and want your tuition money — and that we've compiled for you in Appendix A. If you're thinking about going across the border to the United States for university, your job is somewhat more difficult. There are approximately 3,500 colleges in the U.S. ("colleges" is the more generic term for "universities" there).

We give you the straight goods about virtually every Canadian university in Appendix A, "Directory of Universities and Colleges." (It's the section with the yellow pages toward the back of the book. You can't miss it.) If you want a list of colleges in the United States, you can check out any of those huge directories in your high school counsellor's office — try the *College Handbook* (from the College Board); *Barron's Profile of American Colleges; Peterson's 4-Year Colleges; ARCO, The Right College;* and many more. Your local library probably also has copies. See Chapter 17 for more on applying to and paying for U.S. colleges and other international schools.

Start, ideally before you even begin high school, by choosing names from your much larger list of possible university choices. Keep this smaller list in a safe place. In fact, we advise you to create a special "University Applications File," and put your list there. You'll update the file as you go. We describe this important file in Chapter 6.

Your list will get smaller and smaller until, early in grade 12, it will contain only the names of the universities to which you'll apply. By then, your University Applications File will likely be chock-full of other key information as well — about programs of study, residence, and financial aid. If you want to look ahead, Chapter 6 gets you thinking about the huge variety of courses you can take; Chapter 9 takes you on a campus tour, where you consider various housing options amid many other things; and, as we keep reminding you, pretty much *all* of Part IV is devoted to the financial side of university.

You're Checking Personalities

A key part of your search, probably the most important part, is the personality check. After you find universities that (on paper or on a computer screen) look like they may be right for you, you need to check them out in person to make sure.

You have your personality. Each university has its own personality. You must decide whether your personalities mesh or clash.

The personality check takes time, so allow at least two days for each school you're checking. But don't think of your visits in terms of just driving through a campus, looking at the pretty maple trees, and saying, "This is a nice place." That would be a waste of time, not to mention gas.

You have to get out of the car and talk to people. Even live with them for a while. These are the people with whom you'll spend four years. Are they good guys or jerks?

If you don't take the time for a personality check and then wind up in a community of jerks, the only people more disappointed than you will be us. It will mean that, despite all your other preparation, you're still unhappy with your university choice. It will also mean that you'll probably be itching to transfer to another university by October of your first year. That's an awful lot of hassle to go through just because you forgot to do a simple personality check.

The personality check is so important that we devote an entire chapter to the subject. If you want to jump ahead, check out Chapter 9.

You're Looking for Universities

The subtitle of this part of the book is, "Finding the Right Universities." Yes, that means *more than one* university. No single university is right for you, so don't panic if you can't find it.

What you will find, as your lists grow smaller and smaller, are several schools that seem as if they can give you everything you need. As you check them out in person, you'll be convinced that three or four — or maybe six or seven — of these schools are places where you can thrive. These schools are the "right" universities for you!

Sure, you'll have one or two favourites. But you'll apply to more, just in case your top choices decide they don't want you or you can't scrape up enough money to attend them.

We want you to feel comfortable with your decisions when you send in your applications. You won't be biting your nails, like your less-prepared friends, fearing the rejection letter that could ruin your life. You'll know that wherever you wind up, you'll be at a right university, a campus where you can thrive.

Why You're Not Choosing a University

If you're tempted to add a university to your list for any of the reasons described in the following sections, resist it. Or, you can yield to the temptation, add the school to your list, and then carefully check out the school to see whether it really belongs there. None of these reasons, by itself, has any validity in identifying a school at which you can thrive.

Someone else likes the university

Someone else isn't you. Just because thousands of other students decide that they want to go to Simon Fraser University doesn't mean it's the place for you. It's very possible that Mount Allison University is right for you, but that has no relation whatever to how many other students like it.

If all your friends are flocking to a particular university and you think you'd like to be with your friends, fine. Put that university on your list. But don't apply to the school just because your friends do. You're dealing with *your life*, not making plans for a great party. Sure, see if the university that all your friends are raving about has what you need. See whether your personalities mesh. If this university is not a good fit for you, tell your friends you're going somewhere else. Maybe they'll follow you. Don't be scared to assert yourself. It's sometimes better to be the leader instead of the follower anyway.

If an older sibling or friend you respect recommends the university she's attending, that's a perfectly good reason to put it on your list for a hard look. But such a recommendation is not a good enough reason to rush to the admissions office, application in hand.

The university has prestige

If you want to go to the University of Toronto, or McGill, or UBC, just so that you can say you studied there, fine. Apply to whichever university you think has the most prestige and then sit back and wait for the acceptance offers to come rolling in. But if you're going to do this, then you don't need this section of the book. The prestige of a university in the eyes of the world at large has absolutely no bearing on your ability to thrive on its campus. All three of these universities are world-class, but they may not be right for you.

Prestige or no prestige: It's the education that counts

A friend of ours is a great example of how *not* to pick a university based on prestige.

Beth was happily learning at a small university. She attended classes regularly, did her homework every day, and consistently earned an impressive 85 percent average, sometimes higher. Life was good. But there was a problem. Beth's mother wanted her to come home to the city where she lived and attend the larger, more prestigious, university there. Her mother was a teacher and a graduate of the university. She kept pressing the point. She meant well, and thought she knew best.

There was another problem. Beth's boyfriend of four years wasn't happy with her going to a smaller out-of-town university either. The weekend trips back and forth on the bus certainly didn't help things. He also wanted her to come home — not least because he was going to the same big, prestigious school Beth's mother wanted her to go to. So, after her second year at her dream university, Beth moved back to the big city and enrolled in the more prestigious university.

Although the big university was right for her boyfriend — he liked the big city and he enjoyed his engineering studies — Beth hated the new environment. Not only did she miss her old friends, but also she missed the small, collegial environment at her old school. She had gone from a small school where everyone knew her to a large, impersonal university where she felt lost in the crowd. Less than two months into her third year, she realized the move had been a big mistake. She was miserable.

Her marks dropped, taking her from a solid *A* average to a low *B*. Beth began to feel inadequate and helpless as she could no longer meet and chat with professors. Classes were far too big and Beth felt as if she were nothing but a number.

Although Beth finished her bachelor's degree at the prestigious school (and managed to get her marks back up a little), she remained miserable. She went to a small university in the United States for her master's degree and found happiness once again. The lesson? It's important to do some soul-searching before you decide on your choice of universities. It's also important to stick to your guns and do what's right for *you*.

True, sometimes graduates of high-profile universities have a better chance of finding jobs in their chosen field. And if you have a field in mind, part of your search process is to identify universities that seem to be favoured by those employers.

Likelihood of employment is a valid ingredient to toss into the pot you're stirring to find a university. And, occasionally, likelihood of employment is linked to a school's prestige. But the likelihood of employment is just one of many ingredients in the recipe. If you choose a university only because it gives you a good chance of finding work, you may be gainfully employed in four years, but you may be miserable until then.

The university is tough to get into

For some reason, the prestige of a university often is measured by how tough it is to get into. The number used in comparing that toughness is the school's *admission rate,* which is the percentage of applicants who are accepted. The lower the number, presumably, the better the school. When you think about low admission rates as an indicator of the better schools, though, that kind of comparison doesn't make much sense.

If you go to a university's Web site, you may see the admission rate expressed in the form of the number of students who applied to the university for that given year versus the number of students actually accepted. Since you're good at math, you know that statistics can often be used to confuse just as readily as inform. Think about it. If lots of students apply to a particular university because it's in a big city or has a terrific medical program or whatever, but there's only a certain number of first-year places, few of these students will be granted spots relative to the huge number that applied. So it seems as if that university is more exclusive. But there could be several other reasons why the admission rate is so low: It might be that the university was really popular that year, for one reason or other, or that it did a better job of recruiting applicants. (One reason that prestigious schools recruit applicants is so that they can publish lower admission rates in the university directories and their Web sites, thus appearing even more prestigious.)

A low admission rate has absolutely no correlation to the quality of education (or enjoyment) you will receive from a given university.

So, as usual, the choices are yours. There are solid reasons why some universities have more prestige than others. We just want to be sure the reasons you might apply to a prestigious university are the right ones for you — and only you.

Your parents want you to go to the university

Some of our best friends are parents. While neither Caryn nor David are parents themselves, they both *have* parents, and can remember what kind of influence parents like to assert. Parents as a group are generally well-meaning folks, but we're all fully aware that, occasionally, they can cause trouble. This trouble is natural. Your parents want the best for you — even if it doesn't seem like it, sometimes. Many a troublesome argument has arisen between loving parents and loyal kids over university choices.

A few reasons to consider a prestigious university, and a few reasons not to

Prestige is earned. A prestigious university has proven itself over time.

We're talking about lots of time here; decades, sometimes even *centuries*.

The university's reputation could have just as easily slipped as grown over time.

Is the university you're considering resting on its laurels? The prestige may still be deserved — just not in the programs you want to study.

Prestigious universities look good on your résumé.

Many prestigious universities are recognized around the world. This may help if you want to work internationally or go on to an international graduate school.

It won't help if you choose a prestigious school at the expense of one with a better program in the field you want to study.

Try explaining this in a job interview. It's better to have a top-notch understanding of your field than a prestigious name on your diploma.

Prestigious universities usually have more money and resources.

Thanks to rich alumni and other donors, more money and resources usually aren't far away. The University of Toronto has more than 60 libraries, some generalized and others specialized. Robarts Library, one of U of T's larger, general collections, has over 3 million books, maps, videos, and other items. It's one of the largest collections in the world. Even one of U of T's smaller libraries can have more books and other items than a smaller university may have in its entire collection!

Just because the university has more resources doesn't mean you can access the materials you need.

Finding a *specific* book at a large library is often a challenge. The University of Toronto's Robarts Library, for example, is spread over 12 floors of floor-to-ceiling racking so extensive it's colour-coded so that the librarians in charge of re-shelving books can find their way around.

You may also have difficulty finding books that are up-to-date — say, published within the last 15 years. Older universities have been stocking up their libraries for a long time, and some of the books have been there, gathering dust on the shelves, for years. Our editor had to write a paper on Chaucer's *Canterbury Tales* and couldn't find a book on her particular topic published after 1968!

Sometimes it's the students themselves who hold you back from finding the books you need. Caryn found that the University of Victoria law library operated on something of an honour system; students willingly shared reference materials with each other. Meanwhile, some of the books at the University of Toronto law library have had pages ripped out by excessively competitive students.

Prestigious universities may be the only ones that can afford to hire famous faculty.

All other things being equal, super-intelligent scientists, philosophers, and business leaders are often attracted to large schools (where their own professional reputations can continue to grow).

There's little chance of a first-year under-graduate student ever catching a glimpse of these people.

Famous scientists are at that university to do research and make the school famous — not to teach a bunch of 18- or 19-year-olds.

Plus, just because they're smart (or famous) doesn't necessarily mean they can teach. Some of the worst courses Caryn and David suffered through were taught by professors who are household names in Canada. Problem was, they couldn't teach their way out of a paper bag. Sad but true.

Prestigious universities usually have a lot of old, vine-covered, appealingly musty-smelling buildings.

Admit it, it feels good walking around those buildings — following in the footsteps of who knows how many students who came before you. Prestigious schools are also often symbols of the cities where they're located. They have romantic histories and large, imposing campuses (imposing in a good way). This is probably due to the fact that most newer universities, having been built after the Second World War, bear more than a passing resemblance to bomb shelters.

Those impressive buildings may be old, cold, and decrepit.

What was a state-of-the-art heating system 50 years ago can leave today's students a bit chilly during our cold Canadian winters. And let's not even talk about air conditioning. Old residences simply weren't designed for this type of luxury. Older buildings may have been recently up-graded, but don't count on it.

Parents frequently think they know best where their beloved offspring should go to school. After all, they've known what's best for you all these years and they can find no reason why the fact that you're growing up should diminish their wisdom.

Well, sometimes this parental wisdom works, and parents and kids agree. But, just as often, it doesn't.

Well-meaning parents often overlook one little item. When you, their charming child, go off to university, they get to stay home. (This is when they'll unroll those blueprints to take out the wall between your bedroom and the bathroom to make way for their new hot tub.) Parents don't have to commit four years of their lives to a strange place where they've never lived. It's the student's life — *your* life — that is on the line, and picking a university has to be *your* decision.

At university time, your parents become advisors. They're very important advisors, to be sure. Please accept their advice willingly and consider it thoughtfully. But, in the end, there's only person who will know what's right for you — *you*.

When a parent gives you a piece of advice and you think it's the worst thing you've ever heard, take a moment to think of the following. Parents have been doing their thing for much longer than you've been doing yours. It's possible they could be right and you could be wrong. At least consider the possibility. When Caryn or David get what they might consider somewhat half-brained advice from their parents, they try to remember Mark Twain's quip about his parents: "The older I got," he said, looking back at his long life, "the smarter my parents became." It's reasonable to conclude his parents didn't actually get much smarter; rather, Twain's appreciation of them matured. Yours might too, so go easy on your parents and try to keep the sarcastic remarks to yourself — your parents are just trying to help.

Your parents are also very likely to be your financial backers. Without their savings, you may well be going nowhere. And their advice on how much they can afford will be a key element in your decision.

If Mom graduated from Dalhousie and is urging you to go there to keep the family tradition alive, fine. Put Dalhousie on your list. Give it a good, hard look. Consider that your chances of being accepted might be (slightly) higher because you're the child of an alumna — even though the university admissions officers deny this. But if, after checking it out thoroughly, you decide that Dalhousie is not the right university for you, advise Mom politely that you're going somewhere else. If you'd rather not tell her yourself, hand her this book and we'll do it for you:

"Hey, Mom! Your son's not a kid anymore. You did such a good job raising an intelligent young man that he's now ready to make some choices on his own about how he'd like to lead his life. Back off from that Dalhousie stuff and have the confidence in him to let him choose the right university for himself."

The university ranks high in magazines and newspapers

You've seen them. They're a lot of fun to read. They're the lists in magazines, newspapers, and other printed sources that appear every so often ranking universities by whatever criteria the editors select. These lists tout the best universities, the cheapest universities, the best engineering universities, the best university values, the best tiny universities, and so on.

The rankings serve some useful purposes. They give university presidents something to complain about. And the presidents take advantage of every opportunity to complain about how meaningless it is to try to compare universities, whatever yardsticks are used.

The rankings also keep university public relations offices busy. While their presidents are out complaining, the PR folks at schools ranking high on the lists churn out press releases and recruiting literature trumpeting the news that their institution is in the Top Ten of Best Universities with Red Brick Residences That Offer Vegetarian Meals. Okay, so maybe this exact list doesn't exist, but you get the point.

One list we've never seen in a magazine is Best Universities for You. We'll bet you haven't seen one either. Only you can compile this list.

How many applications?

How many applications should you send? Does a university know whether you apply somewhere else? Does it hurt your chances to apply to maybe a dozen schools? Students often ask these questions as they start thinking about university. And students who don't ask these questions aloud are probably thinking about them, too. They're just keeping the questions to themselves.

The short answer is: Don't worry about sending out too many applications. Every university in the country hopes it will be the only one receiving an application from you, but every university also knows it won't be so lucky. Most students these days apply to at least three or four schools.

If you live in Ontario, an organization called the *Ontario Universities' Admission Centre (OUAC)* takes care of all university applications in the province (including the Ontario College of Art and Design but not including the Royal Military College). The OUAC charges $80 for the first three Ontario universities you apply to — $85 if you are applying from outside Ontario — and $25 for each university after this. The system is different in other provinces: Each university has its own system, its own application forms, and its own application fees.

Realistically, the number of universities you apply to is limited only by the time that you have to complete the applications and the money you can afford in application fees. Most universities these days want $40, $50, or $60 in a non-refundable fee just for considering your application. Only you and your parents know how much you can afford. Our best advice is not to spend the money if you're fairly sure you don't have a chance of making the school's cut-off mark.

It's best to apply to more than one university. Even if you have your heart set on a particular school, don't put all your eggs in that one basket. What if that school says no? You'll have to scramble (pun intended) to find other universities that have space left.

When you reach the end of the process of finding your right universities, in Chapter 9, you'll have about four schools on your list. We suggest that you apply to all four and then find two more that should also get your application.

Six is not a magic number. You'll know, after you complete the process, how many schools feel right for you. Apply to all of them, even if they number a dozen. The best course to follow is to get great marks so all the schools will offer you acceptances. Then you can afford to pick and choose.

Some information in some of the magazine rankings will be useful to you. In the fine print, a few show you the data that they've gathered to come up with their lists. And "total books in a university library" or the "percentage of full professors per student" certainly is good to know, but these numbers (and many like them) are hardly the information on which you would base a final decision.

The criteria used by magazines to rank universities will most likely not be the same criteria that you, after careful thought, will use to decide which universities fit you best. And those rankings that purport to tell you the value you get for your education dollar don't know how many dollars you will be required to spend. All they know is each school's published sticker price, which may or may not be what you spend considering factors such as scholarships, student loans, and other financial factors. We'll repeat that because it's so important. The rankings tell you which universities offer the best value in relation to their direct costs alone. They make no mention of other important factors such as number of students who leave after their first year; living costs in the community; after-university employment; or dozens of other useful facts.

So read the rankings. Enjoy them. Chuckle over them with your friends when you see that your university didn't make the coveted "Best Universities for Polo Players" list or "Universities with the Cleanest Campuses" list or whatever other list is offered. But don't use them to decide where you'll go to university.

Chapter 6

Grade 9: Starting Early

. . . .

In This Chapter

▶ Building your University Applications File

▶ Accepting the ugly truth: Universities look at *all* your high school marks

▶ Choosing the right courses

▶ Thinking about your major

. . . .

You're just starting high school, bright-eyed and bushy-tailed. You're excited about all the new activities you're about to experience, the new courses you'll study, and the new people around you. You're probably a little nervous about your new surroundings. Do you really have to start thinking about university already?

In a word: Yes!

University will (hopefully) be your next step after high school. You need to make sure you can take that next step — and the only way to be sure is to prepare well ahead. If you get to the point of writing your applications and suddenly discover that you don't have a high enough average to even be considered, you'll regret the time you wasted when you could have been preparing yourself. If you realize in grade 12 that you want to apply to an engineering faculty but discover that you don't have the science and math requirements because you dropped them back in grade 9 or 10, you'll be upset that you didn't know in advance how to get ready for university.

Lucky for you, this book has all the pointers you need. In this chapter, we let you know what you need to do both in school and outside of school. In school, take the tougher courses, get to know your teachers, and get the most out of your classes. Outside of school, discover what subjects you love and learn more about them.

Start Your University Applications File

When university admissions officers look at applications, they divide them into four piles: *yes, no, maybe,* and *incomplete.*

We deal with avoiding getting into the *incomplete* pile in Chapter 11, when we take you through the process of filling out an application. Those in the *yes* pile have magnificently high marks and have taken the right subjects. Those in the *no* pile don't have the minimum average necessary to be considered. Different universities and even different programs within universities have different minimum standards, but most arts and sciences faculties require at least a 65 percent average from at least six grade 12 courses, and usually at least a 70 percent in English and sometimes in a math course. This doesn't guarantee that you will get in with those marks, but it does pretty much guarantee that you *will not* get in if your marks are below that level.

Those in the *maybe* pile are borderline. For this large group, the university admissions officers often need to look beyond marks to determine whether to transfer them to the *yes* pile or to the *no* pile. If your application is in the *maybe* pile, you want the university admissions officers to have as much supplementary information about you as possible to make sure you stand out as an exceptional student.

Where does this supplementary information come from? We're glad you asked. It comes from your University Applications File, which you should start in grade 9 — or even earlier.

In this file, keep:

- ✔ Report cards;
- ✔ Notes from teachers about your performance;
- ✔ Special notes about any odd marks that you receive (see the sidebar, "But what about that low mark in chemistry?");
- ✔ Information about any awards you receive;
- ✔ Personal notes about all your activities — perhaps in diary form;
- ✔ Anything else that could be used to demonstrate your excellence or smooth over any questionable areas on your high school transcript.

Later, you will add to the file all your research on specific universities, plus all your ideas and newspaper clippings relating to your potential majors or careers. You will eventually need to organize it into a series of files, but start out with just the one.

Get yourself a labelled file folder and notebook, and choose a specific space to store it for easy reference. Keep it in the same place so you can refer back to it as you progress through high school.

Universities Look at Your Entire High School Career

Think your grade 12 marks are the only important ones? Think again. Universities across Canada look at the marks you receive in every year of high school. The admissions officers will know what courses you chose, what grades you earned, and how many times you had to take each course.

But what about that low mark in chemistry?

Having a few low marks will not end your dream of attending university. High school is a time of self-discovery as well as a time of prescribed education. Believe it or not, university admissions officers know that. You may find that you are simply no good at, for example, chemistry. Well, if you eventually apply to a business administration faculty, the admissions officer will see your low mark in chemistry but may be inclined to disregard it.

That is, he or she may be inclined to disregard it if told in an accompanying letter that you discovered during this class that you had no interest in or talent for chemistry and intend never to study it again, but instead have a fascination for business administration as demonstrated by your high marks in other courses and constant activity with the Young Entrepreneurs' League in your school. Sometimes, it's all in the spin.

Similarly, you may have a low mark in a course that you loved. Unfortunately, it had a 100-percent final exam and you wrote it even though you had pneumonia. Get a doctor's note verifying your sickness and keep it in your University Applications File. Get another note from your teacher verifying that you were an excellent, inquisitive, and intelligent student who simply must have had a bad day. Later, send a copy of the doctor's and teacher's notes along with your application and written explanation. It certainly can't hurt your chances of being accepted at a university.

It's a good idea to track any low marks you receive throughout your high school career, and note the reasons why. They don't have to be as obvious as illness. If you went through a personal trauma, such as a death in the family or parental breakup, universities may overlook certain problem marks you received during this time.

Other reasons can be frequent moves from one location to another, abuse, personality conflicts with a teacher, or a later-diagnosed learning challenge — especially one that can be compensated for, such as hearing loss, visual impairment, or dyslexia.

In fact, since you will likely apply to universities about halfway through your grade 12 year, your marks in grade 11 are almost as important as your marks in grade 12. With the marks required to gain university admission steadily rising over the past few years, it is becoming more and more important to show an excellent scholastic record *throughout your entire high school career*. That means that you need to start working to raise your average and keep it high right from the first day of high school.

Take the Tougher Courses

In pretty much every school, there are courses known as "bird courses" — so easy that even a bird could get a passing grade. These are not the courses you want to take.

We know, you figure you can take them to bump up your average — but it will only hurt you in the long run. There are many reasons why it is better to take the more difficult courses, both to help you get into university and to prepare you for eventually attending university. From personal experience, Caryn and David can both say they felt better for challenging themselves. As an added benefit, the challenging courses were the ones that (usually) meant something to them.

Tougher courses increase your odds

Higher-level courses are usually prerequisites to get into your preferred field of study in university. If you take only general level science in grades 9 and 10, you may not be allowed to take the higher level physics, chemistry, or biology courses in grades 11 and 12. At least one of these courses is required to get into most science-related university faculties. If you don't have the prerequisites, your application will go into the *no* pile.

If you develop a special interest in an advanced level course — biology, for example, let your teacher know about it and ask for a reference letter. Stash it away in your University Applications File. Reference letters can give you a leg up when you apply to universities, both for admissions and especially for scholarships — you must be a pretty exceptional student if your biology teacher raves about you like that, right? (Hey, you might even get a better mark in the course, too!) We talk more about reference letters in Chapter 11.

What if you love that "bird course"?

We don't want to dash your dreams and tell you that it's only acceptable to take courses that will help you look good on your applications. That would be like telling you not to study French romantic poetry in university because it won't lead to a job in the business world. It's your life and you have a right to pursue your own interests and goals.

However, you do need to recognize the consequences and prepare for them. If you take that basket-weaving course, make sure you shine in it — and definitely get a reference letter from your teacher. If this is your true passion, you'll want to do basket weaving as an extracurricular activity, enter competitions, write articles about the art and history of basket weaving, and generally become an expert in the subject.

With all this supplementary material presented, the university applications officer will know that this was not a "bird course" to you. Rather, taking it was an expression of your focus and determination.

Tougher courses prepare your mind

Taking the tougher courses also helps you prepare for the experience of studying at university. Not to frighten you, but the academic level at university is a *huge* jump above the academic level in high school. Demands and workload are much greater, as is the competition.

Don't Drop English or Math

English and at least one math course are required for admission to almost every university in Canada. Usually, universities require you to have higher grades in these two subjects than in other courses. For example, many universities require that applicants have a minimum average of 65 percent in grade 12 to be considered for admission. However, they might also require that both your English and math marks are no lower than 70 percent.

While most high schools require students to take English every year, math is often considered an elective. If you have even the *slightest* wish to attend university you should consider advanced or enriched math to be a required course.

Prepare for Your Major

Okay, you know universities look at *all* your high school marks from grade 9 onward, you've set it up so that you'll take the harder courses, and you've promised yourself that you won't drop English or (gulp!) math. You've set up your University Applications File and stored it in a safe, easy-to-remember place in your room. What's next?

Well, it's time to think about your university major. Wait a minute — before you protest that you're only in grade 9, take note that we did not say you have to *choose* your major. Still, it's a good idea to start thinking about it.

Why should you think about it now? Well, because, after graduating from high school, university is the next important step in your life. Before you take any step, you should think about where you are going. Otherwise, you might waste time on a misstep.

Setting goals

Enough with the stepping metaphors! The reason to think about your university major in grade 9 is so you can take the right courses, certainly. But, it is also so that you can start investigating, understanding, and realizing your dreams in life. Studies show that people with specific goals are more likely to become satisfied with themselves than those with no clear idea of what they want to do.

Unfocused people often drift from one thing to another, from one major to another, from one job to another, without ever finding what gives them passion and satisfaction in life. Now, we're not saying that your life will turn out perfectly if you think about your major in grade 9. But you are more likely to do well in university if you have chosen your major carefully after a few years of contemplation and research. You are also less likely to waste time on majors that are clearly of no interest to you.

Let's say you think journalism is the career for you. You find out which universities offer journalism as a major and check out the course descriptions. You might sit in on a lecture at a local university and visit your local newspaper. Gradually, you may discover that journalism is not the glamorous career that you originally thought it to be. So, you rethink your choice and move on to considering another option.

On the other hand, you may discover not only that you love journalism, but also that you want to focus on political journalism. You write letters to the editor. You start making contacts at the newspapers and magazines that you visit. They may allow you to write a guest column for them. You write for your school newspaper, eventually becoming the editor. You offer articles and commentaries to online publications and some are posted on Web sites. Suddenly, you are a journalist! And, when you apply to the university of your choice, your wealth of experience will go a long way in convincing the university admissions officers that you are exactly the sort of student they want in their faculty. Improving your writing ability won't exactly hurt you in university either!

Thinking ahead allows you to strike the wrong options off your list. It also gives you more time to gather important information about the subjects that you intend to study, so that you will be more comfortable making your final choice of university major — and more capable of doing well once you get there!

Choosing courses

If you discover that you truly love journalism, you will know in advance to take the courses best suited to it. Take English and media studies, history, and economics. You'll still need a math course as well. (Thought you'd get off easy, huh?) And learning French would certainly be a boon if Canadian politics is going to be a focus for you. If you think ahead like this, you will approach your university education with eager anticipation, while many of your less-prepared fellow students will approach it with little more than a shrug of the shoulders.

Get your family and adult friends involved in your research! Learn more about what you may want to study by taking advantage of programs such as "Take Your Child to Work" days. If you already know what your parents do for a living, and you decide it isn't for you, try to find people who work at jobs you find interesting. Ask them to let you tag along at work for a few hours or a whole day. If you feel shy about asking, tell your parents about your idea and enlist their help. Most adults are flattered when anyone finds their work fascinating — give them a chance to show off!

If you continue to find a particular type of work fascinating, try to arrange another, longer visit, or get a part-time job doing what (you think) you love.

No one said you have to be exclusive

As you keep reminding us, you're only in grade 9! There's no reason to limit yourself to one possible major. In fact, you should consider as many as you can. Think about what it would be like to do biochemistry research. Or operate a sports facility. Or teach medieval studies.

Consider everything that interests you — and open your mind to topics that are new to you. How can you know whether pharmacology or economics or Hindu translation are right for you until you check them out?

Faculties and majors

If you haven't researched all the different options for faculties — sometimes called *programs* — and majors before you have to apply, you may be in for a bit of a shock. There are an awful lot of options. And many of the majors listed in a university calendar may not even be recognizable to you as words.

What is *kinesiology*? What about *human geography*? Can you really get a degree in *midwifery*? And is *general arts* the same as *liberal arts*?

It may seem like a never-ending stream of possible options, and you can't even tell what some of them are, let alone whether or not you want to study them. Relax. University majors tend to fall under the category of either *arts* or *sciences*. Some universities divide arts into *humanities* and *social sciences* as well.

Most universities also have a variety of faculties that are separate from the vast arts and sciences faculties. These smaller faculties are sometimes harder to get into because there are fewer spaces available. We have listed a few of them here with a brief explanation as to what each of them means and where they might lead you. As for the majors, there are far too many to list but it's not that tough to research them.

A research tip: Start by looking up any unfamiliar words in the dictionary, then on the Web, and then in the particular area of the university Web site where the major is offered. Ask your teachers and counsellors about all majors that sound interesting. You can even fire off an e-mail to the professors or faculty advisors for the major in question. Don't be shy. This is your future you are planning. Make sure you can make an informed decision.

University Faculties

Faculty	What You Learn	What You Can Do with It
Architecture	Building, space, and landscape design	Become an architect
Arts	Everything from English to philosophy	Depends on your major — and on you
Business administration	Economics and business strategy	Become a manager, a consultant, or an entrepreneur (open your own business)
Commerce	Accounting and economics	Become a chartered accountant
Engineering	Applying science and math to design products or systems	Work in the technology industries, design products, or do research
Humanities	Arts, excluding the social sciences	Depends on your major
Journalism	Researching, writing, the media world	Become a journalist
Music	Mastering a given instrument, music theory, and composition	Become a professional musician, teach

Faculty	What You Learn	What You Can Do with It
Physical education and health	Kinesiology (how the body works), sports training	Become a sports administrator, teacher, or physiotherapist
Sciences	Everything from astronomy to zoology	Depends on your major — the sky's the limit
Social sciences	Anthropology, economics, psychology, sociology	Depends on your major

The nice thing is, you have time. You don't have to research your potential major in a weekend. Eventually, you'll have a list of several majors that sound interesting to you. Keep that list and we'll refine it further in Chapter 7.

Start Your Mull List

Now is not a bad time to start thinking think about your university choices. Get out a pen and a pad, or sit down at your computer. You're about to make your Mull List.

In Chapter 2, we introduced the basics of what to think about when considering a university. Now it's time to rank those things in terms of their importance to you. Use your Mull List to keep track of these rankings. They will change over time as you do. Let's take distance as an example. Do you think you might want to study far from home, or stay close by? If you decide that you really want to live at home for your university years, then there's no point in collecting extensive information about universities on the other side of the country. See what's happening? You're going to use your Mull List to narrow down your choices of universities. Here are some other categories that should be on your Mull List, as well as the sorts of questions you should ask yourself about each:

- **Size:** Is a big campus okay as long as you have a small faculty?
- **Location:** Small town, big city, or somewhere in between?
- **Distance:** The city where your family resides, the other side of the country, or somewhere in between?
- **Major:** Is the course of study you want offered and will you be able to get into the program?
- **Housing:** Can you get into residence? Can you get a single room? Does the university have coed residences? Is it easy to get a place off-campus?

TIP

> ✔ **Students:** What kind of people go to this university? Is there ethnic diversity? Is the attitude cool, laid back, sophisticated, or just plain wrong for you?

Give each category a rating — either by letter (A to E) or number (1 to 5). Include comments to remind yourself why you answered the way you did.

Once you've got some idea of what's important to you, it's time to start researching. As your first step, take a look at Appendix A, the "Directory of Universities and Colleges," in the back of this book. It's full of information on virtually every university across Canada.

After that, go online. The directory lists the URL for every university and college covered. Check out Appendix C, "Useful Web Sites," as well. And just in case you want more to do, bone up on your online researching skills by reading Chapter 8. You'll find ways to save time while you research, and organize what you find into a package you can use.

REMEMBER

What you put in your Mull List isn't carved in stone. What was an absolute necessity in grade 9 might be less important by the time you apply in your final year of high school. For example, in grade 9, when you are 14 years old, you may think it would be terrifying to go to university on the other side of the country. However, a few years later, you might welcome the prospect of getting away from your parents' house. Your list will likely go through several versions before you reach the "definitive" version a couple of years from now. So don't worry about getting it right. Just worry about *writing stuff down*. Your list will change and evolve as you do.

A Mull List

Here's an example of a Mull List made by Lynn, a hypothetical high school student. Lynn is rating what's important to her in a university. Note she's using letters to rank the various factors, and including comments beside each.

Item	Rating (A–E)	Comment
Distance	B+	300 km from home
Size	A	Not giant, not tiny
Location	A	Small town
Major	B	Offers environmental science but hard to get into
Housing	C	Hard to get single room in residence
Students	D	Not much diversity

Chapter 7

Grades 10 and 11: Starting Later

*I*t's begun. You're already deep into your high school career. Your grade 9 record is on the books. You can do nothing to change it.

Relax. Even if your marks were terrible in grade 9, and even if you haven't been taking the tougher courses, there's still time to pull yourself together. Besides reminding you about getting into (and staying in) the right courses, in this chapter we focus on two very important lists that have taken up residence in your University Applications File. First is your list of all the universities you may be interested in applying to when the time comes. In this chapter, we show you how to narrow that list down to a manageable number — the final cut that you'll favour with an application. The other list — equally important (all the lists we suggest you make are important!) — is your list of majors you might want to study for three or four years at university. Yup, you need to start narrowing this list down, too.

Take the Right Courses

Well, grade 9 may be over, but the rest of your high school transcript is still a blank slate. The marks you receive from here on in are the most significant portion of the high school record that you eventually send to universities. And one thing that impresses a university admissions officer is a record that improves each year. Such a record shows that you are peaking at the right time. To find out more about how universities look at you, see Chapter 10.

If your academic record is not as sparkling as you'd like it to be, you still have time to do something about it. A strong finish after a slow start looks better than an excellent record in grade 9 that deteriorates in later years. So, work on your academics now. Make the rest of your high school career stand out.

As you begin grade 10, you need to think hard about the courses you are taking. If classes have already started, you may not be able to jump from basket weaving to biology. However, you can probably move from a general English or math course into an advanced one.

By saying you *can* make the move, we mean that your school will probably let you change courses if you prove that you can handle the extra challenge. Yes, it requires a little extra effort on your part, but it's definitely worth it. Study longer hours. Ask for extra help. Get a tutor if necessary. But get into those advanced classes!

Make sure you take the right high school courses, and start preparing for them as soon as possible. Most universities require a grade 12 (or OAC) English and math on an applicant's high school transcript, and many high schools require advanced grade 11 math to get into grade 12 calculus or algebra. So, it's like we said. If you want to study, for example, math or science at university, you've got to start working your way up to it by grade 11.

Refine Your List of Universities

Once you've gotten yourself on track scholastically, it's time to narrow down and refine the list of universities you're considering. You're about to take the initiative and let some universities know you are seriously interested in them. To do this, you must trim your list to a number that's workable. That way, you can start to communicate with universities without giving up time for important things, such as getting an *A* in chemistry.

Do your research. Use all the resources we describe in Chapter 8 to collect as much information as you can. Read this information through carefully and then categorize your material in terms of:

- Best choices
- Possible choices
- No chance

Write a brief assessment of each of your best and possible choices, along with a list of questions about them. Tuck this away in your University Applications File, which you started in grade 9. It should be getting pretty full by now. Hey, you may even have to start a new one to handle the overflow!

Consider this

Check out Appendix D, "The Mull List," at the back of the book, and do just that — mull things over. Think about what you want out of university and what you want out of life. It may not be the same thing — so consider wisely.

Perhaps you want a fun, party atmosphere at university. You've seen all sorts of college movies and you've heard stories from your older brother about frat parties and football games. It can be quite a draw.

Then again, you know you're intrigued by genetic engineering — perhaps enough to make it your life's work. Through your research, you've found a professor with a stellar reputation in the field. But she teaches at a small university with no football team or fraternities. What should you do?

In the end, the choice is yours. Yes, we know we keep telling you this. Get used to it! If you're passionate about genetic engineering (or whatever it is you happen to be passionate about), and you're 99 percent sure it's what you want to do with your life, then it may be worth giving up football games and frat parties at one university to go to the university with that amazing prof. But remember that you're only in grade 10 or 11. You might change your mind by the time you have to send in your university applications. That's okay.

Go for a stroll on campus

Grade 10 or 11 is not too early to start checking out university campuses. This isn't a formal visit, when you make appointments to see certain people at the university. Think of this first visit as a window-shopping excursion. It's an opportunity to get acquainted with the feel of the campus and gather information about the school. We discuss the who, what, when, and how of the more formal campus visit in Chapter 9.

Go to a university in your area and spend an hour or two walking around. Drop in to the student centre. Check out a residence or two. Read the bulletin boards to see what's happening. Pick up a copy of the student newspaper to see what's current on campus.

Keep your eyes open and observe as much as you can. Talk to people, if you get the opportunity. Don't be shy about jotting down a few notes while you chat. Stroll into the admissions office and see what information it's giving away.

But don't try to push your way into a formal interview. Grade 10 is too early — for you *and* the university — to talk seriously about your plans. Even the beginning of grade 11 is too early. That talk comes later, in the spring of grade 11 or the fall of grade 12, as we discuss in Chapter 9.

If an older friend or relative lives in a university residence, try to elicit an invitation for an overnight visit. The best way to find out how university students live is to live with them.

Our advice? Put both schools on your list, for now, under *possible choices*. Keep thinking about it. You're going to pare this list down significantly by grade 12, but that's still some time away.

Talk their ears off

There are lots of people you should be pumping for information to help you narrow down your list of possible universities.

✔ **Your guidance counsellor:** Part of his or her job is to know about universities and the university application process, and to impart that information to you.

✔ **Your teachers:** Ask them where *they* went to university. Get them to share their insights about university life.

Build a rapport with one or two of your teachers. You can fall back on this if you need to ask for a letter of recommendation to beef up your university application. We talk more about recommendation letters in Chapter 11.

✔ **Your parents:** Find out their opinions. Perhaps they went to a university that is on your list — or one that isn't. They might have a friend that went to one of your choices. You'll never know until you ask.

Your parents may have specific rules or requests concerning your university choice, and they should let you know about them as soon as possible. Remember, parents aren't perfect, and you may have to negotiate a few points with them. Your parents may stipulate that they'll pay your tuition only if you go to a certain university, or if you live at home while you're at university.

Get more information

So you're talking to lots of people and making notes about your conversations in your University Applications File. You should also be hunting down other sources of information:

✔ **University literature, including application packages:** Make note of any features of particular universities that you find attractive. Familiarize yourself with the set-up of the application. (Don't worry, we take you through the process of filling out one of these lovely documents step-by-step in Chapter 11.)

While you can go online and request this information from the universities, we suggest you write them a letter. Yes, this is old-fashioned, and yes, it means a bit of extra work for you. But there are good reasons to do it this way.

- **A letter requesting specific information about the university will yield more than a generic online request:** The package you get sent from your online request may be missing important extras that may affect your choice — extras such as information about the student newspaper and pamphlets about the town or city where the university is located. If you write a letter, you can ask for this information by name.

- **A letter lets you start up a dialogue between you and the admissions office:** This is a good thing. University admissions officers like to grant admission to students who show enthusiasm for their school. Your letter will most likely be kept on file at the university. This file will grow bigger every time you write.

- **A letter can boost your application:** It won't be the deciding factor if your marks are nowhere near the minimum requirements. But, if your application is in that borderline *maybe* pile, it can only help. University admissions officers are human and they like people who like their school.

  Hey, it's not that much more work. Keep a form letter on file on your computer and just change the addresses and the names of people. No sweat.

- ✔ **University directories:** They're big, they're cumbersome. But they're probably in your school library and are a great source of information.

- ✔ **Web sites:** By all means, keep checking university Web sites: While we suggest you don't communicate with universities through their Web sites too often (it's too impersonal), there's a wealth of great stuff online that you just won't find anywhere else. See Chapter 8 for tips on navigating university Web sites.

- ✔ **Computer programs that screen universities based on criteria you set:** These are expensive, but your school library might have one or two you can try out.

Refine Your List of Majors

Hopefully, you've been thinking about subjects you may want to major in since grade 9. You have probably made a list of a few that sound interesting and put it in your University Applications File, right beside your universities list. Maybe you've even started to investigate some of these subjects in greater detail.

And what an investigation! The more you research, the bigger your list gets. There are so many possible majors to choose from. Your options range from aeronautical engineering to business to medieval studies to zoology — with sometimes as many as 100 others in between, depending on the university. Now that you're in grade 10 or 11, how do you narrow it down?

There are some majors you will rule out immediately — depending on your interests. You might cross off languages, or engineering, or business and commerce, for instance. (If you really are interested in any of these topics, ignore what we said. We were just using them as examples. But you get the point. Some things just don't turn you on.)

Figuring out what you really like

Take a step back and write down all the things that make you happy — that give you a charge. Then write down what it is about them that you like. Don't take the easy way out and simply write down the obvious answer. Sometimes what we love is far from obvious. For example, if you love debating you could study subjects as different as law, drama, or politics.

Once you've figured out what you love to do, you can translate this into a potential university major. We've played around with a couple of scenarios in Table 7-1. Your list will probably be much different, but this should let you see what we mean.

Table 7-1	Translating What You Like into a Possible Major	
Activity	*What You Like about It*	*What Major It Leads To*
Debating	Outwitting your opponent with brilliant arguments	Law
	Performing before an audience	Drama
	Convincing people about important issues	Politics
Computer games	Redesigning them to make them even better	Computer engineering
	Comparing how accurate the game is to real events, such as battles	History
	Answering the questions in the news trivia games	Journalism
	Doing simulations	Urban planning or architecture
Skating	Exploring different body movements	Kinesiology
	Helping younger kids improve	Education
	Competition and performance	If you're good enough, maybe you should delay university and try out for the Olympics

GOOD TO KNOW

Fair well

Attending a *university fair* is a great hands-on way to get information about a particular university or group of universities. You can meet with representatives from the university, ask questions, pick up pamphlets, and generally get a pretty solid impression of the school.

University fairs are usually held in larger city centres over one or two days in the fall (when all the grade 12 students who haven't had the benefit of this book are scrambling to plan for the year ahead. But that's not gonna be you — no way). Although individual universities do mount their own fairs, you'll also find groups of universities banding together to do larger ones. For example, the universities in the Atlantic provinces put on a road show in September or early October, stopping in major cities from Montréal to Vancouver.

University fairs are not as popular in Canada as they are in the United States. Down south, colleges put on travelling road shows that go coast to coast in an effort to promote the school and recruit students. These fairs can be quite the extravaganzas. Here in Canada, however, we are rather more low-key. In fact, many Canadian versions aren't known as *fairs* at all. They go by names like *information sessions*, *university tours*, *meet-the-faculty events*, or some other suitably sedate — dare we say, "Canadianized"? — name. We use the term *fair* in this book, but watch for it to go by other names.

Dates, times, and locations of upcoming fairs are posted on university Web sites. Check the sites frequently, especially in the fall, and ask your counsellor to let you know about any you may have overlooked. Appendix A, "Directory of Universities and Colleges," includes the Web sites for all of them. Even if you've pretty well crossed a particular school off your list, you should go to a fair anyway and just poke around. Maybe you got the wrong impression of the university from the Web site and brochure. Talking to people from the university face to face could be a real eye-opener for you. Hey, it never hurts to get a second opinion. Give it a try!

REMEMBER

Taking the time to figure out what you really like is the biggest step to eventually choosing your major.

This doesn't mean your decision is made

If only it were that easy! Leave some room on your list of potential majors, because between now and grade 12 we're sure you will add and delete subjects from it many times over. You're changing, after all — figuring out what you really want to do. You may find that these interests are merely passing phases — something will happen in the future that might change your thinking entirely. For the moment, however, keep the subjects you've identified as options for your major in university. And look, you've narrowed down the first version of this list quite a bit, haven't you?

What You're Not Worrying About

We know, we know, we've been telling you to get busy — making lists, putting them in files, changing what's on the lists, starting new files to handle the overflow. Well, we thought we'd let you know that there are some things that are still too early to worry about in grade 10 and 11. They're not important yet.

Money

Eventually you'll worry about money, but not yet. Grade 10 or 11 is too soon to eliminate the idea of going to university because of the cost. It may be a good idea to sit down and have a chat with your parents about whether or not they will be able to help you pay for university, just so you have your expectations set at the right level. But remember, Canada is a wonderful country for students — tuition is relatively low and there are all sorts of options to help you get a university education. So let's face it: Worrying about cost at this point is a waste of valuable energy. (You can read about finding money in Chapters 13, 14, and 15.)

Selectivity

As you narrow your list of universities, you're not bothering to look at the percentage of applicants a particular school accepts. (Maybe you do, out of curiosity, but you're not writing the number down.) A university's *selectivity*, usually measured by its acceptance rate, has no bearing on whether it's a right university for you.

A low acceptance percentage means only that a whole lot more students apply than get in. This percentage is directly related to the popularity of a university among last year's grade 12 students. And last year's grade 12 classes' opinions — unless you're getting one in person from someone you know and trust — are not particularly important in your search.

The Final Cut

It's spring of grade 11. You've put in a lot of work over the last three years collecting information. Each of the 18 universities to which you wrote responded with a packet of literature about its campus, its courses, its housing, and its costs. Most universities also sent catalogues describing course offerings and included applications for admission.

GOOD TO KNOW
V+

Should you take the SAT I? (Does anyone care?)

It is a curious difference between American and Canadian culture that the *SAT* — a college preparatory test that measures your ability in English and math — can mean so much in one country and next to nothing in the other. (*SAT* stands for *Scholastic Aptitude Test* but is almost always just called the SAT.) In the United States, it's pretty much mandatory to take an updated version of the SAT (called the "SAT I"). Most students usually take the test in grade 11. Your score is a key factor in getting into an American college — the higher, the better. Canadian universities, on the other hand, never ask for SAT I scores, and students rarely offer them voluntarily.

Still, there are good reasons to write the SAT I:

✔ The SAT I can bolster a less-than-stellar academic record — if your applications are likely to fall into the borderline *maybe* piles of your favourite universities.

✔ You can choose whether or not to submit it. You have to submit your transcript, but you can wait to see if you get a terrific mark on the SAT I and then use it as a tool to boost your record…or not.

✔ The SAT I will give you experience writing high-pressure, timed, standardized tests — something you will do a lot of in university.

✔ The SAT I is similar to post-graduate admission tests you might have to take if you go on to law school, medical school, business school, or another post-graduate degree.

If you choose to write the SAT I, pick up a copy of *The SAT I For Dummies,* 3rd Edition, by Suzee Vlk (Hungry Minds, Inc.). We know this is a shameless promotion for our publisher, but if you bought this book you probably like the *…For Dummies* series, so what's wrong with spreading around some good advice?

So, what's the verdict? Should you take the SAT I or not? It's something extra to add to your application, and it's a good learning experience. In fact, it can't hurt you — it can only help you! (Remember, you don't have to submit your score if it's not so hot.) We say, go for it!

Don't expect high SAT I marks to get you scholarship offers if you have a 65-percent average in high school. But if the choice comes down to you and another student, both with the same average, and you've also provided stellar SAT I scores, they may help push your application over the edge into that coveted *yes* pile.

You tried to read everything. Occasionally, now, you feel as if you have information overload and your brain is full.

Now you need to trim the list again. You can decide what information you don't need, clear it out, and toss it away. The next cut — the final cut — will produce a list of universities that you like well enough to visit for a personality check.

Go back to your University Applications File — the one we suggested you start in grade 9. Take out your list of potential universities plus all the brochures, catalogues, and notes stored with it. As you glance at the names of the 18 universities on your list, you get the feeling that this decision may be easy.

You already have a few emotional favourites, universities that lit a spark when you read about them or talked to their people at a fair (the sidebar earlier in this chapter, "Fair well," tells you about the many good reasons to visit university fairs). One university comes highly recommended by your favourite English teacher. As you read the catalogues, three others impressed you with their journalism programs. You look at your list and start crossing out those that have given you no reason to think about them any longer. You find you've crossed out 11 of the 18 names.

You go back to your notes to refresh your memory. You notice that two of the remaining seven universities have enrollments under 2,500. Now, you think that may be a little too small for you, and neither of the two is among your top choices. Those two go and your list is down to five.

But how do you decide if you can thrive on their campuses? The best way to find out is to visit them. We give you some tips on how to make the most of your visits to universities in Chapter 9.

Every university has a personality. You can find out whether your personalities mesh or clash by spending some time with each other.

If you can't get all the way across the country to visit a university, contact the admissions office again and tell them you are extremely interested in their school. Ask if there are any *alumni* (people who have graduated from the university) in your city with whom you can chat about life on campus. Most will be happy to oblige. This also helps you further ingratiate yourself with the admissions officer! Once you decide which universities to favour with an application, it's time to start filling them out. We take you through this process in Chapter 11.

Chapter 8

Researching Online

· ·

In This Chapter

▶ Picking your first online destination

▶ Getting a virtual feel for the school

▶ Going beyond the official Web sites

▶ Finding financial aid online

▶ Organizing your information

▶ Corresponding with your favourite schools

· ·

*T*his chapter discusses how to extend your search for universities or colleges online, how to navigate around a university Web site, how to find information online that could really help with your ongoing search for your best schools, and the cool behind-the-scenes look afforded by some unofficial university sites.

Not only can this online information help you refine your search for your best schools, but you can also start checking out some other important matters, such as tuition costs, financial aid, and even picking a residence! True, using the Internet can never (and should never) replace an in-person visit to the campus itself (see Chapter 9 for more information about tips for campus visits), but you can give yourself a leg up in the planning process by going online — not to mention save a bundle of time.

One of the most daunting challenges facing any student thinking about university is deciding what to look at first. There seems to be so much information out there, from the schools themselves, your parents, magazines, TV, your high school counsellor, and even advertisements on public transit shelters! We know that sometimes it seems like so much information is coming at you that it's easier just to throw up your hands and shout, "Enough already!"

Well, we hear you. Loud and clear.

If you're this far along in the book, you probably understand our general philosophy about planning for post-secondary education. Start early, collect all the relevant materials, do some soul-searching, and then make a decision. Sounds simple, doesn't it? It is, when you remember the old Taoist saying, "The journey of ten thousand miles starts with a single step."

The good news is that you've already taken a lot of steps so far. Our job in this chapter is to show you how to augment the research process you've already started by using the Internet and the Web.

Of course, not every site is easy to navigate, so you may find it frustrating trying to find the information that is relevant to you. As well, some sites may be — let's just say — less than accurate. Relax. We've got some tips for finding the hidden information and for deciphering what you can and can't believe.

So, get ready. Get online. Go!

Get Ready for Your (Virtual) Trip

Before you embark on your (virtual) travels, there are a few things you need to pack.

You need to launch a Web browser such as Microsoft Internet Explorer, Netscape Navigator, or a similar product. Next, you need to visit your favourite search engine on the Web.

Whether you use Google, Yahoo, AltaVista, Excite, or any of an increasing number of search sites, you should know that your results will be slightly different based on which one you choose. If you choose to start your search on Excite, you will get different results than if you search Yahoo for the same search criteria. This is because each search engine uses a different strategy to catalogue Web sites.

When you consider that there are well over *one billion* Web pages on the Internet these days, it's easy to see how even the largest search engine can miss a great number of sites. The lesson? Always use more than one search engine to get the best results. Some search engines may even have links to other search engines. Use them.

We talk more about what to look for specifically on each university Web site later in this chapter (we list the Web sites of the universities, colleges, and technical institutes we profile in Appendix A, "Directory of Universities and Colleges"). For now, though, these are some of the basic features you'll find on most of the sites:

- Every university site has an introductory page welcoming you to its site. This page usually has pictures of the campus, its students, and probably some of its buildings. Often, links to university news items or other current stories are posted as well. Sometimes current weather and sports news is also included.

- Most sites have admissions information, usually separated into under-graduate and graduate categories. Each site is often further divided by faculty, as in, arts, science, math, engineering, and nursing.

- Some sites have course calendars, describing each course at length, its duration, scope, and prerequisites. Although Web sites are very helpful, remember that the *printed* version of the school calendar is the official word. When in doubt, check out the printed version of the calendar in your counsellor's office or local library. The university might charge you (between $5 and $10) to have a printed calendar mailed out to you.

- The site may list the e-mail addresses and telephone numbers of its faculty and staff by department. You can use this list to arrange appointments during your campus visits, as we discuss in Chapter 9.

- Most university sites also have tuition and financial aid information about each program. Study each area carefully.

Some university Web sites have information that has not been updated in years. Almost none will have the updated tuition rates for the following year available until a couple of months before the term starts. If you want to find out how much the school will really charge for tuition, you must get a printed package and keep in contact as the fees change.

Where to Go First

Surprise! It really doesn't matter where you start to look for a university, as long as you finish where you should be (for you, of course).

Maybe you'll choose the university that's geographically closest to you. If you live in Calgary, for example, this will likely be the University of Calgary. If you live just east of Vancouver, you may be starting your search at Simon Fraser University. And if you live in Antigonish, St. Francis Xavier University may be first on your list. You get the idea.

Perhaps your first choice will be where your mother or father lived, met each other, or went to university. It's possible you've heard about a great school on a TV show and want to check it out on the Web. Maybe a teacher or high school counsellor has recommended a particular university to you. And, yes, maybe your first university destination online is where all your friends are going. Just be sure you don't settle on a university only because your friends are going there.

What was that URL again?

Can't find Mount Allison's Web site? Or Laurier's? There are a few URL conventions that apply to most university Web sites. Keep them in mind while you surf and search:

✔ The (pretty much) universal URL convention for Canadian universities is to have the letter "u" (for university) added to the one-word name of the school plus the Canadian suffix ".ca". So, we get www.ucalgary.ca as the main URL for the University of Calgary. The University of Toronto can be found at www.utoronto.ca.

Most Canadian universities follow this convention, although some abbreviate or truncate their name in the URL. St. Francis Xavier University, for example, can be found at www.stfx.ca; Saskatoon's University of Saskatchewan is at www.usask.ca.

✔ Sometimes, when the word "University" comes at the end of a university's name, the "u" portion ends up at the tail end of the university's URL. The URL for Peterborough's

Trent University, for example, is www.trentu.ca. You can find Halifax's Mount Saint Vincent University at www.msvu.ca.

✔ Some schools simply have the name of the institution in the URL, without the "u." Toronto's Ryerson Polytechnic University uses this convention (www.ryerson.ca), as does Sudbury's Laurentian University (www.laurentian.ca).

✔ There are schools that abbreviate their names and tack on the ".ca" suffix. Memorial University of Newfoundland is at www.mun.ca; the University of British Columbia is at www.ubc.ca, and the University of Western Ontario is at www.uwo.ca. Medicine Hat College, in Alberta, is at www.mhc.ab.ca.

A good place to start your general search is the Association of Universities and Colleges of Canada (AUCC) Web site. Here you'll find links to all the universities across Canada. The URL is www.aucc.ca.

Whatever your first choice may be, you'll find an amazing amount of information about courses, programs, campus life, residence, and lots of other stuff — all for the asking, er, downloading. All you have to do is find the right site. Fortunately, this is pretty easy.

We list all the contact information for Canadian universities, colleges, and technical institutes (including telephone numbers and URLs) in Appendix A. However, if you leave this book at home one day when you go to the library to do some research, you should know a few handy shortcuts to find just about any Canadian university or college on the Web.

While you're visiting each university's Web site, keep an eye open for important things such as application deadlines and program prerequisites. If you haven't already figured out which courses you need in high school to follow a particular program in university, this is the place to do it. Most universities these days list program prerequisites based on high school courses. Don't forget to talk to your high school counsellor, teacher, or someone else you trust about your course choices. If you find an interesting site you didn't know about (or a site with one of those l-o-n-g URLs), simply bookmark it for future reference.

Whatever your first destination is on the Web, it definitely won't be your last. If you're like most students, you'll surf to one university site, do a bit of reading and printing, and then go off to another site just to compare. As you narrow down your choices, you'll probably return to some sites more than others. No pressure, though. At this stage, you're simply collecting information and looking around.

How to Read University Web Sites

Now that you know where each university is on the Web, you can start surfing and researching. Keep in mind that each university's Web site is published by the university itself. Like just about all the sites on the Internet, university sites are not subject to any kind of independent verification.

We're not saying that university Web sites are there to mislead you. On the contrary, the vast majority of school Web sites are accurate and portray an honest picture of what university life is all about at the particular school. However, don't believe everything you read. Some parts of the site may not be completely up to date. Other parts may be written by someone who is more enthusiastic than accurate. You wouldn't believe everything you read in the newspapers or see on TV, would you? Right! A healthy degree of skepticism is always a good idea. Also remember that Web sites aren't subject to the same amount of fact checking and editing as the university's printed materials are. So if you encounter a discrepancy between the Web site and the printed version, stick to the hard copy. Better yet, get in touch with the school and find out.

When in doubt, ask questions. Make a printout of specific pages from the Web site and ask a university official about the things you don't understand. Send an e-mail or telephone the school with your questions. Remember to write down everything you find out, including the names and titles of the people with whom you converse. By the time you apply, that helpful clerk who spent half an hour with you could have retired, or transferred, or quit.

Navigating the site

Okay, so you get to a university Web site and see a logo, some smiling people, and a bunch of options to click. Chances are it looks something like Figure 8-1, the home page on Memorial University of Newfoundland's Web site (www.mun.ca). What do you do now?

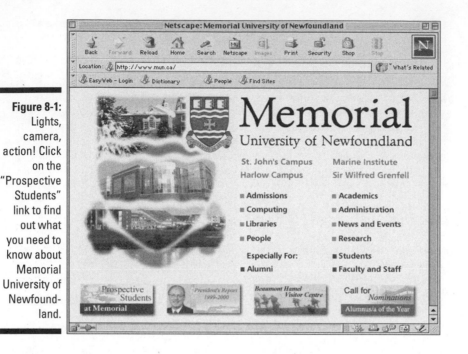

Figure 8-1:
Lights,
camera,
action! Click
on the
"Prospective
Students"
link to find
out what
you need to
know about
Memorial
University of
Newfound-
land.

There's probably a link specifically for "prospective students" or "applicants" or something similar. Click there first and collect all the information you can.

We suggest you put together a list of the different types of information you want to collect, and check them off as you get them. Here's a sample checklist of what you should find out from a university or college Web site:

✔ **Application:** Download the digital version and ask for a package to be sent to you.

✔ **Application guidelines:** This includes the *minimum* high school marks required for admission, courses required, and application deadlines.

✔ **Contact information:** This includes the correct spelling of the name of the school, its full address, telephone number, fax number, and e-mail addresses. There may be a different address for financial aid and residence information, so mark those down as well. You should also note the names of the people who work in the admissions office — they're the ones who will evaluate your application, so you don't want to mess up your spelling there! (There's more on filling out the application in Chapter 11.)

✔ **Extracurricular activities:** This includes information about athletics, fraternities or sororities, and other organizations on campus.

✔ **Major:** Collect information about areas of study that you think you are interested in.

- ✔ **Maps:** Download and print maps of the campus itself and all around it. These will be especially helpful on your campus visit.

- ✔ **Residence:** This includes information on the price of a room in residence and any associated costs such as meal plans or living in a single-sex residence (they tend to be more expensive).

- ✔ **Scholarships and financial aid:** Collect information on what sorts of programs are available.

Bookmark the most relevant pages, such as the place to apply online or the site of the student newspaper, if that interests you in particular. This allows you to go back to a page quickly and easily.

After you collect all the information you need, look around the rest of the site. Go back to the site's main page and explore the other options. Figure 8-2 shows the main page of Grant MacEwan College, in Edmonton, Alberta. Once you've collected the more obvious information about the different programs and courses available and how to apply, you may want to check out what sort of special events the college has going on. You might be surprised at what you find out.

Go to the news and events pages to see what's happening around campus on a day-to-day basis. Read the student newspapers to get the attitudes of the student body. Enter student forums to find out why people on campus are griping or celebrating.

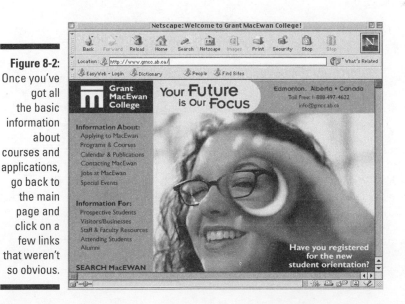

Figure 8-2:
Once you've got all the basic information about courses and applications, go back to the main page and click on a few links that weren't so obvious.

Check out the page about alumni activities to see how active the alumni are in the affairs of the university. Perhaps there is a famous alumna that you would dearly love to meet — who happens to be very active in university activities. Look at the section about professors to find out who might be making judgments about you for the next four years. Track a few of the professors in the subjects that interest you most and search to find out what else they have done. Most professors publish their research — see if anything interests you.

Looking critically at a Web site helps you get an idea of the university's core values and its personality. Take note of how the university or college chooses to promote itself. What's on the front pages and what is hidden in the back? Is it most proud of the look of its buildings, the age and traditions of its institutions, or the quality of its alumni? Does its home page sport a serious-looking professor at a chalkboard or a bunch of smiling students having lattes in a tree-lined quadrangle?

After you have looked around the site, move on to any links the site may provide. Many schools have links to clubs and teams — even to restaurants that operate on campus or nearby. Check out the section on unofficial Web sites later in this chapter to help you figure out where to go next.

You can probably book a campus visit online. Many schools offer different types of campus tours. Some tours are designed for prospective students (these are the ones you probably want). Other tours are for general tourists (you know, folks who are just visiting the city and want to see all the sights). Other tours are targeted at alumni of the university (who the school hopes will donate money). When the time comes to visit the university (as we discuss in Chapter 9), check out the Web site for details first to make sure you get the most from your visit.

Some things to look for online

There might be 100 (or more) pages on a large university site sitting there just waiting for you to look at them. Do all of them apply to you? Probably not, but it's not a bad idea to look around at things that wouldn't ordinarily concern you. Even if classical music isn't your thing, browsing through the Web pages for the university's music faculty may give you some clues about the other cultural happenings at the particular university.

Try to look at a variety of things on each university's Web site. Think about the subtleties, as well as what's obvious. While the actual content of the site is probably most important for you, *how* it's presented might tell you a lot about the school itself. Is the site so cool that it absorbs you for hours, or does it bore you silly in a few minutes? It might be an indicator of things to come. Ah, subtlety! Here are some not-so-obvious things to look for on a university or college's Web site:

✔ **What pictures has the school chosen to place front-and-centre on the home page?** Does it have lots of friendly pictures of students enjoying themselves — or are most of the pictures filled with old beautiful buildings? Graphics may illustrate what the people running the school feel is most important. Then again, it may just be that the school has some rather nice-looking buildings and they are really proud of them. It might be that the few people who were assigned to operate the Web site love to show smiling people. Still, it's a good piece of information to file away.

✔ **What do the residences look like?** You might see pictures of residences on the site. Do they look old (and beautiful) or new (and plain)? Keep in mind that old buildings might impress your parents (after all, they *are* beautiful), but you may not enjoy living in a drafty room with old-style heating. Perhaps those spacious rooms you see on the site are actually meant for *two* people sharing? Could it be that the room is so small the photographer had to stand *outside* the room to take the picture? Will you have space for you *and* your books? Think about these points when checking out the residences online.

✔ **Can you see pictures of the lecture halls and classrooms?** Are they huge (first-year classes in some large universities may have over 1,000 students!) — or cramped-looking? Will you feel under pressure to join in the discussion, even if you don't like saying things in class?

✔ **Do the students pictured on the site reflect the diversity you want?** These days, most universities at least try to *look* as if they have a diverse student population. All other things being equal, larger schools tend to have more ethnic variety. This is usually because large schools are located in large cities (go figure) and draw from a larger general population that is itself more diversified.

✔ **If you're physically challenged, is there evidence that the school will accommodate you?** Sometimes, older schools have been slow to add ramps, elevators, and other assistance devices to older buildings.

✔ **What is the area around the campus like? Can you see yourself being at home there?** Web sites can also speak volumes about the neighbourhood around the school.

- The Web site of a school smack in the centre of a heavily populated urban area such as Toronto or Montreal might emphasize things such as its "bustling city neighbourhood" as an advantage. You're close to lots of shops and theatres, as well as to transit services and 24-hour drug stores and supermarkets. Unfortunately, you're also close to the big city's core, so there's probably going to be more crime and other stuff you might not want to see (or experience), especially if you're from a small town.

- The Web site of a school located in a rural setting may emphasize its clear skies, its pollution-free environment, and the town's friendly people. What it may not mention is that the university is located

30 kilometres out of town and the bus to civilization runs only once every hour. Weekends could be even worse: you might be forced to bum a ride (or cab it) to get into town on Saturday or Sunday. Oh well, that also means there's more time to do your laundry and catch up on writing that term paper!

These, and probably dozens of other personal factors that only you know about, will affect your judgment about which university sites you like and which you don't. As you narrow down your choices, you'll likely get a sixth sense about which schools may be a good fit for you and which ones you'll probably skip.

Too good to be true?

In university, you'll probably learn a term called *cognitive authority*, essentially the degree to which you can believe and trust a given piece of information based on its source. It's a pity teachers don't teach this valuable life skill in high school, because it's useful for a great many things, including the online university search process.

You probably already know not to completely trust what you hear on TV or read in newspapers and magazines. Reporters, writers, and analysts often slant the news and other reporting with their own viewpoints. This *bias* can lead consumers of this information to make bad or uninformed decisions. It's hard to get rid of all bias in writing and reporting because, behind the stories, every writer or reporter is just a person, each with his or her own set of experiences and exposures to life.

You likely also know not to trust advertising, either. Rather than supplying unbiased information to consumers, advertisements are often nothing but seductively misleading half-truths designed to suck money right out of your wallet. Okay, okay, maybe it's not that bad, but remember that advertisements are enticements to buy a product or service paid for by the manufacturers of those very products. Well, guess what? While they're terrific sources of information, university and college Web sites are also — let's face it — advertisements for the particular school.

Here are a few questions to ask about the information you find on a university's Web site that will help you decide whether you can trust it or not:

> ✔ **What is the source of the information on the site?** Does the source of the information have a vested interest in swaying your opinion? If you're reading rave reviews about a particular university's academic life from the university's own Web site, you may want to ask yourself, "Why am I hearing from only the successful graduates — where are all the unsuccessful dropouts? Why did they drop out?"

✔ **Can the information on the site be independently verified?** Try to verify *every* piece of information that's key to your making a decision about a school. Just because one Web site (or person) tells you something
doesn't mean it's necessarily true.

✔ **When was the information on the site published?** How long ago was the information you are reading (or hearing) gathered and published? Sometimes statistics lag behind results for a year. That's okay. But if the statistics are more than a few years old, they're probably inaccurate, which means your decision — if you base it on those statistics — might also be inaccurate.

Pros and cons of using the Web for research

The good news:

✔ The Web gives you quick and easy access to all the universities in Canada.

✔ The Web makes the application process easier. Almost all universities make their application forms and guidelines available online and allow you to apply online, too.

✔ The Web makes it easier to compare schools because the information is available in digital format.

✔ The Web is always available (assuming you have access to a computer with Internet capabilities). You can conduct your research at any time.

✔ The Web lets you visit the campus *virtually* — the next best way to get a feel for the school's personality if it is impossible for you to visit in person.

✔ The Web gives you unfettered access to information not always available through more traditional channels.

✔ And did we mention that just about everything on the Web is free?

The bad news:

✔ The Information on the site may not be completely up-to-date.

✔ Online forms are often more cumbersome than paper versions. And printing out all those fancy forms will cost you big bucks in printer ink or toner.

✔ You can make quantitative comparisons online, but not qualitative ones. You can compare the cost of residence rooms, but you can't compare other factors such as size, view, and the overall comfort level.

✔ The Web can be addictive. You shouldn't be up really late at night researching universities. No sleep equals bad decisions and could affect those all-important grades.

✔ Virtual campus tours are great, but they're not, as they say, "the real McCoy." If you're serious about studying at a particular university, you really should try to visit the campus in person.

✔ There may be a technical problem on the Web site that disables links to important areas of the site, such as admissions information.

✔ The online portrait of the university or college may not be wholly objective.

What Else Is Out There: Unofficial Sites

Okay. So that we're clear about things, we should explain that there are ways to go beyond the official sites. *Unofficial sites* — those not operated or officially sanctioned by the school — may be a good resource to check to get a more complete picture of a specific university.

Students at a university usually run unofficial sites for a particular purpose. Although you probably won't find *really* weird stuff out there (after all, they are usually linked to the main university page), you can get an idea of the scope of activities and pastimes at the school.

Here's a smattering of what some schools have online:

- ✔ Religious sites, which serve the different religious groups on campus;

- ✔ Sports sites, such as the swim club or curling club;

- ✔ Political sites, such as the local chapter of the Liberal Youth (clubs such as this are where many future political leaders learn the ropes);

- ✔ Hobby and recreational sites, such as the movie club, computer club, audio visual club, chess club, Latin club — and many others.

If you check out these unofficial sites, you'll discover which schools are more active in which areas. For example, you might discover that Toronto's York University has a far more active (and boisterous) political culture than the University of Toronto, despite the fact that they are located in the same city and arguably serve the same market of students. Other schools are really into their sports teams, and their Web sites reflect this focus. Still others seem to place more emphasis on academics and host more sites related to educational subjects and the transition from school to career. If you see more references to sites such as *The Commerce Students Union* and fewer references to *The Swing Dance Society*, you might conclude that one school is more "serious" than another (notice we didn't say "better").

Getting the straight dope on courses

Many large universities, or ones with active student bodies, publish *course evaluations:* frank, objective, student-written commentaries about all aspects of the course in question — from the topics covered, number of assignments, and how hard the final exam is, to whether or not the professor can teach. These are sometimes called *anti-calendars,* a play on *university calendars.* More and more universities are making these course evaluations available on their Web sites. We suggest you check them out — bookmark the page, even. They're one of the best ways to get the straight dope on the courses a university offers.

Even in small universities, there are likely to be dozens of extracurricular activities, each with its own Web site. In a large university, there could easily be over 500! Keep a folder of your impressions of various Web sites — official and unofficial. Store it in the same folder on your computer where you store downloads from the universities.

Don't limit your online research to university-related Web sites. Newspapers and magazines across Canada are now online and quite often contain items of interest to students. You may find articles concerning cost of living and employment opportunities in the area where one of the schools you are interested in is located. You can also check out the local housing situation using a newspaper's online classified section. Street maps — available online for all big cities and many smaller centres — make looking for accommodation a bit easier, especially if you're not familiar with the neighbourhood.

Many TV and radio stations are also online. If your computer and Internet connection can handle the software requirements, streaming audio and video — or just downloaded clips — can offer a better way of bringing a yet-unknown community to life. Rather than looking at static pictures of a given city or neighbourhood, you can watch movies of recent events and news items, and even check out commercials for local bookstores, restaurants, and pubs!

Finding Money Online

Although surfing university Web sites can be fun, it's also serious business. Picking your courses or choosing a residence aren't the only aspects of your university life. You must also figure out how to pay for this life.

We discuss financial aid and scholarships extensively in Part IV of the book — especially in Chapters 14 and 15. Besides the Bank of Mom and Dad (and, of course, your own savings), there are generally two ways to pay for post-secondary education: getting money from the university, college, or technical institute you attend, and/or getting money from the government. Information about both sources is available online.

Money from the university

Each university's Web site has a section on financial aid, with information on how it calculates tuition rates and other fees. Most have a link directly from the home page — if not, simply go to the site's search function and enter a keyword such as "finance," "tuition," "financial aid," or "scholarship." It's unfortunately true that, for many universities, the search engine won't provide what you are looking for. In these cases, keep looking in areas such as courses and programs, the registrar, or the bursar. If that doesn't work, simply send an e-mail to the address we've listed for your particular university in the Directory of Universities and Colleges.

Once you find the right area, you'll first have to work out how much tuition you will pay depending on your course load, programs, and other factors. Then you'll want to find out what kind of scholarships are available and whether you can get financial aid. Some universities have an online form you can fill out that calculates how much financial aid you can expect, while others simply refer you to the Web site of the government agency that administers financial aid.

You'll likely see references to awards, scholarships, bursaries, and other grants in the financial aid section of the Web site. You should have a look at these areas and see what each school offers by way of assistance well before you apply. Unless you (and your family) are particularly well off, you will probably want to offset the costs of your university education with as many scholarships and grants as possible. A discount is better than paying full price!

Tuition rates vary from university to university and, within a given university, from program to program. Do as much research as possible so there'll be no surprises when you start to apply. Check out the bursar's page (the folks that you write your cheques to) when you're surfing to get more ideas. We take a closer look at the different tuition rates in Chapter 12.

Money from the government

We cover the provincial and national student loan programs in-depth in Chapter 14, but you might want to get a head start by looking at these programs now. Most university Web sites have links to the federal government's Web site, or to the Web site of the provincial government in question.

The university and government financial aid Web sites have a wealth of materials (sorry for the pun!) that can tell you what loans, scholarships, grants, and bursaries are available, what their requirements are, and how much they pay. In addition to listing the deadlines by which to apply, some of the sites let you apply online.

As an added bonus, if you apply for a student loan online you don't have to pay the $10 application fee! If you send in the paper forms, you must also send in the money.

To get you started, we've found useful information about a few of the bigger loan programs at these Web sites:

✔ Information about Alberta's provincial student loans can be found at the Alberta Learning Information System (ALIS) at `www.alis.gov.ab.ca/learning/FinancialAssistance/`;

✔ Information about the British Columbia Student Assistance Program can be found at `www.gov.bc.ca/studentservices/`;

✔ Information about the Ontario Student Awards Program is at `http://osap.gov.on.ca`. Note that there is no `www` in this URL.

The sites for the rest of the provinces and additional financial aid sites are listed in Appendix B, "Money Sources."

Organizing Your Information

Earlier in this book, we mention that it's a good idea to keep track of your university packages as they come in, preferably stashing them neatly away in your University Applications File, which has been with you since grade 9, right? Well, you need to organize the research you've been doing online, too. We suggest you store this important stuff in two locations: on your computer and in your file.

Keeping track of your digital details

First, just as you did with your paper materials, create a University Applications Folder on your computer. Inside this folder, create subfolders titled "Me," "Universities," and "Other stuff."

TIP

All those slick, glossy brochures

Most university Web sites have a section where you can request those glossy brochures you may have seen in your high school counsellor's office or library. Go ahead — fill out the forms, wait a few days, and then check your mailbox. Request a package from a variety of schools as soon as you can. Sometimes the mail takes weeks to arrive, so it's best to ask for this stuff well before you need it.

Things change. Often. Any information you get today could be out of date tomorrow. Check the fine print to make sure you've got all the bases covered. It's very possible that a new school year will bring with it different prerequisites and other academic challenges.

Just because you've read a brochure once doesn't mean the information will be current by the time you go back to it.

When you start getting stuff in the mail from the universities, date each piece so you know when you received it (and how old it is).

- The "Me" subfolder should contain your personal information, lists you've made about your university decision, your digital diary, perhaps a subfolder on employment or career-related materials, and whatever else relates to you but not to any particular university.

- The "Universities" subfolder should contain a list of all the universities you are investigating, with the dates that you communicated with each noted.

  - The "Universities" subfolder should also contain other folders within it — one for each university that interests you. In these folders, store all the materials you download or receive from universities.

  - Each university subfolder should have its own subfolder, labelled "Correspondence." In these subfolders, store copies of *every* e-mail you send and receive from the universities. Don't worry about how irrelevant the e-mails seem right now, just save them. You never know when you'll need to prove that you really did send that request for information about residence six months ago!

- The "Other stuff" folder contains, well, other stuff. Materials that don't quite fit into any other section do just fine in here, thank you very much. In this folder, save newspaper articles and statistics about any aspect of university that interests you.

Make sure that everything you store on your computer has a meaningful name and a date. Calling a file called "G&M.doc" may tell you that it came from the *Globe & Mail,* but it doesn't tell you anything about its content. That means you have to open it to read it just to find out what it is. After a while, you'll have dozens or hundreds of files, and you won't want to open each one to find the specific file you need. Calling the file "G&MFirstYearGradesF23.doc" tells you that it is an article from the *Globe & Mail* about first-year grades that was in the newspaper on February 23. Not bad for a file name!

No matter what you choose to include, don't forget to keep the relevant dates and contact information on file!

Ideally, you should pretty much know your top three or four picks by the end of grade 11, so our advice is that you send away for the information packages by the end of the fall term (at the latest). This way, you can puzzle things out all spring, go on a few campus tours (they're usually held all through spring), and generally prepare for university with plenty of time on your hands and a good idea of what to expect.

Of course, you can send away for the packages earlier, too. This might be a good idea if you want to keep your choices as wide open as possible — or if you're considering applying to an international university where deadlines for standardized testing (such as the SAT I) and scholarships can be months earlier than their Canadian counterparts.

Sometimes in Canada the mail takes a few weeks to get to where it's going, especially if it's during a holiday season when letter carriers are stretched to their limit. Sometimes the mail takes a long time because universities wait for a few weeks and then send out a large batch of packages to get a better postal rate. Hey, sometimes the mail takes a long time just because you're waiting for it.

The paper trail: Expanding your University Applications File

You're not going to store your information only on your computer; some of it you will probably want in hard copy, as well. In fact, we suggest that you keep printed copies of important documents such as application forms and financial aid information. You never know when your computer might crash. When you consider that you're going to be storing all the stuff you download from university Web sites along with the packages the schools send you in the mail, plus a bunch of other stuff, what has happened becomes clear. You've outgrown your University Applications File — at least in its present form. You need to get a bigger one.

Should you go out and buy a big three-ring binder? Maybe you should shell out a few bucks for a plastic file case with lots of file folders. Perhaps you might be able to organize things really well with one of those ugly (yet, oh so functional) brown accordion files.

Or do you simply get an old shoebox and stuff everything inside?

We advise you to put one of those accordion files into a bigger box and label all the sections of the file. The front sections of the accordion file should be set aside for this book and your own personal notes, Mull Lists, and other plans. The next sections should be reserved for your high school transcripts, doctors' notes, awards, and related materials. Then, keep a section of the accordion file set aside for each university of particular interest, and keep the remaining materials organized in the rest of the box. Don't forget to cross-reference everything in the files with the materials you have saved on your computer.

Organize your materials in any way that makes sense and feels comfortable to you. The point is to group your information so you can find what you need when you need it.

Keep everything about a particular university in one place. The glossy brochures you get in the mail should be referenced to the material you gleaned from the Web site. This way you don't lose sight of the big picture.

Communication: More Than an Art, It's a Necessity!

We realize that there's been a lot to digest in this chapter. It's no problem to re-read stuff if you find your eyes glossing over because your brain is full. Before we close out this chapter, however, we just want to leave you with a couple of suggestions about corresponding with universities and colleges.

The administrative staff at universities are very busy at certain times of the year:

- **September:** When they must deal with the huge wave of incoming students on campus;

- **Late October and early March:** The mid-term exam periods, when some students crash and burn and go to the administrative offices for help;

- **December and late April:** The final exam periods. Enough said;

- **June:** Graduation.

Savvy students keep this in mind when they make information requests and pose questions.

Remember to get some kind of written confirmation of what you're being told. When you can't use paper correspondence, use e-mail as much as you can, since this provides a (virtual) paper trail of what's been said — and by whom.

If you start early, you'll have plenty of time to get things happening smoothly and without much fuss. If you leave things to the last moment…well, we know you won't let *that* happen.

Chapter 9

Getting the Feel of a Campus

· ·

· ·

Going to university is a commitment. You're agreeing to spend three, four, or more years of your life at a certain place with a certain group of people. If you live to be 80, that's still 5 percent of your entire life that will be spent at university. Would you commit to buy a car you haven't seen or given a test drive? Of course not. So don't decide where to spend your university years without first meeting the university. As a smart parent once joked, "Have a date first before you rent a hall for the wedding."

Armed with all the research you've been doing (and probably a thousand questions), you're ready to start pounding the campus pavement. But first, we should answer the question that comes up 99 percent of the time when we talk to students. Invariably, someone in the crowd asks, "Why should I spend time going to *see* the campus?"

You Won't Know Until You Go

You may think that you like a certain university that's in the mountains, on the edge of a small town, with about 1,500 students. From its glossy brochures, the school sounds like an idyllic spot to earn a degree. Then you get there and find that it's dominated by neat freaks who get haircuts every week and ridicule roommates who leave socks on the floor.

Neat freaks aren't reported in the university brochures. And they didn't show up on that cool Web site you saw. But neat freaks may make you uncomfortable. Depending on your personality, they may make you *very* uncomfortable. If you show up in first year without visiting the campus before you apply, you're stuck in Neat Freak Land for at least nine months. And those nine months you spend there will be miserable — you'll be hoping all the while that another university will take you as a transfer student.

The truth is, many students transfer after their first or second year of university. If you talk to transfer students candidly about the reasons why, the most common answer is that the first university "wasn't what I expected." And if you ask the logical next question, you'll find that their expectations came without the benefit of a campus visit.

Tales abound of students heading to a prestigious university, or to the university where their crowd is going, with no idea of what lies ahead. They're unhappy from week one. Go figure.

You're not looking for a university because it has prestige or because it's popular with your friends. You're looking for a university that's right for you, where you can grow academically, socially, and emotionally. If your friends decide to go there, too, so much the better. But if they don't, and it's a right university for you, you'll quickly make new friends. You'll see.

Personality Check: A Reprise

The biggest test in locating a right university is the personality check. That bears repeating — and remembering. Be sure to test the university with a first-hand personality check. To do so, visit the campus, meet officials, talk to students, eat in dining halls, and, if you can manage it, spend the night.

The concept of a university "personality" was not invented for this book. Students have been using the word in this way for years. A campus visit is one of the best ways to see if you like the school (and perhaps even if the school likes you).

As you've been going along, you've probably whittled that list in your University Applications File down to between four and six schools. With a campus visit, you can find out how right they are for you. This way, you can get to know the schools for yourself, up close and personal.

Those four to six schools may be your favourites, but there's no reason to apply just to these schools and nowhere else. Thousands of students apply to 15 or more universities just to ensure they eventually get in somewhere. We discuss this approach in more detail in Chapter 11.

Set Your Visit in Spring or Fall

The best time for *you* to visit universities, in terms of convenience, is during the summer, when you're not burdened by the pressures of high school. But, at most universities, summer is the worst time for a personality check. Nobody's on campus in the summer. Well, hardly anybody is. A few students who are taking summer classes and the professors who are teaching them are sweating through June and July, but by mid-August they're gone, too. In the summer, you can get a nice view of tree-lined paths, stroll through empty residences, visit the student union, if it's open, and not much else.

The best time to get a genuine feel for a university's personality is when all students are on campus, all classes are in session, and all systems are go. That's spring and fall. Ideally, you've identified the universities you want to visit in the spring of grade 11. So the ideal times for your visits are during March and April of grade 11, or September and October of grade 12.

You know those *professional development (PD)* days your teachers let you have off so they can get together and discuss students? Well, why not arrange your campus tours during these days? While your classmates are off playing video games or just plain sleeping in, you can be soaking up the ambience at a university. If your particular school doesn't have any PD days, arrange to take a day or two off anyway. Checking up on where you're going to spend the next four years of your life is very important. Your teachers will probably help you plan around tests and assignments. As an added benefit, they may even think you're a more serious student. And having a teacher take you more seriously sure can't hurt!

Check the university catalogues to see when classes end for the summer. You don't want to visit during final exam week, because no one will talk to you. At some schools, finals are as early as the end of April. On other campuses, they don't come until June. Allow two days for each campus visit, because staying overnight — even if it's in a motel or hotel — is important. If the university is within easy driving distance, plan to drive there in the morning, spend the afternoon, evening, and following morning gathering information, and then drive home the second afternoon. Even if the university is in your hometown, you'll probably want to take the full two days.

Of course, if you're that unwilling to skip school — wow, we're impressed — perhaps you can schedule your campus visit for a Friday/Saturday period. A couple of things to keep in mind, though: many universities have fewer classes scheduled on a Friday, because some professors don't like lecturing on Fridays. Also, considering the usual Friday- and Saturday-night parties, you may not get an honest feel for the school if you visit over a weekend.

Don't make your visit a spur-of-the-moment trip. Plan it at *least* two weeks in advance. After selecting dates that are good for you, call the university admissions office for an appointment. One of the most essential of all the essential items in your visit is a two-way chat between you and a university admissions officer. If you show up unannounced, you may find nobody home. Or, an admissions officer may adjust her schedule to fit you into an already busy day. Being human, she'd find that adjustment a bit irritating. Her first impression of you would be negative, and that's not the impression you want to create.

With a few weeks' notice, an admissions office can usually schedule sufficient time for a leisurely chat. Call for the appointment and then build the rest of your campus visit around it.

Do Mom and Dad Really Have to Come Along?

Your parents, we're sure, are fine people. And they have key roles to play in helping you find the right universities.

Go back and read that last sentence again. They have key roles to play in helping you find the right universities. Notice that word *helping*. Your parents certainly can be a big help, but that's all they can be. Finding a university must be your effort and your decision. After all, it's your life on the line. It's you who will be attending classes, writing term papers, and living in residence. When decision time comes, only you can figure out what's right for you.

As they read this section, some parents are scoffing. They're thinking, "My kid can't decide where she's going to university, because she's not paying the bill." When they think about it a little longer, they'll realize that's only half true. The "kid" is paying with her time. Remember, it's you who will spend three or four years at university — not your parents.

Of course, your choices may be limited by the amount you — and your parents — can afford to spend, but within that limit you have to decide what's right for you. And that monetary limit will become flexible if you decide to borrow money for university. (You can read much, much more about all this money stuff in Chapters 12 through 18.)

So, should your parents go along on your campus visits? If it's at all possible, yes, absolutely. Parents will see things and hear things that you don't. Simple arithmetic tells you that six eyes and six ears see and hear more than two of each. And parents will think of questions to ask that may not occur to you.

Back in the motel or hotel room, or on the drive home, you can compare notes and come up with better opinions about the university than if you were gathering information with no help.

Should your parents accompany you to your appointments? Yes, for all the preceding reasons. At the financial aid office, they'll definitely think of questions that you won't. No biggie. They're just older and wiser. As an added bonus, they'll probably be able to offer a more accurate description of their financial condition than you would.

Campus visits produce the best results when you and your parents work enthusiastically within your separate roles. You are the customer. You are inspecting a product to see whether you want to buy it. You also are trying to decide where to spend four years of your life. Apply the information you collect toward those two goals.

Your parents are advisors. Welcome their advice. You might sometimes think they're a pain, but they act the way they do because they want what's best for you. Consider their advice seriously, because they undoubtedly are wise people. And they definitely have more experience than you do — even if one or both of them didn't go to university themselves. And it might be nice of you to thank them for helping you out. But it's still your decision.

Cover the Four Essentials

To accomplish its purpose, each campus visit requires four essential elements. Make sure that you:

- ✔ Plan a chat with an admissions officer.
- ✔ Arrange a talk with a financial aid officer.
- ✔ Find opportunities to talk to as many students as you can.
- ✔ Stay overnight, preferably in a residence.

Other things you can do, such as talking to professors and sitting in on classes, can help you gauge the university's personality. But the four elements we just mentioned are essential.

The admissions office

The admissions office does much more than read applications and decide who gets into its university. It's the liaison between the university and all potential students at all stages of the university-seeking process. Admissions officers try to recruit you at university fairs. They send you brochures with pretty pictures of smiling students. They answer your requests for course catalogues and other information. And they will try to recruit you once again, after they decide you are their kind of student.

Your appointment with the admissions officer is a two-way street. Each of you — the student and the person representing the university — is trying to impress the other while also trying to decide whether you really like each other. While, as we've mentioned before, your marks are by far the most important factor for Canadian universities when evaluating your application, many universities now use interviews and supplementary material to decide if the students who are currently in the borderline *maybe* pile can be offered admission.

If you have sailed through high school with a 90 percent average (and you've kept your marks up in your final year), the admissions officer will be happy to see you, chat for a while, and perhaps even discuss what academic programs you might want to pursue. If, on the other hand, you have a sinking feeling this the university is a *reach* for you (or, worse still, *out of reach* for you), you would be smart to figure out how to supplement your marks with a face-to-face meeting and an explanation of why you did poorly in, for example, grade 12 geography (or another subject).

If you've had personal troubles recently, bring a note from a doctor, counsellor, or clergy member attesting to this fact. If you've seen your marks drop in your final year because of family financial difficulties, explain this as well. Use the meeting as a way to put your best face forward, explain away any problems, and generally assure the admissions officer that you can hack it at his university.

Canadian universities prefer to receive written letters rather than using an interview process. Every university is different, so ask the admissions office at the particular university what works best for them — and follow their advice. Admissions officers have regular meetings in which students with marginal marks (note, we didn't say *marginal students*) are discussed. Even if you have had a bad final year, you still might get admitted to the university of your choice if you can explain why you had problems — and what you've done to fix them.

The financial aid office

You haven't thought about money all this time. (Right?) Now you need to give money a thought.

Eventually, you must decide where you'll go to university based on which schools have accepted you and how much each expects you to pay. The financial aid officers are the folks who decide how much their university expects you to pay — that is, how close to the sticker price your tab will be. When you visit the campus, you need to begin a conversation with these folks.

After you make an appointment with the admissions office, you can call the financial aid office and ask for some time to chat. On most campuses, the two offices are in the same building. In some schools, the admissions officer and the financial aid officer are the same person.

Tell the financial aid officer that you have an appointment with the admissions office and, while you're there, you'd like to get information about your prospects for financial aid. He will probably welcome you eagerly because he doesn't get much company — at least, not as much as his admissions counterpart. Very few student-visitors think about dropping in to the financial aid office. Indeed, very few prospective students know that the financial aid office exists until they receive news about their grants and loans after they're accepted for admission. But that's not you.

During your visit, offer some information about your family's financial condition: your parents' income range, their ballpark net worth, and any money you have stashed away. With that general information, the financial aid officer can at least estimate whether you'll receive any cash from the school. Some brave financial aid people may even venture an educated guess as to how much money you'll receive. Still, no one knows for sure how much aid you will get until your application data get pushed through a computer.

But, believe it or not, that's not the main reason you're there. (If you read Chapter 14, you'll know how to make the same financial aid calculations yourself.) No, you dropped in to meet a financial aid officer and to let him meet you. You hope he'll remember you favourably. When the time comes to assemble your financial aid package, an image of you as a nice, friendly person can't hurt. The financial aid officer will be dealing with thousands of students whom he knows only as names on a computer screen. If he can put a pleasant personality with a name, so much the better for you.

And when you need to call the financial aid office with questions, you'll be more comfortable knowing the person on the other end of the telephone line — and knowing that he knows you. Don't forget to send a thank-you note to the financial aid officer when you get home.

The students

Before you left home, you nailed down firm times for two important appointments on campus: at the admissions office and at the financial aid office. But during the rest of your visit you want to wing it — you're on a freelance search for information. One of your best sources will be the people most plentiful on campus: the students.

University students are among the most opinionated of human beings. They usually have strong feelings about what's right and what's wrong with their schools, and they have no problems about sharing those views. Some students who are now in university say they found out more from other students on their campus visits than from any other source. No surprise.

Be sure to seek out students wherever the opportunity exists — the library, a cafeteria, a walk across campus. If students look like they have time to talk, talk to them. Ask about the classes, the professors, the social life, and the housing conditions. Don't be pushy, just firm. Trust us, you probably won't have to ask many questions to produce a stream of opinions.

You can find out a lot about students as you talk to them. And that's important because the key ingredient in a university's personality is its students. Their collective approach to life determines whether a university is a party school or nerd haven, liberal or conservative, clean-cut or grungy. In conversations with students, you can quickly get a feel for which way the campus leans in these and other areas that may be important to you.

If you're leaning toward a particular field of study, look for students majoring in that area. A good way to find them is to hang around the building where that department is located and its classes are held. In large universities, personalities can differ from faculty to faculty, and from department to department.

The overnight stay

The best way to discover a person's true personality is to spend a night at his place, wake up in the morning, and see how he acts at breakfast. The same is true of a university.

The overnight stay is the most important way to find out exactly what you want to know about the school. No other part of the visit will have as much impact on your opinions.

The reason you're visiting the university is to decide whether it's a place where you can thrive and be comfortable for three or four years. You can find out a little about a university by walking around for a few hours talking to people. You can find out much more by spending the night in a residence, if you can manage it, or at a local motel or hotel. The overnight stay gives you a feel for

TIP

A group tour? Why not?

When you visit a campus don't be surprised if other students are there looking, just like you. Some may show up at Queen's University the same day as you. Indeed, the university admissions office may have arranged it that way.

When you call for an appointment, an admissions officer may suggest that you arrive in time for a tour with other visiting students. If it fits your schedule, do so. A group tour is harmless and can be another information source.

Group tours are held several times a week in the busy visitor seasons of spring and fall. Call well ahead and book your place, if possible. Prospective students are assembled in a meeting room, hear a brief talk about how wonderful the university is, and then are introduced to a student who leads a campus tour.

The tour offers live views of scenes you have already seen in brochures. The student escort is working for the admissions office and will probably describe the scenes in words written by the admissions office. When you ask a question, it's likely to be one for which the admissions office has supplied an answer.

The student tour guide, though, can help you start the rest of your personality check. Ask where students hang out in their spare time. Ask about the most popular student cafeteria. If you haven't lined up a residence room for the night, ask your guide about the chances of arranging to stay in one. She may be working for the university, but she's still a student. And one reason she was hired for the job is because she likes to talk.

the campus after hours, when classes end, professors go home, and students do whatever they do.

A night in a residence gives you the best view of how students live. For a few hours you can experience life as a student at this university. And what better way to know whether you like something than to try it?

Many universities will arrange an overnight residence stay if a visiting student asks for it. Some won't, citing space, insurance, and a whole list of other concerns. Sometimes a brother, sister, cousin, or other relative may already be at the university and can make this happen for you. Whatever your situation, you won't know the answer until you ask. Almost all universities require advance notice. When you call the admissions office to set up your appointment, ask whether staying overnight in a residence room is possible.

If the university can't arrange it, you're on your own. Through your family and friends, try to find a student who can give you a spare bunk or a floor to spread out a sleeping bag.

 There are potential dangers to a residence visit, too. Drugs and alcohol may be part of campus life, but you don't have to indulge just because you're trying the university on for size. Date-rape drugs are virtually tasteless, so beware of accepting drinks from people you don't know, even other females. And just because you're a guy doesn't mean you are immune from campus predators. Always be careful and *only stay in residence with someone you know or if the school has made arrangements for this to happen.*

Meet the other students in the residence. Find out the personality of the residence you're staying in. Ask about the other residences. What are the students' interests? What do they talk about? Complain about? You're going to want to know about the residence that goes without heat until February even though the temperatures dip below freezing soon after November.

Now is also a good time to find out if the university has a *walk safer program.* These programs provide building-to-building escort services to locations on and off-campus. Although first developed for female students, most schools have made the service available to males as well. The program goes by different names from school to school, but the idea is the same, and it's a very important one.

You Can Do Even More

The four essentials of a campus visit (described in the "Cover the Four Essentials" section) won't take all of your time. You'll have a few hours to look elsewhere for information. Here are some things you can do.

Visit a professor

If you're leaning toward a particular university major, you'll want to find out more about the school's courses in that area than what you can read in the catalogue. You also may want to get a sense of the types of people — professors and students — involved in this field of study.

Students aren't the only ones who like to talk. Professors do, too. Talking to students is a large part of their daily lives. If you're leaning toward chemistry, call the chemistry department before you leave campus and ask whether you can visit a professor. Mention that you're thinking about a degree in chemistry. The person answering the phone, probably an administrative assistant, either has the authority to schedule an appointment or can suggest a good time to drop by when professors are available.

When you chat with a professor, try to do two things:

✔ Get information about the chemistry curriculum and the requirements for a chemistry major. Professors are busy, though. Don't pester them with questions you should already have answered by now by reading the department brochure or other university material.

✔ Tell the professor *why* you're interested in chemistry. Talk about what you've accomplished in chemistry as a high school student. Don't use this time to kiss up — professors see this all the time and aren't impressed. Simply let the professor know that you're a great student who really likes the subject.

A fact of university life is that faculty departments covet students who major in their areas. And the better the student, the more fervent the coveting. The more students a department has, the easier it can justify its existence to administrators who prepare budgets. If you impress a professor as the kind of student she would like to have, she could drop a note to the admissions office saying so. Perhaps you might even suggest this idea to her. That note will go into your file at the university. When your application arrives, this professor's note will become part of the package reviewed by admissions officers who decide whether you get in.

The note can go a long way. Recommendations from faculty are not treated lightly.

Audit classes

By *auditing* classes, we're not talking about anything to do with accounting (unless, of course, you're visiting an accounting class). By auditing, we're talking about attending a class and simply listening to the lecturer, getting a sense of the course and its dynamics, and generally figuring out if this is the kind of class you would to attend. Classes, after all, are the reason you'll be going to university. Sit in on one or two while you're there to see what vibes you get. You're going to be spending a lot of time either in classes or on your way to classes for a couple of years — you'd better find out what they're like.

When you talk to a professor, ask whether you can visit one of his classes. If he doesn't have one soon, he may refer you to a colleague who does. Interest in attending a chemistry class is clear evidence of a sincere interest in chemistry. Go figure.

If you can't get into a class with a professor's help, try some students. If you spend a night in a residence, ask one of them whether you can tag along to class the next day.

Unless you're at a small university, where classes tend to have fewer than 30 students, you should check out both large and small classes. Your reactions will be different in each. Find a large class of several hundred students in an auditorium with a professor lecturing from a stage. Ask yourself whether you're comfortable in that kind of setting. Do you like the idea that the professor has no way to find time for individual attention to several hundred students?

Sit through the class. Think about the situation. The experience may change some items you think are important about a university. You also can ask the admissions office for a list of classes required for first-year students and show up at one of those.

Read the student newspaper

A good source of campus information, available without talking to anyone, is the student newspaper (or newspapers, on larger campuses). The student newspaper is usually available in the student centre, residence lobbies, and other popular campus spots. The student newspaper can give you a quick briefing on the current hot campus issues and a feel for what students at the university think is important.

Some student newspapers are now reproduced on the university's Web site. If you have access to the Internet, try to read the school's paper in advance. That can give you a feel for the campus and suggest some questions you may want to ask when you visit.

On many campuses, the student paper is a self-supported activity, free of control by the university administration. In those papers, student journalists are inclined to discuss issues as candidly as they would in their residence rooms.

Journalists and writers, as a group, tend to be more outspoken than the rest of the population, and student journalists are no exception. That makes the student newspaper office a fine source of information. Drop into the newspaper office, explain who you are and why you're there, and ask for a copy of the paper to read. Then, unless everyone seems to be scurrying to meet a deadline, strike up a conversation with a staff member or two. You might be surprised by how much you can find out so quickly.

Add It to Your File

You may think you'll remember all the details of your visit, but as you go from school to school the details of each visit will blend into each other. Pretty soon you'll be asking yourself, "Which was the school that had that *really* cold cafeteria?" or "Which university had really cramped residence rooms?"

To help you remember all these important details, we've put together the checklist in Figure 9-1, a couple of pages over, for you to complete for each school you visit. You can photocopy these two pages and use them when you visit each school. Store the completed checklist in your University Applications File.

Finding the true school (it's around somewhere)

Underneath all the hype, colourful brochures, and snazzy Web sites lies the true university. Your job on all your campus visits is to find it. To use a metaphor, we can provide you with the shovels, but you must do the digging. Your parents can hold the map for you, but you alone must figure out where to excavate. You get the idea: You have to sift through all the glitz and look at what's important — for you.

All Around Town

If you're new to the university *and* the city, you should figure on spending a bit of time during your visit looking around off-campus. Of course, you probably won't have a lot of time in that two-day span, but you can use what time you do have to check out the city or town that is home to the university — and potentially home to you for several years.

Is the area cosmopolitan or is it country? Is it urban or rural? Is it dirty or pristine? Artsy or sterile? Does it look as if there's lots to do there, or are you likely to get bored in no time flat? Keep in mind that your university life won't be 24-hour studying. (You're surprised to hear us say that, right? Well, it happens to be true. You know what they say: All work and no play….) It's all about matching personalities. The point of the campus visit is to figure out if your personality matches that of the university. The city or town that houses the university is in many ways an extended campus. Does its personality match yours?

Even if you're from the same town or city as the university you're visiting, you might want to spend some time in the immediate university area. This area is sometimes called the *student ghetto*. Get a sense of the culture. It's probably different from your own neighbourhood. Are stores open late? Does it look safe?

Here is a list of things to check out off-campus:

- **Cultural activities:** You can always benefit from a little cultural inspiration, right? From ethnic events to the latest Andrew Lloyd Webber extravaganza, find out what kind of entertainment is around. Don't forget to find the local first-run and repertory movie house. Most universities also have the occasional movie night for students to enjoy.

- **Green space:** If you love to get away from it all in the forest or anywhere outdoors, find out what sort of scenery is in the neighbourhood and how difficult it is to find the kind of scenery you want.

University: _____   Date visited: _____

What are your first impressions of the school?

_____

_____

_____

_____

If you have a car, how expensive was the parking? Safe? Well-lit?

_____

_____

_____

_____

Did the campus look safe? Does the university have a walk safer program? Were there working emergency phones installed throughout the campus? Does the school have its own police or security force or does it use the local city police to patrol the campus? Are you able to see crime statistics for the campus? (Some universities post these stats in libraries, residences, and other public buildings to alert students and staff to criminal behaviour.)

_____

_____

_____

_____

How are the classrooms and buildings? New? Old? Secure? Wheelchair accessible? Clean? Dirty? Functional? Cramped? Smelly? Confusing? Well-lit? Cold? Warm? Hot? Drafty? Crowded?

_____

_____

_____

_____

Did you enjoy the classes you attended? How big were they? Did the professors speak well? Did they hold the students' attention or were students bored? Did the professors engage you and make you want to learn the subject they were teaching — or did you find yourself looking at your watch constantly and trying to stay awake until it finally ended?

_____

_____

_____

_____

How are the residences? New? Old? Secure? Wheelchair accessible? Clean? Dirty? Functional? Cramped? Smelly? Confusing? Well-lit? Cold? Warm? Hot? Drafty? Crowded?

_____

_____

_____

_____

Are the students friendly? Private? Surly? Helpful? Cute? Shy?

_____

_____

_____

_____

How was the food at the cafeteria? Hot? Tasty? Cold? Chewy? Bland? Healthy? Mostly junk food? Tasted like cafeteria food? Surprisingly delicious?

_____

_____

_____

_____

How was the gym? New? Old? Secure? Wheelchair accessible? Clean? Dirty? Functional? Cramped? Smelly? Confusing? Well-lit? Cold? Warm? Hot? Drafty? Crowded? Does the gym hold recreational classes that interest you?

_____

_____

_____

_____

What are your other thoughts about the university? How would you score this university against other ones you've visited?

_____

_____

_____

_____

Score:

_____

Figure 9-1:
Campus visit
checklist.

- ✔ **Hobbies:** You don't want to give up your passion for skydiving just because you are going to university, so make sure it's available nearby!

- ✔ **Local restaurants:** You can check out the university hangouts, plus discover some personal favourites.

- ✔ **Off-campus housing:** You will probably live out of residence at some point, so get prepared. (We discuss housing options outside of residence a bit later in this chapter.)

- ✔ **Places of worship:** If you attend a place of worship regularly, you'll want to make sure there is one near campus. Your priest, minister, rabbi, mullah, or other spiritual advisor should be able to help you on this one.

- ✔ **Stores and shopping:** You need to make sure you can get your favourite stuff (or good substitutes!), the books you need, and everything else that's important to your lifestyle.

- ✔ **Touristy spots:** You may never do them again, but it does give you a taste of the city. Gastown in Vancouver, Harbourfront in Toronto, or Vieux Québec in Quebec City, to mention only a few spots to visit.

- ✔ **Work opportunities:** You may need to work part-time while attending university. Many universities have work or career centres that you can check out.

The businesses and organizations that advertise in the campus newspapers are usually close by and definitely student-friendly. The newspaper is a great place to start your neighbourhood tour planning.

Hunting Down Housing

Another reason for the campus visit is to figure out where you're going to live during your university years (or at least the first year, anyway). You won't do well at university unless you have a good home to come back to every day. You won't be able to sleep well if your neighbour is the drummer for a grunge rock band. You won't be able to study if your kindly old landlady wants to talk your ear off every day because her own kids don't call her often enough.

Generally speaking, you have three housing options at university:

- ✔ Living in residence.
- ✔ Living in your own or a shared apartment off-campus.
- ✔ Living at home.

During your campus visit, give some thought to where you want to live. Are the residences really roomy and full of old-world charm? Is there a thriving off-campus population that really seems to know where it's at? If the university is in your hometown, does it just make more sense to bunk in with your parents? (Maybe they'll let you convert those couple of rooms in the basement and you can move down there — after you clean out all those boxes full of stuff your Mom and Dad affectionately call "knick-knacks.") The campus visit is a good time to start mulling this over.

Life in residence

Our opinion is that you won't really fit in to campus life without living on campus — and this usually means living in a student residence, at least for your first year.

Staying in residence has advantages and disadvantages. On the plus side, living in residence gets you out of your family home and on campus, where you can concentrate on the matters at hand: learning, growing, and having fun. Residence makes you feel like you're part of the university community. Everything's closer when you live on campus. The lecture halls, the library, the gym, and yes, other students, too. You can grow some pretty strong bonds with your friends in residence, which enhances your university experience. It may sound corny, but it's true.

Everybody in first year does not live in residence and there are often not enough spaces for everyone even if they wanted to live there. When you apply to university, make sure you indicate whether you want a place in residence. That way, you get on the list as soon as you are accepted. We talk more about this in Chapter 11.

Living in residence is not always as warm and fuzzy as it sounds. It's expensive. Room and meal-plan fees can easily reach $5,000 per year. In some schools, it costs even more. This is on top of tuition, books, and other expenses. For many students and their families, this is a significant barrier to university study.

Some students enjoy residence life a little too much. The temptation to party, date, and generally goof off is just too much for them. Instead of soaring at university, they bottom out. Instead of heading to their lectures, they head home.

Life off-campus

If you want to live off-campus, there are a number of things you should check out:

 ✔ **Safety:** Take care. Living off-campus is likely to be less safe than living in residence or at home. Take your parents when you go looking for places to stay. For many students, their first year of university is the first time they're living away from home. They may not be completely equipped to understand all the intricacies of rent, utilities, and the other "pleasures" of renting your own place.

 ✔ **Roommates:** Consider living with a friend off-campus. There will be days when you just need to talk to someone. Living in residence, you have plenty of people to chat with (some of whom you might actually learn to like or love). Living off-campus, you sometimes have to be your own support group. Picking the right roommate is important.

 ✔ **Expenses:** Even places nicely referred to as "student accommodation" can be very expensive. Rent is one factor, of course, but you also need to anticipate the unforeseen costs of repairs. (See the sidebar entitled "Removing the wallpaper: A true off-campus housing story" for a cautionary tale about living off-campus.) When you factor in the expense (and hassle) of buying furniture (or dragging that old bed from your parents' attic), perhaps living in residence isn't so expensive after all.

Removing the wallpaper: A true off-campus housing story

Our friend Bob and his fiancée, Linda, decided to move off-campus after spending first year in residence. Neither had much money to rent a great place, but they wanted to live together and have their own space. After moving all their stuff into a basement apartment in a rather seedy part of town, they decided to redecorate their humble abode to give it a homey feel. First up was that tacky wallpaper in the kitchen. After soaking the circa-1960 design with special wallpaper remover, Bob decided to grab the top corners of the existing wallpaper and pull.

Suddenly Linda started screaming in horror. Bob quickly looked at the wall and immediately dropped the piece of wet wallpaper. Underneath the small patch of uncovered wall were *dozens* of cockroaches, all running for cover. One terrified roach actually ran up Bob's shirtsleeve!

Bob and Linda stayed in that basement apartment for the rest of the year. They put up with more cockroaches (there's never just one roach), unbelievably loud disco music from the upstairs neighbour (they got earplugs for studying), and a freezing cold winter (they coped by bundling up). Still together after 20 years, all they can do is laugh at their inexperience and naïveté when renting their first apartment.

The lesson? Take your parents and inspect the place with them. Look under kitchen and bedroom shelves for telltale pest droppings. Flush the toilet while running the shower: how much does the water pressure drop? Pay for your security deposit and rent by cheque and get a receipt. Never pay in cash. Make sure you have good locks on the doors and plenty of outside lighting for security.

A key advantage of living off-campus is that you get to keep your place over the summer. Students in residence typically have to move out a few days after final exams every summer. If you live off-campus in a traditional apartment, you won't have to move. Of course, your landlord will probably want you to rent for the full year, making it necessary to either sublet the apartment (if your lease allows this) while you go home for the summer, or stick around for the summer and work in the big city.

Life on the home front

There are certainly advantages to staying at the Mom and Dad Hotel for the next four years. First and maybe foremost, the price is right. Even if your parents start charging you a few bucks for your room and board, it's not likely anywhere near what the university residence or your landlord will charge you. With so many other changes taking place in your life (university is *very* different from high school), it might be nice to have a bit of stability.

Next up is food. Even if the parents charge you for room and board, you'll probably do well by eating at home. Sure, it won't be as glamorous as eating in cafés near the school. You also won't be paying $7.50 for a cup of coffee and a bowl of cereal.

Mom and Dad may actually want you to stay home and study. There are some students who do particularly well by just going to school and returning home. They may lose some of the feeling of "community," but they balance that by scoring high marks in first and second year. Only you can determine if remaining at your parents' will help or hinder your university experience.

For most students — especially those in first year — living in residence is an important part of the university experience where lasting friendships and relationships often form. Marks are very important (as we might have mentioned once or twice elsewhere in the book), but you also need to strike a balance between academic growth and personal growth.

If You're a Mature Student

A campus visit is just as important for students whose high school years are in the past. You, as much as your younger colleagues, need to see whether a university's personality fits your lifestyle. You need to know whether it's a university that enthusiastically welcomes older students or one that focuses only on the young. The best way to find out is to visit the school.

When you visit a campus, an admissions officer can fill the same role as the high school counsellor. She can offer good advice on whether her university is the right place to pursue your goal. (If it isn't, she can steer you to potentially more appropriate places.) She can talk about the courses you need and, if necessary, set you up with a professor to talk in more detail. She can tell you how the admissions criteria differ for you as an adult and offer a realistic estimate of your chances of being admitted. She can tell you what activities and organizations exist to serve older students.

After talking to an admissions officer, don't forget those people who have the most intimate knowledge of any university, its students. Stroll the campus and drop in to the student centre to see how many older students are in view. Chat with a few of them about the opportunities and problems that mature students face. You'll likely find out just as much from other adult students about how you will fit in at a university as you will from the admissions office.

Don't Drop the Ball

The universities you visited have not forgotten you. Don't forget them.

Within two days after your return, drop notes in the mail to everyone you talked to at length on campus, including the admissions officer, the financial aid officer, professors, and other folks. Remember to send thank-you notes to the students, as well. Thank them for giving you their time and advice. Try to mention something specific from each conversation so that it doesn't read like a form letter. Your note will convey the impression that you're a considerate person, a doer, and someone they would like to have on their campus. The letters will help your cause if you eventually apply to the particular school.

A file with your name on it exists in the admissions office. It was created when you first wrote for a brochure or catalogue. By now, it contains any notes made during your appointment with the admissions office, perhaps some notes sent over from the financial aid office, and possibly a note from a professor. When your thank-you note arrives, it will go into the file. So, eventually, will your application for admission, which we get to in Chapter 11.

When an admissions officer opens your file to decide whether you should be accepted to his university, he'll see the thank-you note from your visit. Little things count.

University research checklist

Okay, so you're researching universities. You're visiting them — virtually or otherwise. You're gathering information. You're asking questions.

But before that, you have to figure out what information to gather. What questions should you ask? What will be really important to you that you need to find out? How can you know what you need to know before you get there?

Well, that's why we put together this checklist. For each university you wish to research, this is the information you want to gather. Check off each piece of information as you receive it. Don't worry about assessing the universities yet. Just get the information first.

Info Received   **Topic**

The Basics

❏   Name

❏   Address

❏   Phone numbers

❏   Fax numbers

❏   Web site address

❏   Contact information for registrar

❏   Contact information for residence

❏   Contact information for financial aid

❏   Admissions requirements

❏   Application dates

❏   Application fees

Info Received   **Topic**

Materials Arrived or Downloaded

❏   Application

❏   University package

❏   Residence information

❏   Financial information

University Assessment

❏   Campus visit

❏   Size (overall and first-year admissions)

❏   Focus/programs/faculties

❏   Student–instructor ratio

❏   Number of spaces available for residence

❏   Special considerations

Financial Information

❏   Cost range for first-year tuition

❏   Cost for residence

❏   Cost for books

❏   Cost-of-living index

❏   Scholarships available

❏   Financial aid available

Opinions

❏   Mine

❏   Parents

❏   Friends

❏   Teachers

❏   High school counsellor

❏   Others

❏   Overall university reputation

What If You Don't Visit the Campus?

You live in Québec. You're bummed out because you can't afford the plane fare to visit two of the universities on your list, Simon Fraser University and the University of Victoria, both in British Columbia. You're especially disappointed about UVic (as it's called), which you've heard has a terrific English program.

Don't worry. All is not lost. Ask friends, relatives, teachers, and counsellors if they've ever been to SFU or UVic. These people know you pretty well and will give you some indication whether the universities' personalities mesh — or clash — with yours.

Since there are relatively few universities in Canada (compared to the more than 3,000 colleges in the United States), it's likely that you'll track down a few people who have studied at either school.

Some smaller universities have programs that put you in contact with an alumnus of the school (a graduate). These informal programs are designed to overcome the objections some students (and their parents) have when considering smaller schools.

Part III
Crunch Time: Getting into University

"Our selection committee simply couldn't agree on which one of you should get the last opening at the University. So, if you'll just hold the spoons there for as long as you can... Martin—are you timing this?"

In this part . . .

This part is where you work on making yourself look exceptional. Of course, nothing in this book can make you look exceptional on its own. You have to take the steps to make yourself attractive enough so that the universities you want will want you, too.

Chapter 10 explains what universities find attractive about students. If you have a 99 percent average throughout high school, you can probably get into any university you choose. However, for the vast majority of students, who don't have such high marks, it's important to know how to best present yourself. Chapter 11 takes you through the actual application process, including a step-by-step stroll through a typical application form.

Chapter 10

How Universities Look at You

In This Chapter

▶ Zeroing in on your marks

▶ Taking your awards, jobs, and activities into account

▶ Including a great recommendation from your teacher or high school counsellor

▶ Factoring in your special circumstances

So, what do you need to make it into your universities of choice? What kind of person do you have to be? There are a lot of myths circulating out there about who gets into university and who doesn't, and why this is so. We think a lot of these myths are out there to confuse and intimidate you. Well, maybe no one is targeting you personally, but frequently people like to make processes appear more mysterious than they are — that way, these people look more impressive because they know the answers. This book is here to give you the real scoop — simply and without any mystery. We'll tell you what you really need to know.

It's not difficult to understand what makes some students more attractive to Canadian universities than others. Some universities may try to make you believe the admissions process is a dark, mysterious undertaking that you, the poor uninitiated applicant, are just too green to comprehend. When you ask them how they decide who to accept, they'll answer you with vague generalities such as, "The most important thing we look at is your high school record." What exactly does that mean? Just your marks? The courses you took? Are your school activities part of your record? If your record is "most important," does that mean they also look at other things that they consider less important but still important nonetheless? This chapter gives you the rest of the story.

If you ask an admissions officer to show you the scoring system her university uses to grade applications, she may deny that one actually exists. (They do exist. Pretty much all schools have one.) Or she may say something like, "It's proprietary information that we don't share with the public." Hey, that means you. You're the public. Of course, you're also the buyer of the services the university is selling.

What Universities Are Really Looking For

You may have heard that a particular university gives preference to:

- ✔ Students applying from certain high schools.
- ✔ Students who are children of successful (meaning rich or well-known) alumni.
- ✔ Students who are star football players (or hockey players, or skiers, or . . . you get the point).

Most of these "solid facts" are solid *fiction*. Canadian universities, unlike their American counterparts — whose elaborate admission procedures take a multitude of factors into account — base their initial admission offers almost solely on your marks.

Universities are looking for the same thing, essentially. They want good students. Good students make professors happy. And the last thing an admissions officer needs is a bunch of professors complaining about the quality of the students in their classes. Good students also warm the hearts of university presidents, who can brag about them on fundraising trips to alumni groups. And good students make it easier for universities to fill their primary roles — places of learning through an interchange of ideas. So a good student is every university's first priority.

Marks, marks, marks

When an admissions officer says your high school record is the most important item in your application, you'd better believe her. Your high school transcript is the first piece of paper to be scanned during your application's 15 minutes of fame, when it's being considered for admission. Every university's first priority is to enrol good students. Your high school transcript tells the admissions officer what kind of student you are. It doesn't tell her what kind of person you are, just the kind of student you are.

The admissions officer will look at your grades, of course. The more *A*s she sees, the better. She'll frown if she sees a lot of *C*s and *D*s. She will also look at which courses you've taken — and how difficult they were. Final-year calculus is harder than a generic math credit — universities know this.

The same thing goes for grade 12 chemistry or biology versus general science courses, which are known to be easier. And what about your communication skills? Universities put a lot of emphasis on English (or French, if you're applying to a French-speaking university). After all, if you can't communicate effectively at the high school level, how will you be able to communicate effectively in your university courses?

At most Canadian universities, your marks are the main attraction, pure and simple. However, once they have made the basic decisions about which students will definitely be offered admission and which students definitely won't, most universities then look at other factors.

These other factors are:

- Awards;
- Extracurricular activities;
- Jobs;
- Other stuff.

At some universities, however, marks are the *only* thing admissions officers look at. The other factors don't enter into the equation. Sorry.

Which bucket are you in?

Each university naturally wants to admit only the best and brightest of available students. Most universities in Canada admit *every* student who applies with a 90 percent average or over; *most* students with an 80 percent average or over (depending on the program); and *some* students with a 70 percent average and over. They also admit *a few* with a 60 percent average or over.

Think of a series of empty buckets on a staircase. Once the "90 percent and over" bucket on the top stair is filled, the school fills the "80 percent and over" bucket on the next stair down, and then the "70 percent and over" bucket. Finally, the "60 percent and over" bucket is filled — assuming at every step along the way that there's any water (or, in the case of admissions, *space*) left.

Now, let's say a student has an average in the mid to high 70 percent range. His marks wouldn't fit into the first two buckets, but they would fit into the third. The challenge this student has is to ensure his application floats to the top of the "70 percent and over" bucket by becoming visible.

This is where the meetings with admissions officers and testimonial letters we talked about in Chapter 9 come into play. Every admissions office has ways of letting those students in the *maybe* pile get admitted. Perhaps it's after-school leadership (provided you want to take politics or sociology). Maybe it's volunteering at the local seniors' home (provided you want to study gerontology). Perhaps you want to go into nursing and you volunteer as a candystriper at the local hospital.

Although every admissions officer we spoke with stressed that high school marks are the best indicator of future university success, they also said they would be willing to listen to a *reasonable* explanation of why you blew that mid-term in chemistry. Your explanation better be good, though, and backed up by solid documentation. After all, admissions officers don't want to hear stories such as "The dog ate my final report" or "My mom washed the jacket I had my student notes inside." Do you think they were born yesterday?

If you are a borderline student whom the admissions officer is unsure about, extra material detailing your achievements in the other factors we mention can make or break your application. For some health-related programs, a personal interview is required. For performance-related programs such as music, an audition is required. And, as we discuss in Chapter 17, international universities work on a completely different admissions system where high school marks are only one factor involved in granting you admission.

Students who do more than just study

Despite all that we've been saying about high marks, universities want students who do more than study. They want students who get out of their rooms in residence and mingle. A typical university takes pride in being a community and wants students who will be productive citizens of its community. It looks for students who are likely to:

- Volunteer
- Join organizations
- Assume leadership roles
- Work for the newspaper
- Shoot photos for the PR office
- Help when help is needed
- Get involved in things other than classes

However, since these admirable skills are very difficult to quantify, Canadian universities base their admissions decisions primarily on marks. It may not seem fair that a well-rounded, solid *B+* student gets passed over for a nerdy *A+* kid who has no real life skills and probably couldn't survive in the real world — but who said life was fair? The important thing is to understand the system and work within it.

If you're a mature student, you can signal to the admissions office your solid eligibility by proving that you've excelled at a challenge (preferably academic) you've experienced in real life. Perhaps you've spent ten years raising your kids and now want to gain part-time admission because you've always wanted to better yourself — for you *and* your kids. Maybe you had to drop out of high school because your family was having financial difficulties. Now that your small business has grown into a going concern, you want to return and take a commerce degree.

Whatever the reason, the admissions office can judge you only on the information you supply. If you supply mediocre marks (from an old high school transcript) and neglect to add that you were awarded the best-instructor award at the local community college, you're missing out on a valuable opportunity to blow your own horn.

If the admissions officer is concerned about your ability to handle the work at the university level, she may suggest you enrol in a *transitional-year program*. These programs are designed to get folks who have been out of the academic world for a little while back in the loop with courses in core subjects such as English and math.

What Universities Don't Judge You On

This is the part where we systematically tear down a bunch of myths about what universities judge you on when considering your application. You already know what matters to universities (your high school marks). And you already know what you need to do to give yourself the best shot at getting in (get the best marks you can). Well, you might want to cast an eye over this section, because here's what *doesn't* matter.

Your class rank

In addition to grade 12 marks, every university likes to see where you *rank* (or place) within your grade. In times gone by, a student's class rank was almost as important as his overall average. This is not the case anymore. Universities realize class rank doesn't tell them how good everyone else in your school is, just in your particular class. As well, class rank could make a student who slacked off look good (assuming others in his class slacked off as well). The opposite could also be true.

Class rank is somewhat of a holdover from the past, where some schools were more rigourous and marked harder than others. The class rank was an attempt to level the playing field by assuming the best student in one school was probably roughly equivalent to the best student in another school — regardless of overall marks. Although a laudable attempt, the class ranking system can lead to inaccurate comparisons between supposedly "tough" schools and "easy" ones.

Universities, with a few exceptions, will note your class rank on their academic scorecards (when they are able to get it from your high school). That said, the ranking isn't anywhere near as important in determining their final decision as your overall average is. In fact, many schools ask counsellors for the information on class rank only for students in the top 5 percent of the class, for the purposes of offering admission scholarships.

If you feel that your class ranking will help you (let's say you scored at the top of your class), write a letter to the director of admissions and explain this, accompanying your letter with a backup letter from your teacher, counsellor, or principal, confirming your claim.

Your high school's rank

Time to shoot down another myth. You know, the one about there being some kind of master list ranking every high school in Canada, which selective universities use to pick their students. Well, there is no such list.

Students, and more often parents, ask about this list every year. They've heard about it from a friend, whose aunt's hairdresser heard it first-hand from a reputable source. You know how it goes. They want to know where their kid's high school ranks on this list, and if it ranks low, is that why he can't get into U of T or UBC or Harvard or wherever. We repeat, there is no such list. Even if we wanted to compile one (and Caryn and David have both thought about it), where would we start? How do you compare high schools? What criteria do you use to rank them?

Now that we've destroyed that myth, we'll offer you a fact. Some high schools prepare their students for the rigours of university better than others. Universities can spot the difference, and yes, they come to know which ones these high schools are. What does this mean to you? If you have high marks, your high school's rank means nothing in the eyes of the universities to which you apply.

If you're a borderline applicant — a *maybe* — the past experience of a university applications officer with students from your high school may help get you in. But so might other things such as a positive recommendation letter from a teacher or counsellor, or even from a professor at the university where you're applying if you became friendly enough with one during your campus visit. There's more about getting a good recommendation later in this chapter.

Your test scores

Unlike American colleges, which rank students according to their results on standardized tests such as the SAT (now called the SAT I), Canadian universities focus on high school marks to ascertain if you have what it takes to join their elite ranks. Canadian universities don't demand SAT I scores — and most are surprised when students submit them.

In fact, the only time a Canadian university typically sees any SAT I scores is when an American student submits them. Remember, American students live and die by their SAT I scores. In Canada, we use high school marks almost exclusively.

While we encourage you to take tests such as the SAT I to prepare you for things to come in university (and these tests are required if you want to study at an American university), Canadian universities simply don't use them.

If you decide to go on to medical school or law school (still considered undergraduate degrees, technically speaking), you will likely have to write the *MCAT (Medical College Admission Test)* or *LSAT (Law School Admission Test)*. We say "likely," in the case of the MCAT, because not all medical schools require it. McMaster University and the University of Ottawa, for example, do not require it. Don't get your hopes up about the LSAT, though. That's one test you have to write, no matter where you are applying. If you want to go on to graduate school to get a master's degree, you will probably have to write a *GRE (Graduate Record Examination)*. Admission to a university's *M.B.A. (Master of Business Administration)* program usually requires you to write your *GMAT (Graduate Management Admission Test)*. Taking the SAT I is good preparation for all of these tests.

When a Great Recommendation Counts

A recommendation from your teacher or counsellor can be the most overlooked and underrated item in your university application, depending on your status. A great recommendation gains importance if your application is borderline, teetering on the fence between getting you in or locking you out. Note how we say a *great* recommendation.

Avoid a bad one

Some lazy teachers and lackadaisical counsellors kiss off student recommendations as chores to get out of the way. They don't think much about what they're saying. They use non-specific, trite sentences that give the impression they've written the same letter 75 times. And they probably have. It's easier for a busy teacher to compose a one-size-fits-all letter than to try to individualize recommendations for 75 students.

Those letters don't help you. In fact, they hurt. The admissions officer will conclude that you must not be much of a student if a teacher can't come up with anything more than a few platitudes about who you are. Keep in mind that you have some control over who writes the letters and what they say. If you're unlucky and have a poor counsellor, you're probably stuck with that person, unless you feel like complaining to your principal. But you can choose which teacher you want to recommend you.

Get a good one

By the time you apply to universities, you have probably developed a rapport with a few teachers whom you respect and who know you well as a student and a person. Pick one and ask him to write a letter for you. Give him a few weeks' notice so that he doesn't have to do it overnight after grading papers. Chat with him about what he might tell the university that will enhance its knowledge of you. Tell him why you're interested in that particular university. Remind him of things you've done. You can even give him a list of stuff you've accomplished or even a draft of the letter as you would prefer it to be written. Teachers are busy people who sometimes forget things. There's no harm in doing some of their work for them!

Remind the teacher or counsellor who is writing your recommendation that the university doesn't want to read stuff about you that it already knows. If they ask how you know that, show them this book.

Yes, We Know You're Special, But Will Universities Think So?

Hundreds of university applicants fall into categories outside the normal scoring process. Universities like to call these applicants *special*. In the admissions office, being *special* often means being *attractive*.

Maybe you've had great marks until grade 12. In grade 12, someone in your family died, or you were in a bad accident. Your marks suffered, but they're not that bad. And anyway, it wasn't your fault. You were overtaken by *extenuating circumstances*, and you should let the admissions office know. Admissions officers are caring people, but they're overworked and sometimes miss students who otherwise should be admitted. If you let them know, you may suddenly find yourself in that special category.

If there's something special about you — your marks, your home situation, your school — let the admissions officer know. This is not a time to be shy. Send information about your special circumstances when you apply. If you bring up your problems only after you have been refused entry, you lose credibility. Besides, by the time the university gets around to re-reviewing your application, all the spots may be filled. (See the sidebar, "Which bucket are you in?")

You can begin a dialogue with the admissions officer before you apply, explaining how much you want to attend their university and asking for their advice on how to avoid being overlooked because of the difficult events of this challenging year you've just been through. The admissions officer will certainly respond, and will likely remember you when your application arrives.

Summing Up

Your high school record, starting in grade 9, is the first and most important thing a university looks at when it's deciding whether to let you come study there for a while and earn a degree. If you're not in grade 9 yet, you still have time to plan what you take in high school. Work out a curriculum path that will give you a lot of the tougher courses by your final year. Talk to your counsellor, teacher, or principal. Include your parents in your high school, university, and career decisions wherever possible.

If grade 9 is in your past, some of your high school record is already written in stone. Sorry (or perhaps, happily), there's nothing you can do about it. But you can still work on the unfinished part. A record that improves as you move through high school is looked upon favourably. The opposite — a strong grade 9 or grade 10 followed by a steady downward slide — won't impress many admissions officers. Go figure.

The most important year on your high school transcript is your senior year: grade 12 (or your OAC year, if you're in Ontario). Universities like to see your academic record getting stronger every year. This means you're performing at your best as you come to them. Many universities, especially the more selective ones, want to see your grades for the second half of your final year — even after they've offered you a preliminary (or early) admission. They'll ask your high school to send over your final transcript. Only then — if your average hasn't dropped significantly — will they give you a final, confirmed offer of acceptance.

Different schools have different application deadlines. In Ontario, an organization called the *OUAC (Ontario Universities' Application Centre)* takes care of many of the transcript details, so you must be aware of the OUAC deadlines. In the other provinces, each university handles its applications slightly differently, most with separate forms, fees, and instructions. Make sure you check (and re-check) all deadlines. When in doubt, ask someone who should know. This means you'll probably ask your counsellor, teacher, the university's admissions officer, or somebody else who hopefully knows what she's talking about. Don't bother asking your friends. They might think they know, but they could steer you in the wrong direction.

Some universities offer a first, second, and even third round of admissions. You want to be in the first round (sometimes called *early admission,* which is usually made in late April). If you are given early admission, all you have to do is keep your marks up and you're in. Students who have overall averages of 90 percent or more are usually in this admission round. Sometimes, students in the high 80s are given provisional admission in this first round as well.

If your marks aren't high enough for first-round admission, you could be offered admission in the second round, typically made in May. This is when the majority of students hear from each university, although a few Canadian universities notify students a bit later than this.

In theory, there is a third admission round in the summer, usually in June or July. In practice, however, popular programs at large schools fill up quickly. If you've missed the first two rounds of admission, you know there's a problem. You should talk to anyone you can about getting into *any* university. You might also want to explore other options, such as working for a year, or taking a year off altogether and reapplying when you've had some time away from the education treadmill.

Lots of students are hedging their bets in the face of this tough competition and applying to many more universities than they need. The OUAC processed approximately 239,000 program choices from 60,511 Ontario high school applicants for the 2000/2001 academic year. While many students made only three program choices, well over 10,000 students selected all 17 of Ontario's universities plus the Ontario College of Art and Design (whose applications are also administered by the OUAC)! These students thought they were beating the system. They thought they had a sure-fire chance of getting in somewhere. What they may not have known was that each university admissions officer was told exactly what ranking each student placed on each of his 18 choices. What do you think the admissions officer of the university whose name appeared as the 18th choice felt about this particular student's application? We're guessing not much.

It cost each of these students $455 to apply to all 18 of these schools — more if they applied to more than one program at each university. Unless you are *really* concerned about not being able to get into any university, be a bit selective when choosing which schools you will honour with an application.

Just because you've received the offer of admission doesn't mean you can slack off. High school seniors who kiss off their spring semester because they think it doesn't matter have been shocked to find their university offers withdrawn due to their poor performance. Borderline students — remember the *maybe* pile? — are often admitted on the condition that their full final-year grades remain satisfactory.

Chapter 11

Grade 12: Making It Happen

. . . .

In This Chapter

▶ Finalizing your short list

▶ Figuring out when to apply (timing is everything)

▶ Filling out the application

▶ Including supplementary materials

▶ Applying to a university in another province

▶ Guarding against mistakes on your application

. . . .

*O*kay, so you've been following this book faithfully since grade 4, and you've already researched all the universities in the country — and maybe several colleges and technical institutes, too. Maybe you're so on the ball that you've looked even further afield, at international universities, as well. You've made your choices as to which you most want to attend. Then again, maybe you've had a few other things to do and you're not *quite* ready yet. Hey, it's even *possible* that, here it is, your final year in high school, and you've hardly even *thought* about applying to universities.

Don't worry. Whatever the case, we'll get you through the big application process.

Step 1: Getting Ready to Apply

If you haven't narrowed down your short list of universities yet, take a look through the earlier parts of the book. Go through the processes, make the lists, and ask yourself all the questions. Make sure you have decided that you want to go to university in the first place, and that you want to apply now. Come back here when you've done all that stuff. It's okay, we'll wait.

Here are some things to think about as you research universities and mull over your list. You should be able to shorten your list considerably based on how important these factors are to you and where the universities you are evaluating rank in relation to them:

- **Distance:** Do you want to leave home? If so, how far would you like to go? Or, how far are you *willing* to go? Does how often you return home matter to you? Is it important to you to remain in your hometown or province? Depending on how you rank distance, you can eliminate those universities from your list that are either too close or too far, whichever applies.

- **Housing:** Do you want to live on campus? Can you get space in residence? Is it important to you to be part of a campus where life revolves around residence and student activities? Or do you care whether most of your fellow students commute? Housing is one of the most important — but often most neglected — decisions about university. Two people can take the same programs, attend the same classes, and interact with the same students, but have totally different university experiences based on whether they live on campus or off.

- **Location:** Do you care about where your university is located? You can find schools in big cities, suburbs, and small towns. If the location of your university is important, remind yourself why.

- **Major:** Do you know what field of study you'd like to pursue at university? You may not have made a firm decision yet, but now is the time to give it some thought. If you're leaning toward a specific area of study, you want to look at universities that offer programs in that area — preferably schools that are known for excellence in it.

- **Personality:** This is probably the most important thing to think about. Yet it's easy to forget because a university's *personality* can be hard to describe and is certainly intangible. Does the university's personality mesh with yours? How do you *feel* on campus? Do you fit in? Do you like the students and the professors and the atmosphere? Is this a place where you can feel at home? It should be. It's where you'll be spending the next several years of your life.

- **Size:** Is the number of students at your university important to you? Big schools and small schools each have their pros and cons. Would you feel more comfortable on a large campus offering a wide array of activities, social life, and cultural opportunities? Would you prefer the small classes and individual attention that are more prevalent at smaller schools? Or would you be happy with a little of both worlds at a medium-sized university?

How many applications?

By now, you probably have one or two universities you're leaning toward. You have made your "best" choices — those schools where you find yourself most comfortable with all aspects of the campuses, such as the curriculum, the professors, and the students. You especially enjoyed your night in residence. But a couple of other universities that you feel could serve your needs nicely are out there as well. You could be happy and thrive at either of them if your top-choice universities don't accept you.

Susan narrows down her list

Susan is heading to university next year and she needs to pull together a short list of schools to which she'll apply. She lives in Calgary and she's adamant that she'd like to stay in the West. She knows she wants to live in residence — both to get out of the family home and to soak up the whole university experience.

She would like to be on a campus with a substantial number of students and a variety of activities, yet one that is still small enough that a professor might know who she is. She wants to study general arts: maybe business, maybe philosophy, but she's not sure yet. And she wants to live in a big city with lots of cultural activities.

The factors Susan rates highest are location, size, and housing. She has no strong feelings yet about a major and, other than being in the West, distance does not appear to be a factor either.

What should she do? She should look at the research she has compiled — perhaps starting with the yellow-coloured "Directory of Universities and Colleges" in the back of this book. She should check out where each university is located, its size, and its residence facilities.

If we consider the provinces of Saskatchewan, Alberta, and British Columbia to be "the West," then Susan determines that she can attend:

- University of Regina
- University of Saskatchewan
- University of Alberta
- University of Calgary
- University of Lethbridge
- University of British Columbia
- University of Northern British Columbia
- Simon Fraser University
- University of Victoria

That's quite a list! But, since Susan really wants to go to university in a big city, she can strike several of these schools off her list, leaving the University of Alberta, the University of Calgary, the University of British Columbia, and Simon Fraser University, all of which have residence programs with spaces available (she's checked!). So, Susan ends up with a workable short list of four universities. What's more, since the first three all have student populations of more than 20,000 and Simon Fraser's population is barely over 10,000 it will probably be her first choice, recognizing her wish for a medium-sized school.

Susan will also add her *reach* university as well as her *safety net* school to complete her program choices. We describe both of these in this chapter in "Step 1: Getting Ready to Apply."

Okay, you have identified four "right" universities for you. Now apply to all four and see what happens.

Whoa! We know what some of you are thinking. Why not just apply to your top two choices and, if they turn you down, go on to the next two? Bad idea for one big reason: If you wait, you may be shut out. What if, for whatever reason, your top two choices turn you down? Meanwhile, the other two universities on your list (where you haven't bothered to apply) are busily accepting students — without you! The other two universities may be full by the time you eventually apply. That's not the right way to begin your university career.

The most efficient approach is to submit all your applications at the same time. Ideally, that time is by December of your final high school year.

Sending four applications does not require four times the work, contrary to what you might think. Much of the information you provide is pretty general in nature, and is required on all applications. In fact, if all the universities you apply to are in Ontario, you need only fill out one form. (We provide a copy of the application form for Ontario universities later in this chapter.)

If you are considering applying to a college or technical institute in Ontario, you're in luck, too. Just as for universities in Ontario, there is a common application form for many Ontario colleges and technical institutes through the Ontario College Application Service. Log on to www.ocas.on.ca to download the form.

Remember that, except in Ontario, four applications *does* mean four times the money. In Ontario, you can apply to up to three university programs for an $80 application fee. Each additional university program on your list costs an extra $25. In every other province, you send a separate fee along with your application, usually in the $35 to $70 range. These fees are non-refundable, by the way, so you won't get your money back if the university doesn't want you or you don't want the university. If you have a budget of a couple of hundred dollars for application fees, four is no problem. If your budget is tight, the application fee is a factor to consider.

Go for the reach

Then there's that university (or program) you really like, but you feel is probably too tough to get into. With your high school record, your chances of getting in look like a long shot. Last year, the minimum average required to get into the program was 82 percent. You have an 80 percent average.

In admissions-office language, this university or program is a *reach* for you. This means you may not get in, but your credentials are close enough that it can't hurt to try. If you have an experienced high school counsellor, ask her about the chances of getting in with your marks. She may have seen others in your situation try. If you feel it's worth a gamble, send Reach U an application. What's the worst that can happen? Reach U may say *no*. But you could get lucky. It's a gamble where you have little to lose and much to gain. As one of our mothers says, "If you don't ask, you won't get." Words to live by.

Don't forget, another application means another application fee.

Everyone needs a safety net

You now have five universities on your short list: two that are your top choices and best hope, two others that are backup if your top two say *no*, and the reach. You still have one more university to identify, however. This is the school that needs to be on every student's list, because it's the place you're sure you can get into if all else fails. It's your *safety net*. Imagine the worst-case scenario. All the schools that you applied to (hypothetically) in the preceding sections of this chapter say, "Sorry, we've filled our class with other people." What a horrible thought! But in case it happens you need to be prepared.

How do you determine your own safety-net school? Look for one that accepts students with a low enough average that your own average makes acceptance a sure thing. We're not talking about the minimum averages for consideration — you need to investigate a little more and find out the range of averages that actually get *accepted* by the school. Some universities post this information about the last school year — some don't. However, generally, admissions officers will help you find this information. Remember, the averages are different every year and for every program, but they often stay in about the same range. It pays to do your research and keep up to date!

Hopefully, you won't even need your safety net. But you want to be certain that when your friends head to university, you aren't staying home.

Last year, the Ontario University Application Centre (OUAC) processed applications from just over 60,000 students, with a combined total of almost 240,000 choices. While some students applied to only a single university, most applied to several — and more than 10,000 applicants applied to all 18 schools (Ontario's 17 universities plus the Ontario College of Art and Design, for which the OUAC handles applications) on the OUAC list!

Looking forward to graduate school

One other thing you should give some thought to when applying to universities is whether you want to move on to graduate or professional school after your undergraduate degree. You don't have to make a firm decision in high school, but you should think about your options. If you want to get a graduate degree in the subject you are majoring in during your undergraduate degree, it's usually easier to remain at the same school and work with the professors who you already know. It's a good idea to check out the quality of the graduate studies programs — and whether they exist at all! — before you apply to the university.

Considering graduate school?

Some people believe they are more likely to be accepted to a graduate school if they attended the same university for their undergraduate degree. At first glance, this theory seems to make sense. Universities like to form bonds with their students, and how better to do so than by keeping the student for a few more years of study?

Unfortunately for those students who think they need such an edge to get into their chosen professional program, it's just not true. A university's graduate school is usually completely separate from its undergraduate counterpart. There is little communication between them when it comes to admissions, except, of course, concerning marks and faculty recommendations.

Generally speaking, graduate schools look at your undergraduate marks and your admission test scores — the *LSAT (Law School Admission Test)* for law school, the *GRE (Graduate Record Examination)* for many master's programs, the *GMAT (Graduate Management Admission Test)* for M.B.A. programs, and others.

Graduate schools may also look at a few more factors to determine your acceptance. They may require you to write an entrance essay, supply personal references, even go in for an interview. They're far more inquisitive than undergraduate admissions officers — but they have to be choosier because space is more limited in professional or graduate schools. However, this is no reason to ignore the possibility of going to graduate school. You can often take graduate-level courses in your later undergraduate years, but before you even get to university you can

investigate what sort of graduate programs may be offered at the school of your choice.

Sometimes, undergraduate students will meet a professor with whom they want to study for their graduate degree. If you're already at the school you like for graduate work, this works out even better for you. Universities sometimes unconsciously slant admissions toward alumni, even though there's nothing to suggest this in their official material. By rating their own undergraduate programs as more difficult than others, graduate schools may be less demanding or more forgiving of students from their own school — especially when a student tries to explain away a low mark or two.

The upshot of all this? If you think you might want to try graduate school, you should start thinking about choosing an undergraduate university and choosing a graduate university — and whether these schools might be the same. You may want to go to a small school for your undergraduate years and then go to the "big city" for graduate work. You may feel the opposite is true: After four years of hustle and bustle of the big city, a small-town graduate school will let you concentrate on your schoolwork.

Whatever you decide, you can add the possibility of going to graduate school to your Mull Lists. You already know you have a better chance of gaining admission to university if you plan for it early. Now you know you will have a better chance of getting into graduate school if you start doing the research before you even get to university.

If you want to get into a *professional degree* program (such as medicine, law, or education), it doesn't really make a difference which university you attend for your undergraduate degree. This said, you *should* consider whether or not you wish to remain at the same university (in the same city) for both degrees.

After four years at the University of Toronto, Caryn didn't apply to either her alma mater or York University for law school. They both have excellent law programs with fine reputations, but Caryn wanted to try out another city. Luckily, the law school with the programs and personality she wanted was as far away from Toronto as you can get while still remaining in Canada!

Step 2: When and How to Apply

Get ready. This is the start of a whole new ball game. You have identified six universities, including a *reach* and a *safety net*, to which you're going to apply. Now you must tell them about yourself in a way that will make them eager to have you as a student.

You don't have much of a choice as to when to apply to university. The universities set their own deadlines and time frames for considering applications. You either meet their schedules or get left behind, as we discuss in the sections below. Depending on the university, however, you may have a choice on *how* to apply. For example, more universities each year allow and even encourage you to apply online.

The early bird gets the worm, er, edge

The best time to apply depends on the universities to which you're applying and the admission systems they use. If a school has a firm, published application deadline, be sure that your application gets there before then. Don't just *send* your application by the deadline; give it some time to arrive. Tardiness is not a desirable trait.

Most deadlines are in January or February for the class arriving the following September. Some deadlines are as early as mid-December. Some are in mid-March. Look at the deadline and mark it on your calendar. This is a very important date! Now move back at least a month. Circle *this* date. By preparing your application as closely as possible to this early date, you increase your chances of admission. Don't rush, you'll only make silly errors.

The vast majority of university applicants wait for the deadlines to send off their stuff. But you're no dummy. You're going to help your own cause by submitting your application a few weeks early, before the mailbags start piling up on the admissions officers' desks. (If you do procrastinate and wait until the last minute, you may want to consider an overnight delivery service to guarantee your application's arrival.)

If you're applying to a university that uses *rolling admission*, get your application in as soon as the school will take it. Rolling admission means applicants are considered, and accepted or rejected, as their applications are received. It's essentially done on a first-come, first-served basis. If you wait too long, the first-year class could be full.

Universities that use a rolling admission list a deadline close to the end of your final high school year, say in June, although it may be as late as August. By that time, they are almost invariably full. Don't wait that long! Find out the *earliest* time you can send in your application and send it in then. Admissions officers will be impressed by your eager attitude and will have more time to look at your application.

What a break! A common application

Applying to universities in Ontario is somewhat easier than applying to universities in all the other provinces because of an organization called the *Ontario Universities' Application Centre (OUAC).* It administers a common application for all 17 Ontario universities plus the Ontario College of Art and Design. You can flip forward a few pages to see what the standard application for full-time attendance looks like (Figure 11-1).

You fill out the two-page form, listing the universities and programs you wish to apply to, and send in the application, along with your application fee. The OUAC charges $80 for application to three university programs, but you can apply to as many as you like for an extra $25 per application. Out-of-province Canadian students who wish to apply to Ontario universities pay a slightly higher fee: $85 for three choices, $25 for each additional program choice.

This common application applies to those 18 Ontario schools only. If you want to apply to a university outside Ontario, you have to do so separately. Sorry.

Note that despite the fact that the Royal Military College is considered a university because it grants degrees, it is not on the list of universities administered by the OUAC. You have to apply to the RMC through your local Canadian Forces Recruiting Centre. We discuss the option of a military education in Chapter 16.

Copies of the OUAC application form are sent each year to every Ontario high school's counselling office — and to many schools outside Ontario also. If your school runs out, check with your counsellor about ordering more or send the OUAC a request for your own copy. You can find the organization online at www.ouac.on.ca.

British Columbia has something similar to Ontario in the form of the *Post-Secondary Application Service of British Columbia (PASBC)*. Its Web site is located at www.pas.bc.ca. You register to get a log-in account, enter your basic information, and then go on to apply to any of 18 British Columbia universities, colleges, or institutes, including the four universities and six colleges in Appendix A, our "Directory of Universities and Colleges." You still have to pay each school's application fees separately, but at least this is a central place from which to apply.

Applying online

Pretty much all universities in Canada — including the OUAC — use the Internet for the application process. Be sure to check out a university's Web site for application instructions concerning the best way to apply online. Some universities have the entire application visible onscreen and you just fill in the spaces. Others have you download the form, fill it in, and mail or e-mail it back to them. Still others have secure online applications that require you to fill in one field at a time until the application is completed.

All of the universities, colleges, and technical institutes listed in Appendix A, "Directory of Universities and Colleges," post their applications on their Web sites, along with instructions on how to fill them out, application fee amounts, deadlines, and other stuff. It's not always easy to find exactly what you want because there are so many different application options available. However, perhaps the process is a bit convoluted for a reason. After all, if you can't figure out the application process, chances are you won't be able to understand what is taught in your university courses.

Even if you apply online, you can still submit supplementary materials through the mail. You can certainly send your application fee through the mail, so send your extras with it. You'll know for sure that your supplementary materials arrived when your cheque clears!

Step 3: Anatomy of an Application

Enough with the preliminaries. It's time to make yourself look beautiful — on paper or on a computer screen. In this section, we go line by line through the sections of a typical application form. We bring important parts to your attention and highlight areas where it's easy to mess up. If you'd like a visual cue as you read through this, you can refer to Figure 11-1, the Ontario Universities' Application Centre's common application form.

| RETURN TO: À RETOURNER AU:
ONTARIO UNIVERSITIES' APPLICATION CENTRE
CENTRE DE DEMANDE D'ADMISSION
AUX UNIVERSITÉS DE L'ONTARIO
650 WOODLAWN ROAD WEST
P.O. BOX 1328, GUELPH, ON N1H 7P4 | APPLICATION FOR
ADMISSION TO AN
ONTARIO UNIVERSITY
FOR APPLICANTS ATTENDING
AN ONTARIO SECONDARY SCHOOL | DEMANDE D'ADMISSION
À UNE UNIVERSITÉ
DE L'ONTARIO
CANDIDATS PRÉSENTEMENT INSCRITS
À UNE ÉCOLE SECONDAIRE DE L'ONTARIO | REFERENCE NUMBER NUMÉRO DE LA DEMANDE
2001
REFER TO THIS NUMBER ON ALL CORRESPONDENCE
NUMÉRO À CITER DANS TOUTE CORRESPONDANCE |

TITLE TITRE | **LEGAL SURNAME** NOM | **ALL LEGAL GIVEN NAMES IN FULL** (UNDERLINE NAME COMMONLY USED) PRÉNOMS (SOULIGNER LE PRÉNOM USUEL)

GENDER SEXE | **DATE OF BIRTH** DATE DE NAISSANCE | YR. AN | MO. MOIS | DAY JOUR | **SOCIAL INS. NO.** N° D'ASSURANCE SOCIALE | **SECONDARY SCHOOL STUDENT NO.** NUMÉRO MATRICULE | **MINISTRY IDENTIFICATION NO.** NUMÉRO MINISTÉRIEL

MAILING ADDRESS ADRESSE POSTALE
- APT.# APP. | NO. & STREET N° ET RUE
- CITY VILLE | PROV. PROV. | POSTAL CODE CODE POSTAL | AREA CODE & PHONE NUMBER INDIC. RÉG. ET N° DE TÉL.

HOME ADDRESS ADRESSE DU DOMICILE
- APT.# APP. | ☐ CHECK BOX IF SAME AS MAILING ADDRESS LA MÊME QUE L'ADRESSE POSTALE | NO & STREET N° ET RUE
- CITY VILLE | PROV. PROV. | POSTAL CODE CODE POSTAL | AREA CODE & PHONE NUMBER INDIC. RÉG. ET N° DE TÉL.

COUNTRY OF CITIZENSHIP PAYS DE CITOYENNETÉ
- 0 CANADIAN CITIZEN CITOYEN CANADIEN
- 1 PERMANENT RESIDENT RÉSIDENT PERMANENT
- 2 STUDENT AUTH. PERMIS DE SÉJOUR POUR ÉTUDIANT
- 3 OTHER (SPECIFY) AUTRE (PRÉCISEZ)

STATUS IN CANADA STATUT AU CANADA

MARITAL STATUS ÉTAT CIVIL
- 1 SINGLE CÉLIBATAIRE
- 2 MARRIED MARIÉ

FIRST LANGUAGE LANGUE MATERNELLE
- 1 ENGLISH ANGLAIS
- 2 FRENCH FRANÇAIS
- 3 OTHER AUTRE

LANGUAGE OF CORRESPONDENCE LANGUE DE CORRESPONDANCE
- 1 ENGLISH ANGLAIS
- 2 FRENCH FRANÇAIS

IF NOT BORN IN CANADA, ENTER DATE OF ARRIVAL IN CANADA
SI NÉ HORS CANADA, DATE D'ARRIVÉE AU CANADA | YA | MM

COUNTY | C. OF CITZ. | ADJ.

HIGH SCHOOL CURRENTLY ATTENDING ÉCOLE SECONDAIRE ACTUELLE | MIDENT

	COURSE TITLES NOM DU COURS	COURSE CODES COTE DU COURS	COMPLETION DATE CONCLUSION DU COURS	CREDIT VALUE EQUIV. EN CR.	MARK % NOTE %	G. TYPE TYPE N	FR FR	DELIVERY MODE	C. TYPE TYPE C	NOTE COMMENTAIRES
1										
2										
3										
4										
5										
6										
7										
8										
9										
10										
11										
12										
13										
14										
15										
16										
17										
18										
19										
20										
21										
22										
23										
24										
25										
26										
27										
28										
29										
30										
31										
32										
33										
34										

TO BE COMPLETED BY THE SCHOOL OFFICIAL À ÊTRE REMPLI PAR UN MEMBRE DE LA DIRECTION DE L'ÉCOLE | NUMBER OF COURSES WHERE THE LANGUAGE OF INSTRUCTION IS FRENCH NOMBRE DE COURS DONT LA LANGUE D'ENSEIGNEMENT EST LE FRANÇAIS

THE APPLICANT HAS EARNED THE O.S.S.D. LE CANDIDAT A REÇU LE DESD. | **1** | **OR OU** | UPON COMPLETION OF THE CURRENT PROGRAM THE APPLICANT WILL BE QUALIFIED FOR THE O.S.S.D. À LA FIN DU PROGRAMME ACTUEL LE CANDIDAT AURA COMPLÉTÉ LES EXIGENCES DU DESD. | **2** YES OUI | **3** NO NON | **TCR**

PLEASE PRINT NAME ÉCRIRE LE NOM EN CARACTÈRES D'IMPRIMERIE | TITLE TITRE | DATE

TO BE COMPLETED BY THE APPLICANT / A ETRE REMPLI PAR LE CANDIDAT
CHOICES 1 TO 3 - TOTAL $80.00 / CHOIX DE 1 À 3 - TOTAL DE 80 $

UNIVERSITY AND PROGRAM SELECTIONS (CONSULT THE INFORMATION BOOKLET) CHOIX D'UNIVERSITÉS ET DE PROGRAMMES D'ÉTUDES (SE REPORTER AU LIVRET EXPLICATIF)

CHOICE CHOIX	CODE COTE	CO-OP COOP	UNIVERSITY NAME (AND COLLEGE NAME IF APPLICABLE) NOM DE L'UNIVERSITÉ (ET DU COLLÈGE S'IL Y A LIEU)	PROGRAM TITLE TITRE DU PROGRAMME	SUBJECT OF MAJOR INTEREST DOMAINE D'INTÉRÊT	EXPECTED ENROLLMENT DATE DATE PRÉVUE D'INSCRIPTION	FULL-TIME PART-TIME TEMPS COMPLET TEMPS PARTIEL	IF YOU APPLIED BEFORE, ENTER YEAR SI VOUS AVEZ DE JA DEMANDÉ L'ADMISSION, DONNEZ L'ANNÉE	RESIDENCE INFO REQ'D RENSEIGNEMENT SUR LES RÉSI-DENCES REQUIS
1									1 YES/OUI 2 NO/NON
2									1 YES/OUI 2 NO/NON
3									1 YES/OUI 2 NO/NON

ALL CHOICES AFTER 3 ARE $25.00 EACH / REMETTRE 25 $ POUR CHAQUE CHOIX AU DELÀ DES 3 PREMIERS

									1 YES/OUI 2 NO/NON
									1 YES/OUI 2 NO/NON
									1 YES/OUI 2 NO/NON

APPLICANT'S E-MAIL ADDRESS - ADRESSE ÉLECTRONIQUE DU CANDIDAT

APPLICANT DECLARATION - DÉCLARATION DU CANDIDAT

HAVE YOU EVER ATTENDED A POSTSECONDARY INSTITUTION?
AVEZ-VOUS DÉJÀ FRÉQUENTÉ UNE INSTITUTION POSTSECONDAIRE?   YES/OUI 1   NO/NON 2

IF "YES", PROVIDE THE FOLLOWING INFORMATION FOR THE POST-SECONDARY INSTITUTION ATTENDED.
SI OUI, FOURNIR LES RENSEIGNEMENTS DEMANDÉS POUR L'INSTITUTION D'ÉTUDES POSTSECONDAIRES FRÉQUENTÉE.

			YEAR LEVEL NIVEAU SCOLAIRE	PROGRAM PROGRAMME D'ÉTUDES	DIPLOMA / DEGREE DIPLÔME / GRADE
FROM/DE : YR AN	MO	Name & Location of Institution / Nom et lieu de l'établissement			
TO/À : YR AN					

DO YOU AUTHORIZE THE UNIVERSITY TO FORWARD TO YOUR SECONDARY SCHOOL ACADEMIC DATA REGARDING YOUR PERFORMANCE WHILE AT UNIVERSITY? THIS INFORMATION WILL BE KEPT CONFIDENTIAL AND WILL BE USED BY THE SECONDARY SCHOOL FOR CURRICULUM RESEARCH AND GUIDANCE PURPOSES.

PERMETTEZ-VOUS À L'UNIVERSITÉ DE TRANSMETTRE À VOTRE ÉCOLE SECONDAIRE LES RENSEIGNEMENTS RELATIFS À VOTRE RENDEMENT À L'UNIVERSITÉ? CES RENSEIGNEMENTS DEMEURERONT CONFIDENTIELS ET SERVIRONT UNIQUEMENT AU SECONDAIRE À DES FINS DE RECHERCHE DANS LES PROGRAMMES D'ÉTUDES ET LES SECTIONS DE L'ORIENTATION.

YES/OUI   NO/NON

TOTAL NUMBER OF YEARS IN ALL ONTARIO SECONDARY SCHOOLS
NOMBRE D'ANNÉES D'ÉTUDES DANS LES ÉCOLES SECONDAIRES DE L'ONTARIO   1 ☐ 2 ☐ 3 ☐ 4 ☐ 5 ☐ 6 ☐ 7 ☐ 8 ☐ More than 8/Plus de 8 ☐

TOTAL NUMBER OF YEARS IN AN ENGLISH LANGUAGE OR CANADIAN SCHOOL SYSTEM NOMBRE D'ANNÉES DANS UN SYSTÈME SCOLAIRE DE LANGUE ANGLAISE OU CANADIEN	IF OUTSIDE CANADA PLEASE SPECIFY WHERE VEUILLEZ PRÉCISER L'ENDROIT SI L'ÉCOLE (N'ÉTAIT PAS AU CANADA)

DO YOU INTEND TO APPLY FOR FINANCIAL ASSISTANCE FROM THE ONTARIO STUDENT ASSISTANCE PROGRAM (OSAP)?
PRÉVOYEZ-VOUS FAIRE UNE DEMANDE D'AIDE FINANCIÈRE AUPRÈS DU RÉGIME D'AIDE FINANCIÈRE AUX ÉTUDIANTS DE L'ONTARIO (RAFÉO)?   ☐ YES / OUI   ☐ NO / NON

DO YOU INTEND TO APPLY FOR THE "AIMING FOR THE TOP" SCHOLARSHIP PROGRAM? PRÉVOYEZ-VOUS PRÉSENTER UNE DEMANDE POUR UNE DES BOURSES « SOMMET DE L'EXCELLENCE »?

☐ YES/OUI BY CHECKING "YES", I AUTHORIZE THE ONTARIO UNIVERSITIES' APPLICATION CENTRE TO DISCLOSE MY GRADES TO THE STUDENT SUPPORT BRANCH (OSAP) OF THE MINISTRY OF TRAINING AND COLLEGES AND UNIVERSITIES FOR THE SOLE PURPOSE OF DETERMINING MY ELIGIBILITY FOR THIS SCHOLARSHIP, IF I APPLY. EN COCHANT « OUI », J'AUTORISE LE CENTRE DE DEMANDE D'ADMISSION AUX UNIVERSITÉS DE L'ONTARIO À DIVULGUER MES RÉSULTATS SCOLAIRES À LA DIRECTION DU SOUTIEN AUX ÉTUDIANTS (RAFÉO) DU MINISTÈRE DE LA FORMATION ET DES COLLÈGES ET UNIVERSITÉS DE L'ONTARIO AUX FINS DE DÉTERMINER, MON ADMISSIBILITÉ À RECEVOIR CETTE BOURSE SI JE PRÉSENTE UNE DEMANDE.

☐ NO/NON

I HEREBY CERTIFY THAT ALL STATEMENTS ARE CORRECT AND COMPLETE INCLUDING MY DECLARATION OF CITIZENSHIP AND STATUS IN CANADA. I UNDERSTAND THAT I MAY BE REQUIRED TO SUPPLY DOCUMENTATION AT SOME FUTURE DATE TO SUBSTANTIATE MY CLAIM, AND THAT ANY MISREPRESENTATION OF THIS DATA MAY RESULT IN THE CANCELLATION OF MY ADMISSION OR REGISTRATION STATUS. I AUTHORIZE THE SECONDARY SCHOOL AND THE MINISTRY OF EDUCATION AND TRAINING TO FORWARD ALL ACADEMIC INFORMATION, SCHOOL RECORDS AND RECOMMENDATIONS TO THE APPLICATION CENTRE AND TO THE UNIVERSITIES OF ONTARIO. I UNDERSTAND THAT IN THE CASE OF SUSPECTED MISREPRESENTATION OF APPLICATION INFORMATION, OTHER CANADIAN UNIVERSITIES MAY BE CONTACTED.

JE CERTIFIE QUE LES RENSEIGNEMENTS DONNÉS SONT EXACTS ET COMPLETS Y COMPRIS MA CITOYENNETÉ ET MON STATUT AU CANADA. JE SAIS QU'ON POURRA ME DEMANDER DE FOURNIR DES PREUVES À L'APPUI ET QUE TOUTE FAUSSE DÉCLARATION PEUT ENTRAÎNER L'ANNULATION DE MON ADMISSION OU DE MON INSCRIPTION À L'UNIVERSITÉ. J'AUTORISE L'ÉCOLE SECONDAIRE ET LE MINISTÈRE DE L'ÉDUCATION ET DE LA FORMATION À FAIRE PARVENIR MON DOSSIER SCOLAIRE AU CENTRE DE DEMANDE ET AUX UNIVERSITÉS DE L'ONTARIO. SI UNE FAUSSE DÉCLARATION EST SOUPÇONNÉE, JE COMPRENDS QUE D'AUTRES UNIVERSITÉS CANADIENNES POURRONT ÊTRE CONSULTÉES.

DATE :   APPLICANT'S SIGNATURE:
DATE :   SIGNATURE DU CANDIDAT :

PLEASE NOTE: THE BASE APPLICATION SERVICE FEE OF $80 (CDN), PLUS ANY APPLICABLE ADDITIONAL CHOICE FEES, MUST ACCOMPANY THIS APPLICATION FORM IN ORDER FOR YOUR APPLICATION TO BE PROCESSED.
NOTA : LES DROITS DE SERVICE DE 80,00 $, AINSI QUE LES DROITS DE SERVICE POUR TOUT CHOIX ADDITIONNEL, DOIVENT ACCOMPAGNER CE FORMULAIRE POUR QUE VOTRE DEMANDE SOIT TRAITÉE.

Figure 11-1: The application you fill out to apply to universities in Ontario.

REMEMBER

Request two applications from each university you apply to, or at least make a photocopy of each. One copy serves as your rough draft. The other will be the polished version you'll use to wow the admissions officers.

We haven't included all the possible permutations of the application in this section. If we had, the book would be about 1,000 pages longer than it is. Nor do we discuss how to fill out an application for a college or technical institute. That's because the forms are fairly similar, for the most part. They ask you to provide the same types of information. You can log on to www.ocas.on.ca to view and download the common application for Ontario colleges. Unfortunately, as with universities, there's no such universal application for colleges in other provinces. But you can check them out by going to the particular college's Web site. We include the URLs for selected colleges and technical institutes in our "Directory of Universities and Colleges."

If you are from another country besides Canada, if you want to transfer credits from a non-Canadian university, or if you have other exceptional circumstances, speak with an admissions officer about what else you need to provide.

Vital statistics

The first section of the application is just what you expect. It asks for your identification information. Fill it out. Fill it *all* out. Make sure every box has something in it, unless the box is marked "optional." You may think it's obvious that you are a "Mr." if your first name is "John," but tick the box anyway. If something is missing, that makes your application incomplete. It will not be processed until the information is tracked down — by an admissions officer who is probably not too thrilled by the prospect. You don't want to mess up unnecessarily in this straightforward part of the application.

Name

Use your legal name; the name that appears on your social insurance card and birth certificate. Don't use nicknames or short forms.

Be careful about name changes. Just because your mother remarried and you have started using the last name of your stepfather doesn't mean that it's your *legal* last name. Unless you've legally changed your last name to your stepfather's, put the surname you were given at birth on the form. The form has a place for a former last name. If you have one, fill it out. If not, put a straight horizontal line through the field (yes, with a ruler or other straight edge).

Never put "NA" for "not applicable," because there may be people out there with the last name "Na" — and the harried applications officer will have to contact you to find out if this is the case. Hey, it's happened! Of course, if you *have* legally changed your name, put your new (legal) name in the top box for your name, and put your previous name in the box designated for a former name. It's pretty straightforward.

This is a good time to confirm that your high school is using your full and correct name and has accurate contact information for you, as your transcript will be sent to the universities from there. If the name you supply on your university application form can't be matched to the name supplied by your high school, you're looking at some unnecessary delays.

Address

Fill in all the fields, striking out those that don't apply to you. Don't forget to include your area code when filling in your phone number. Write the name of your city in full — it's West Vancouver, not W.Van.

There may be separate spaces for a mailing address and a home address, and a box to check if they are the same. Put a check in the box if your mailing address and home address are the same (they likely are) instead of filling out the fields twice.

If you enter an e-mail address, make sure it is one you check frequently. The universities may send you important information or even try to contact you about some aspect of your application. Don't let the university's call go unanswered!

Status and other information

Fill in your gender, date of birth, social insurance number, immigration status, marital status, first language, language of correspondence, and whether or not you are applying as a mature student. Wow! Nosy, huh? (Just wait until you see what they ask on financial aid applications. If you're curious, flip ahead to Chapter 14 and check it out.) The universities do have a right to ask you these questions, nonetheless. Do you have a right to refuse to answer? Sure, but only if you are prepared to have your application marked incomplete. If you don't provide the information they ask for, they don't have to consider your application.

Make sure the information you provide is accurate. Check your social insurance card to make sure the numbers are correct and that you haven't transposed any digits. If English is not your first language, don't lie about it to get around having to write the TOEFL (Test of English as a Foreign Language — we tell you more about that later in this chapter). Lying about anything on your application is a big no-no.

If you are not a Canadian citizen, you will be asked to fill in your immigration status, country of citizenship, and date of arrival in Canada. You may be asked more questions later. Get out your immigration documents first and make sure you are entering the information correctly. If you hold citizenship in more than one country, use the country that appears on your most recent immigration documents. Otherwise, there will be a discrepancy when the folks at the university check your status — and they will.

Program selections

You decide the answers to the next set of questions on the application form. That's a nice change, isn't it?

- ✔ Enter the academic term and year that you want to start attending the university. There are two terms (sometimes called *semesters*) in the regular academic year: fall and spring. If you hope to begin university in September of 2003, for example, enter fall 2003.

  Sometimes, schools give you a choice between *winter* and *summer* terms. If you want to start in September (a "normal" school year), then you mark *winter* on the application form. Summer school for universities can start as early as May.

- ✔ Enter whether you want to study full-time or part-time.

- ✔ Enter the faculty to which you are applying (such as arts, sciences, engineering, or another faculty). You probably don't have to declare your major yet, but you do have to choose a particular faculty and, depending on the school, your intended program of study. If you are unsure about which program to indicate, ask the university admissions officer.

Depending on the university, choosing your program incorrectly now may exclude you from eventually getting into the one you want. When in doubt, always ask.

On the OUAC common application form, you also have to:

- ✔ Enter your university choices, ranked from 1 to 3, and so on.

- ✔ Enter the university program codes (listed in the OUAC calendar under the application guidelines for each Ontario university), along with the program title (or name), and your intended major — yes, you have to fill this in for the OUAC form.

- ✔ Enter whether you are interested in a co-op work program, if applicable to your program of study. Not all universities — and not all programs — offer a co-op opportunity, so make sure the university and program to which you are applying is one of the few that do. We tell you all about co-op programs in Chapter 16.

High school attendance

Make sure you enter the full name of your high school — it's on the school's letterhead and it's also on your transcripts! If you've attended other high schools previously, make sure that the one you list on your application is the one from which you're graduating. You will be asked to indicate the province and country where the school is located. You also need to enter whether your high school is semestered, and your intended graduation date. If your school is semestered, then the universities will know that the marks you receive at the end of December are final and that they need to request records for a different set of courses in the spring.

If you're not in high school, enter the last calendar year you were. Mature students have a different set of guidelines to follow, allowing them to send in more information about their life experiences since they left high school, so make sure you get the proper guidelines and application forms from the university.

Don't worry about entering your high school's address if the application doesn't request it — although the *name* of the high school must be correct. The universities each have a master list of all the high schools in Canada. They'll use this list to contact your school and request your transcript.

You will likely have to provide this information for every high school you have attended. This is another one of those times when starting your University Applications File early really pays off. If you've done this, all the information we're talking about — transcripts, addresses, and other stuff — will be in one easily accessible place. This saves you time and frustration.

Past college/university attendance

You have to tell the universities whether you have attended other post-secondary schools, in Canada or anywhere else. Even if you failed every course and never want to think about that horrible episode in your life again. Even if you attended for only a month and then dropped out. You still have to disclose the name of the university (or college, or institute), its location, your dates of attendance, the type degree or diploma you received, and your major.

The admissions officers don't care so much about how well you did or didn't do in your past post-secondary career — mature students can bolster their applications by supplying letters of intent and other supplementary information. What the admissions officers *do* care about, however, is whether you have any disciplinary action on your record. What might you do that results in disciplinary action? Well, failure to disclose this very information is one thing. Lying on any part of your application form can do it as well. Being caught cheating, hacking into the school's computer servers, or performing other acts contrary to the school's moral code will all result in a mark against you in your file.

If you have such negative reports on your record, send along a letter of explanation and a reference letter from a trustworthy source. Perhaps you were going through personal problems at the time. Perhaps, after being caught hacking the servers, you saw the error of your ways and voluntarily reworked the network security for the entire school's system. Get the dean or president to send a letter about your miraculous transformation and unparalleled talent.

Residence and special needs

Most universities have a section on their application forms asking you whether you want to live in residence if you are accepted. If the university accepts you, the information about residence is sent to you with your offer of admission. For some schools, you have to request residence information separately. For all universities, you need to apply separately for a place in residence. After all, not every first-year student wants to live on campus; the school has to figure out how many residence offers it needs to make.

There is usually a section asking you if you have *special needs*. What are special needs, and how do you know if you have them? If you are physically challenged, for example, you might get a residence room on the ground floor in the residence that has wheelchair access. If you're hearing challenged, you may need special fire alarm devices in your residence room. If you're visually challenged, you may need accommodations for an assistance dog. Don't be shy about asking the admissions officers what allowances their school makes for students with special needs.

Payment

Pay the application fee with a cheque, money order, bank draft, or credit card. Don't send cash. Staple the cheque, money order, or bank draft to the front top of the application form to ensure it does not get lost when the letter is opened. If you're paying by credit card, be sure to fill in the field asking for the name of the cardholder, even if the card is in your name. And don't forget to sign the space indicating the school has authorization to charge your card!

Make sure that your cheque doesn't bounce. Don't use a maxed-out credit card. That really makes an applicant look bad!

Other stuff

Some universities ask questions on the application to help them out in their marketing efforts. They may want to know how you heard about the school and why you chose to apply to it. We know, we know, you hate filling this kind of thing in. Although not doing it won't adversely affect your application, we suggest you take a few extra minutes and do it anyway. It's usually just a few extra checkmarks. If it makes the applications officer just a little bit happier, it will be worth your time.

Declaration

This is where you sign and date the application form. By signing your name to it, you confirm that you have read the information and instructions on the application and filled it in accurately, and you guarantee that the information is complete and correct. Your signature here also grants the university authority to verify any of the information you provide on the application and to use or release the information for statistical analysis.

All declarations include a statement like this:

"I acknowledge that withholding relevant information or providing false information on this application or submitted with it may be considered grounds for non-admission or, after admission, grounds for dismissal."

About those recommendations

You may have signed the declaration, but your application isn't quite ready for the mail. Now you have to enlist the help of your high school counsellor. He needs to write a few things about you on your application. What your counsellor says (and doesn't say) can affect everything from whether you get offered a scholarship from the university to whether you get in at all. The recommendation can be a few lines in the space provided on the application, or a full-length letter attached separately.

Most universities offer entrance scholarships. To determine who gets these, universities look at marks and some other criteria, including the types and levels of courses you took, your rank within your class, and personal recommendations. To find out this last stuff, the universities want to hear from someone other than you, and the school counsellor is usually a good person to ask. In this, your counsellor can be a big help to you — or a big hindrance.

The counsellor will be asked where you rank in relation to the top 5 percent of students in your class. Of course, there is also a box that states "Our school does not rank students," and a few lines for the counsellor to comment about you. You want the counsellor to say glorious things about you, so how can you ensure that he does so?

Develop a relationship with your counsellor. Even if the two of you haven't met before now, it's not too late. Enlist your favourite teacher and ask her to help you convince the counsellor what a model student you are. Make sure that your counsellor has enough time to write a fitting recommendation about you so that you can get it in before the deadline. Start talking with your counsellor as soon as you can — at least a month before you want to send in your application.

You may want to write the recommendation yourself or combine forces with your favourite teacher. As long as everything you say is truthful, chances are the counsellor will use it, at least as a basis for your letter. After all, any busy counsellor will be happy to have some of his work done for him.

What does this mean? Simply put, if you lie anywhere on your application — either by saying something you know to be incorrect or by intentionally not responding to something that's asked for that you don't want to tell — don't expect to be accepted. Of course, the university might not find out that you lied on your application until later. No problem. As soon as it does find out, it can kick you out of school if it thinks your situation is serious enough to warrant this punishment.

Even if you have attended the university for two or three years, it may still kick you out. And, in *really* serious cases, a university could conceivably even take away the degree you received years before!

Universities understand that honest people make honest mistakes, so they probably won't kick you out for forgetting one of your seven middle names. However, if you deliberately lie on your application, don't expect any sympathy.

Step 4: Padding Your Application (Umm . . . Sending Additional Materials)

There are also other things you may want to send along with your official application to bolster your chance of getting into the university of your dreams. These are the things you have been hoarding in your University Applications File all these years. Well, it's time to get them out!

Send your additional materials in the form of a letter with copies of the other materials we mention in this section attached. The letter should be divided into subheadings, perhaps like the ones we list here. You can send the same letter to each university, as long as you change the contact information. But you'll probably want to personalize each one a bit. Remember, universities like students who like them!

Awards

Mention every award you received in high school, small or large. Don't forget that certificate you earned in Latin class, the Lions Club Student-of-the-Month award, and your prize in the science fair. And mention the award your school newspaper won while you were the number-two editor. That's a school-related honour, too.

In case you're wondering, don't include the blue ribbon you won for your dog's trick at the local dog park activity day. And don't list the trophy for winning the local under-17 female singles tennis tournament. Those are fine accomplishments, but they're not *scholastic* honours. (Okay, if you won *Wimbledon*, let them know. Admissions officers can be wowed by celebrities just like anyone else.)

Jobs, achievements, and talents

If you worked during high school, or even beforehand, let the admissions officer know. This is especially important if your job was related to the subject that you wish to study. A stint working at a lab on an aspect of the Human Genome Project suggests that you will probably do well in first-year genetics.

If you had to work during high school because of financial need (instead of for your love of watching free movies while ushering at the local Cineplex), let the admissions officer know this, too. It might go some distance in explaining why your marks are not quite as high as you'd like them to be, and you may still be considered for admission.

Tell the admissions officer what makes you special. Do not recount a long list of mundane activities that everyone else can do. Be selective and be compelling. If you have spoken at a conference on the topic you wish to study at university, this will impress the admissions officer. If you have been a student journalist for the local newspaper, this is relevant to your application to the journalism program. If you have designed an intriguing online game, provide the URL and let the admissions officer know why a degree in computer engineering is so important to you.

Even if your activities are not exactly related to your intended studies, they can still work in your favour. Tell the admissions officer about volunteering in the children's cancer ward at the local hospital for the last three years. Everyone should have something that sets them apart from the crowd. Let that part of you shine through.

Attach supplementary materials to back up your claims, such as a conference brochure listing your name, or a thank-you letter from the conference organizer, clips of your articles, or anything else you might have.

Explanations

If you have inconsistent grades or grades that are not quite up to par, this is where you explain them. Don't beg or whine or blame anyone else for your problems. Simply state that there were unavoidable factors that contributed to the lower marks and you want to explain them. As with the other items, back up what you say with letters from reputable sources, such as a doctor, teacher, religious advisor, or other relevant adult.

Step 5: Considering Your Special Circumstances

If you take a stroll around pretty much any university in Canada, you'll encounter a diverse collection of people. There are people from all over the world whose first language is something you may never have heard before. There are people with different philosophical, political, and religious beliefs. There are people of all ages, from different income levels, with different interests, talents, and experiences. All are welcome at the university.

It's a fantastic opportunity and a fantastic place. Universities encourage diversity. If you are applying from another province or country, if you speak another language, or if you're an older applicant, your application procedure, and your life at university, may be a bit different.

Applying from another province

Students who are not residents of the province where they go to university are called *out-of-province students*. Universities tend to be perfectly open to applicants from other provinces. However, out-of-province students are sometimes required to pay a slightly higher tuition rate than people applying from their own province. We cover tuition rates in Chapter 12.

Applying from another country

Your tuition fees will be much higher if you come from another country — usually at least twice as much as Canadian residents pay. You also have to get a student visa as well as an entry visa, and you may have to get a medical certificate showing you have a clean bill of health.

On the plus side, because of the extra cash universities take in from foreign students, they tend to be eager to accept them.

TOEFL: The real English test

If English is not your first language and you are applying to an English-speaking university, you will likely be required to supply evidence of your facility with English, so you can complete your courses and get your degree. You generally need to pass a standardized English-language test — the *Test of English as a Foreign Language (TOEFL)* is the most common of these, but there are others as well. Here is a list of several of them, along with contact information for test centres:

✔ **Test of English as a Foreign Language (TOEFL):** This is a standardized test administered through TOEFL/TSE Services, P.O. Box 6151, Princeton, New Jersey, 08541-6151, USA. You can find out more at the Web site at `www.toefl.org`.

✔ **Certificate of Proficiency in English (COPE):** This test is administered through COPE Testing Ltd., 7B Pleasant Boulevard, P.O. Box 1164, Toronto, Ontario, M4T 1K2. The Web site is located at `www.copetest.com`.

✔ **The International English Language Testing System (IELTS):** This test is administered through the IELTS Office, University of Cambridge Local Examinations Syndicate, 1 Hills Road, Cambridge, CB1 2EU, UK. The Web site is located at `www.ielts.org`.

✔ **Michigan English Language Assessment Battery (MELAB):** This test is administered through MELAB Testing, 3020 North University Building, University of Michigan, Ann Arbor, Michigan, 48109-1057, USA. The Web site is located at `www.lsa.umich.edu/eli/melab.htm`.

Make sure you contact the universities you are applying to before you write these tests to determine their specific requirements for scoring and reporting. Many universities have special codes that must be used to ensure your scores are sent to them. If you don't know the code, your results will not get to the university and your application will be incomplete. Some universities do not accept all the tests we list, either. Ask the university before you write!

Applying later in life

Not every university student goes to university right after high school. If you have taken only a year or two off before applying, your application will likely be placed in the same group as those of all the students applying directly from high school. However, if you've been absent from the formal education system for longer than a couple of years, you will probably be considered a *mature student.*

Every university has a different set of standards for classifying students as "mature," and for allowing them entry, so check with the admissions officer if you have been out of school for any period of time.

If you are a mature student and you haven't completed high school, you can still apply to university. In some cases, universities ask for your score on a special, standardized high school equivalency exam called a GED (which stands for General Education Development test). Alternatively, mature students may be asked to complete a *qualifying-year program* rather than a GED. Qualifying-year programs are designed to bring students who have been out of high school for some time up to university speed. Since every university has its own unique set of admission requirements, ask the school's admissions officers about your particular situation.

Complete the application and, if required, send your high school transcripts with it (and, if applicable, the results of your high school equivalency exam). You are also encouraged to send supplementary materials, such as a biographical letter explaining what you have done in your life, your accomplishments and challenges, why you want to attend university, and what you intend to do in the future.

Many universities like dealing directly with high schools, especially for marks and transcripts. In these cases, the university will make its own arrangements to get your high school marks.

Step 6: Silly Mistakes That Are Easy to Make

In the earlier parts of this chapter, we talk about making your application look good. But we wouldn't be doing our job if we didn't also tell you how to avoid making it look bad. Little mistakes can add up and sway an admissions officer's opinion about you in the wrong direction. Don't let your application fall prey to these unnecessary blunders.

What does that say?

If the university admissions officer can't read your application, you've got problems.

She won't necessarily put it in the *no* pile just because of poor penmanship. However, she may end up filing your application incorrectly. It may appear that you wish to study anthropology when you are really applying for archeology. Even worse, she may not be able to decipher the correct spelling of your name. This could spell trouble when your high school submits your marks to the university. They might not match up with your application. Horrors!

Type your applications and any correspondence you have with any university! If you can't get access to a computer or typewriter, print everything carefully in block letters. If you're downloading forms, printing them out, completing them, and then sending them back, use a laser printer or a high-end inkjet printer (with lots of toner or ink).

The big blank space

An application with missing information is put in the *incomplete* pile and is not considered for acceptance until all the information is supplied. It takes the already-harried admissions officer extra time and effort to track this information down — which usually involves tracking *you* down. While she is gathering, confirming, correcting, and otherwise fixing your application, other students (the ones with complete applications) are being accepted to the school you want to attend.

The stuff you neglect to mention may not be important to you, but it is to the applications officer. Maybe it's obvious to you that your hometown of Victoria is in British Columbia, but there's another Victoria in Prince Edward Island, you know. Think it doesn't matter that you can't remember when you received your landed immigrant status — it was years ago, right? Well, think again. Track down the information and fill it in. And be polite when the admissions officer hunts you down. She's had a long day trying to find you and your missing information.

Don't leave any field on the application blank unless it is marked as optional to fill in.

Make sure your information is accurate

If you can't remember the date you received your landed immigrant status, for example, you can't just make up a date and put that in the application. Remember what we said before about the declaration that every applicant must sign? You are guaranteeing that the information you are providing is true. If it's not, you can be in trouble at any time — from the first moment the admissions officer reads your application all the way to several years after you have graduated. Don't lie. Don't embellish. And, if you don't know the answer, find out.

Get rid of typos

Make sure you know what you are going to say before you fill in the application. You may want to make a copy of it and fill out a rough-draft version first. Check your facts and get someone else to look it over before completing the final form.

Carefully type your information on a computer or a typewriter. If you are using a computer, make sure the information is accurate before you print (use the program's spell check module!). If you are using a typewriter, make sure it is a correctable typewriter so that you can fix errors as you go by backspacing.

Whatever you do, don't pour or brush Liquid Paper or other correctable liquid on your application forms. These products are useful for some documents, but not for a university application. You want your application to be pristine.

Looks count. You may not be able to make yourself look brilliant through a perfectly typed application form, but you *can* make an otherwise strong application look sloppy and foolish because of a couple of spelling mistakes. Make sure the only thing that stands out on your application is your achievements.

The mysteriously changing name

Keep a copy of all your correspondence with the universities you apply to (in your University Applications File, of course), and use the same name every time. Check with your school to make sure that your transcript is sent under the exact same name as the one you are using on your application forms.

Some of us use different versions of our name on different pieces of documentation. You might have one version on your driver's licence, another on your social insurance card. This is the case of the Mysteriously Changing Name, and it can cause problems for you and your application.

Let's say John Smith applies to a particular university providing all his names as requested: John Ivan Jones Smith. Later, he sends supplementary material, signing only with the name he generally uses for correspondence: John Smith. When his transcript is sent, it appears that his school used his hyphenated name: John I. Jones-Smith. When he does not hear back from the university in the expected time, he calls asking about his application. He uses the name he generally goes by when talking with people: Jack Smith. What do you think he discovers? The university has no idea where his materials are! And it may not even know who *he* is!

Just give the answer, already

It may sound obvious, but answer the question that is being asked. If the form has a space for you to put the name of your high school, put the name of your high school there. Every year, certain applicants put something else, such as "See letter from principal." They think that forcing the admissions officer to get the name of the high school from an accompanying rave recommendation letter will likewise force her to read that letter.

Well, maybe so, but it is not likely to get the result you want. Instead of being impressed by the letter and by your ingenious manner of drawing attention to it, she is more likely to be frustrated by the missing information and steamed that you chose to waste her time this way.

Don't beat around the bush. Just answer what you're being asked.

Get it there on time

Universities have deadlines for admissions. If your application has not arrived by the deadline, you will not be considered.

Sure, after a particular university has considered all the other applications, one of its admissions officers *may* choose to look at your application, if the school has any remaining spaces. But, do you really want to take that chance?

Send your application in at least a few weeks early and then call to make sure it has arrived safely.

Step 7: Signed, Sealed, and Delivered

Congratulations! If you've completed the steps in this chapter, then you've likely got a pristine application (or maybe several) signed and ready to go. All you have to do now is address an envelope, find some postage stamps, and put your carefully prepared documents (on paper or disk) in the mail. If you decided to apply online, this final step is unnecessary. You're finished. Not all that tough, right?

Make a copy

Wait a minute! Before you send in those applications, photocopy them and keep the copies in your University Applications File. File them under "Correspondence" for each individual university. You can refer to them if you find yourself answering questions from an admissions officer. It doesn't hurt to keep a log of the name of the person you spoke with, the date, and what was discussed, as well.

The wait

The hard part starts now. The waiting. If your university asked for applications in mid-January and announces decisions in early April (at the earliest), you've got at least ten weeks in limbo. Some waiting periods are shorter; some longer. But for these weeks, you'll be in the dark with no clue as to how well your application is going over.

You're not alone. A few hundred thousand other students are pacing and biting their nails along with you. Sure, it would be nice if an admissions officer called you the day your application arrived to tell you how it fared. But it doesn't work that way. Get on with your life in high school and keep your grades up. Remember, if your university accepts you, it will want to see the rest of your grades for your final year. We talk about waiting lists and what to do when the responses start arriving in Chapter 19.

Good work!

Part IV

Please Report to the Financial Aid Office: Paying for University

The 5th Wave   By Rich Tennant

"My daughter's university education is costing me an arm and a leg and over 60 noses a year."

In this part . . .

Here comes the nasty word: money. You need some to go to university. Not a big surprise, right? But you might not need as much as you think. In this part, we give you a good idea of how much money you really need to have — whether you choose to attend university in the city where you live or on the other side of the country. We also give you advice on how to find the money you need if it's not waiting patiently in your bank account.

Chapter 12 takes you through a detailed listing of what you should expect to pay, including tuition, books, residence, incidentals, and more. We've also included a chart comparing the costs of various different universities. Chapter 13 is something you and your parents should read well before application time. There are tips and strategies to help you plan years in advance for the financial side of university. Chapters 14 and 15 deal with the money you can get from outside sources — loans, bursaries, grants, and scholarships. Chapter 16 looks at co-op work terms and the military as options to earn your tuition as you study. Chapter 17 takes you through the costs and requirements of going to an international university. And Chapter 18 offers tips that you can use during your university years to help you reduce or eliminate the debt from student loans, which often weighs down graduates long after they've left those hallowed halls behind.

Chapter 12

Shake Off the Sticker Shock (Remember, It Costs More in the U.S.!)

. . . .

In This Chapter

▶ Discovering the range of tuition fees

▶ Factoring in other university costs

▶ Adding in what you need to live

▶ Figuring out how much you'll really pay

▶ Becoming acquainted with financial aid

. . . .

*I*t's time — yes, it's finally time — to talk about the dreaded topic we all try to avoid: money. Now, don't rush off. We know you don't have an appointment or have to go wash your hair or some other excuse. Learning about the costs of a university education isn't as bad as you think.

The costs themselves are probably less than you think, as well. You may have read about students graduating with a debt load of hundreds of thousands of dollars. Those are *American* students. In Canada, tuition is far less. In fact, the only way you can wind up hundreds of thousands of dollars in debt is if you buy a new Porsche every year to get to your classes. So, calm down.

In this chapter, we take you through the different ways universities compute their tuition rates and then add in all the other costs of getting a university education. There are extra fees the universities charge — some are optional and some are not. There are basic costs of living — whether you live in residence, with your family, or off-campus. And there are adjustments to be made for the cost of living — things cost different amounts in different places.

You may be able to cut your costs by getting financial aid through scholarships, loans, or other means. We introduce those here and explain them in greater detail in Chapters 14 and 15. You can reduce your debt in other ways, too, through working or tax planning. We discuss those methods in Chapters 16 and 18. Right now, we're going to help you figure out the full amount that you will have to pay to get an education at a Canadian university, college, or technical institute. Let's get to it!

How Much Do You Need?

Can't you just contact the school and ask how much it charges? Sorry to break it to you, but there's a lot more to consider:

- ✔ **Tuition:** Tuition is not always a fixed amount, even for a first-year, full-time student. It may vary depending on where you are from (that is, in-province, out-of-province, or out-of-country), what programs you wish to follow, and what courses you want to take. There are a variety of other fees beyond tuition that are related to your being at the school. These include administration fees, college fees (some universities have a *college system,* where you belong to a particular college within the university), insurance fees, fees for use of the school's facilities, books, lab fees, and more.

- ✔ **Housing:** Well, you have to live somewhere, don't you? Perhaps you'll live in residence, perhaps you'll live at home with your family, and perhaps you'll live in an apartment off-campus. Wherever you live, you have to pay for it somehow.

- ✔ **Food and clothing:** You also have to pay for food, clothing, toothpaste, laundry, and the other necessities of life. Of course, *living* is made up of more than these necessities, so you will also pay for buying living accessories, going to movies, treating yourself to a nice meal in a restaurant once in a while, and the costs of your hobbies — assuming you have time for hobbies.

- ✔ **Travelling home:** You may want to travel home to visit your family once in a while, as well. If you live at home, well, you're already there — so there is no cost beyond public transportation or the expenses of your car. If you have a car, that is another expense — and don't forget about the cost of parking, especially on campus! If you go away to university, travel will be a little more costly. You may have to fly across the country — and back — probably both at winter break and for the summer. And you'll still need to foot the bill for public transportation or driving around the city where you go to school. It all adds up.

- ✔ **Dependents:** If you have a family and have to take care of dependents, you will also have to take care of their expenses. You are usually more entitled to receive financial aid in these circumstances.

Tuition: Different Universities Charge Different Amounts

So you know you want to go to university and you want to know how much tuition will cost. You request application packages from all sorts of schools. You think they will tell you exactly how much you will need to pay for a year of education. Think again. It's not that easy.

You probably figured the tuition amounts would be different if you are a part-time student — after all, you won't be taking as many courses, so you shouldn't have to pay as much as a full-time student. That's absolutely true: All the universities post different rates for part-time students. For the sake of convenience (and because we don't want to saddle you with a bunch of extra reading — you've already got *that* in school), we calculate the tuition amounts for a full-time student only. Get in touch with an admissions officer at the schools you are interested in attending to find out about tuition rates for part-time students. Pay special attention to incidental fees, if you are a part-time student. You may not have to pay all of them.

Some universities have a set price for a full-time, first-year course of studies in a particular faculty. While the different faculties — arts, engineering, music, or journalism, for example — may charge different amounts, everyone who attends first year in, say, arts or sciences pays a set tuition fee.

Not all universities base their tuition on an annual, or even semestered, approach. At some universities, you have to figure out your own tuition based on a particular set of guidelines.

These universities have a set rate per credit, so you have to add up the amount of credits you will be taking for the year and multiply it by the *per credit* fee. Notice we do not say that they charge a rate "per course." Some courses run for half a term, some for a full term. Some courses are worth a full credit, others are worth only half a credit. Some may even be worth two credits. It depends.

At Nippissing University, for example, what would be called a half-credit course at some universities (lasting only half a year) is actually a three-credit course, and a full-year course load is generally considered to be 30 credits (three credits times five courses times two terms). This makes sense: Most first-year, full-time programs have the equivalent of five full credits, however you slice and dice the numbers. Check your program and your courses to figure out what each credit is worth.

Most programs have a few *required* courses for the first year and only one or two *optional* courses, so this makes it a bit easier to determine a full course load.

Nippissing University charges a set amount for a three-credit course and double that for a six-credit (that is, full year) course. There are no discounts for taking more courses. At the University of Northern British Columbia, on the other hand, tuition is charged *per credit hour* depending on how many hours of instruction the course requires.

It may sound complicated, but the vast majority of universities simplify the process by publishing a sample *fees list* that a full-time, first-year student in a particular faculty will pay, even if this is calculated by adding together a bunch of individual credits. Unfortunately, only some universities make this information easy to find. Often, you have to hunt around the Web site or within the materials you have been sent to find the basic tuition rates. The best place to start your search on the university's Web site is under "Admissions" or "Financial Aid."

We've collected these tuition amounts and printed them, along with a bunch of other information you should know, in Appendix A, "Directory of Universities and Colleges."

What if you are from another province?

It may be surprising to discover, but all Canadians are not charged the same tuition at all Canadian universities. Most universities are *province-blind,* meaning it doesn't matter which province you come from; out-of-province students pay the same tuition as in-province students. The universities in Québec, however, are not province-blind. They charge out-of-province students more.

Québécois students pay $1,670 or thereabouts in tuition fees at most universities in Québec, while students from all other provinces pay around $3,708. At Bishop's University, Québécois students pay $2,390, while out-of-province Canadian students pay $4,430. At the Université de Montréal, Québécois students pay $61.31 per credit, while Canadians from outside Québec pay the same fee — plus $73 more per credit. This discrepancy may disturb Canadians from other provinces. However, the final price paid at Québec universities by students from Manitoba, New Brunswick, and the other provinces is fairly comparable to tuition at universities in the rest of the country.

What if you are from another country?

International students pay far more in tuition fees than Canadian students. Usually, the rate is a bit more than double — sometimes even triple — the price of tuition for a Canadian student, and obviously a lot more than that at Québec universities. On average, Canadian universities charge about $8,500 to $12,000 for full-year tuition for a non-Canadian student, although rates can be a few thousand dollars higher or lower depending on the institution.

Why is it so much more expensive? The Canadian federal and provincial governments subsidize university education — a lot. For Canadian students, about three-quarters of the cost of a university education is government-subsidized. The rest comes from tuition and university endowments. Since "foreign" (international) students (and their parents) are not contributing toward these costs by paying Canadian income taxes, it seems only fair that they pay their way in the form of higher tuition fees.

Even paying these higher fees, international students still get a break at Canadian universities, since some government money is used to subsidize their education. These students are faced with much, much higher tuition fees at American universities.

The amount you pay is determined by your residence status, not where you were born. If you are "resident" in Canada according to the *Immigration Act*, then you get all the advantages of the province in which you live — and that includes paying the regular tuition rate rather than the non-discounted rate for international students.

What if you have First Nations status?

There is no difference in the basic tuition rate for First Nations students versus all other Canadians; however, those with First Nations status can get some significant benefits to reduce the final amount they have to pay.

The *Post-Secondary Student Support Program (PSSSP),* established in 1989, provides financial support for tuition, travel, and living expenses for people with First Nations status. The PSSSP has an annual budget of $293 million. It may cover the bulk of your university costs, including tuition and university fees (this includes books and other supplies), as well as travel and living expenses for you and any dependents.

To qualify for this program you must be a *Status Indian* under the *Indian Act*. To find out more, you can contact the Ministry of Indian and Northern Affairs Canada online at www.ainc-inac.gc.ca.

Beyond the PSSSP, there are a wide variety of scholarships and grants open to First Nations students only. Many are offered by the universities themselves, although others may be offered by provincial governments, organizations, banks, corporations, and private individuals. You can find listings of these at www.ainc-inac.gc.ca in a downloadable document called "Scholarships, Bursaries and Awards for Aboriginal Students."

To figure out your tuition fee, you need to know:

- What faculty you will be in;

- Whether you are a part-time or a full-time student;

- Whether the university's tuition is based on a set annual fee, a semestered or term fee, a fee per credit, or a fee per credit hour;

- How many credits your courses are worth, and what your total amount of credits will

be at the end of the year (assuming your university works on a credit system);

- That you will pay a surcharge if you are attending a university in Québec and you are resident in another province;

- Your immigration status, if you are from another country. If you have Canadian residence status, you pay the same tuition fees as Canadian citizens.

At certain universities in Canada — including the University of Saskatchewan, the University of Alberta, and others — there are a certain number of spaces set aside for First Nations students. You follow the same application procedure as everyone else, except that you establish your First Nations status and compete for those spaces with other First Nations applicants exclusively.

Other University Fees

Did you think that was it? No, no, no! Tuition is just the beginning. Added on to tuition fees are other fees a university charges its students. Most are mandatory, but they are kept separate from tuition fees for some administrative purpose, we're sure.

The fees are for the upkeep and betterment of campus. The purpose is to make the university experience better for every student. Most make a lot of sense, such as fees for medical and health services on campus so students don't have to go trekking around an unfamiliar city trying to find a doctor in their time of need. Other fees may seem somewhat less urgent. Athletic fees may be money down the drain for someone who never sees the inside of the gym, but all students have to pay into a general athletic fund (although part-timers generally pay a bit less).

The feeling is that a university is a community. Whether you use any of its "optional" services, universities maintain that they are there for you — and you have to pay for them.

Generally, the universities tell you in advance how much these "incidental" fees will be, but they rarely spell it out clearly. Most universities include the fees in the final total they tell you to pay at admissions time, while for some you'll have to cut a separate cheque to a different department.

Student association fees

Student associations are made up of student governments and the clubs and organizations that fill out a student's life — when he's not studying. Don't be too critical of having to pay this fee, as one of these student organizations compiles and publishes the course evaluations that rate the various classes and professors to help you choose the best courses for you. Other university clubs may help you meet other students in your field for valuable career networking or even put on dances to meet that special someone.

Medical and health fees

Some universities operate campus-based clinics where students can get treated for everything from broken bones to depression. Others offer supplemental health insurance. The actual facilities vary from university to university, so check out what is available at your favourite universities. As we discuss in Chapter 17, many universities outside of Canada require proof of supplemental health insurance before they will confirm enrollment.

Athletic facilities fees

A healthy mind is best kept inside a healthy body. All universities have centres for sports and fitness, and most are quite extensive. You are likely to be able to find facilities for synchronized swimming, fencing, and curling, along with the more mainstream sports such as jogging, aerobics, and weight lifting.

This fee generally also covers the costs of the sports teams that you can try out to join. Some are highly competitive, while some are for more casual intramural pickup games. It's not just the obvious sports, such as football and hockey, that are represented. This category covers squash ladders, diving competitions, and sometimes even rodeo.

And, yes, you have to pay for this. Even if you are a couch potato and intend never to set foot inside that building where people actually sweat, you are still required to foot the bill. Maybe, just maybe, you should try to foot the *ball.* After all, you paid for it.

Program or college fees

Some universities collect all the incidental fees that we have mentioned above and make one total fee for all of them. You pay it as a contribution to your program. At the University of Toronto, for example, the arts and science faculty is so large it is divided into a variety of smaller "colleges," and each one determines its own fee. The fee pays for everything from all we include above — campus radio, membership at the athletic facilities on campus, membership in the students' association — to several social and cultural events of the college itself, including *frosh week*, where newcomers are "initiated" into the university life.

Lab fees

You need more than a lab coat — you also have to pay for the use of the lab. While these fees are often more expensive for engineering or science majors, students of all types may be charged for use of computing labs or other facilities. There may also be a libraries fee that everyone must pay, since everyone is *supposed* to be using the libraries.

Miscellaneous fees

Then there are fees charged for the campus newspapers and radio stations and all the other organizations that have been granted funding by the university. Some universities will incorporate these fees into tuition, but most assess an extra lump sum to account for them.

Books

Some students get by on second-hand books for at least some of their classes, but most professors include the latest editions of textbooks as required reading. Figure on about $900 per year for books but be prepared to increase that amount depending on your field of study — and your ability to find bargains.

Tools of the trade

Most students could not imagine going to university without a computer. You can get access to computers at most universities, but a personal computer really has become a necessity for organizing your work and writing essays and reports. In fact, Acadia University provides the use of a personal laptop computer for every student — and includes the extra cost in tuition fees.

Of course, with the cost of a computer comes the cost of its upkeep, including software, upgrading, and accessories such as printer cartridges. You'll also need notepads, pens and pencils, and other materials specific to your courses. You may need protective clothing, such as a hard hat and goggles for engineering, or a lab coat for chemistry.

When tabulating costs, we won't include the price of a computer. Many students already have one by the time they get to university and, besides, it is a one-time cost as you probably won't need a new computer every year. You will need to maintain it and upgrade it, but a new computer every year is overkill. That is, unless you are studying computer engineering or design, in which case add a few thousand dollars to your total for extra tools of your trade.

The Cost of Living

Somehow, otherwise highly intelligent university students sometimes have a tendency to forget the fact that, while they are attending university, they are also doing other things — such as living. They count up the costs of tuition and other university fees. They add in an allowance for books and supplies. Okay, maybe they add the cost of residence and a meal plan.

But there's more to life than that. A lot more. And during your years at university, you should be finding out what all there is to life. University life is a whole new experience, so your mind is already opening to new academic possibilities. Open it further and take in the social, political, cultural, and other influences that are so richly represented on a university campus.

Our advice is to drink in the opportunities of university life — but lay off the booze. It's well known that alcohol plays a part in many university activities. We're not going to lecture you — we're sure you get enough lectures at school and home. This part of the book is about money, so our point is that all these activities will cost you something. They will cost you for the materials, club memberships, and other incidentals. However, they will also cost you time. We've seen far too many students bomb out because they spent too much time partying and not enough time studying. It's up to you whether you will squander your time in mindless activities or invest your time in making yourself the person you truly want to be.

Besides, if you pay for an education, you should make sure you get it. It's up to you to make the most of your time and get the best return on the money invested in your education. The following are the living expenses that you should plan for when figuring out how much you need for your university education.

Housing

There are three basic options for housing when going to university:

- ✔ Living in residence;
- ✔ Living at home with your family; and
- ✔ Living off-campus.

Living in residence

Residence life is an excellent way to start your university career. You get thrown — hook, line, and sinker — into the middle of campus life and you can either sink or swim.

The cost of residence is variable depending on the city and the options you choose. Residence in Montréal, Toronto, and Vancouver is more expensive than residence in Brandon, Saskatoon, and Prince George. It's not that the residence rooms are that much better in the big cities — it's just that the cost of living is higher there.

Most residence estimates you will see in admissions packages or on university Web sites include a meal plan. This is because pretty much everyone who lives on campus buys a meal plan. However, as we discuss below, you (sometimes) do not have to buy a full meal plan just because you live in residence. Check out your options before you buy.

There are generally several different residences you can choose from and there is usually a different price associated with each. You may choose a single-gender residence or a coed one, a modern building or a place that looks like a castle, a place with only double rooms and a washroom down the hall or a residence made up of apartments with kitchens and bathrooms.

Don't blindly opt for the lowest-priced option — it may be cheap because its heating system hasn't been updated since there was a world war — and we mean the first one!

Living at home

About 60 to 70 percent of students at Canadian universities come from within a 100-km radius of the university campus. University types call this the *feeder area*. It makes sense to a lot of students — and their families — to live at home while attending university. It's less disruptive at a time when you should be concentrating on your studies. It's convenient because you don't have to move and you can enjoy all the comforts of family life — including Mom's cooking and laundry service. And it's less expensive. For many families, this last point is the deciding factor.

Not having to pay for residence can cut up to $6,000 off the cost of a university education. You may have to pay a bit more in public transportation charges and you may wish to buy a limited meal plan. Besides, the family will still have to foot the bill for Junior's food at home, but it will not be nearly as much as the cost of residence and a full meal plan. Plus, Mom and Dad probably haven't installed a cash register at the fridge. This will come *after* you graduate and they start hinting around for you to leave already!

Living off-campus

Many students prefer to live in residence or at home for their first year or two of university and find their own accommodations in second, third, or fourth year. By that time, they often have a friend or group of friends with whom they wish to share an apartment. It's fun, it's exciting — and it costs money.

Without the support net you are used to, you will have to become responsible for all the costs of a home; these include utilities, furniture, telephone — don't forget long-distance charges — maintenance, and a lot more.

However, off-campus housing often proves less expensive — especially when you share accommodations — than living in residence. Of course, the cost of an apartment varies drastically depending on the city where you live and the level of luxury — or liveability — you require. Most universities have housing offices where you can get help finding a place to live near the university. Often, students congregate in areas known as *student ghettos,* where housing is relatively inexpensive.

Many universities have cost estimators built into their Web sites. They provide an estimate of your expenses based on the information you provide. You can fill in the numbers or go with the estimate they provide as a default.

Food

A lot of people make jokes about the eating habits of students as a solid diet covering the four food groups: Kraft Dinner, ramen, pop, and doughnuts. In fact, there's the well-known "first-year spread" — the ten pounds or so that students tend to gain during their first year at university. However, over the years, both universities and students themselves have started to become increasingly aware of nutritional matters. That doesn't necessarily mean you won't be wolfing down a significant number of doughnuts while attending university. It just means you'll be more aware of what you are eating.

Just like for housing, there are three main ways to get your daily human intake of calories:

- ✔ The meal plan;
- ✔ The Mom plan; and
- ✔ The make-it-yourself plan.

The meal plan

Contrary to popular belief, you do not have to live in residence to get a meal plan. University officials know that students will spend a healthy portion of their day on campus even if they live off-campus. They want to encourage this behaviour, because the more time spent on campus the more time the student can go to class, study in the libraries, meet with other classmates to discuss courses, and generally learn.

To make sure these students don't faint from hunger while they are busy learning, a variety of different meal plans have been created at the universities across Canada. People in residence often get a full meal plan, but many come in different sizes — there is no reason for you to pay for lunches if you intend never to eat them. Many meal plans have been created on the credit basis — no, you don't get course credit for eating breakfast, these credits represent a specific amount of value and every time you eat at a campus facility your meal card gets swiped to take off a certain number of credits.

Sometimes the credits are based on a meal — if you eat breakfast, it is the same fee regardless of whether you have just a banana or a stack of pancakes with sausages and toast and eggs and all the fruit you can carry. Other meal plans assess a certain value to each different food, so you can graze your way through the day without being charged for a full meal every time you want a snack.

More and more residences are being built with kitchen facilities, allowing you to do your own cooking. Of course, this means you have to buy your own food and take the time to prepare it, but this is often preferable for some students — especially those with specific food requirements.

Check out what is available on your particular university campus and talk to the residence admissions officers to find out all your different options. Feel free to contact them before you have been granted admission to the university. Most of their work comes after the admissions acceptances are sent out, so they will have more time to talk with you from, say, October — after students have moved in and stopped moving around — through December — before students who have been accepted frantically try to elbow their way into the best spaces in residence.

The Mom plan

Or the Dad plan. Or the Family plan. The point of this plan is that, just as you do in high school, you eat with the family and have access to all the great food that is in the kitchen. Of course, you'll still have to spend a considerable amount of time on campus, so you will have to bring or buy food at least part of the time. Most students carry backpacks, so it's probably not a hassle to lug around an apple and a sandwich in case you get peckish. However, sometimes you're going to want a hot meal.

You might want to consider getting a credit-based meal plan to allow you to benefit from the subsidized cafeterias and dining halls — generally much less expensive than off-campus food — and spend more time with your friends in residence. Of course, we mean that you will be able to discuss that political science assignment over lunch — yeah, that's what we mean.

The make-it-yourself plan

If you live off-campus without your family — whether in an apartment, a fraternity house, or even a separate area of your family home — you will have to be responsible for your own food. This means you'll have to buy the food — including all the condiments and spices and other things that your mom always just seemed to have around.

You'll also have to get tools for cooking — pots and pans and dishes and cutlery and soap and all sorts of other things. You may not need a mushroom brush and the little doo-dads that Martha Stewart considers indispensable, but there are more than a couple things you'll have to pick up. The nice thing is, they can be used for years to come. This is not just a university expense — this is an investment in your life.

It's obviously more expensive to buy and cook your own food than it is to have your family supply it for you. However, many students find it less expensive to prepare their own food than to get a full meal plan in residence — but that is often because the quality of food students cook for themselves is somewhat lacking. On the other hand, students in residence tend to overeat simply because there's a huge buffet in front of them every day.

More Costs of Living

Consider your clothing budget — perhaps you are moving to a colder climate and need warmer gear. You'll need toiletries and cleaning supplies, bedding, newspapers, prescription and over-the-counter drugs, glasses or contact lenses, laundry, and all sorts of other basics of life that you have just gotten used to having around the house.

If you stay with your family, perhaps all of that will still be provided for you. If not, you have to think of it — and buy it — yourself.

Transportation

There are two general categories for transportation:

- ✔ Travel to and from your hometown
- ✔ Travel around town

Travelling to and from your hometown

This one comes into play only if you have gone away for university. If so, you will probably need two round-trip tickets a year — for the summer and for the holidays. You may choose to travel home more frequently depending on how much time you have, how much money you have, and your personal family situation. Whether or not you go home more frequently also depends on how far away you have moved.

When considering airfare, you should know that the price always goes up at the holiday season — because that's when everyone wants to fly! Try to book ahead to take advantage of seat sales whenever possible. Find out when your exam schedule is as soon as possible in the year — often if you fly before December 15th or 18th you can take advantage of a lower rate.

Travelling around town

You may spend most of your time on campus, but once in a while you have to get out. Many students get a bicycle, which is a big help until serious winter weather comes along. Public transportation systems exist in all cities with universities in Canada — the bigger the city, the more extensive the public transportation system. Usually, you can get a student transportation card at a discounted rate.

If you drive, you've got to cover the cost of car payments, insurance, maintenance, gas and other fluids, parking, and incidentals. Many universities sell a parking pass for students, allowing them to park in any of the designated spots on campus. Check for details, as some of them may be crucial. For example, the University of Alberta, in Edmonton, offers two types of parking passes: with electrical plug-in for $360 for the academic year, or without plug-in for $336. People from southern climates might not realize the value of a plug-in until it's too late — it allows you to plug your car battery heater into an electrical outlet so the goo in the car battery doesn't freeze and leave you stranded with a non-starting car.

Embellishments

Then there's the personal stuff. Maybe you love going to movies. Maybe you want to take up scuba diving. Maybe you want to eat out at fine restaurants every night. We have no idea what you like and how much of it you can afford. If you're independently wealthy and want to jet off to Tuscany for a week of soaking up all the Italian culture — you know, for your fine arts degree — go right ahead.

Most students live pretty inexpensively, so we're not going to estimate a huge amount for your embellishments. When calculating your need for a student loan or other financial aid, these embellishments are really not considered at all. There's an amount estimated for your living expenses. Beyond that, you're on your own.

Putting It All Together

There's no way we can be completely accurate about all your expenses, because we don't know what you consider the necessities of life. So we took the liberty of assuming a few things about you when we put together the information in Table 12-1. We assume you are a full-time, first-year student in arts or sciences, living on campus in a double residence room with a full meal plan. We used the estimates given by the universities themselves whenever possible. Our sample schools are a cross-section of institutions from coast to coast, to give you an idea of what you'll pay in the West and in the East, as well as somewhere in between.

We also assume you have the same personal expenses in each city, but that they vary in price due to the cost of living. We factor in a few extras in the bigger cities, because we know you are more likely to spend more when you live there.

Caryn recalls that when she attended the University of Victoria, there simply weren't as many things to spend money on as there were when she attended the University of Toronto. Free time was spent on the (free) beach in B.C.; at the ballet in Toronto. Since the beach was considerably less costly that the ballet, less money was spent on "entertainment" in Victoria.

We haven't included amounts for travel to and from your hometown, so if you are going away to university you'll have to add these amounts.

Also incorporate your own personal cost of living increase (or decrease) depending on whether you simply must have the latest fashions and several mochaccino lattes a day, or whether you are happy to live on Kraft Dinner and wear thrift-store outfits.

Table 12-1

The Real Cost of University

Item	Victoria	Lethbridge	Manitoba	Toronto	McGill	Mt. Allison	Sheridan College
Tuition	$2,265	$3,964	$2,847	$4,029	$1,668	$4,390	$9,000
Additional fees	$200	$220	$185	$750	$0*	$185	$2,868*
Room and board	$4,600	$3,731	$3,500	$6,000	$6,000	$5,850	$7,100**
Books and supplies	$845	$1,000	$1,371	$700	$2,250	$750	$0
Personal expenses	$2,500	$2,000	$2,000	$3,500	$3,500	$2,500	$3,500
Total, in-province	$10,410	$10,915	$9,903	$14,979	$13,418	$13,675	$22,468
Out-of-province increase	$0	$0	$0	$0	$1,770	$0	$0
Total, out-of-province	$10,410	$10,915	$9,903	$14,979	$15,188	$13,675	$22,468

*Additional fees and costs for books and supplies are estimated together.

**No meal plans are offered at Sheridan, so room and board is $4,600 for residence and an estimated $2,500 for food. By the way, we are using the average costs for a bunch of the multimedia programs at Sheridan as an example. Tuition for programs at the college can be as low as $1,720 or as high as $17,000.

As you can see, the cost of tuition is only a fraction of your costs for the school year. For the purposes of financial planning and calculating financial aid, we are doing some averaging and approximating to say that a typical university student will require about $12,000 for a full-time, first-year education in arts or sciences at a Canadian university.

The costs we have included are for the academic year only — September to April. You're on your own for May, June, July, and August. Hopefully, you can find a job to both earn your living and help you save up for some of your expenses over the next school year. Hopefully, that job is fulfilling and will help you look ahead to your future career. We talk more about earning enough money to stay out of debt in Chapter 18.

Financial Aid: The Basics

We discuss financial aid in greater detail in Chapters 14 and 15, but now that you are looking at the numbers involved with getting an education we wanted to let you know that you will probably not have to pay the whole shot. Everyone can benefit from government savings incentives (discussed in Chapter 13) and, besides, you are probably going to get some sort of financial aid.

What? You? Financial aid? You'd never take a government handout. Besides, you may be wondering if you even qualify for financial aid, since your total family income is above the poverty line. We admire your honesty, but we want to clarify what we mean by *financial aid*. In many cases, financial aid is a handout to less well off Canadians to help them get an education they could not otherwise afford. A long time ago, say 40 years or so, that's all financial aid was. Nowadays, though, financial aid is a lot more.

Definition =

The term *financial aid* has evolved to include anything that makes up the difference between what a student pays and the total cost of a university education. Financial aid can be a government grant, a subsidized loan, a collection of private scholarships, or a tuition discount offered by a university. All of these items, taken together, are considered financial aid.

Are those horror stories and myths for real?

You may have heard horror stories about the trauma of applying for financial aid, about filling out the reams of forms that ask for all kinds of personal information. You probably have also heard some myths about applying for financial aid. Some of the most popular myths are:

- Obtaining financial aid is too traumatic, so why waste time?
- Obtaining financial aid is too difficult, so why waste time?

✔ My parents make too much money, so I won't get any aid.

✔ Getting financial aid is just another way to borrow money, and I don't want to go into debt.

✔ I've been out of school too long for them to consider me eligible.

None of these is necessarily true. Allow us to clear up the rumours and shoot down the myths, one by one.

The "trauma" myth

Yes, you need to fill out forms when you apply for financial aid. And, yes, those forms ask a lot of personal questions about your income, your bank accounts, and your parents' assets. But the universities and government agencies administering financial aid are asking for the same information — and less of it, by the way — than the Canada Customs and Revenue Agency expects you and your parents to provide on your annual tax returns. The CCRA wants the information to take away your money. The financial aid people want it to give you money.

Plus, there's a bright side, if you look at it this way: When you dig out your financial records and apply for financial aid in January, you'll have much of the work done for your (and your parents') tax return in April.

The "too hard" myth

Applying for financial aid takes time, true. But it doesn't take much time. All they're asking for are a few numbers on a few pages. There are no essays, no personal choices to make, and no tough math questions to sweat through. There's none of that heavy-thinking stuff that will confront you every day in university. All you have to do is dig the numbers out and write them down.

You won't get any money unless you ask for it. Asking means filling out forms.

The "too rich" myth

This may be the most prevalent myth of all. Too many students believe they aren't eligible for financial aid because they — or their parents, really — make too much money. And these are parents with incomes in the $60,000 to $70,000 range. Boy, do they need this book!

You may be surprised to know that right now, as you read this book, students from families with *six-figure* incomes are receiving financial aid at many of the universities in the country. This aid is based on financial need. And they're getting the money legitimately, without cheating. And you can, too!

The "just another loan" myth

First of all, some financial aid is given away in scholarships, bursaries, and grants. These are not loans — you don't have to pay this money back. They are given for academic excellence, for leadership, or for an interesting combination of factors. The thing is, every year some of these aid packages are not given away, because no one bothers to apply for them. We'll be talking about these forms of financial aid in Chapter 15.

However, the other form of financial aid is indeed a loan. But a student loan is by no means "just another loan." It's quite different. It's interest-free. That means you get the use of the money for the entire time you are in university and you don't have to pay interest on it until you leave school. The government subsidizes your education by taking care of the interest.

If you're older

When it comes to money, adults are no different than students going to university directly from high school. The cost of attending is the same, and the available financial aid is the same. The rules and eligibility for aid programs apply to all students of any age.

When you, a mature university student, read about financial aid in this book, everything you read applies to you, too.

One thing is important to remember. In Chapter 14, we explain how to determine whether you are considered a dependent or independent for financial aid purposes. If you are married or living in a common-law relationship, or if you *have* a dependent, you are automatically considered independent. This generally makes it easier to get financial aid.

Tax credits to the rescue

The government wants to encourage Canadians to get an education, so it gives them incentives to save their money for education, and to spend less, as a bonus for going to school. We tell you about the savings incentives in the next chapter. The bonuses are in the form of *tax credits*.

Canadian tax law gives tax credits to those who are responsible for the bills of someone going to school. If you are paying your own bills and are considered independent for the purposes of financial aid, then you can claim the tax credits. If you are dependent and your parents are paying the bills, then they can claim the tax credits.

Now, don't get too excited. You can't include all the costs we outlined in this chapter as expenses. However, you can include tuition and all ancillary payments you make to the university. There's also a monthly tax credit for general expenses.

As we emphasize throughout this section, always consult a tax lawyer, accountant, or other qualified professional when making financial decisions.

There are two forms of tax credits for tuition-paying families:

- ✔ An *education tax credit* of $200 per month while you are going to school.
- ✔ A *tuition tax credit* for all mandatory amounts you pay to the university for educational purposes, including tuition, athletics fees, student services fees, and more. Optional fees for clubs and student organizations are not included.

As an extra bonus, you can carry forward all unused portions of these tax credits to be applied against future income. That means if you have no income while you are going to school you can save the tax credits for a year when you do have income and decrease the tax you pay in that year.

Don't forget to plan

Going to university is often a team effort involving your whole family. Up until this chapter, this book is mostly about you working to be able to gain admission to university or college and choosing the right schools for you. In the next chapter, we talk about how parents can plan ahead and save money to help you out financially during your years at university. You can also work together to plan the best way to have the most family wealth before, during, and after you head off to the hallowed halls of post-secondary education.

You are more likely to get a student loan or other assistance if you are independent, but this may not be the best way for your family to maximize its wealth. The interest-free loan may not set off the benefits of allowing your parents to claim the tax credits, for example.

There's a lot more to tax planning and financial planning than we can cover in this book, so make sure you consult with your accountant, lawyer, investment planner, or financial planner to figure out the best options for you and your family.

All of these professionals will probably tell you that the best advice for sound financial planning is to start well in advance. Parents should start thinking about their children's education as soon as the kids are born — if not sooner! And, despite the fact that we tell you many times in this book not to *worry* about paying for your university education, there's no reason you can't start *thinking* about it as soon as you figure out how something like interest works.

Since we figured you'd want to know about your long-term financial planning options, we wrote a whole chapter on it. Just turn the page and start saving!

Chapter 13

Long-term Planning (Parents, Read This!)

*W*hen you talk about money for university, two inescapable facts leap out.

✔ Fact #1: You and your parents must pay some of the bills.

✔ Fact #2: Your chances of getting financial aid to help pay the bills are good.

We discuss fact #1 in this chapter and fact #2 in Chapters 14 and 15. This chapter answers the question, "Where will you get the money to pay your share of the bill?"

Why is it so important for you and your parents to put away money for your post-secondary education? After all, if you can get financial aid, why bother to save money and do financial planning?

It's never guaranteed that you will receive money that you will not have to pay back. Scholarships, bursaries, and grants are awarded every year, certainly, but if you are depending on getting one in order to pay for university you may be in for a nasty surprise. Even if you have fantastic marks, there's always the possibility (often a good possibility) that someone else will have even better marks. Even if your high school average this year is high enough to trigger a scholarship from a particular university, the university may have raised its minimum average requirements by the time you eventually apply.

Is a university education really important?

Sure, going to university is costly, but the vast majority of graduates find they get their money back though higher wages and more disposable income. Recent studies at the University of Toronto show that university graduates realize an average *after-tax annual rate of return* of 10 to 15 percent on their education.

This means that, after taxes, university graduates have between 10 and 15 percent of what they paid in tuition left over as disposable income — over and above the amount of disposable income of those who did not go to university.

If you paid a total of $20,000 for your four years of university, you will likely see an extra $2,000 to $3,000 (roughly 10 or 15 percent of $20,000) remain as disposable income, after paying taxes.

Besides, not going to university can be even more expensive. Statistics Canada research shows that higher education significantly improves the chances of finding well-paid employment after graduation and lowers the likelihood of unemployment.

It might not be such a sure thing. As standards and tuition levels are rising, students are becoming more aware of available scholarships. That means the competition for them is getting tougher.

Even if you get a scholarship, bursary, or grant, you probably won't get enough money for all your expenses. Don't forget, you need more than tuition and residence fees to get by.

You have to pay back most of the financial aid that is available to you. Over half of the people who attend a Canadian university take out a loan to pay for their expenses. Most are interest-free while you stay in school, but eventually they must be repaid. And, as soon as you leave school, interest on the loan starts to accrue. Do you really want to start out your life as a university graduate mired in debt?

We didn't think so! Okay, so it's agreed. Let's do some financial planning!

One more thing before we continue in this chapter. Canadian tax laws change frequently and so do people's individual financial situations. Always consult your accountant, lawyer, or other trained and knowledgeable professional when constructing a personal financial savings plan for your or your child's university years.

Planning Is Key

If you're already in grade 12, this chapter is not for you. This chapter is for the folks — students and parents — who will face bill-paying time 2, 4, 10, or 20 years down the road. When the time comes, wouldn't it be great if you could simply write a cheque to cover each year at U Willpay as you enrol? With some careful planning, you may be able to swing it.

Planning, in this case, means that boring word, *saving*. Face the facts: The more money you put away in an investment, bank account, or other safe place, and the earlier you start stashing your money, the better your chance of being able to write those pay-as-you-go cheques. It seems obvious. And, to most people, it is. The problem is that too many people just don't do it.

A survey by *Money* magazine shows that half of all parents don't save for university at all, and only 25 percent are saving by the time their child is eight years old.

Since long-term planning is not something we expect from an eight-year-old child, the rest of this chapter is going to be directed toward your parents. Now, don't get uptight. After all, most of the book is devoted to you, and we go right back to concentrating on you from the next chapter onward.

Figuring Out How Much You Will Need

How can you possibly determine how much a university education will cost several years from now? In most provinces, tuition fees are going up even more than the cost of living. There are new forms of education these days, with distance learning and different universities, colleges, and institutes cropping up all over. Who's to know what sort of education to prepare for — and who's to know how much money it will cost when your child is ready?

We're afraid we don't have a perfect answer for you. The truth is, nobody really knows how much money you'll need in the future. Even the people who set tuition rates at universities every year have no idea what they'll be charging two years from now.

Universities are at the mercy of their respective provincial governments for funding contributions. The problem is that these contributions have been slashed in recent years and show no sign of increasing. Universities also have to rely on the generosity of alumni and other private donors to cover the costs of running the university. It's difficult for the universities to predict how much funding to count on from these sources. So what does that mean for you? The best you can do is to make some educated guesses, along with the rest of us.

How much is tuition increasing?

Tuition rates have gone up a lot in the last decade and show no signs of stopping. How much they go up is hard to predict, and many parents and students are working hard to pressure the government to put more money into education. Over the five years from the 1995/1996 academic year to the 2000/2001 academic year, full-time tuition in arts or sciences at Canadian universities generally increased by approximately 24 percent. Dividing that by five years, we get an annual increase of close to 5 percent. Table 13-1 illustrates tuition increases province by province.

Table 13-1	Change in Tuition Rates across Canada, 1995–2001	
Province	*Change in Tuition, 1995–2000*	*Change in Tuition, 2000–2001*
Newfoundland	43% increase	No increase
Prince Edward Island	23% increase	No increase
Nova Scotia	39% increase	9% increase
New Brunswick	41% increase	4% increase
Québec	No change, or slight decrease, depending on the institution	
Ontario	60% increase	Range of increases and decreases, depending on the institution
Manitoba	24% increase	6% decrease
Saskatchewan	18% increase	Range from no change to 14% decrease, depending on the institution
Alberta	41% increase	Negligible increase
British Columbia	No change	No change

Is it that simple? Not by a long shot. For example, in many provinces and many specific institutions, there was no increase at all in the last year, having experienced the entire increase in earlier years. In Québec and British Columbia, there were no overall increases over the entire five-year period. As well, the amounts of the increases vary drastically depending on both the province and the institution. During that five-year period, Université de Montréal tuition actually went *down* by 9 percent, while at Acadia University tuition rose an incredible 66 percent, and the average increase in Ontario was 60 percent.

You also have to look at other factors when considering these numbers. At Acadia, the university introduced a program so that all students get use of a personal laptop computer. The increase makes a bit more sense in light of that fact. However, there is no such program at the Ontario universities. Tuition just plain went up.

How much is the cost of living increasing?

The cost of living is not going up nearly as much as tuition. This means that the other costs of sending your child to university will not rise as much — although they will certainly rise somewhat. The present annual *consumer price index* (the Canadian government's gauge of the cost of living) is about 3 percent.

So, what does all that mean for you? Plan for at least a 5 percent annual increase and make adjustments as you can by watching the changes over time. Are 5 percent increases likely? Well, it's a good guess, but it requires some averaging and estimating with the numbers we mentioned above. If the consumer price index or tuition rates rise drastically, you'll need to save more. And if the pressure being exerted on the government by student activists (and others) works and tuition increases slow down, you'll have some money left over. Meanwhile, if the inflation rate starts going up wages tend to follow suit.

Estimating the cost of tuition, room and board, and other expenses to be in the neighbourhood of $12,000 today means that annual bumps of 5 percent will put it in the $29,000 neighbourhood in 18 years. Considering you will want to be ready to pay for four years of study, that brings the total to about $116,000. (Increases over the four-year period will be offset by interest you can make on your savings.)

By the way, that $29,000 a year is not necessarily the amount you will have to pay. After all, your child can earn a scholarship, get a bursary, or earn enough money herself to pay for or contribute to the total costs. (Now *that* would be nice, wouldn't it?) Or maybe another relative may choose to help foot the bill. But, in case none of that happens, it's best to be prepared to pay the full amount.

Settling on How Much You Should Save

There is no ideal savings plan for university. Just as each student must find her own right universities based on her own priorities, each family must determine its own savings plan based on its own financial situation. Here are some questions to consider:

- How much can you afford to put away each week, each month, each year?
- How much time do you have until the first tuition bill arrives?
- How receptive are you to the idea of borrowing money to pay for university?

Mull over these numbers

Mull over these savings scenarios. One of them may work for you and your family.

- **Set aside $10 every working day, starting the day your child is born.** Invest the money where it earns 8 percent, and by the time your child is 18 you'll have $110,000. You'll have what you need and a little breathing room, in case tuition fees skyrocket even more. If $10 each working day (or $200 a month) is too steep, make it $5. You'll still have a nice $55,000 nest egg at university time.

- **If your child is in grade 2, put away $460 a month.** By the time he walks across the stage for his high school diploma, you'll have $100,000 tucked away. Stash aside only $115 a month, and you'll have a total of $25,000.

- **If Junior is in grade 8, $680 a month will produce $50,000 by tuition time.** A mere $270 a month will add up to $20,000.

- **If university is two years away, you can still build up a $25,000 savings account by putting away $1,000 a month.** All these calculations assume that you're earning 8 percent on your savings. If you have an astute broker who can get you a better return, you won't have to save as much.

A work-free income source

Saving money on a regular monthly basis is the simplest, but probably the most painful, method of planning to meet university costs. Nobody likes to save. Human instinct is to spend a dollar as soon as it enters one's pocket. Humans need some discipline to suppress that instinct and put away some money.

Saving is a way to get paid for doing nothing. It's a work-free source of income. We talk about some fantastic savings incentives later in this chapter.

Your Financing Options

There are two main options: saving and borrowing.

Within both of these options, there are a variety of different ways to achieve each goal — and the way you save or borrow can make a big difference to how much money you have when university time rolls around.

You should save money if you possibly can. We know it's tough and there are bills to pay and mortgages to make, but university is important. If it's a choice between basic living expenses and saving for university, we're not going to tell you to stop paying the rent or feeding your family.

That would be ridiculous.

But, if it's a choice between getting Johnny those $200 sneakers or putting the money away in his university fund — well, enough said.

Can't I get more if I have less?

Don't we also say in this book that financial aid is almost always available to those in need who can't pay for a university education? Doesn't that mean it would make more sense to appear completely destitute at university time so that the government will foot the entire bill?

Not on your life! Just because financial aid is likely to be available doesn't mean that you won't have to pay it back eventually. The money available to students that does not have to be paid back is based on merit — scholarships awarded for getting top marks in high school or grants for some other special achievement. We talk about these in Chapter 15.

Most financial aid that is available to students who can't afford university is available as a *loan*. After the student stops attending university, the money must be repaid. And, while interest does not accrue while the student continues to go to school (unless you have a bank loan, which we talk about a bit later in this chapter), it will begin to accrue soon after he or she leaves the institution. And this money *must* be paid back. If you fall off your repayment schedule, the money owing will be taken out of any income tax refund you may be expecting. It's the government — it will get its money any way it chooses.

You can certainly choose to get a student loan — indeed, depending on your financial circumstances, you may not have a choice — but saving money earlier is a much better option. Not only does it give you some peace of mind, you can also benefit from the various savings incentives set up by the government.

So many ways to save, so little time, it seems

There are many ways to save. You can hide money in the garden or under your bed, but you won't make any interest that way. Some other options are:

- ✔ Setting up a savings account for your child.
- ✔ Creating a trust account in your child's name.
- ✔ Making more aggressive (and, therefore, riskier) investments for your child.

Savings accounts: Low-risk investing

Savings accounts don't need to be simple bank accounts, where your interest rate may fluctuate over time. You can buy your child a *guaranteed investment certificate (GIC),* a *Canada Savings Bond (CSB),* or another *term deposit.* You place the money in the account for a set period of time and get a fixed amount of return over that time. There is usually a penalty if you want to take it out early. Savings accounts are safe investments, but the return is relatively low. Because the income is derived from your money — even though you plan to use it for your child's education — it is taxable to you at your tax rate.

Trust accounts

A trust account can be set up at a bank or trust company, and the capital can be used to invest in GICs, CSBs, other term deposits, stocks, bonds, or anything else you may choose. It is a firm commitment, because once you establish the trust, the money belongs to the child — not you. As the administrator, you can withdraw the money only for the child's own use. You can't even transfer the money over to a Registered Education Savings Plan (RESP). The tax situation is somewhat different than basic savings accounts, however. The first level of interest is still taxable to you, but any interest on the interest accrues to the child — after all, it is his money. Any capital gains the investment earns are also attributed to the child.

The child is not required to use money in a trust for the purposes of education. Once he reaches the age of majority (18), he can do whatever he chooses with the money.

Stocks and mutual funds: Higher-risk investing

If you are willing to take some risk with your child's education savings, you can invest in stocks or mutual funds. The return may be greater if you do well, but the risk is also greater. As with savings accounts, the income is still attributed to you for tax purposes.

Whenever you invest in the stock market — including buying mutual funds — you run the risk of losing everything you invest. Stocks are never guaranteed, so get good financial advice before risking your child's education on them. As an added bonus, a good financial planner can help you arrange your taxes in a manner that results in the best possible financial situation for you, through income splitting, setting up trusts, or creating other legal ways of arranging your income and assets.

RESPs: Your Best Option

The best option is to take advantage of the federal government's *Registered Education Savings Plan.* It offers virtually tax-free investment along with a grant program (Canada Education Savings Grants) that gives you extra money just for saving money.

The government wants parents to save for their children's education, so it created Registered Education Savings Plans (RESPs). These plans let people (typically, the child's parents or grandparents) invest money virtually tax-free for use when their child is ready to use it for education. A Registered Education Savings Plan is exactly what it says:

- ✔ **"Registered":** While the money can be deposited at your bank, through your broker, or through other so-called *promoters* (companies that are allowed to offer RESPs), you fill out a form to register it with the federal government in the name of a specific recipient — it can be your child or anyone else, depending on the type of RESP you choose.

- ✔ **"Education":** The money must be used for post-secondary education at some point in the future. The money does not have to go toward university — it can be a college or a technical or vocational institute as well — but it does have to be a post-secondary educational institution considered eligible by the government.

- ✔ **"Savings Plan":** It's a way to help you save. You can invest money in a lump sum or set aside a little every year, month, or week — however you prefer. The money does not just sit there waiting to be used several years down the road. Just like with the better-known *Registered Retirement Savings Plans (RRSPs),* you can invest your money in a variety of different ways. You can put it into stocks, mutual funds, and bonds, or simply earn straight interest on it depending on how much risk you wish to take. Every promoter provides different options out of those that the government deems qualified, so shop around for what is best for you. You can choose to get a *self-directed RESP*, which allows you to choose the investment options, or a *group RESP,* which is administered for you.

There is a current limit of $4,000 per child per year that you can contribute, and there is also a contribution cap maximizing at a lifetime limit of $42,000. The interest or income from any money you put into a RESP is exempt from taxation until it is taken out. When it *is* eventually taken out, it is considered part of the taxable income of the recipient — the student, who usually is making very little income, if any. That means there is usually no tax paid on RESP investments.

There is no limit on the amount of *foreign content* that can be held in a RESP, unlike the maximum 30 percent rule for RRSPs! Foreign content refers to shareholdings of companies that are not based in Canada.

Each child named as the recipient on a RESP must have a valid social insurance number and be a Canadian resident at the time the contribution is made.

How are RESPs administered?

There are two options when setting up a RESP: a *self-directed RESP* or a *group RESP*.

Self-directed RESPs

Self-directed simply means that you can determine where the money goes in terms of investment — in stocks or bonds, GICs, CSBs, or even a cash account. Self-directed RESPs can be set up at most major banks, through your stockbroker, or through mutual fund companies or trust companies. Shop around, because different institutions administer RESPs differently. Generally, there will be an administration fee for setting up the RESP, and there may be a minimum contribution limit as well.

Group RESPs

A group RESP allows you no control over investment, except for the amount you choose to invest. Instead, your contributions go into a pool of capital that is invested by a trust company and you get shares in the trust. The investments are made in only extremely low-risk investments, such as government T-bills, bonds, and mortgages, that are government-guaranteed or insured. This means the investments have lower risk but also generally lower return. Group RESPs are administered by selected non-taxable entities in Canada

Canada Education Savings Grants (CESGs)

For the first $2,000 of an annual contribution you make to a RESP, the CESG program will contribute a matching sum amounting to 20 percent of your contribution. This means that your first $2,000 earns a matching $400, for a total of $2,400 in the account (per child per year). You can choose to carry forward any unused portion of your grant, so if you do not make a contribution — or enough for the maximum grant — in a given year, the grant money can be available next year.

For example, if you make no contribution in 2003 but make a contribution of $4,000 in 2004, you will not get the grant money in 2003, but in 2004 you will get the $400 grant money for both the first $2,000 and for the second $2,000, which will be considered a carried-forward contribution from the year before. That means you will get a total of $800 in CESG that year. There is a maximum of $800 that you can receive in any one year, so you can't invest the entire $42,000 when your child is 17 just to get the maximum CESG.

The child must be under 18 years old to qualify for the program. There is a lifetime maximum of $7,200 in grant money available per child, regardless of how many people set up RESPs in his or her name. The annual limits also apply to the child — as opposed to the contributor. If more than one person has a RESP in a child's name, the grant will go to the first one to make the contribution that year. If there is any grant room remaining, it will go to the RESP of the second contributor.

Of course, this money can earn interest through investment in the savings plan, just like the rest of the money in the RESP. This means that if you contribute the maximum amount possible every year starting when your child is born and get that same conservative 5 percent interest, your RESP would end up with an *extra* $11,816 — that's the original $7,200 grant plus $4,616 worth of interest!

The $7,200 is not included in the $42,000 lifetime maximum you can contribute to a particular RESP, so it is effectively simply a bonus for saving!

You can transfer the grant money along with your RESP to another eligible recipient if your child does not pursue a post-secondary education. However, if you don't transfer the RESP and your child does not go to university, college, or another designated institution of higher learning, the grant money returns to the government.

including Canadian Scholarship Trust, Children's Education Trust of Canada, Heritage Scholarship Trust Foundation, Universitas Foundation of Canada, and USC Education Savings Plans. You pay administration fees for the group RESP as well.

For the group RESP, when your child enters university your contributions (less administration fees) are returned to you to pay for the first year's tuition and other costs. When your child enters second year, she receives the amount the shares have earned in the form of a scholarship that must go toward her education.

Check the fine print and details for each different trust company. Some RESPs have high up front or administrative fees. Some require that the child enter school by age 21 and terminate the trust if the student decides to take some time off before going to university or even during studies. Other plans require constant investment and terminate the trust if investment stops, returning to you your contributions only with no interest — and deducting penalties and administration fees!

How much will the RESP earn?

Assume you start saving for your future university student as soon as he's born. Starting at birth, you make the maximum $4000 contribution possible every year until you reach the limit of $42,000 (when your child is 11 years of age). Even if the investment earns only a modest 5 percent annual interest, the fund will have grown to $81,005 by the time your child is 18!

Added to that, you will have saved all of the taxes on the income you earn. If your income tax rate is 25 percent, you will have saved an extra $9,751. Contributors with a 50 percent rate would save an extra $19,502. If you've got the money to save, this is the best way to do it — not bad for filling out a simple form.

What if I decide to discontinue the RESP?

Perhaps you suddenly find yourself in dire straits financially. Perhaps you simply decide you don't want to finance the child's education anymore. Whatever the reason, let's say at some point you decide you don't want to continue the RESP. What can you do?

You have two options:

- ✔ **Redesignate the recipient.** Change the name of the child to be someone else whom you wish to get the money. However, this child must take the money out within 25 years of the establishment of the RESP. If a RESP has not been paid out within 25 years of being set up, you can designate which educational institution you wish to have receive the money, but it will no longer be eligible for distribution to a child.

- ✔ **If the RESP has been in existence for at least ten years, simply break the RESP and take back the money.** Until it has been removed for education purposes, it remains yours and not the child's. However, if you do so, you will have to suffer the consequences of paying all the income tax on any income your contributions have earned, along with returning all CESG payments and the income earned on them.

As we mentioned at the beginning of this chapter, always consult your lawyer, accountant, or other knowledgeable professional before taking any financial step.

Can I extract my money from the RESP if my child doesn't go to university?

Or college? Or an institute? Is the money lost? Nope. You can get your contributions back at any time. As for your interest or other "growth income" earned in the fund, contributors who have contribution room in their Registered Retirement Savings Plans (RRSPs) can transfer up to $50,000 in RESP interest directly into a RRSP. There are some prerequisites, though: you must be resident in Canada, the plan must have been in existence for at least ten years, and the designated beneficiary must be 21 or older and not enrolled in a post-secondary institution. If you don't have the contribution room, you still won't lose all your money. You do have to pay back all CESG payments and the income earned on them, however, and start paying taxes on the amount of income you have socked away.

It used to be the case that, unless the child could use the money for post-secondary education, all growth income would remain in the plan and parents would get back only the amount they contributed. The rules have changed.

RESPs are transferable, so if one child does not end up going to university, the entire amount can be transferred over to the name of another eligible child with RESP room as long as the money is used for post-secondary education within 25 years of creating the RESP. There may be different rules that apply depending on the type of RESP you have set up and the particular agreement you have made with your promoter, so make sure you read the fine print when setting up your RESP.

Your child does not have to go to university in Canada to benefit from the RESP. Post-secondary institutions in the United States and other countries are eligible under the RESP rules as long as your child is enrolled in a post-secondary-level course that runs a minimum of 13 weeks.

Working it all out

Take a look at this five-step scenario to see how investing in a RESP can pay off:

1. Assume you make the maximum $4,000 RESP contribution every year from your child's birth. At the end of 11 years, you will have socked away the contribution cap of $42,000 ($4,000 for ten years and $2,000 in the final year).

2. Assume you get a conservative 5 percent return on your investment and this is compounded over the years. At the end of 18 years, your interest will amount to approximately $39,005.

3. Meanwhile, you have been receiving the maximum CESG amounts of $400 per year, for a total of $7,200.

4. You get compound interest on that money as well. Still assuming it to be a conservative 5 percent interest rate, that earns you another $4,616.

5. The total you will have accumulated by the time your child is 18 years old is $92,821. If you are going for that $116,000 we mentioned earlier in this chapter, this takes you almost all the way!

Along with the savings, grant, and interest, you will also get all those income tax savings because you will not have to pay tax on the income you make in the RESP!

Borrowing

When the time comes to go to university, if you have saved enough for your child's education you will not need to borrow a dime. If your child happens to earn scholarships, bursaries, or grants, well, there's extra money available for residence, books, or anything else.

However, if you have not saved enough for your child's education, there's always the option of borrowing. Your child can apply for a Canada Student Loan. If he or she does not qualify or still needs more money even after receiving the provided amount of the loan, you can try to borrow privately. We discuss this in Chapter 14.

Every dollar saved means at least a dollar earned — usually closer to two after it grows.

Juggling for Money

There are other sources of money that you and your child can plan ahead to access. Canada Student Loans are interest-free while your child is in school, so if she needs to borrow from anywhere, that's the place to do it. Of course, not everybody can get a student loan — it's reserved for those who really need it. So, if you (or your child) have millions of dollars in your bank account, she probably won't qualify.

And how, you might ask, does an 18-year-old get millions of dollars in her bank account? Well, unless she was one of those wunderkind dot-com millionaires, the money probably came from other people. Perhaps you, her parent, gave her some extra money to reduce your own taxes, or perhaps grandma gave her some money for her future education.

Now, if your daughter does have millions rightfully in her own name, then she won't need to borrow for university. But what if it's only a few *thousand* — and you know that your family might be in dire straits in a few years when you and your spouse retire? Your child should probably borrow for university so that the rest of the family won't have to suffer. In that case, you should juggle the money so that she is better able to qualify for financial aid.

If you're skeptical about this idea, you should know that nothing we are about to suggest is illegal, unethical, immoral, or frowned upon by picky financial aid directors (or the folks at the Canada Customs and Revenue Agency). Some of the pickiest directors who have written their own advice books suggest some of the same steps. Just as careful tax planners take advantage of the tax laws to pay the minimum required by law, careful university planners can take advantage of the financial aid rules to get the maximum allowed by law.

Put your money in the right place, in the right name

Let's say you contribute the full amount you can to your RESP, but you still have some money left over to save. Where are you putting it? Whether you choose to invest in mutual funds, stocks or bonds, or simple bank accounts is up to you. But you should pay special attention to whose name the account it in. If you think you're being nice to your eight-year-old son by putting the money in his name, think again. He will be less eligible for a student loan when the time comes, because the financial aid officers will see the large amount of money invested in his name.

On the other hand, you might be able to save a bundle in taxes by transferring money over to your child's name. Investment income in your name is usually taxed at a higher rate than investment income in your child's name, because your child will have less overall income and, therefore, be in a lower tax bracket.

 Financial aid administrators don't ask you to report the amount of equity you have in a family residence, so you may be eligible for more financial aid by contributing toward your mortgage instead of placing extra money in a savings account.

Overall, you need to do some strategic planning to balance your tax needs with your university-cost needs. If you believe your child will not need to qualify for a student loan in the future and you can save a lot of money by transferring money to your child, do it. If you and your entire family will be better off using the extra money on other things, do that. The bottom line is to get some professional advice to help you invest wisely to end up with the greatest wealth in the long run.

Say "no thanks" to gifts

If Grandma wants to give Stephanie Student a $1,000 savings bond for university, don't reject her generosity, but ask her to please wait awhile. Suggest that Grandma write Stephanie a nice note (grandmothers are good at nice notes) saying she has a $1,000 bond squirrelled away for her university education. When the time comes, Grandma will write Stephanie a cheque. Meanwhile, the bond stays in Grandma's name and nobody will ask about it. When calculating financial need for university, her money will not be counted.

Teach

It's not an option for everyone, but generally people who teach at universities — professors and instructors alike — get free tuition for their dependents. That means that if you're an accountant the university hires to teach first-year accounting once a week you may get more than your paycheque: your kids could get to attend the university for free.

Your kids don't get an entirely free ride, as they still have to pay for incidentals, living expenses, and books — but not having to worry about tuition is a big help. Oh yeah, they still have to gain admission the regular way — this benefit affects only how much they pay once they get to university.

Not all universities offer the same *perquisites* (benefits) to all faculty, so find out for sure when negotiating your position. Generally, the benefit applies to children of any age along with your spouse or spousal equivalent.

Get some good advice

"Get some good advice?" You might be thinking, "But that's why we bought this book! We expected you to give us good advice." Well, thanks, but there's only so much we can tell you in a book. Every family has a different financial situation, so everyone needs advice that's specific to them. Talk to someone at your bank about planning for the future. Talk to your broker about financial planning goals and strategies. Talk with everyone you can to get as much advice as possible.

Financial planning checklist

Here are the steps to take in financing your university education:

For parents:

- Plan ahead by saving through RESPs.

- Get the maximum Canada Education Savings Grant every year.

For students:

- Save money yourself by working after school and in the summers (unless you need to take that time for studying — don't sacrifice your opportunity to get into university just so that you can pay for it!).

- In the years before university, find out how much you are likely to pay for tuition, room and board, extra university fees, and general living expenses. Figure out how much you will need by the time you get to university using the formula we suggest in Chapter 12. Then deduct the money you anticipate you will have available by the time you get to university. The amount you have left is your *financial gap*.

- Do everything possible to get the highest marks you can get. All Canadian universities offer entrance scholarships to students with the highest marks — usually 85 percent or above, or the top 5 percent of the graduating class at your high school.

- When applying to university, search out and apply for all the scholarships, awards, and grants you can find, even if you believe your chances of getting them are slim.

- If you are in financial need, search out and apply for bursaries.

- After you have exhausted all other sources and find you still need money to attend university, apply for a loan. Apply through your provincial student loans association for both a provincially sponsored loan and a federal loan through the Canada Student Loan Program. These loans are interest-free while you remain in school.

- If you can't get government-sponsored student loans, or if you need still more money, search out and apply for other loans. Unlike the government-sponsored loans, bank loans carry a substantial interest rate — that will not be waived while you are in school. If you use a traditional bank loan to finance some of your university education, you will continue to accumulate debt while you are studying biochemistry, taking an exam in 19th century Russian literature, or just hanging out at the student pub.

As you plan for your child's university education, while at the same time planning for retirement and planning to save on taxes, your best-laid plans can contradict each other. It's a wise idea to seek advice from an expert financial planner, and *Personal Finance For Canadians For Dummies,* 3rd Edition, by Tony Martin and Eric Tyson (published by CDG Books Canada, Inc.), is a good place to start.

Chapter 14

Getting Financial Aid

. . . .

In This Chapter

▶ Making sense of the terminology

▶ Finding sources of money

▶ Applying for a bursary or grant

▶ Getting a student loan

▶ Remembering that you need to ask in order to receive

. . . .

So, we've established that you need money to go to university. We've even helped you approximate *how much* you will need, whether you are going to university next year or ten years from now. And, we've told you and your parents how to plan ahead to have enough money when you eventually get there.

But what if you don't have enough? Are you sunk? Do you have to give up on your dreams of getting a university education and go to work in a sweatshop? Not on your life! There are lots of options to help you pay for your university education. We'll talk about work-study, or co-op, programs in Chapter 16, and working during university in Chapter 18.

However, in this chapter and the next we'll talk about getting money through loans, bursaries, grants, and scholarships. All this comes under the general category of financial aid, although we have separated out scholarships to talk about in Chapter 15. Despite the fact that each option is somewhat different from the others, every option represents money you might be able to get just by filling out forms and asking.

The people who administer financial aid don't have to give you the money, but typically they will if you truly need it or if you truly deserve it. We'll tell you how to demonstrate your need to the holders of the purse strings.

And it's not exclusive. You can apply for all sorts of scholarships and grants and ask for bursaries and loans at the same time. Of course, you are required, for example, to tell loan administrators how much money you are getting in the form of scholarships, as it might cut down on the amount of loans to which you are entitled.

But we're getting ahead of ourselves. First we are going to discuss what financial aid is and who qualifies for it. Then we'll look at how to find financial aid — both the obvious options and in places you might never have imagined.

What Is Financial Aid?

Financial aid — or *financial assistance* — is money you get to help you go to university. It comes in many forms for many purposes. We could divide it into two categories: The Type You *Don't* Have to Pay Back and The Type You *Do* Have to Pay Back, but we prefer to make a different distinction.

- **Merit money:** There's money you get for being special — called scholarships or awards. In the United States, people call this *merit money* because you get it only when your results merit it. Getting this kind of money is entirely dependent on your marks and, sometimes, who you are. How much money you and your parents have or make doesn't matter. This is money you do not have to pay back and, if you keep your marks up, you often get more of it every year you go to university. We talk about this kind of financial aid in Chapter 15.

- **Need money:** In this chapter, we'll talk about *need money* — the money you get because you don't have enough to go to university. You don't have to be particularly smart or have really high marks to get need money. You just have to be a qualified student in financial need. This can be either the type that you don't have to pay back — bursaries and grants — or the type that you do have to pay back — student loans.

Now, you might think it's odd to talk about need money before we talk about merit money. After all, if you can get enough merit money, why bother with need money? It's true. The thing is, most people can't get enough merit money to cover all their costs. They have to supplement it with money from their own sources and, often, must look for need money. It's a fact that more than half of all Canadian university students have a student loan.

Besides, when most people think of financial aid, they think of need money. They don't think of merit money. So, we figured, why confuse anyone? If you're reading this chapter and you want to know more about merit money, you now know enough to go on to the next chapter. And let us emphasize how important it is to go on to the next chapter.

Every year, millions of dollars in scholarships, awards, and grants are available to be given away. Every year, lots of that money is *not* given away because no one bothers to apply for it. Your marks can't be too low to apply! Everyone can apply! And, if no one else bothers to apply, you can get the money.

Bursaries, Grants, and Loans — Oh My!

Need money comes in three different forms — bursaries, grants, and loans. Let us explain what they are, how to find them, and how to apply for them.

The administrators of need money want to find out your level of need. They want to find out how much you will have to pay for an education and your general living expenses, how much you (and your parents) have saved, how much you (and your parents) earn, how much support you get from your parents, and how much you can expect from other sources. When put together, this tells them your *need*.

But the three forms of need money are *very* different. Here's why:

- **Bursaries:** These are gifts of money provided to students who can establish financial need by universities, corporations, institutions, or private individuals. They may be available for anyone in need; however, most have a specific focus. For example, Maritime entertainer Rita MacNeil provides a bursary at the University College of Cape Breton for a student who is the child or spouse of a coal miner. There are lots of bursaries available for all sorts of different types of people.

- **Grants:** These are also gifts of money for students who can establish financial need, but they are generally given out for a specific purpose, such as research into a particular topic.

Canada Study Grants, however, are mostly provided simply on the basis of need to students who fall into one of four categories:

- Students with permanent disabilities;

- Students who are *high-need* part-time students;

- Female students in certain doctoral studies;

- Student-loan recipients with dependents.

You apply by filling out a form to obtain a Canada Student Loan and requesting that you be considered for a Canada Study Grant as well. We go over a standard student loan application later in this chapter.

- **Loans:** As the name suggests, these are not gifts — they must be paid back. Most students are familiar with the concept of a student loan, administered by the government, for which no interest is payable until the student leaves the university. It is much easier to qualify for loans than for bursaries or grants.

Millennium scholarships

Millennium scholarships administered by the federal government have been set up for Canadian full-time undergraduate students who have completed their first year and want to continue their studies but have excessive financial need. While they are called scholarships, they are actually bursaries. Those who apply for financial assistance through their province will automatically be considered for a millennium scholarship if they have completed their first year with at least 60 percent of a full course load at a recognized institution. You can find more information on the millennium scholarship program at www.millenniumscholarships.ca.

The words used to identify the different types of financial aid are mixed up a lot. You'll often find bursaries and grants used interchangeably. Sometimes bursaries are given the name "scholarship" or "award" — possibly to make the recipient feel better about receiving it. In fact, in the United Kingdom, "bursary" is the name generally used for scholarships, and sometimes the usage crosses the pond. Whatever it is called, find out who is eligible, how it is administered, the application procedure, and whether or not it has to be paid back.

Bursaries and Grants

There is a wild and woolly assortment of bursaries and grants available. Your provincial financial aid office will tell you about some of them, universities themselves will tell you about others, and the rest you just have to find on your own.

A good place to start your research is at http://studentawards.com, where you enter your personal interests, talents, and other details, and the search engine provides you with a list of bursaries, grants, and scholarships to apply for. The search process for bursaries and grants parallels the search for scholarships, so read the next chapter for pointers on locating scholarships.

Bursaries and grants may be offered to part-time or full-time students, Canadians or international students, top students or those who just barely got accepted. Most are interested in your financial status, as bursaries and grants are made available to help those in need. Often you will have to provide detailed financial information about you and your family, as well as a budget showing your need over the academic year.

Apply for bursaries and grants as early as you can. Some organizations hand out money on a rolling first-come, first-served basis. This means anyone who fits the criteria gets the money until the organization has none left. If you delay, there may be no money left for you by the time your application is read, even though you may be an ideal candidate for the bursary.

While financial need is important to get a bursary, there will often be other qualifying factors. Typically, bursaries have been set up for a particular purpose. It may be to encourage athletes in a particular sport or it may be in memory of a particular individual, so it is awarded only to students from the same town, of the same ethnic origin, or to kids of people in the same profession. Bursaries are also created to recognize superior achievement *outside* of the academic arena. They may be awarded to students who have shown extraordinary leadership, volunteerism, or courage in the face of difficult circumstance.

Ask your university financial aid department about bursaries and grants offered in your particular field of study. Generally, private individuals who donate money to fund a bursary do so to the university they themselves attended.

Corporations and associations may set up bursaries to help out the families of their employees and members. Make sure you ask your parents, grandparents, and other relatives to provide you with a list of all employers and associations with which they have any affiliation. Then you contact them and ask about whether or not they offer any support. Remember: If you don't ask, you won't get.

Don't think bursaries and grants are just for the kids. Most bursaries are *age-blind,* so mature students are just as likely to get them as anyone else. Besides, certain grants are set up specifically for single parents and certain bursaries are set up specifically for mature students. Ask at your university financial aid office what options are available for you.

Bursaries and grants are taxable on amounts over $500, so you must include them as income in your tax return.

First Nations students receive financial aid through the Post-Secondary Student Support Program (PSSSP) operated through the Department of Indian and Northern Affairs Canada. They are entitled to apply for Canada and provincial student loans along with all other Canadian citizens, but a *Status Indian* as defined under the *Indian Act* will get a much better package through the PSSSP. Many universities also offer bursaries specifically to First Nations students. Check the document called *Scholarships, Bursaries and Awards for Aboriginal Students* at www.ainc-inac.gc.ca/ps/ys/pdf/sbaas_e.pdf for more information.

Student Loans

There is nothing wrong with taking out a loan to pay for university. University is an investment in your future and can increase your income potential by far more than the cost of tuition. Obviously, it would be better to obtain money you don't have to pay back by getting scholarships and awards, but you may not have the qualifications. Even if you do get some merit money, you may not get enough to pay all the bills while you go to school.

There are several different types of loans available to students:

✔ **Canada Student Loans, sponsored by the federal government;**

✔ **Provincially sponsored student loans, sponsored by the province where you live;**

✔ **University loans, from the university you attend;**

✔ **Bank loans;**

✔ **Personal loans, from individuals.**

Federal and provincial student loans

You apply for a Canada Student Loan (a federal loan) and a provincially sponsored loan using one application form, issued by your home province. The application is reviewed by the people in your home province's central processing office, who apply a set formula to determine how much money you will get from the federal government and how much you will get from the provincial government.

You must reapply every year. There is no obligation on the part of the loan officers to provide you with funds, even if they have done so the year before.

Student loan programs change every year, and they may change *during* the year. It's up to you to ensure you have the most up-to-date information. If you don't do your research, you may miss a valuable opportunity or ignore a crucial detail.

These loans have a few highly relevant advantages that make them so popular among university students:

✔ **Government loans are interest-free while you attend university:** This includes time you spend working during a university-operated co-op program, or over the summer between the end of the spring term and the beginning of the fall term.

  ✔ **Government loans give you an interest-free grace period after you finish university:** Interest does not begin to accrue until six months after you finish your studies, whether you graduate or drop out.

  ✔ **Government loans have a lower interest rate than other types of loans:** Even once interest begins to accrue, the government limits it to a set rate that is lower than what most banks charge for other loans.

  ✔ **Government loans have ways to help you out if you can't repay right away:** Some people are eligible for debt reduction and interest relief from the excessive load of repaying their student loans. This is a rare situation and not to be expected, but those in need should ask at the central processing office for details.

Loans from the university

Universities want to make sure their students can survive while attending school, so they have set up loan programs. The University of Toronto, for example, has even gone so far as to declare that no student accepted at the institution will be denied an education because he can't afford it, and has set up an expensive financial aid program to back up that statement. For each university, talk to the financial aid (or bursar's) office to find out what is available.

Most universities will help out their students in emergency situations with short-term loans. These are for circumstances where your regular source of financing has been delayed and you have an immediate need for basics such as food and accommodation.

Bank loans

If you can't get a government-sponsored student loan and your university will not help you out either, you may have to try to get a loan from a bank. You'll realize immediately how much more preferable the government-sponsored loans programs are to private loans.

You have to provide a lot more information to banks and you will probably have to get a *co-signer* or *guarantor*, an individual who has wealth — enough to cover your loan at least — who agrees to pay back your loan should you default. Typically, the co-signer or guarantor is a relative, but you can ask anyone sympathetic to your cause.

Of course, banks charge interest on their loans from the day the loan is made. You have no interest-free period, no grace period. The rate of interest is likely to be higher than that offered by the government, and no one is going to offer you debt relief.

Shop around at various financial institutions to make sure you get the best rate and the best terms you can. If your guarantor has a lot of money invested with the particular financial institution, ask him or her to help you negotiate a better rate for your student loan. Chances are the bank will want to keep one of its preferred customers happy.

Personal loans

If you know someone who is ready, willing, and able to lend you money for university, this may be a better option than taking out a bank loan. You can work out the interest rate between you — probably somewhere between what you would have to pay in interest and what she could get in interest on the money if invested.

If you can get a government-sponsored student loan, however, it is preferable to do so rather than take a personal loan from an individual. The government loan gives you the use of the cash interest free for the duration of your university education. Even if your personal beneficiary offers you an interest-free loan, she will be taking the hit for you by not earning interest on her money while you are at school. If you take out a government-sponsored student loan, the government takes the hit.

Applying for a Government-Sponsored Student Loan

As we've mentioned, you apply for Canada Student Loans by applying for the government-sponsored student loans in your home province or territory. In the Yukon, you apply through the *Department of Education's Student Financial Assistance Unit (YESNET)*. In Ontario, you apply through the *Ontario Student Assistance Program (OSAP)*. In Alberta, you apply through the *Alberta Learning Information Service (ALIS)*. All the provincial or territorial student assistance offices are listed in Appendix B, "Money Sources." The financial aid or bursar's offices of all Canadian universities carry the applications as well, as do many high school counsellors' offices.

Québec, Nunavut, and the Northwest Territories administer their own student loans programs independent of the Canada Student Loans Program. The forms remain much the same and students still obtain loans through their provincial or territorial student assistance office.

There is a $10 fee to apply for a government-sponsored student loan, but the fee is waived if you apply online!

Who can apply?

You! Okay, we don't know that for sure. Maybe, somehow, this book found its way to a foreign prison where a non-Canadian, non-student with seriously bad credit happened to pick it up. Sorry, if that's you, well, you aren't going to get a Canada or provincial student loan.

For everyone else, here are the necessary criteria:

- ✔ You must be a Canadian citizen or a permanent, legal resident of Canada.
- ✔ You must be a resident of a province or territory participating in the Canada Student Loans Program. As we mentioned above, Québec, Nunavut, and the Northwest Territories administer their own student loans programs — residents can still apply for a student loan, they just won't get a Canada Student Loan.
- ✔ You must be enrolled in a university (or another designated educational institution) carrying at least 60 percent of a full-time course load of 12 weeks or more. (For students with permanent disabilities, the limit is 40 percent of a full-time course load.)
- ✔ You must show that you have financial need.
- ✔ You must keep your marks up.
- ✔ You must pass a credit check if you are over 21 years old and have never applied for a student loan before.
- ✔ You must not have defaulted on a loan in the past.

If you want to see if you qualify and how much you can likely obtain, try the Student Need Assessment Software (SNAS) at the CanLearn/Canada Student Loans Web site at www.canlearn.ca.

How do the financial aid officers decide how much I'm eligible for?

Once you have obtained and filled out the Canada Student Loan application, it goes to the provincial central office to be processed. In four to six weeks, you will get a letter from the office telling you if you meet the standards of eligibility and, if you do, how much of a loan you can expect to receive.

You should know how the people in the office process your request along with the requests of thousands of others. After ensuring you pass the basic eligibility requirements, the loans staff determine a few things about you.

Who probably won't get student loans

Even though we emphasize that student loans are available for everyone in need, that's not completely true in every case. There are a few categories of people who are not eligible for student loans that are funded by the federal or provincial governments:

✔ **International students:** Part of the process of obtaining a student visa to attend a university in Canada is showing that you have sufficient financial resources to meet the burdens of tuition, room and board, other fees, personal living expenses, and a return trip home. If you *can't* show that, you can't get a visa. If you *can* show that, you don't need financial aid. (In emergency situations, most universities will respond by helping out the student directly.)

✔ **Students with poor credit ratings:** Canada student loans and those administered by the provinces operate by having the governments provide the loan to a student, although banks or credit companies may administer the debt. When repayment becomes due, the student pays the bank or credit company, but the loan is still guaranteed by the government. Obviously, the government would prefer not to guarantee loans of students likely to default, so it examines your credit history. Of course, if the government doesn't find you eligible for a student loan, your chances of getting one from a bank or from the university you wish to attend is virtually nil, unless someone else is willing to act as your guarantor.

✔ **Part-time students, sometimes:** Most part-time students are not eligible for these interest-free government student loans. To make up for this gap, there are part-time Canada Student loans that have the disadvantage of not being interest-free. Interest starts to accrue 30 days after you receive the loan. However, you apply for them in the same offices as regular government-sponsored student loans. Most universities have set up programs offering loans to worthy part-time students in need, as well.

✔ **Your category:** You are put into one of a set number of categories: dependent living at home, dependent living away from home, independent living at home, independent living away from home, and single parent. Each category has a different priority in terms of the offer of funds.

✔ **Your costs:** Your idea of the costs of attending university may be very different from those of the people in the loans office. They figure out what you need for basic existence while attending the particular university you specify. This amount varies depending on your category.

✔ **Your contributions:** Any scholarships, awards, grants, and bursaries go directly into this category. You are also expected to contribute all your savings, along with any earnings you make working part-time or during the summer — in fact, they will consider how much you earned and determine what you should have saved from your jobs. Even if you blew your savings on a vacation or something else, you will still be assessed as having a reasonable savings from your job and this will lessen the amount of loan you can expect. You are also expected to contribute the money you have from all other sources — savings, trusts and inheritances, benefits (including Family Allowance and Employment Insurance), and whatever else you may have.

✔ **Your family's contributions:** This amount depends on a lot of factors, including:

- How much your parents earn;

- How much your parents have in savings and equity;

- How many siblings you have, whom your parents must also support;

- Whether one parent is the sole supporting custodial parent, after divorce;

- What child-support agreements have been made between divorced parents.

From this, the financial aid officers determine your need, or how much money you will be offered as a student loan. Your need equals your costs minus your personal and family contributions.

You can always appeal the decision if you have been refused a loan or if you were offered one that will not cover your actual needs. You will find that the people in the loans office are quite willing to give you another look if there has been a significant change in your information since you applied. For example, if your parents suddenly divorced, leaving only one custodial parent as the sole supporter of you and your three siblings, the loans office will likely revise its assessment. If you suddenly have an accident that stops you from working over the summer at that high-paying job — or if you get laid off from that high-paying summer job and don't have the contribution money you expected — the loans people will be sympathetic.

If you decided just to blow your savings on a car, don't expect a lot of sympathy and don't expect to get any more money.

Filling Out the Application Form

While the various provincial application forms are somewhat different in the way they look, all ask for basically the same information. Let's go through the application, step by step.

First things first

Make sure you get the right application form. You need to obtain a form from the office of the province in which you are resident — not the province where your university is located (unless, of course, they are in the same province). There are different forms for different people and they are very well explained in the offices. If you are in doubt, ask one of the financial aid officers to help you figure out which form to use.

Apply online, if you can. This saves the financial aid officers the tedious task of inputting your data, and they are so grateful they will waive the administration fee for everyone who applies online.

If you can't apply online, print clearly in black ink. We know, we told you that you could print your university applications using a computer and printer. However, on the forms you are asked to print in black ink and we've learned that it is always the best policy to simply do what is asked.

If you're not applying online, make sure you attach payment with your application. Your application will not be processed until your cheque clears.

Personal information

It starts out quick and easy but soon the information requested gets a bit personal. Get used to it. It gets even *more* personal later on in the form. Enter your vital statistics, including your social insurance number and student number, if you have one from your university (do not enter your high school student number). Enter your name, address, and telephone number. Enter your date of birth, preferred language of correspondence (you can choose only English or French), and citizenship status. Indicate whether you have disability issues such as hearing impairment, and whether you have any outstanding student loan and/or bankruptcy issues. Also enter the last dates you attended (or will attend) high school and/or post-secondary studies.

Don't lie on this form. Rest assured that the financial aid officers will check (and often recheck) your responses before giving you any money. If you are found to have intentionally misled them, you will find it difficult to get financial aid — for the rest of your life! Honesty is more than the best policy — it makes the best business sense.

Just as when you are filling out your university application, be sure to answer *every* question, except those that say an answer is optional or the sections that you are not required to fill out. If the answer is $0, write $0. Don't make some mark with a circle and a line through it. Don't write "nil." Remember that any unanswered question or incomprehensible response will cause the computer to kick out your application and return it as incomplete. You'll have to resubmit it with the question answered. The process of figuring your need will be delayed by about a month.

Current status information

Whether you are considered *dependent* or *independent* will affect how much loan money you get. The options and details are:

- **Married:** Regardless of age and with whom you are living, marriage makes you considered independent. You must submit a copy of your marriage certificate and your spouse must fill in part of the form.

- **Common-law or same-sex relationship:** Similar to being married, this too will make you considered independent. Your partner must fill out part of the form and submit an affidavit confirming you have lived together in a conjugal relationship for at least three years or confirming you are raising children together.

- **Sole-support parent:** You must provide evidence of this, but this automatically makes you considered independent. You are likely to get additional assistance.

- **Separated, divorced, or widowed with no dependent children:** You won't get additional assistance, but you will be considered independent.

- **Out of high school for at least five years as of the date of the academic year for which you are applying:** This automatically makes you considered independent.

- **Out of high school for at least four years as of the date of the academic year for which you are applying:** You will likely be considered dependent. Your parents' situation will be a factor in determining your eligibility.

- **Have not been a full-time high school or post-secondary student for at least two 12-month periods:** You will likely be considered dependent. Your parents' situation will be considered in determining your eligibility.

- **Crown ward:** You are considered a *Crown ward* if both of your parents are deceased and you are under the age of majority in your province or territory. You will be considered independent.

- **None of the above:** This fits the bill for most students going to university from high school. You are considered dependent. Your parents' situation will be considered in determining your eligibility.

Residency

Financial aid is administered by the province where you are resident. Since the provincial financial aid officers do not want to give away money to people from another province, you must confirm your residency and, if applicable, that of your parents or partner. To be considered eligible, you or your parent(s) or your partner must have lived in the particular province for at least 12 consecutive months prior to the start of the post-secondary education. If that is not the case, you may be eligible in another province.

Previous post-secondary studies

You must indicate all relevant details of any previous post-secondary education. Indicate the name of the institution and your program, dates of study, what type of program it was, whether you completed your studies, your percentage of a full course load while you were studying, and, of course, the amount of government-sponsored student loans you received.

You are not asked to indicate how much remains owing on the student loans, simply what you received from the Canada Student Loans program and from the program of the particular province.

You must fill in this information for all post-secondary institutions you attended, regardless of whether or not you received financial aid.

Applicant's children

Indicate the number, names, and ages of your dependent children. In this case, children are considered dependent if they are of preschool age (this means any child too young to attend elementary school), if they are under 16 years of age and attending elementary school or high school, if they are 16 years of age or older and taking at least 60 percent of a full course load in high school or a post-secondary school, or if they are 16 years of age or older and have a permanent disability.

You are also asked to indicate your expected payment for child care while you are attending school.

Next of kin in Canada

This is mostly for emergency purposes. Your children and partner cannot be considered next of kin for the application.

Financial data

This is an important part. First, you must declare the value of your assets including vehicles, bank accounts, amounts saved in RRSPs, investment properties, and most other assets. You should not include your principal residence, clothing, furniture, and personal belongings.

This is a significant loophole that can be used to your advantage in financial planning. You can own outright a home valued at $1,000,000 and, as long as it is used as your principal residence, it will not be considered (or even noticed) by the financial aid officers.

Next, you must declare your income from the previous year and your expected income for the upcoming study year. This includes more than simply employment income. You must also declare *all* other taxable income, as well as child-support and alimony payments, government benefits, lottery winnings, monetary gifts, scholarships, awards, bursaries (excluding certain federal bursaries), grants (excluding certain federal grants), and any other income.

Intended institution and course of study

You must indicate where you will be going to university, in what program, when the term will start, and various other details. You must also indicate if you will be living with your parents while studying. If you are classified as *dependent* and you will attend a university in the same city as your parents, you will be expected to live with your parents while studying and money will not be granted for residence or other accommodations. If you will attend a university in another city, money for accommodations can be included in your loan package. If you are attending a university in another city, you must also indicate the cost of travel to and from your hometown.

Information from partner

Your spouse or your common-law or same-sex partner must fill out this section of the application. The information required is basic identification, the date the marriage or living together began, employment or student status, and gross income for the previous year.

If your partner will not be living in Canada during your study period, then you are not considered to be "married or equivalent."

Consent to release personal information

The consent for the financial aid officer to collect and use your personal information is coming up later. This section allows you to make your information available to others, such as your partner or parents, so that they can be involved in the administration of your loan. It is optional.

Information from parents

If you are or may be *dependent*, your parents (or other legal guardians) must fill out this section. They must indicate their basic identification, marital status, the number of dependent children they have, and their dates of birth. They also must provide certain financial information about their incomes as reported on their tax returns for the previous year.

The number of dependent children obviously indicates how much of a strain is already placed on the parents' incomes. The dates of birth are important because the older your parents are, the more assets they can protect because the government assumes they'll need the money sooner for retirement.

Other programs

If you wish to apply for other grants and bursaries, some will be included in the provincial financial aid form. If you think you might be eligible, you might as well apply. All it takes is ticking off a couple of boxes and filling in a few additional words of information. However, make sure you are eligible. The millennium scholarships, for example, are only available for students who have completed at least 60 percent of a full course load in a post-secondary institution.

Declarations, consents, and signatures

There's one section each for partners, parents, and the applicant. Similar to the declaration in the university application forms, these declarations are guarantees that everything you have stated in the financial aid application is true. However, there's more to it.

You are also granting permission for the administrators to collect and use your personal information — and so must your partner or parents, if applicable. The financial aid officers must conduct due diligence to confirm what you have said. They may not choose to go poking around in your bank accounts, your tax records, and all other personal information they can find — but then again they might. Basic information is checked; the officers also investigate a certain number of applications at random. Any applications that appear suspicious are investigated automatically.

Don't forget to ensure that all signatures you need are on the form. Since each individual is making two declarations — that everything stated is true and that permission for collection and use of personal information is granted — two signatures are required from each person. As always, if any information is missing the application cannot be processed and you will get a request to complete the application properly. This delays the process and means you will not get your money until later.

Deadlines for government loans are strictly enforced and providing information too late could mean you lose the opportunity for funding for that entire year. Check the deadlines for your particular provincial program scrupulously and get the information — all of it — in on time!

Application fee

You have to tell them how the fee will be paid. Remember, your application won't be processed until your fee is received.

Supporting documentation

You have to prove what you claim. In each section, the form spells out exactly what you need to send along, depending on which circumstances apply to you. Here are the most frequently required items:

- ✔ Photocopy of your social insurance card

- ✔ Photocopy of your Canadian immigration record (if applicable)

- ✔ Medical or other official document proving permanent disability (if applicable)

- ✔ Marriage certificate, separation or divorce agreement, or affidavit from common-law or same-sex partner confirming you have lived together in a conjugal relationship for at least three years or confirming you are raising children together (if applicable)

- ✔ Evidence of being a sole-support parent (if applicable)

- ✔ Letter from your trustee in bankruptcy showing you are not in default of another loan through the provincial or a federal program, and confirming that any funds provided through the provincial or federal assistance program will not be seized (if applicable)

Financial aid planner

To apply for financial aid, this is the information you will need to have ready. Do your research and pull together all of your materials before you fill out the forms.

✔ **Category (which are you?)**

❏ Single dependent living with family

❏ Single dependent living away from family

❏ Single independent living with family

❏ Single independent living away from family

❏ Married or equivalent

❏ Single parent

❏ Status Indian

✔ **Costs (research the amounts in advance)**

❏ Tuition and other university fees

❏ Other university costs (books, materials)

❏ Room and board

❏ Other reasonable living expenses

❏ Travel expenses to and from the city where your university is located

❏ Costs for dependent family members

✔ **Personal contributions (track down all your personal wealth information)**

❏ RESPs: Total value of all monies in RESP accounts set up in your name, including contributions, CESGs, and investment interest

❏ Trusts in your name: Total value that you will receive when you go to university

❏ Parental contribution: The amount you have been promised by your parents (or anyone else who is concerned with your welfare)

❏ Personal savings: All that you have saved over your life that can be used for your education. It does not include primary residence, furniture, and personal items

❏ Earnings from employment: How much you will make weekly/monthly at your part-time or summer job (if applicable) while attending university. Provide details if applicable, such as scheduled contract termination date

❏ Scholarships, bursaries, and grants: The total you will receive for each

❏ Other sources

✔ **Family contributions (if you are dependent, a percentage of your family's financial capabilities will be assessed as an expected contribution)**

❏ Parents' status: Married or common-law; divorced; separated; widowed; both parents deceased

❏ If parents are divorced or separated, what is the support agreement? Less family contribution is expected if a parent is the sole support of the family — in fact, this status can trigger offers of greater amounts

❏ Number of siblings being supported (along with any special circumstances such as special needs of any of the siblings)

❏ Family savings: This amount is independent of the amounts reported under personal contributions. It does not include primary residence, furniture, and personal items

❏ Family earnings: How much your supporting parent(s) earned in the last taxation period

Easy, wasn't it? You now have completed the only form you're likely to need to get the financial aid you deserve — although you can certainly fill out more applications to try for other funds. After all, you have all the information you will need right in front of you!

Getting the Money

You will hear whether you will receive a loan, and how much you will receive, about four to six weeks after you submit your application. Make sure you keep a copy of your application and contact your provincial office if you have not heard back within that time.

The last day Ontario universities have to inform students that they have been accepted is July 15, while the people at OSAP tell us that students who have not applied by July 31 will not receive their funds by the time they have to pay for tuition in September. They can still apply and may get a loan, but the funds will likely not arrive in time and the student must make other arrangements with his or her university.

As to how the money will be paid, the situation changed as of this year. Previously, banks, credit unions, and caisses populaires issued funds for the Canada Student Loan Program. Instead, from now on the funds will come directly from the Government of Canada through the National Student Loans Service Centre. They will either issue and send you cheques or you can supply them with a void cheque and the money will be deposited directly into your account.

Repaying Your Loan (the Part Everyone Forgets)

Okay, sit down and take a deep breath. What we're going to tell you next isn't easy to hear. Loans are not grants — eventually, you have to pay back your student loans. Just because they are easy to get doesn't mean you don't have to worry about paying them back.

What's more, you have to start paying them back quickly. You may want to take some time off after you graduate and before starting your career to travel around the world and "find yourself." Sounds like a great idea, except that your student loans started accruing interest six months after you finished university. If you don't have a job by that time to help you start paying back the loans and the accruing interest, your debt will grow even greater.

You will repay your loan directly to the government office that provides it. To assist you in figuring out a schedule for repaying your loans, you'll find a

Canada Student Loan repayment calculator (along with a debt management calculator) at the Human Resources Development Canada Web site at www.hrdc-drhc.gc.ca/student_loans/.

Many universities have financial planners available online for prospective students. Try out the financial aid worksheet Web site from the University of Toronto at www.utaps.utoronto.ca/financial_aid/.

You know that University Applications File you started back in grade 9? Start a similar file, just for student loans. Keep in it your copies of applications, all correspondence you receive (and send), and any statements you may receive. You need to include your student loans — and their interest and repayment — in your taxes.

The student loan you receive will apply toward your needs over a full year. You will get much of it (usually 60 percent) up front and the rest mid-term. That means you might not need all of it immediately. Invest the amount you don't need in a no-risk, interest-earning account such as a GIC or other term deposit. The amount of interest you make on the investment can help you pay back the loan. Of course, you'll have to declare the interest on your taxes and as income when you reassess your loan eligibility.

MONEY MATTERS

Why not just declare bankruptcy?

There is a rumour going around that you can get out of repaying your student loan by simply declaring bankruptcy at the end of your university career. Let us dispel that one. Bankruptcy is not a good strategy from any angle.

First, you are just starting out in your career. If you declare bankruptcy, you are saddled with the stigma of loan default. This means you can't get a credit card. It also means you will have extreme difficulty getting a loan of any sort for many years to come — forget about getting a car loan, mortgage, or business loan to finance your new venture! In fact, you will find it difficult even to get an apartment, as many landlords now do credit checks on prospective tenants before offering them a lease. It's completely legal to refuse to offer tenancy to someone with a bad credit rating.

Some employers check credit ratings as well, especially in industries where you will be in a position of trust or in a position to deal with other people's money. The legal, financial, administrative, and even service industries and sales may be difficult to break into after having declared bankruptcy.

Remember, the bankruptcy laws were not made for you. You must pay back your student loans!

If you have defaulted on your student loan, your debt will be turned over to a credit agency that will hound you for payment. Your credit will be negatively affected. And the federal and provincial governments have the right to withhold your income tax refund and apply the amount toward your debt until the entire amount plus interest is paid off. Not a cheery prospect. The moral of the story? If you are having problems paying back a loan, notify the folks who own the loan and see if you can work out a modified repayment strategy.

Chapter 16

Working Your Way through University

● ●

In This Chapter

▶ Deciding if co-op work programs are for you

▶ Joining the military and getting your degree for "free"

● ●

*T*his chapter has two topics: co-op work programs at university and joining the military to earn your degree. Why put these two seemingly disparate topics in one chapter? Well, it's because both options let someone else pay for your years at university — and this part of the book is about financing your university education. This chapter helps you figure out whether either option is right for you.

First on the agenda are university co-op programs. In a co-op program, an employer pays for your education (or, at least, a large portion of it) by hiring you for a four- or eight-month period during the semestered school year. Co-op programs are increasingly popular in Canadian universities, but not every school offers them. We'll point you to a list of schools that offer co-op programs.

The second part of the chapter deals with joining the Canadian Forces, and getting the taxpayer to pick up the tab for your university education. Of course, there's no such thing as a free lunch — and there's no such thing as a free education, either. In the case of the military, rather than pay for your education in actual dollars, you pay for your education in time served with the Canadian Forces.

I'm about as Co-operative as the Next Guy...Co-op Programs Explained

While perusing a university calendar, you may have read about *co-operative work programs* (usually just shortened to *co-op programs*), and wondered what they are. Alternatively, you may have heard about them from TV or the radio and found the idea of working while going to school intriguing. This chapter discusses the pros and cons of these popular programs and gives some advice on figuring out if these programs are for you.

First things first. What is a co-operative work program? According to the Canadian Association of Co-operative Education, co-operative education is defined as "a program that formally integrates a student's academic studies with work experience in co-operative employer organizations." In other words, co-operative education has elements of both the school side of things and the job side. For many students, co-op education is the best of both worlds!

If you're accepted into a co-op program, you go to school for a few semesters and then spend a formal *work term* at a nearby employer. During your work term, you are paid and treated more or less like a standard employee at the particular job. Your co-op term could be spent programming at a communications company, building robots at a manufacturing plant, or working at one of dozens of jobs for interesting Canadian companies. It depends on the program.

You repeat this cycle of learning and working until your degree is complete. Since there is more time spent "in the field" (that is, actually working), a co-op program typically takes a few months longer to complete than does the traditional four-year degree. Again, exactly how long you have to spend completing your degree varies with the university, but it can be eight months or more. On the bright side, though, you gain valuable experience as you continue your academic studies.

If you're interested in co-op work programs, you should find out early on if the universities of your choice offer them. It's easy to find out, because the universities that offer co-op programs tend to be very vocal about it. Consult the university calendars. Hit the Web sites of the schools that are on your list. Or, simply check out the Web site of the Canadian Association of Co-operative Education at www.cafce.ca.

What do co-op programs offer?

The jobs you have in your co-op program let you gain valuable work experience while you earn money in the "real world." Not only do you gain great experience doing the things you've been learning about in books, but also you make good contacts at the particular co-op work placement. Since your co-op work is related to what you're studying, you also build your résumé with some impressive credits. Sounds good, eh?

Each work situation is developed and approved by the university's co-operative educational department as a suitable learning situation. This means, for example, that the employer can't hire a third-year co-op engineering student just to haul bricks at a construction site. Conversely, the third-year engineering student can't just show up and expect to get paid for hauling bricks. It's a two-way street. Both the student and the co-op employer must work together to provide an environment in which everyone benefits and the student gets *useful* on-the-job experience.

Co-op jobs are directly related to what you are studying in university. They give you valuable experience working at the kinds of jobs you'll probably do in the future. This is very useful when you graduate and find yourself looking for a fulfilling job in your field.

There are dozens of different co-op programs at universities across Canada. They differ by location, subject, employer size, degree of school supervision and reporting, and other key factors. This said, just about every co-op program has a few things in common:

- Co-op students must be actively involved in productive work related to their field of study.

- Co-op students get paid for the work they perform. Although the pay won't be equal to that of a really experienced worker, the student does get paid at a reasonably competitive rate.

- Co-op students' progress on the job is tracked by their school. This monitoring is important as the work term is treated as part of the entire educational experience for co-op students. Co-op work terms are not simply a series of unrelated summer jobs; they are aimed at providing progressively more experience in your program.

- Co-op students' progress on the job is tracked by their employers, too. In many cases, employer evaluations serve as the basis for your mark in your co-op work term.

- Co-op work terms can comprise up to 50 percent of the total time spent at university. Co-op terms are taken quite seriously, and it's very rare that a given co-op student spends less than 30 to 35 percent of his or her total university time on the job. Whereas a traditional (i.e., non co-op) student may spend three months every summer at a job (about 25 percent of the year), co-op students can spend double this amount of time on the job. In short, co-op students usually have to work a bit harder than those who follow the traditional path of university education.

How are co-op programs viewed after university?

It depends. As with a traditional job, how your co-op experience is viewed after you graduate depends on the type and quality of the work you did during your work terms.

If you applied yourself, worked hard, and received good employer (and university) evaluations, your co-op terms are likely to be viewed extremely positively, putting you well ahead of those students with no direct experience (co-op or no co-op).

For obvious reasons, most employers want to hire experienced staff who have proven themselves in the job market. Having impressive co-op work-term evaluations tells your prospective employer that you understand how the real world works and are prepared to do the job.

How much money do they pay me?

It depends on a number of factors, including your experience level, the type and size of co-op employer, and other things including your academic major or specialty, how in-demand your skills are at the moment, and even if this is your first work term or a subsequent one.

Co-op employers determine the salary paid to the co-op student, not the university. Salaries vary based on your program of study and work-term level, but usually increase as you become more experienced. This is because you become more valuable to your prospective employer as time goes on.

Just about every university involved with co-op programs prepares a list of salary averages and ranges according to academic program and work term. This list is available to both employers and students, and serves as a guideline for student remuneration.

Naturally, salary is an important consideration in choosing a co-op work-term placement. It doesn't take a commerce major to figure out you want the highest-paying job you can get. After all, the more money you earn during your co-op work term, the less money you'll have to come up with from other sources such as the folks at Canada Student Loans and the Bank of Mom and Dad.

On the other hand, you don't necessarily want a high salary to be your *only* influencing factor. Try to look for a position that also provides you with some solid experience and transferable skills. The entire point of the co-op educational program is to provide you with experience in your chosen field of study and to give you a leg up on the competition who haven't had the benefit of co-op.

Can a co-op placement turn into a "real" job?

Yes. Although it's certainly not guaranteed, doing well at your work term is the best way to turn the co-op placement into a permanent position. After all, what better way to prove yourself than by actually doing the job?

You can't, however, simply assume you will get a permanent job just because you did well during your work terms. Things change, companies expand and contract with the economy, and jobs that were available during your co-op term may not be there when you graduate.

Are the placements guaranteed?

No. Although co-op programs at most Canadian schools are highly organized, there is the distinct possibility of not getting a placement for a particular term. Like a traditional job search, it is important to start your co-op job search as early as you can. Most co-op programs have formal job finding (and approval) services, interview clinics, and a detailed follow-up infrastructure.

The folks at the university's co-op department do what they can to help you find a co-op placement, but *you* have to get (and keep) the job yourself. If you don't get a co-op placement you simply return to school or do something else for a couple of months.

What do you mean I have to pay a fee? I thought they would pay me!

Since a given university's co-op infrastructure can be extensive, the student must usually pay a *co-op term fee* to offset the costs involved in the program. This is not a placement fee (since the placement is not 100-percent guaranteed). Rather, the co-op term fee is a way for the university to recover some of the costs it incurs in administering and delivering the co-op program.

These administrative costs include equipment, postage/courier, printing, copying, publicity and promotional material, subscriptions and mailing lists, telephone and fax, and even office furnishings. From a student point of view, the fee goes toward employment preparation courses, job-search counselling, access to job postings, interview arrangements, access to job databases such as Campus Worklink, work-term monitoring, work-term evaluation, and usually the use of telephones and fax machines for your job search. Whew!

Co-op term fees vary widely depending on the university, the work term, and other factors. Check with the specific university to find out how much you're expected to pay.

In the 2000/2001 academic year, the University of Guelph charged its students $200 per co-op semester. Ryerson's co-op fees for the 2000/2001 school year were $1,875 in total, but were *amortized* (or broken up) — over three to five years depending on the particular student's academic program. Ryerson says this strategy minimizes administrative costs and smoothes out student fee payments over a longer period. The University of Calgary uses yet another system, charging its students $384 per co-op course.

Within one university, there may be wide variations in co-op fees by faculty or department. As an example, the Université de Moncton's faculty of social sciences charged its students $710 per co-op program in the 2000/2001 school year. The nutrition and sciences department charged a whopping $2,312 for its co-op program.

Our point? As we've said throughout this book, ask lots of questions, get names of people you talk to, and keep accurate records of who said what (and when). You don't want to get into a co-op program and suddenly find out that the fees are vastly different from what you had assumed.

Being ineligible for a loan because you work too much

You might remember from Chapter 14 that interest on outstanding Canada and provincial student loans is applied immediately following your withdrawal from full-time studies or graduation. The Canada Student Loan Program now recognizes an *approved* co-op work term as an integral part of your studies. Therefore, you might want to talk with your bursar or other financial aid official at your school to figure out how earning money during your co-op terms will affect your ability to get financial aid.

Effective August 1, 1995, Canada Student Loan funding — including co-op terms organized by your university — is limited to 340 weeks of assistance. This won't affect you as an undergraduate but it might pop up later if you intend to go on to graduate studies. If you take a total of 208 weeks (four years) to get your undergraduate degree (including co-op work terms), and then another 104 weeks (2 years) to get your master's degree, only the first 28 weeks (much less than a year) of your Ph.D. degree will be covered by Canada Student Loans.

Since a Ph.D. can take three, four, or even five years to complete, you can easily run out of loan deferrals before you get out of school. As we said, you don't need to worry about this now. It's just good to know and file away for future notice.

Join the Military, See the World, Earn Your Degree

Hey, have you heard there's a big organization that sends qualified students to university for free, gives them a part-time job while they're at school so they can earn some pocket money, and then sends them overseas to exotic places?

As an added benefit, students can be 100 percent sure of a job after graduation from this outfit. And, get this: *the job is pretty much guaranteed to be in your field of study*. Perhaps best of all, the organization has been around for more than a century, so there's little chance it will be shut down.

Sound too good to be true? Surprise, it's the Canadian Forces. And they want you!

How does this work?

The Canadian Forces has two programs of interest to high school students who are thinking about getting a university education and would like to serve their country: the *Regular Officer Training Plan (ROTP)* and the *Reserve Entry Training Plan (RETP)*.

Signing up for the ROTP (and, to a much lesser extent, the RETP) is the main way students are granted admission into the Royal Military College in Kingston, Ontario. Granted, there are fewer program and course choices at RMC (since it's primarily designed to graduate officers in the Canadian Forces), but there are a surprising number of non-military programs. See the sidebar entitled "What can I take as an officer cadet at Royal Military College?" for additional details about courses as well as other non-RMC programs of study.

The Forces' ROTP is the admission plan under which the majority of Royal Military College students are enrolled. Applicants who have been accepted for entry at RMC will be enrolled as *officer cadets* in the *regular component* of the Canadian Forces.

The RETP, on the other hand, provides a *limited* number of vacancies at RMC for those who would like to undertake military training along with their education — but who don't want to make the regular five-year commitment to the Regular Forces after graduation. Under this alternative, you must pay for your education, very much like a traditional university setting (although your fees will be noticeably less than a traditional university).

What can I take as an officer cadet at Royal Military College?

Note: courses and programs are changing at RMC. Check with your counsellor or with RMC directly to get the latest scoop on degree programs.

Although you don't have anywhere near the same choices you do in a civilian university, you do have some degree of choice at RMC:

You have the choice of the following arts programs:

- A four-year *bachelor of arts degree (B.A.)* in humanities, including specialties such as English, French, and history

- A four-year B.A. in social science, including specialties such as political science and economics

- A four-year B.A. in business administration

- A four-year B.A. in military and strategic studies

As you can see, with the exception of the last option, all B.A. degree programs have direct civilian applications.

And, in case you're wondering, the last program is designed for students who want to spend their career in the military.

You have the choice of the following science programs:

- A four-year *bachelor of science degree (B.Sc.)* in general science

- A four-year B.Sc. degree in honours science, including physics, chemistry, and mathematics specialties

- A four-year B.Sc. degree in space science

You have the choice of the following engineering programs:

- A four-year *bachelor of engineering degree (B.Eng.)* in civil engineering

- A four-year B.Eng. degree in mechanical engineering

- A four-year B.Eng. degree in chemical and material engineering

- A four-year B.Eng. degree in electrical engineering

- A four-year B.Eng. degree in computer engineering

Currently, all degrees are taught as four-year programs. Soon, the Royal Military College will be granting three-year degrees, although little information is available about when this new system might be implemented. If you follow a three-year program, your total years in the Canadian Forces will drop from nine to eight. There are two exceptions to this: if you have trained as an air navigator or as a pilot. See the section, "How long do I have to serve after I get my degree?" for details.

It is sometimes possible to study outside of the RMC when the military needs officers in specific career categories that the RMC doesn't teach. These include physiotherapy, pharmacy, nursing, and personal selection (think human resources). This said, there was only one (!) position available for the 2001/2002 academic year in physiotherapy, and only four in nursing.

Other programs, such as the *Medical Officers Training Program (MOTP)* and the *Dental Officers Training Program (DOTP)* are available — although these are *extremely* competitive. Ask at your recruiting centre for details.

If you are accepted into the ROTP, you can expect to attend a seven- to ten-week *basic officers training camp* (think "boot camp"). After your summer working with the Forces, you enter university life at RMC. If all proceeds according to plan, you complete your degree in four years and begin serving your *obligatory service*. More about this a bit later in the chapter.

Under the ROTP (and some other plans, such as the *Medical Officers Training Program (MOTP)* and the *Dental Officers Training Program (DOTP))*, the Canadian Department of National Defence pays the costs of tuition, uniform, books, instruments, and other essential fees. In addition, each officer cadet is paid a monthly salary. Medical and dental care is also provided. Sweet.

Upon successful completion of your particular academic program, officer cadets are awarded their degrees and granted commissions as officers in the Canadian Forces. You're in the army (or navy or air force) now.

How long do I have to serve after I get my degree?

All graduates of the ROTP are obliged to serve for a minimum of five years in the regular (or full-time) component of the Canadian Forces after graduation. This period of service is called obligatory service and means that your *minimum* total commitment is nine years: four years at school and five years serving in the military.

Depending on which program you're in, however, you may have to serve longer. Programs such as *air navigator* and *pilot* are programs where additional investment is made in your training. Since you receive additional training, you are expected to give additional service. In the case of an air navigator, the additional service period is two years, making a total of 11 years from the start of your first year at RMC to the last year as a navigator. In the case of a pilot, the total commitment is 13 years (four years for your RMC degree, and nine years in pilot training and service).

This is obviously a big chunk of your life. It's not something you should consider without a great deal of thought.

Not that I'm considering it, but how can I get out of my commitment?

If after joining the Royal Military College you decide that the Canadian Forces are not for you, you may apply for release, without obligation, after the first day in November of your first year but prior to the beginning of your second academic year. You may continue in school until just before the start of the second year (after serving your summer work term).

Just before you start your second academic year, you will be asked to sign your obligatory service contract, binding you to attend RMC for the next three years and further binding you to your additional five, seven, or nine years of service after that.

If you leave after completing your first year, the Royal Military College will send you a retroactive tuition bill for your year at school. You get to leave but you still have to pay for your education. As we said, there's no such thing as a free lunch!

After you sign your obligatory service contract, you are committed for the next eight years. It would take extraordinary circumstances to be released.

Can I go to RMC and not serve in the military?

Not really. RMC is pretty much geared toward graduating military officers for the Canadian Forces. If you want a general university education, you should probably consider going to a traditional university.

However, the Canadian Forces offers another program besides the ROTP. As we mentioned earlier in this chapter, the Reserve Entry Training Plan (RETP) provides a limited number of vacancies at RMC for those who would like to undertake military training along with their education — but who don't want to make the regular five-year commitment to the Regular Forces after graduation.

Reserve entry cadets receive the same education and training as do ROTP cadets, but they are required to pay fees. RETP cadets are required to take summer training, for which they receive pay and allowances. Unless you have transferred to the Regular Forces, you are committed to serve in the *primary reserve* (essentially a reserve military force called up in times of war) upon graduation and commissioning.

How do I apply?

RMC has a rather unique application process. Rather than applying to the college or through a provincial application centre, your application is processed by your local Canadian Forces Recruiting Centre. Remember, this is the military!

The application process includes a full medical, aptitude, and physical fitness test, as well as an interview. Applications are best initiated early in the final year of high school and, since the application deadline varies from year to year, it makes sense to look into this option as early as you can. Your local Recruiting Centre can provide specific information.

A birth certificate and a certified copy of your latest high school transcript is required at the start of the application process. As part of the application process, applicants must also complete an application form for the ROTP or the RETP. You can get information concerning the application process from the Canadian Forces Recruiting Centre (CFRC) nearest you or by calling (toll-free) (800) 856-8488.

Within Canada, applicants not resident in a city in which a Recruiting Centre is located will normally be provided with return transportation and reasonable travelling expenses from their place of residence to the CFRC, and living expenses while at the CFRC.

Application for admission under the ROTP or RETP must be made by early March of the academic year prior to entry, but the earlier you apply the better. Application deadlines may be confirmed with your local Canadian Forces Recruiting Centre. By applying for the ROTP or RETP, you are also automatically applying for residence and for scholarship consideration. Successful candidates will be offered a place in the ROTP or RETP at the Royal Military College of Canada located in Kingston, Ontario. You will be notified of the requirement to attend a seven- to ten-week pre-academic basic officer training course starting shortly after the end of your final high school year. Upon successful completion of the basic officer training course, you will proceed to your academic institution (the RMC in most cases) to commence your university studies.

Do they have to take me?

No. In fact, lots of people are turned away from the ROTP and RETP. The Forces says that only about 25 percent of students who apply under the ROTP — and an even lower percentage of students who apply under the RETP — are admitted to RMC. Plus, the first-year class at RMC is extremely small, especially when compared with large civilian universities such as the University of Toronto, McGill, and UBC. For the academic year 2001/2002, RMC's *entire* first year enrollment was approximately 375 students.

It is for this reason that the Canadian Forces strongly recommends that all students send in applications to several universities in addition to their application to the Royal Military College. If you don't get into the RMC, you can still go to a traditional university. As usual, don't put all your eggs in one basket.

What's life in the Forces like?

Life in the Canadian Forces is a lot different from those old American war movies you might see on late-night TV. It's very different from the new American war movies, too. Canadian soldiers are respected worldwide as effective fighters and peacekeepers. Members of the Canadian Forces have a proud tradition of service and honour to their country.

There is a large physical component to being in the military. From the initial seven- to ten-week "boot camp" and continuing on through your years at school and obligatory service, you are subjected to some rather intensive physical training and discipline.

It's especially challenging for first-year students. Each day starts with a 6 a.m. (yes, that's in the morning) reveille, and the rest of the day is just as regimented. Scheduled (and mandatory) periods are held for showers, bed-making, cleaning, breakfast, dressing, inspection, classes, study, exercise, more showers, more study, and then lights out. Any breach of the rules or regulations is punished. Any "independent" students are quickly brought under control.

As you can tell, attending RMC is a far cry from a civilian university and is *definitely* not for everyone. Some people find the clockwork running of their lives very disconcerting. Others have problems with the strange new rules and regulations. In the past, women and visible minorities have had a tough time of it in this traditionally white male bastion. This is changing (albeit slowly), as more outreach programs are designed and implemented to attract a more diverse mix of people.

Make no mistake about it. Joining the military is a very important decision in your life. Once you've started your second year, it is *extremely* difficult to walk away from your commitment. If you have problems dealing with authority figures, you probably won't be able to cut it in the military. You could be miserable for the four years of school *plus* the additional five, seven, or nine years of military service.

In most cases, you have to volunteer to be sent off to one of Canada's many peacekeeping missions around the world. Otherwise, most of your service will be spent somewhere in Canada (sorry, you don't get a choice of where you're stationed). You are also subject to *military law* at all times. This means a completely different set of rules, regulations, and laws.

Although the Forces may try to put a great spin on things — the U.S. Navy used to use the slogan, "Join the Navy and See the World" — overseas missions can be an unhealthy mixture of mind-numbing boredom punctuated by a few moments of absolute terror. If you volunteer for overseas duty with the Forces, you certainly won't be spending your time sitting on some vacation

Loving the military life

We don't want to sound negative about going to RMC, because, for those who work well under a regimented atmosphere, RMC and joining the Forces can be the best thing in their life. Some graduates report a sense of purpose, camaraderie, and home that they never experience anywhere but in the Forces. They are also able to do things in the Forces — tactical manoeuvres and blowing stuff up — that would land them in jail in the outside world.

Lots of students at traditional universities find there are too many distractions in terms of social life and other activities — consequently, they never get their studies done, or they fail out. That's not the case at RMC. In fact, the regimented study schedule can help you build a solid work ethic that will take you throughout your life.

Going to RMC is a lifestyle choice. It's not a trick to get a free degree. The recruitment officers are very choosy because they need to ensure you know what you're getting into. However, if you love everything about the military, then there really is no life like it.

beach sipping party drinks. You might build bridges in war-torn countries, patrol a disputed border between two countries you never heard about in high school geography, or even fly combat missions over a hostile country.

Whatever you do, you will be given little (if any) choice in the matter. After all, it is the military, and here you're basically told *what* to do, *how* to do it, *when* to do it, and *how many times*.

How will I be viewed when I get out?

It depends. You may decide you like the lifestyle so much you'll re-enlist. Once out, you might find it difficult to reintegrate yourself into the (very different) civilian lifestyle. The Forces now has formal reintegration programs to help soldiers fit back into the mainstream of society.

How you fit in depends on you, the courses you took during university, and what type of specialist you became in the military. Airforce pilots can become pilots of commercial airlines, although they have to be completely re-trained on the civilian equipment. Computer experts often find work at large defence contractors writing classified computer programs. Some ex-soldiers even join the Royal Canadian Mounted Police or CSIS, the Canadian Security Intelligence Service — Canada's spy organization. So instead of your mom cooing to the neighbours, "My kid, the doctor," she can say, in a very quiet voice, "My kid, the spy!"

Chapter 17

International Universities

*E*very year, thousands of Canadian students travel to the United States, Britain, France, Germany, Australia, and dozens of other countries to study, soak up the new culture, learn a new language, and, in general, thrive and have fun. Imagine walking through the hallowed halls of Harvard, studying Chaucer at Cambridge, or reading an early copy of Voltaire's *Candide* at the Sorbonne.

As you might guess, however, studying abroad involves a lot more planning than applying to the local university. If you're applying to any American university, for example, there's the important matter of writing (and scoring well on) the SAT I, a standardized exam that everyone must write.

If you're thinking about studying in London, you have to deal with a fair amount of culture shock. Yes, the English speak the same language we do (or, to be more precise, *we* speak the same language *they* do), but they behave and act very differently than Canadians. There are many important things involved with fitting in, staying healthy, ensuring you can afford to live (after all, things are very expensive in Europe), and dealing with things such as bank accounts, driving on the "wrong" side of the road, hanging out in pubs, and other matters that are very different from what you may be used to in Canada.

And, of course, there *is* a language barrier if you plan to study in a country whose population doesn't speak English. Negotiating the narrow alleyways of Rome on the way to classes sounds a lot more romantic than taking the bus to your 9 a.m. Monday morning calculus class at Memorial, but if you're not completely fluent with both the language and the culture you'll be in for a few big surprises in your first year.

This chapter is designed to get you thinking in the right direction about studying at an international university. It gives you a framework within which to mull things over — and decide if you should consider international study. It also provides some financial aid information as well as some tips on staying healthy in your new home. Are you packed and ready to go?

Why Go Away (Far Away) to School?

There is no single answer to this question. Your parents might have taken you to Boston when you were seven years old and you somehow knew you had to return. Now that you're almost out of high school, Harvard seems a logical choice for the place you should study. On the other hand, you may be an aspiring computer programmer and know some of the best software designers are trained at Stanford University, in the heart of Silicon Valley. There are probably as many reasons to study abroad as there are students.

Here are a few more reasons to consider an international education:

- ✔ **An international university's prestige may translate into a higher-paying job:** The prestige of a large American university such as Harvard, Yale, Brown, Princeton, Stanford, UCLA, Northwestern, or Notre Dame can go a long way in the job market. There are many employers who will pay a little (or a lot) extra to hire graduates of a prestigious American university. Recruiters from large Wall Street (and Bay Street) firms frequently set up career fairs at some of the large American universities hoping to snatch up graduates and install them in plushly carpeted corner offices.

- ✔ **The history:** Sure, you can learn all about French romantic poetry, for example, from just about any Canadian university. But imagine actually studying in the same library as did the French poets you're studying. Imagine strolling down the River Seine looking up at the Eiffel Tower, or sitting near a troupe of mimes by Notre Dame cathedral in Paris. It's inspirational, to say the least.

- ✔ **The culture:** Perhaps England is more your cup of tea. Studying at Oxford or Cambridge University will round out your education in a way that only centuries of scholarly tradition can offer. Here are universities that educated some of the future kings of England! Simply put, sometimes just *being there* adds an intangible, yet important, perspective to your education.

- ✔ **Follow in your parents' footsteps:** Your father may have studied medicine at Johns Hopkins, and you want to carry on the family tradition. Your mom may have gone on an exchange to a university in France or Switzerland, and has been hinting around that you would really enjoy the surroundings. Perhaps you want to learn Cantonese and take over the family import-export business; studying in Hong Kong may be the best of both worlds for you.

Whatever your reasons to consider an international university, you can look forward to one of the best adventures of your life. Opportunities that you haven't even dreamed about can open up for international students. New people, languages, cultures, methods, architecture, food, romance, and possibly a better learning experience can await you if — and it's a big if — you are prepared and know what you're doing.

International universities can cost you, not only financially but also spiritually. Certainly, tuition at international universities is a lot more than tuition at Canadian universities, but the great distances involved can take an even greater toll on you. You'll see your family, friends, and loved ones a lot less than you would if you stayed in Canada. Think about the big changes before you take the plunge.

Now that we've got you all excited to head abroad to university, you should know that being accepted to international schools is no cakewalk. Take American colleges, for example. You can't just pick a college you like, apply, and get in. The process doesn't work that way. You'll be lumped in with all the rest of the applicants from abroad, like you, as well as applicants from their own country. If you apply to Harvard, for example, you'll be one of more than 16,000 applicants! Harvard accepts about 2,100 students each year. You'll be competing with everyone else in the pool for one of those 2,100 acceptance letters.

Harvard, of course, is an extreme. Most U.S. colleges are not so competitive. But the vast majority of colleges have minimum academic criteria and accept only those students who meet their standards. Applying to a college, in most cases, does not mean automatic acceptance.

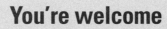

You're welcome

International universities want you. In almost all cases, any Canadian student who wants to attend school in a country other than Canada (and who is qualified to enrol) will find universities and colleges ready to welcome him with open arms. The basic rule of supply and demand is at work, and it applies to everyone. Overall, American colleges and other universities abroad are not getting enough students from their traditional source — their own high schools — so they're actively looking elsewhere to fill their classes. And "elsewhere" includes the other countries of the world such as Canada.

Some American colleges send representatives to big cities in Canada to seek out promising students and help them with the task of applying and enrolling. Almost all colleges have programs on their campuses to make students from other countries feel welcome. Most have special departments to deal with the needs of international students.

Where Do You Start?

Canadians considering going to an international university should start the same way they would start if they were considering going to a Canadian university. Make a list. Identify the reasons you want to go to an international university and what you want from it. Then start researching your options. If you want to go to the United States, pick up a directory of U.S. colleges and look for those schools that meet your needs. If you want to go farther away, use the Web to research the universities in the countries of your choice.

Read the advice that this book offers in Chapters 1 through 9 about finding the universities that are right for you. The advice applies to students going everywhere.

Think about your goals, your dreams, and what you want to do with your life. Think about the adventure of studying in a different country. The sights, the smells, the new experiences! Now, think of the realities. Can you afford to live in Rome? Will your love for Paris overcome the coolness of many Parisians? Can you deal with the gloomy skies of the London winter? Are you going to freeze in Boston? Are you going to fit into the "culture" of Los Angeles? Will you feel smothered by the heat and humidity of Singapore? Only you can figure this out.

Start with research. Expand your Mull List to include international options. Research all of your options: first online, then expand your research by sending away for the brochures from international universities. Find out about the cities where the universities are situated, the political situations in the country, and the history of the people. Convince your parents that you'll be okay so far away from home. If at all possible, consider visiting far-flung cities during school breaks and summertime. If you want to study in the United States, you'll have to write the *SAT I* or *ACT* exams, and these are given only in major Canadian cities at certain times of the year. We discuss these exams later in this chapter.

What You Need to Get Accepted to an International University

This, of course, depends on what school you're applying to, what program you want, what country you want to study in — and dozens of other parameters we can't even begin to list. If we were to outline every scenario (and the appropriate response), you likely wouldn't be able to finish this book before you got to university — even if you started reading in grade 9!

There are, however, a number of things you must do for just about every university regardless of the specific situation. The good news is that you probably already know most of these steps.

- ✔ **You have to apply, like everyone else.** Although the deadlines might be earlier considering you are dealing with universities in different countries, you must apply to the particular university. No matter how good you are (or how high your marks are), the university won't come to you.

- ✔ **You aren't treated the same as everyone else, even though you have to apply like everyone else.** If you apply to an international university, then *you* are the foreign student. You may be subject to language testing, higher fees than native students typically pay, and reduction (or complete elimination) of financial aid opportunities such as grants, loans, and scholarships.

- ✔ **You may need a student visa or other government paperwork allowing you to study in the particular country.** Luckily, these visas are usually easy to get if you've been accepted to a recognized educational institution such as a university. You can get details about visas from the university when you're accepted, or from the local consulate or embassy of the host country. EmbassyWeb provides links to many international embassies around the world at www.embassyweb.com.

- ✔ **You need your transcript to be sent directly to the international university.** Keep in mind that these documents must travel a long way, so you should arrange for them to be sent to the university well in advance. Other universities usually have deadlines for foreign students that are a month (or more) earlier than for domestic students.

- ✔ **You need to be tested.** If you're applying to an American college or university, you will be required to write a *standardized admissions test* — usually in the form of the *SAT I*. More about this test later in the chapter.

- ✔ **You need to speak the language.** Obviously, if you're planning on studying at an American or British university, you probably won't have many problems with the language. Sure, there are local words and phrases that you'll have to learn, but you'll likely have little difficulty understanding your professors, renting an apartment, buying groceries, or taking the bus to school. On the other hand, if you're studying in France, Germany, Italy, Spain, Hong Kong, or another country where English is not the primary language, you had better be fully bilingual by the time you start school. University will be difficult enough without a language barrier.

- ✔ **You need to have enough money.** The immigration officer will want to see some proof that you can support yourself while studying in his country. Bank statements, letters from your parents, a line of credit, or other forms of proof may be required to keep you away from the welfare rolls. Unless your work is directly related to your education and arranged by your university, there is little or no chance of working part time to supplement your income in most countries.

If you have citizenship in the country where you want to study, most of these issues don't apply. If one of your parents was born in the U.K., for example, you are entitled to apply for British citizenship. If you get it, you will automatically get European Union citizenship, which makes it easier to get into universities in other countries, work while studying, and even be considered for financial aid.

However, with advantages come responsibilities. Getting your Israeli passport, for example, might make it easier to study in Tel Aviv, but you may also have to do your mandatory armed forces service as soon as you enter the country, just like every other Israeli citizen your age. Many countries in Europe have mandatory military services for young people. Canadian kids are pretty lucky not to have to give up a year (or more) of their lives in the service of their country.

Student Visas and Work Permits

If you are lucky enough to be offered admission to an international college or university — and you've figured out you can handle the costs — the next step is securing the necessary paperwork to enter, study, and possibly work in a foreign country.

In most circumstances, this is simply a matter of completing a few forms. While sometimes time-consuming, getting a visa (and, possibly, a work permit) is a necessary part of your international school experience. Unless you secure your student visa you probably won't be able to enter the country to study.

If you fail to get a work permit, you may jeopardize your financial aid award since you will be unable to fulfill the work component of your financial aid commitment. It depends on whether your particular financial aid package at the particular university requires you to work on-campus, off-campus, or not at all.

Canadian students seeking admission to an American university should make complete and careful plans for meeting expenses. Immigration regulations and restrictions on off-campus summer employment make it imperative that students know exactly where they can obtain funds (e.g., family resources, government grants, or savings).

When you present your passport, you will be asked why you are coming to the country and whether you have enough money to cover the cost of your stay. You will probably be asked to prove this with a bank statement or sponsor's letter. You will also be asked to prove that you have a confirmed place at the particular educational institution. Be prepared to answer a number of other questions about yourself and your intentions during your stay in the country.

Staying healthy in a new country

If you study in the United States or abroad, you must ensure you have adequate health coverage. In most cases, your provincial health-care program will not adequately cover you from the moment you leave Canada. Many universities must be assured you have proper health-care coverage *before* they will confirm your admission. This extended health care may be quite expensive and must be budgeted for when considering overall costs of university abroad.

Depending on the university (and the country), supplemental health-care fees can easily reach over $1,000 (and more) per academic year. You must add these fees to your overall university costs calculation.

It is also very important for you to have suitable accommodation while you are studying. The standard of your academic work and your health can suffer if your living conditions are not satisfactory. In many areas of America and Europe there is a serious shortage of off-campus student accommodation, so you must start making arrangements as soon as you have been accepted at the particular university.

Most adult residents in Europe are subject to taxation based on residence. For example, U.K. residents have to pay local council tax, which is directly related to the property they occupy. In certain types of accommodation (notably university residences), full-time students do not have to pay the tax because the property is exempt. In other types of accommodation (such as nearby flats or student apartments), however, students will be charged the tax. When in doubt, ask at your university's international students centre or ask your university counsellor.

Finally, when the immigration officer has checked your documents and is satisfied that you are a genuine student, you will get a stamp in your passport showing the length of time you are allowed to stay and other immigration conditions.

Most universities have departments that provide advice and counselling to prospective international students. Check out if your intended university does this early in your research process. You get formal assistance from these departments when you are accepted at the university or college, but there's no reason not to chat with these folks earlier on.

Welcome to America

Most Canadian students who go to an international university go to the United States, so we will focus the rest of the chapter on going to an American school. However, the advice remains the same if you wish to go to university in another country. Find the general information you need; research your particular universities; find out what it takes to get in and how much it costs; make sure you have what it takes on both counts; and apply!

Information sources

You may not have access to the wide variety of directories and reference books that Americans find on the shelves of their neighbourhood bookstores and libraries. Some directories are sold internationally, but you may have to search, or ask in a bookstore, to find them.

One excellent information source comes from the College Board, the most prolific purveyor of material to help students get into college. *The College Handbook Foreign Student Supplement* is a condensed version of the College Board's huge directory of American colleges. This supplement comes with a 30-page, clearly written explanation of many things you'll need to know about becoming a U.S. student. If you can't find it for sale where you live, write to College Board Publications, Box 886, New York, NY 10101-6992.

Other good sources of information include:

- **U.S. embassies:** The U.S. government, through its embassies, operates advising centres in countries from Albania to Zimbabwe for non-citizens seeking information about the United States. People at these centres know a lot about U.S. colleges and regularly deal with requests for college information. Check with a U.S. embassy or consulate for the location of an advising centre near you. The embassies also have information about U.S. college representatives visiting their countries to recruit students.

- **Canadian universities:** Some universities in Canada have close relationships with U.S. colleges. All universities are part of the worldwide higher education community. It's very likely that a Canadian university near you will have information on U.S. colleges, probably in its library.

- **Visiting professors:** U.S. college professors love to travel to Canada. We speak the same language (mostly) and Canadian cities are comparatively crime-free, inexpensive, and far less polluted. They love to do research in Canada. And they love to talk. (They earn much of their incomes by talking.) If you know of U.S. professors working or travelling near you, ask for some of their time to talk about U.S. colleges. Chances are good that your request will be enthusiastically granted.

- **Your friends:** This is the same advice we offered earlier. Talk to friends whose opinions you respect. If you have friends who have been to the United States, ask them about U.S. colleges. Although not the last word in college information, your friends are good information sources.

Can you get in?

Getting into the top schools can be very difficult. When you apply for admission to an American university, you're often competing in a much larger pool of applicants than you might otherwise do in Canada. Table 17-1 shows a profile of the graduating class of 2004 at Stanford University, one of the more prestigious schools in the United States. You can see that not only was there quite a large pool of applicants, but also that their high school and SAT I marks were top-notch.

Table 17-1	Profile of the Stanford Graduating Class of 2004
Item	*Number or Percentage of Class*
Number of freshman applicants	18,363
Number of freshmen admitted	2,425
General admission rate	13%
Number of freshmen who accepted offer of admission	1,599
Overall admission rate	8.7%
Percentage of applicants who were in the top 10% of their high school graduating class	90%
Percentage of applicants who were in the top 20% of their high school graduating class	97%
Percentage of applicants who achieved top SAT I verbal scores of 700 to 800	72%
Percentage of applicants who achieved top SAT I math scores of 700 to 800	76%
Percentage of applicants who had a high school *grade point average (GPA)* of at least 3.8	76%

American schools have very different admission procedures than do Canadian schools. Besides your high school marks, you need to score well on your SAT I, write a great admission essay, have a superior interview with a university admissions officer, itemize related extracurricular activities, and other important things. Not every college or university requires all these components, but many of them do. Ask your counsellor and consult the Web site of the particular university to find out exactly what rules apply to you.

This is why it's really important to start your American college or university application process early. Really early. In fact, there are some colleges in America that have early admission in November and regular admission in December. Stanford University, for example, had an application deadline in the 2001/2002 school year for *early decision* on November 1, 2000 — and an application deadline for regular admission of December 15, significantly earlier than Canadian universities.

Some schools release statistics that break down from which parts of the world their applicants hail. Others aren't so generous, however, so it pays to ask. Figure 17-1 illustrates the geographic profile of the 2000/2001 freshman class at Stanford University, with a section that breaks down the foreign component of the class — the number of students from countries outside the U.S.

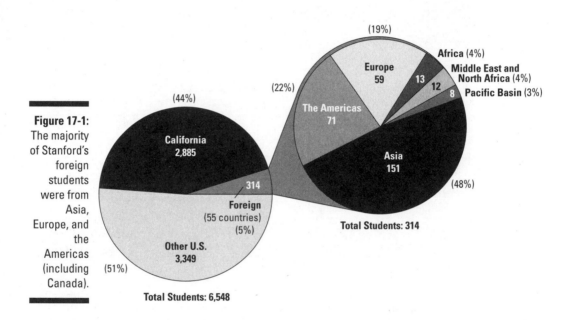

Figure 17-1: The majority of Stanford's foreign students were from Asia, Europe, and the Americas (including Canada).

Canadian applicants are categorized under "The Americas." This means that a maximum of 71 of a total of Stanford's 6,548 graduates were Canadian. This represents slightly more than 1 percent.

Can We See Your SAT I Scores, Please?

You've probably heard something about the SAT I test. It's pretty much required by every four-year college and university in the States, so it's really important to know about it if you're interested in attending an American school.

What is the SAT I and why do I have to take it?

The *SAT I* is a three-hour standardized exam that tests students' ability to handle complex math and "verbal" (that is, English-language) questions. The test is given in SAT testing centres (usually gymnasiums and other large halls) across America and in a few places in Canada and other countries. Usually administered on a Saturday morning, the SAT I is given at regular intervals throughout the school year — but you must sign up for it beforehand. You just can't walk into the testing centre and take the test.

You have to take the SAT I test because it is likely an admission requirement of the college you are interested in attending. Unlike Canadian universities, which use your high school marks as the chief admission criterion, American colleges usually require the SAT I for admission. The SAT I is a standard way of measuring a student's ability to do college-level work.

Nobody knows why this difference between Canadian and American universities exists, but it does — so you have to deal with the weirdness as best you can.

Since courses and grading standards vary widely from school to school, scores on standardized tests — such as the SAT I — help admission officers compare your academic achievements with those of students from different schools — and different countries.

American colleges look at many other things besides your SAT I score when making admission decisions. These other factors include your high school record, an application essay you must write and submit, teacher and counsellor recommendations, interviews, and extracurricular activities.

What abilities does the SAT I test?

The SAT I is designed to measure your verbal and math *reasoning* abilities. There's no memorization involved. The point is to discover how well you think. In theory, your SAT I scores predict how well you'll do at college. As an added benefit, knowing how you scored in relation to other students also lets you (and the college) compare you directly with other students. No pressure, though!

The three-hour SAT I test is made up of:

- ✔ **Three verbal sections:** Two 30-minute sections and one 15-minute section.
- ✔ **Three math sections:** Two 30-minute sections and one 15-minute section.

✔ **One 30-minute *equating section*, verbal or math:** This section does not count toward your score. Rather, it helps make sure that scores on new versions of the SAT I are roughly comparable to scores on previous versions of the test. (This is necessary because the test has gone through lots of different versions in its time, and the organizers need to make sure everyone is being tested, and graded, fairly.) You won't know when you're writing this section of the test, however — it's not marked. So, try to do well on everything.

The SAT I does *not* measure your motivation or drive, your creativity, any foreign-language skills, or other knowledge not specifically asked for on the test. It does not ask about any special talents you have. Despite the fact that these qualities will contribute to your success in college (not to mention your success throughout the rest of your life), the SAT I does not test for them.

What do my SAT I scores tell admissions officers about me?

Your SAT I scores tell admissions officers how you compare with other students who took that same test. Since all SAT I scores are reported on a scale between 200 to 800, test marks for an average student will likely fall roughly in the middle of this range. Let's say your verbal and math scores were each about 500, college admissions officers know that you scored better than approximately half the students who took the test. (To put another spin on things, you scored *worse* than the other half of students who took that particular test.)

Since no single test score can reveal everything about how you tested, percentiles and score ranges are also included on the score reports sent to colleges. Admissions officers can use all this information to evaluate your test score.

Does the SAT I really show how well I'll do in college?

The people who run the SAT I tests know that no single test can predict with 100 percent certainty what any student's grades will be in college. Rather, colleges use SAT I scores to help *estimate* how well a given student is likely to do at its school.

Let's say a student writes the SAT I test and scores 600 on each of the math and verbal components, for a total of 1,200 points. In the first year of college, the same student averages an overall *B-minus* in her courses. The college simply links these two pieces of information, possibly factoring in other details such as the college program she's enrolled in and her high school grade point average (GPA). From this, the college draws some conclusions on which it might base future admissions decisions.

Based on historical data, students who achieve a 600/600 score on their SAT I exams will average a *B-minus* at their college. If the college in this example wants to attract only students who will score *B*+ averages or higher while there, it may raise its SAT I score minimum to admit students who test a bit better. If the school wants more students and is satisfied with *C* average students, it may lower the minimum SAT I scores it accepts.

But how well will you, in particular, do in your first year based on your SAT I scores? Colleges can hypothesize and draw all the conclusions they like, but how well *you* do boils down to a few things: how hard you work, how effectively you study, and how difficult your program is. It also depends on your own capability — *that* is the only factor the SAT I measures. Like an IQ test, the SAT I rates your potential. What you do with it is up to you.

How can I register for the SAT I, when can I take it, and how much does it cost?

If you're currently in high school, the best person to ask about taking the SAT I is your high school counsellor. You can also call the folks at the College Board, who run the SAT I testing program, at (609) 771-7600 between 8 a.m. and 8:45 p.m., Monday through Friday, Eastern time (summer hours are 8 a.m. to 5:45 p.m.). Testing schedules are released in August for the following academic year and all the details are put together in a booklet, which is distributed in September to high schools across the country. The tests are generally held from October through June of the following year — usually mid-October, early November, early December, late January, late March, early May, and early June. Check with your counsellor or the College Board to be sure. There is no testing during the summer months. This means that if you need to get an early decision, you either have to take the test in October or by the previous June.

The SAT I costs $24 US.

These examinations are administered in cities all over the world several times each year. All applicable tests must be completed by the December *preceding* the September of desired enrollment. You must make your own arrangements to take the test, registering at least eight weeks before the actual test date and instructing that the results be sent directly to the particular universities of your choice.

Some American colleges and universities have *early decision* deadlines as early as *November 1*. Since it can take up to eight weeks for your test scores to be processed, you must write the SAT I in *the previous school year* to ensure compliance with the university's application requirements.

How Much of the Green Stuff Do You Need?

We've said it before and we'll say it again: Canadian universities are quite a bargain.

When you compare the price range of $2,000 to $5,500 (in Canadian money) for each year of a four-year Canadian university to the costs to attend a college or university in another country, you will be in for a shock. Not only are the well-known American colleges far more expensive than this — first-year undergraduate Harvard University cost more than $29,000 US in the 2001/2002 school year — you have to pay for "extras" such as residence and health-care insurance as well.

Assuming the exchange rate is approximately $1.50 Canadian to one American dollar, a year of tuition alone at Harvard will cost you approximately $29,000 times 1.50, or a whopping $43,500 in Canadian funds!

Tuition at Stanford is a bit less. The sticker price of each undergraduate year in the 2000/2001 school year was $24,441 US — or about $36,662 Canadian. Then we add the other costs, all in American dollars. Room and board came to approximately $8,030, while the school estimated students spent about $1,080 on books. With added personal expenses (including things such as entertainment, snacks, laundry) of $1,620, the grand total came to $35,171 US, or $52,756 Canadian! See, we said it was expensive!

Even state colleges (heavily subsidized by the taxpayers in the particular state) are comparatively expensive. As you can see in Table 17-2, for the 2001/2002 academic year Florida State University (www.fsu.edu) charged its out-of-state students more than *four times* the tuition it charged its in-state students. This meant that, even though everything else was the same cost for in-state versus out-of-state students, the final totals showed that out-of-state students paid nearly *double* what in-state students paid.

Keep in mind that the amounts listed above are in U.S. dollars and are estimated costs only. Most students will have additional miscellaneous expenses associated with campus living such as long-distance phone bills, pizza, and laundry. And, of course, you have to get there, which means adding the price of return airfare for probably two trips a year. These costs may add up to an additional $3,000 or more per year, depending on lifestyle, budget, and appetite.

Table 17-2	Annual Basic Costs at Florida State University, 2001/2002 Academic Year	
Item	*Cost for Florida Residents*	*Cost for Non-Florida Residents*
Tuition	$2,379	$9,716
Housing	$2,828	$2,828
Food	$2,322	$2,322
Books/supplies	$700	$700
Total	$8,229	$15,566

Few students who apply to Harvard or Stanford (or any other American college or university) have to pay the full amount. Every American college and university has an elaborate system of scholarships, grants, bursaries, loans, work-study, and other financial aid programs to reduce tuition costs to eligible students.

Canadians aren't eligible to get U.S.-government-backed financial aid such as *Stafford Loans* (also known as *FFEL Loans*, or *Direct Loans*) or *Pell Grants* (worth just over $3,000 in the 2001/2002 school year). Both the Stafford Loans and the Pell Grants are the two major sources of money for American students.

More bad news: You're not eligible for Perkins Loans (tuition loans financed at 5 percent interest) or PLUS Loans (an acronym for Parents' Loans for Undergraduate Students) either. Again, these programs are available to American students only.

The good news is that you are eligible to apply the money you have in your Registered Education Savings Plan (RESP) as well as any provincial student loan amounts you're able to secure. This means that you stand a fighting chance of paying for your American university education, if you can get in.

Some financial aid is available

Does the name Hakeem Olajuwon mean anything to you? He's one of the best-known professional basketball players in the United States. He came to the U.S. on a student visa more than two decades ago. Although he didn't complete his degree, because the NBA drafted him after his junior year, the three years he did finish were paid for in their entirety by the college he attended, the University of Houston. Olajuwon received what's known as a *free ride* — three years of college free — because he was an outstanding basketball player.

Athletics is one way of getting a tuition discount, or having tuition waived altogether. Good basketball players from other countries are in demand by those U.S. colleges where winning basketball games is a high priority. Discounts (also called scholarships) are available for other sports as well. Many Canadian students, for example, are riding free at U.S. colleges because they're excellent hockey players.

But you don't have to be an athlete to get financial aid. If you're an attractive student — that is, someone a college would like very much to have in its student body — the college will offer you some of its own money in the form of a tuition discount. Just like American students, you won't have to pay the full sticker price.

Many colleges also offer aid to Canadians based on their financial need. They have special forms for you, different from the financial aid applications used by U.S. citizens, because they want different information about you. In addition to requesting information about your family's income and assets, the form will ask such things as the source of your emergency funds in the United States. If you ask for a financial aid form, a college will send you one. Some send it automatically along with your application for admission.

However, as we mentioned before, Canadians are not eligible for U.S. government aid — Pell Grants, Stafford Loans, SEOGs, and the other stuff. These programs are for U.S. citizens only.

A good source of financial aid information is *Funding for U.S. Study: A Guide for Foreign Nationals,* from the Institute of International Education, 809 UN Plaza, New York, NY 10017-3580.

Additional U.S. financial aid resources

Just in case you think we haven't given you enough to work with already, these are five excellent financial aid information sources you can find online.

- ✔ **Calculators:** Free, accurate, and completely confidential ways of understanding college education financing using their "what-if" exercises: www.finaid.org/finaid/calculators/other-calculators.html.
- ✔ **College Board:** A national association of schools and colleges whose aim is to facilitate the student transition to higher education: www.collegeboard.org.
- ✔ **FinAid:** The Financial Aid Information Page: www.finaid.org.
- ✔ **Project EASI:** Assistance to students and families in planning for education beyond high school, choosing among alternatives, and financing these choices: http://easi.ed.gov/.
- ✔ **The Student Guide:** Financial aid information from the U.S. Department of Education: www.ed.gov/prog_info/SFA/Student Guide.

Chapter 18

Staying Out of Debt

∙∙∙

In This Chapter

▶ Planning ahead for the next four (or more) years

▶ Budgeting while you're at school

▶ Hitting the books and pounding the pavement: working while going to school

▶ Understanding summer job trade-offs

∙∙∙

This chapter deals with the nitty-gritty aspects of dodging debt during and after your university years. Most Canadian students have at least *some* debt when they leave university. In some cases, this can't be avoided. In other cases, students get into debt because they can't (or won't) plan ahead for what is, any way you slice it, a costly educational experience. This chapter explains how to stay out of debt so you can concentrate on learning all you can from university.

People Don't Plan to Fail, They Fail to Plan

Some students amass a staggering amount of debt after three or four years of university. How does this happen?

Today's students pay appreciably more money for university tuition in Canada than their parents did. This is largely due to the fact that provincial governments are subsidizing university education a great deal less than they used to do. It's not just that inflation has eroded the value of the dollar and so a university education therefore *looks* more expensive. University education *is* more expensive for the average student because he has to pay *a greater share* of it on his own.

Save early, save often

In Chapter 1, we mention that students should be reading this book in grade 4. We know, however, that most students in grade 4 have other things to do than plan for their post-secondary education. This is a real shame. If you start planning in grade 4 (when you are probably about nine years old), there is every reason to believe that you and your family can afford just about any university in Canada you choose. And, if you really get going early, you might be able to afford many American universities as well.

But — and it's a big but — you have to start planning early for the magic of compound interest to really work. By planning ahead — no matter how late in the game you start — you at least know what you're up against in terms of staying out of debt.

Find, win, or inherit money

The first step toward staying out of debt (and this holds true for any large purchase, whether it be a car, a house, or a university education) is to understand how much you can afford to spend and construct a workable budget to make it happen. This entire section of the book is dedicated to financing your university education. The options you have for financing your university education are:

- ✔ Savings (including government-assisted plans)
- ✔ Bursaries
- ✔ Grants
- ✔ Loans
- ✔ Scholarships
- ✔ Working part-time while attending school

You will be in a much better position if you start saving early for your university education. We talk about this type of long-term planning in Chapter 13. However, assuming you've gone through all the steps (including reading Chapter 13), you may find that you still don't have enough money for your university education. It is for this reason that we talk about student loans in Chapter 14, scholarships in Chapter 15, and co-operative work programs in Chapter 16. If you haven't read through these chapters and worked out some of the examples, why not do that now? We'll wait right here.

Budgeting 101: Your First Course

As a very rough estimate, you will want to budget at least $12,000 per academic year if you stay in residence at university, and at least $6,000 if you stay at home. Remember that university costs more than just tuition. To your basic tuition costs, you need to add:

✔ Books (between $500 and $1,000 per year);

✔ Food (between $0 and $3,000 per year, depending on whether or not you can sponge off your parents);

✔ Miscellaneous university fees (including incidental fees, health centre fees, and athletic centre fees);

✔ Extracurricular or non-academic costs (including going to the occasional movie, transportation, clothing, and other lifestyle costs).

Your total? Likely between $7,000 and $12,000.

That's not all it costs

Taking all these costs into consideration, you also have to factor in the cost of living in the city where the university is located. Large cities cost noticeably more to live in than small cities do. If you multiply this $7,000 to $12,000 estimate by the three or four (or more) years, you are looking at spending somewhere between $21,000 and $48,000 on your university education.

Sounds like a lot, doesn't it? It is, but it's doable.

It costs even more if you go abroad

These estimates are for the Canadian university experience, and will likely double (or triple) if you want to get your university education from an American, British, French, or other international university. We discuss international fees in Chapter 17, but suffice it to say that students can easily spend $20,000 US (and possibly much more) *per year* studying abroad. Fortunately, most federal and provincial loans available to Canadian students studying at Canadian universities are also available to Canadian students studying abroad.

However, rather than trying to pay off $28,000 worth of debt for a four-year Canadian degree (assuming you live at home), you will be paying off at least $80,000 US worth of debt for a four-year degree abroad. And you won't be living at home during this time, so your ability to sponge off the parental units will be somewhat limited.

If you plan ahead, though, even this huge amount of money is achievable through a combination of savings, bursaries, grants, loans, and scholarships. If you get to your final year of high school and your educational savings account has the grand total sum of $39.53 in it, it's probably dawning on you that you're going to have a financial challenge on your hands to afford university.

Building Your Budget

If this is your first time constructing a budget, relax, it's relatively easy. Take a look at the worksheet in Figure 18-1. You can write on a separate piece of paper or use the one in the book — it's up to you. Fill in the associated costs for your top three university choices, most of which can be found on the universities' Web sites, which we list in the "Directory of Universities and Colleges" at the back of the book.

The difference between what money you have available to you for your university education and what this education will cost (based on your research) is the amount of money you're going to have to come up with above and beyond what you already have. And, depending on your own personal financial situation, as well as the financial situation of your parents, this money may come from bursaries, grants, loans, or scholarships.

- **Tuition fees:** No matter how a university calculates its tuition fees (by course, credit, hour, workload), you should count on a range of $3,500 to $5,500 for a full course load.

- **Books and materials:** This cost will vary significantly by program studied. For example, a civil engineering student will probably need to purchase a CSA-approved hard hat, safety boots, protective glasses, and other equipment necessary for the job. A chemistry student will have to purchase a lab coat and at least one pair of protective glasses. A management student may have to purchase a pricey financial calculator to keep up in class. Many universities approximate these costs to be about $1,000 a year.

- **Incidental fees:** These include items such as student government, college fees, athletic centre fees, campus health fees (or health insurance, if you're studying in America or abroad), computer access fees for the campus-wide network or reaching the Net, library fees, and others. Some universities lump all of these into one "super fee"; others break it all down for you. Plan on at least $300 for this, possibly much more.

- **Room and board:** This will be a major expense for you, unless you live at home. Even then, your parents may ask you to chip in a few bucks every week for the food bill. Your university meal plan may seem expensive — and they usually are — but in many cases universities give students little choice but to accept the plan as given. Add an extra $4,000 to $6,000 to your budget.

- **Computer and computer accessories:** Ownership of a computer is pretty much expected at university. You may have used a typewriter during your high school years, but university is strictly a computer environment. Some universities require that their students have a computer; others merely suggest it. There are even a few schools that include a new

Item	University 1	University 2	University 3
1. Tuition fees	_____	_____	_____
2. Books and materials	_____	_____	_____
3. Incidental fees	_____	_____	_____
Student government	_____	_____	_____
College	_____	_____	_____
Athletic	_____	_____	_____
Health insurance	_____	_____	_____
Computer access	_____	_____	_____
Library	_____	_____	_____
4. Room and board			
Residence	_____	_____	_____
Meal plan	_____	_____	_____
Laundry	_____	_____	_____
Household stuff	_____	_____	_____
5. Computer			
Hardware	_____	_____	_____
Software	_____	_____	_____
Supplies and materials	_____	_____	_____
6. General living expenses			
Clothing	_____	_____	_____
Transportation	_____	_____	_____
Parking	_____	_____	_____
Insurance	_____	_____	_____
7. Entertainment and personal expenses			
Movies/books/magazines	_____	_____	_____
Medical (including birth control pills and condoms)	_____	_____	_____
Contacts/glasses	_____	_____	_____
Miscellaneous	_____	_____	_____
Total	_____	_____	_____

Figure 18-1:
A sample university budget.

computer in first-year fees. Whatever your particular situation, you should budget for a powerful enough computer to get you through the next three or four years of research, word processing — and, yes, budgets.

And while we're on the subject of computers, don't forget to budget for consumables, repairs (or extended warranties), and other hidden costs. With good-quality printers selling for between $99 and $200 but printer cartridges retailing for $35 to $50, it's pretty obvious that the price of these consumables can quickly add up. Depending on your program, you may go through a cartridge a month — and, during peak essay writing times, possibly even more.

While you can get by using the school's computers, which are usually scattered in strategic areas such as libraries and other common areas, you'll be much happier with your own, if you can possibly afford it.

✔ **General living expenses:** These are expenses you have regardless of whether you attend university. These expenses include clothing and transportation (buses, trains, or planes if you live far away, and of course automotive expenses if you're lucky enough to have a car). Add some extra for warmer clothes if you are going to a more northerly climate. Just because you would pay these whether you went to university or not doesn't mean you don't have to budget for them.

Things to watch out for are expensive items such as car insurance (for the under-25 set, car insurance can easily run into the thousands of dollars). Monthly parking expenses on some campuses in large Canadian cities can easily run $100 or more. Even if you have a car, it may make sense not to use it unless it's really cold or some of your friends can chip in for the gas and parking. After all, you're on a budget.

✔ **Entertainment and personal expenses:** You've got to have a life, even at university. Don't forget to budget for those things you love — even if they have nothing to do with your studies. There's nothing wrong with taking a break to go see a movie, or taking a salsa dance class, or even taking a vacation during reading week. In fact, it might be necessary in order to keep you sane! Just make sure you factor the costs for these extras into your budget.

Getting a Part-time Job

To hear your parents or grandparents tell their tall tales of when they went to school, you might wonder how anyone actually *survived* their educational experience, let alone enjoyed it. Walking 20 kilometres uphill in the snow every morning to get to the bus stop is only one variation of the hardships that parents and grandparents claim to have performed on a daily basis in times gone by.

In truth, while it is generally easier to live in the modern era, it is far more expensive to *enjoy* it. Consequently, many students choose to (or are forced to) work during their academic year. This is something your parents might not have had to consider.

The trade-off: Higher marks versus more money

Working during your academic year is a trade-off between getting enough money to cover at least some of your expenses and doing well in your academic courses. There is no doubt that working during your academic year cuts into the time you would otherwise have to study. You might think that students who work hard at jobs while they are at school have lower marks than students who don't work. Interestingly, there is very little evidence to support this theory. There *is* evidence, however, to support a different theory: A healthy balance of work, study, and play makes you into a better student — and a better-rounded adult.

Some universities, especially those in the United States, *expect* you to work while at school, as part of a formal work-study component in a financial aid package. You perform certain tasks at the school (such as refiling books in the library, issuing tickets at events, or other clerical, administrative, or labour-intensive jobs) to "work off" part of your debt load.

In Canada, few schools use this system, but many students supplement their income by working part-time on- or off-campus. From delivering pizzas to lifeguarding at the athletic complex, there are hundreds, if not thousands, of jobs available for students on and around campus.

A great place to start looking for jobs is the campus careers or job centre, where employment opportunities (both on and off-campus) are listed. Depending on your qualifications and experience, these jobs can be relatively lucrative and will help provide at least some pocket money while you study.

The other trade-off: Earned money versus more aid money

Working part-time during university may affect your eligibility to receive financial aid. The provincial and federal student loan systems are based on *need*. If you are working — that is, earning money — the government thinks you need *less* of *its* money.

If you're thinking about getting a job while at school

Working during university is a good idea only if you can balance your academic activities with your working life. There is absolutely no point in working yourself into a frazzle so you can attend university if it makes you miss out on the university experience entirely.

Working during your academic year may interfere with your schoolwork and bring your marks down. This usually happens when you bite off more than you can chew and work more hours than you realistically should. Depending on your course load, program, and other factors, you should probably limit yourself to no more than 10 to 15 hours per week (and probably less until you fully understand what university life is all about).

Many students make the mistake of working to support themselves to the detriment of their ability to study, defeating the exact purpose of why they are in university to begin with.

Talk to your university counsellor or other advisor about job opportunities on campus as soon as you can. Many students coming into university fresh from high school mistakenly assume that the new workload is similar to what they have encountered in high school. In fact, a rather deceptive part of university is that students frequently have far *fewer* hours actually in class than they did in high school. For every one hour of university class you have, you should expect to spend *at least* three hours going over the class notes, reviewing the material, and studying the topic just to keep up.

It is very common in the first two or three months of university life to become so overwhelmed by the sheer workload that life quickly comes to a screeching halt. December exams (mid-term exams for full-year courses and final exams for half-year ones) are the first signs of real trouble. Some students find themselves failing out by Christmas and decide to leave university even before their first year is over. These students are called *Christmas grads,* a not-so-funny moniker for the unfortunate souls who either let homework and studying slip too long or couldn't otherwise keep up with the often-crushing workload in first year.

Ironically, this could lead to a situation where the more you work, the less financial aid you are entitled to receive. Speak with a qualified tax lawyer, accountant, or other business professional to ascertain what your exact situation is with respect to working while receiving student loans. If you are not receiving any form of student assistance, this does not apply to you; however, many student loans are affected by how much work you're doing. The moral of the story is to always research your particular situation as best you can and talk with as many informed people as possible.

Getting a Summer Job

Although getting a summer job is more or less expected of today's students, there are trade-offs involved in the type of summer job you select. As unbelievable as it may seem, some students start thinking about their summer job as soon as they begin university in September. They construct their résumé, verify their references, and start checking out the job boards at the career centre. Why the rush?

You should start thinking about your summer job as soon as you can, provided you have your academic work under control. Consider the trade-offs between accepting a potentially lucrative (but mundane) job versus one that, though it may pay relatively poorly, is nonetheless in your field of study. Pay a visit to your school's career centre early on in the year and drop in often to learn about important summer job opportunities.

If conditions are right, a part-time job on-campus during the year can transform itself into a full-fledged summer job. You might work for a chemistry professor, cleaning the lab for a couple of hours a week during the school year, and then carry on as an assistant to one of the professor's graduate students over the summer.

Many career centres have special clinics to teach students how to look for summer jobs during the school year. Find out when they are held and attend them.

The trade-off in choosing a summer job is the dilemma between gaining valuable experience and making valuable cash. One job may offer great experience in your program or field of study, but another may offer the chance to increase the payments on your student loan and lessen your debt. It's a tough call. Planting trees in northern British Columbia may pay well, but it won't help you become a better doctor or lawyer or mathematician. However, planting trees at $20 an hour will certainly help you pay down your student loans so you can *afford* to be a doctor or lawyer or mathematician. What should you do?

We suggest you go for the experience. It will help you in the long run, and besides, if you've read any of the chapters in this part of the book, you've got a couple of ideas about financing your post-secondary education that will (hopefully) minimize the amount of student loans you need to take out in the first place.

Even though you may get a terrific summer job in your chosen career field, you should know that wages paid to university students are relatively low — usually far lower than what blue collar and/or manual workers earn. So while all your friends who couldn't get into university because they were goofing off are making great money at the car plant bolting bumpers onto next year's car models, you're slaving away washing out smelly test tubes and beakers for $8 an hour. It might not seem fair now, but your university degree *will* come in handy some day, when you graduate, get hired at a major pharmaceutical company, and buy your first car — maybe one that your buddies assembled.

The experience you gain from washing out beakers or helping to run the lab will be invaluable for your first "real" job. Employers look for employees with experience in the field in question. If you plan to be a forester, then having a job planting trees in northern British Columbia is certainly worth considering. However, if you intend to be a pharmacist, planting trees may not have much value to a future employer.

A Last Look at Co-op Education

Co-operative education programs (or *co-op programs,* as they are better known) are an interesting hybrid between academic work and real-life experience. We discuss co-op programs in detail in Chapter 16, so have a look back if you skipped over this section or want a refresher. When considering working during your academic years, you might also consider a university that offers co-op job placements.

While it takes longer to get a degree in a co-op program (since you work as well as study), you gain valuable work experience that's *directly related* to your area of study and chosen career. Not only are co-op students able to supplement their income with a regular paycheque for their co-op work term, they also gain valuable experience and make important contacts in the job market. It is not uncommon for co-op work placements to become permanent jobs after graduation. It's something to think about.

Despite their obvious advantages, not all universities offer co-op programs.

Part V
Dotting the "i"s and Crossing the "t"s: The Final Details

The 5th Wave — By Rich Tennant

©RICHTENNANT

"Ahh — it's that time of year again when students on the waiting list fill the tree outside the admissions office."

In this part . . .

This is the rest of the story. This part is about what happens after the application process is over. When will you hear back? What do the letters from the universities mean? What should you do next?

Chapter 19 helps you organize all your replies and figure out your next steps. If you got into your first-choice university, great! If not, you need to be able to properly assess your various options. Chapter 20 takes you through the all-important rethinking step. Too many students don't bother to stop and think before taking the final plunge into their university education. We're here to make sure you do what's best for *you*.

Chapter 19

Congratulations, You're Accepted! Now What?

· ·

In This Chapter

▶ Knowing when to expect the acceptance letters

▶ Understanding the university's decision

▶ Giving each school a second look

▶ Wising up to the Waiting List

▶ Deciding what to do if some universities want a deposit

▶ Taking the next step if the news isn't good

· ·

The work is over. Now, you've reached the fun part. Four of the six universities to which you applied — including one of the two you like best — have accepted you. The other put you on a Waiting List, and the final university flatly refused you. After a few weeks of nervousness waiting for the mail, you're basking in the glow that comes with knowing you're really wanted. Now you get to decide which of the four universities you'll favour with your presence next fall.

Now the Fun Begins

Once again, you're in control. It's just like the old days, way back last year, when universities were filling your mailbox with pretty brochures pleading with you to apply. For a while there, you relinquished control of the process to the people who were considering your applications. Now you're in control again. Four universities want you, but you can enrol at only one. Within days of their acceptance letter's arrival, all four probably will be in touch reminding you how wonderful they are.

For some of your friends, getting letters is not so much fun. A few of their top-choice universities said no. They opened the mail to find the dreaded one-page letter that begins, "We regret to inform you . . . ."

Some of your friends have only themselves to blame. They didn't do all the work that you did. They haven't been studying as hard as you to get those top marks in the advanced-level courses. They didn't prepare their applications with tender loving care. They didn't bother following the simple instructions for reporting information about themselves. They didn't seek out friendly teachers or counsellors to write recommendations. They didn't read this book.

You might think you're just luckier than your friends. Well, maybe luck played a tiny role in your success. Much more important, though, was the record you compiled through your years of high school — the good grades, the tough courses, the commitment to activities. Without your solid record, luck would have been meaningless.

Okay, savour the glow for a day or two. Then sit down and start thinking again. You need to decide where you'll go to university.

The News Starts to Arrive

Throughout the first section of this book, we assumed some things about you to help illustrate the process of finding your right universities. You start with the vast field of 51 Canadian universities and many more colleges and technical institutes (plus a number of universities abroad, if you want an international education).

Eventually you decide on two that you really like, plus two more where you think that you can be happy and thrive as a student. You apply to all four. Then you follow this book's good advice and apply to two more — a *reach* school, where your academic credentials are close but marginal, and a *safety net* school that will be there for you if all else fails.

You are aware, after you mail your six applications (by January at the latest, unless your school does it for you in December, depending on how and when you apply), that you have a long wait ahead of you for the news. Of the schools at the head of your list, Top-choice U has a *rolling admission* (deciding on applications as they arrive) and Favourite University announces its admission decisions in late April. You really want to go to Top-choice or Favourite — if you can get in and afford it. So, regardless of when you hear from the other four, you know that your final decision will not be made until spring.

The safety net works

The first university you hear from is U Safety, your backup school. In early February, a few weeks after sending your application, you receive a letter from

Safety saying you're in. Not a surprise — but, at least, a big relief. You're now certain that, when next fall rolls around, you can ask professors more interesting questions than, "Do you want fries with that?"

You're not Top-choice's top choice

The envelope from Top-choice U is too thin to be an offer of admission. You open it and feel discouraged. But, wait. It doesn't say *no* after all — it says *maybe*. Remember, Top-choice uses a rolling admission — deciding on applications as they arrive — so only the very cream of the crop will be admitted early. Others, including you, get placed in the *maybe* pile.

While Top-choice says it cannot accept you for admission at this time, it also tells you that, if you're interested, the school will put you on a *Waiting List* in case any vacancies occur. Enclosed is a card you must sign and return to get on the Waiting List. (We're using the term *Waiting List* with capital letters because that's how most universities use it. It's an entity with an official name: The Waiting List.) You're disappointed but not shocked. You knew that getting into Top-choice would be tough. You're pleased that it didn't reject you outright but instead said, "maybe later."

One you didn't make

You're not surprised that you haven't heard yet from the other three universities. You know that Favourite University, Threebie Tech, and Long-reach U all announce their decisions in late April. By April 30, you've heard nothing. Your fingernails are getting a little frayed around the edges, and you think about calling the post office to ask whether it's delivering your mail. Then comes the letter from Long-reach, the school where your credentials are borderline but you applied just in case.

The news isn't good. Long-reach says no. There's no mention of the Waiting List. The letter simply says no. Things aren't looking too good right now. But you're still waiting to hear from the others.

At last! Hooray!

Happily, the word comes the very next day from Threebie Tech, a polytechnic university where you could be happy if your top two choices turn you down. Threebie decided that you would be a fine addition to its campus. That's two out of four, so far. It's not perfect, but it's not bad.

Within the next week, you hear from Fourmost U, the other university on your list in case the top two say no. Fourmost wants you. Your smile starts to get wider. Three out of five is pretty good. But you're also a little worried because you haven't heard back from Favourite University, one of your top two choices.

The next day, finally, the letter from Favourite University arrives. Your eyes start to sparkle a bit when you see how thick the envelope is. It has to contain more than a one-page rejection letter. You rip open the envelope, pull out the first page, and start to read: "I am delighted to inform you that Favourite University is offering you admission to its first year class in September. . . ." Your first reaction is "Whew!" Then the little sparkle becomes a golden glow that spreads all over. And you say to yourself, "Congratulations."

But what about Top-choice?

It's time to decide which university you're going to, but Top-choice still has you on the Waiting List. What do you do? Well, you move on and reconsider all your options. Consider all the universities that accepted you and consider how Top-choice fits in. Perhaps it's not the best school for you after all. Then again, perhaps by the time you have reconsidered all the universities, you will have heard from Top-choice again — this time, with a final decision.

The Missing Piece

You have your choice of four universities. You just have to choose one, fill out the enrollment form, sign your name, and put it in the mail. You rush to your collection of calendars, brochures, and notes to remind yourself what you specifically liked about each university.

Whoa! Back up a minute. A key piece of the puzzle is still missing. If you haven't thought about it yet, one of your parents is probably reminding you right now. It's that nasty word again: money.

When you hear about financial aid

U Safety and Threebie Tech each offered you an entrance scholarship. It won't pay for everything, but it will help. In fact, combined with the amount socked away for you in your RESPs, it will cover your tuition costs and other university fees. You got financial aid information from all the universities that accepted you as part of the offer of admission package. But you've received no offers from Favourite University or Fourmost U. And you know your parents can't pay the tab at those places simply by writing a cheque.

However, U Safety, Threebie Tech, and Favourite University are in the hometown of either your parents or your grandparents, so you can live at "home" while going to any of these. Hmmm.

Suddenly, you get a telegram. You've never received a telegram before so this one is a bit of a shock. It's from Fourmost U offering you a scholarship! And it's even more than you are getting from U Safety or Threebie Tech. Will other offers arrive this way? Unfortunately, we can't tell you that one for sure.

Why the financial aid offers don't always come with admissions offers

If universities could tell you how much money you'll get at the same time they tell you that you're accepted, you would have an ideal situation. But the process doesn't work that way. The financial aid (or bursar's) office has been figuring how much aid you deserve to get ever since your application arrived. But it won't offer you a dime unless the admissions office decides you're in.

You see, the financial aid folks can't make their final decisions about money until they get the final word on who has been accepted. Even then, many schools want to decide how valuable you are to them — compared to everyone else they've accepted — before they offer you an incentive. That's why there is a notification gap. (We cover financial aid in Chapter 14 and scholarships in Chapter 15.)

Revisit Your Choices

While you're waiting for your money offers, you can do things to start the final decision-making process. If you don't think of these items, the universities that want you will remind you. You can check out those five schools (Top-choice is still an option until it clearly says no) to remember their pluses and minuses — and to recall all the factors that put those five on your application list.

Start by going back to your University Applications File — no doubt a little tattered by now. Review the calendars, catalogues, and brochures you got in the mail. Check the notes you made from your research in the directories and from your campus visits. Ask yourself again:

- ✔ How strong is the program in the field you want to study?
- ✔ How closely does the campus fit your desires for size, location, and distance from home?

> ✔ What vibes did you get from the students?
>
> ✔ Are the professors and staff the kind of people you enjoy dealing with?

You already answered those questions once, when you decided Top-choice and Favourite are where you would like to be. But you've had a busy year, and some things might have slipped your mind. Review them so that you remember how you felt when you applied.

You will also be told whether you got into the specific program you requested. Universities will consider you for your requested program first. If you do not qualify for that, they may still offer you admission to the university — just in another program. If you don't get into engineering, you may be offered a place in general sciences, for example. This is another consideration when choosing which school to accept.

The Waiting List

Top-choice U did not accept you. But it didn't reject you, either. The school offered you something in between. The Waiting List may be frustrating to you, but it is absolutely necessary for universities.

What Waiting List means

What Top-choice is saying is, "You're not among the best we got this year; then again, you're not among the worst. If you want to take your chances that some of those better people won't enrol, we'll keep your application alive."

The decision is up to you. If you would like to stay in consideration, sign the card that says so and return it. If the university doesn't hear from you, its Waiting List won't include your name.

The Waiting List is a common phenomenon at universities that have more applications than they need. Each year, these universities try to guess precisely how many students they must accept to fill their first-year classes, but their guesses frequently are wrong. If, year after year, Snow-Capped University gets one-third of the students it accepts, it will send out 1,800 acceptance letters to fill its 600 first-year spots. But, whoops, this year only 500 of those 1,800 enrol by May 1. Snow-Capped U suddenly needs 100 more bodies to fill its first-year classes. Out comes the Waiting List.

Why they use the Waiting List

A Waiting List generally is used for one of three purposes, depending on the university:

- ✔ **As a supplemental acceptance list.** A university intentionally will accept fewer students than necessary to fill its class, as a hedge in case more enrol than anticipated. For example, a university with 600 available spots and a historical one-third enrollment rate should logically accept 1,800 applicants to get 600 first-year students. But if 700 of those 1,800 accept the admission offer, school officials will have very red faces. The school will have nowhere to put these "extra" 100 students. So the university takes *fewer* than 1,800. And when its one-third yield occurs again, it will fill the remaining slots from its Waiting List. The school does the same thing every year.

  Ah, you noticed the term *yield* we tossed into the next-to-last sentence in the preceding paragraph. This word is jargon that occasionally slips into admissions officers' everyday conversation, especially if you are dealing with American colleges. A school's yield is the percentage of accepted students who actually enrol. Harvard's yield usually is around 75 percent, meaning that for every 100 students offered admission, 75 say yes. Stanford's yield is about 60 percent. Canadian universities don't like to advertise their yields. Sometimes you'll hear that Canadian schools don't even track yields — but they do.

- ✔ **As a hedge against a bad year.** A university will accept the students it thinks it needs, but keep a Waiting List against events beyond its control. One such event would be fewer students enrolling than it expects. Another would be fewer students than expected enrolling at another university, say the University of British Columbia. If UBC takes 50 students off its Waiting List, ten of them may have already signed up for the University of Victoria. Suddenly, ten students on the University of Victoria Waiting List get word that they're in. And those ten create ten new vacancies at Simon Fraser. This has a domino effect.

- ✔ **As a (fake) consolation prize.** Some universities rarely admit anyone from a Waiting List. They use the list to make many of their rejected applicants feel a bit better about the eventual final rejection in July.

How do you know which way your university uses a Waiting List? You don't. If you ask, you'll probably be told that it's used to fill vacancies if enough students don't enrol. That will be true. Some candid admissions officers may tell you — if you ask — how many Waiting List students eventually were accepted in the past. But it's unlikely that anyone on campus will offer a forecast of how many vacancies will occur this year. They don't want to get your hopes up. Or down.

An astute high school counsellor who has dealt with the particular university for years will have a good idea how often the Waiting List is used. If you're lucky enough to have an astute counsellor, seek his advice. Ask any friends who are already studying at that university if they have had experiences with the Waiting List, or even have been on the list themselves.

The Deposit Dilemma

Back in February, you got the good news of being accepted at U Safety. But it came with some bad news. It accepted you for admission, but said it needed a $200 deposit to hold your spot. Deposit requests are common in American colleges but not so common here in Canada, and they vary in size with the school. American colleges feel a cash deposit is very clear evidence that you are serious about enrolling.

You had a problem. You knew your two top choices would not give you a decision for a few weeks. But you wanted to be sure that you had a spot at Safety, in case the others turned you down. You called a Safety admissions officer — the same one you chatted with a year earlier. She said they needed the $200 or they would give your place to someone else. But she assured you that if you change your mind later the deposit would be refunded. So you sent Safety its money.

The same dilemma faces thousands of students every spring. One university wants a deposit before another university makes a decision. Most universities understand the spot you're in and will refund your money if you go elsewhere. But ask to be sure. Get the refund policy in writing, if possible.

Call the admissions officer and explain candidly that you can't make a firm decision until you hear from every university. The odds are high that the deposit will be refundable. If the admissions office gets hard-nosed and says you lose your money if you change your mind, that may be a good reason for dumping the school from your list. It's not a customer-oriented attitude.

Wait for the Other Shoe

Now that you have reconsidered the campuses that want you, checked all your old records, and sought more advice from friends, teachers, and counsellors, you still need the missing piece before you can decide where to go. You must find out how much each university expects you to pay and how it expects you to pay it.

What If You Didn't Get into Your First Choice?

Hey, it's not the end of the world, right? Remember, you could have put all your eggs in one (university) basket and just applied for your dream school. You were put on the Waiting List at Top-choice U, but it eventually said no — as you knew it might. But all is not lost. Now, you can move on with other things and pick from the universities that remain.

If you really had your heart (and career) set on Top-choice U, try again. While there may be a legitimate reason why Top-choice rejected your application, you still have a chance of being admitted. Your marks might have been slightly lower than the school's cut-off this year. You might not have met an important deadline because of an illness, family matter, or other mitigating situation.

You can ask for reconsideration. Unless your marks are so low that the admissions officer has no choice but to deny you admission, it's a real option.

Take stock of yourself

Do you *really* want this university? Asking for a second chance at Top-choice — especially when other universities want you — can be a humbling experience. Most students would rather take a trip to the dentist than plead their case in front of a grizzled admissions officer. Apologies to both dentists *and* admissions officers — who are mostly *great* people, but the point we're trying to make is that challenging a negative admissions decision can be a complex and time-consuming process.

Take stock of your academic situation

Do some research on Top-choice U's Web site. It may already have published its cut-off grade for this year. If your marks are nowhere near this grade, you probably don't have much of a chance. Although you're a great student, you didn't score highly enough to get in this year. Hey, it happens. It may seem like the end of the world, but it isn't.

If your marks are very close to Top-choice U's cut-off, you might be able to convince the admissions officer to let you in anyway. But you have to have a good story — and we're not talking about making stuff up. We're talking about letting her know you're a good kid who had a bad year because you were sick a lot, or because a parent died, or because of another situation beyond your control.

The university applications process: an Ontario example

We realize that the admissions process is so complex it can often seem like a question on your algebra final exam. This is to be expected. The main purpose of this book is to explain and simplify things so you can concentrate on the more important things (such as keeping your marks high and thinking about the future).

Here, we outline the admissions process for universities in Ontario. We use Ontario as an example for three reasons. First, Ontario's 17 universities represent one-third of *all* universities across Canada, so outlining the general Ontario experience helps not only the huge number of Ontario students applying but also many out-of-province students who are trying to get into an Ontario university.

Second, although the specific dates vary slightly for each university, the information in this sidebar is meant to illustrate a *general* application scenario. Third, the folks at the OUAC (Ontario Universities' Application Centre) have been so darn helpful throughout the entire process of writing this book, Caryn and David thought they'd plug the organization whenever they could. Thanks, OUAC!

One final caveat: These dates were for the 2000/2001 application process. Each year, application dates will vary a little. As they say on TV, check your local counsellor (and university) for details.

September: Initial information is sent out to students

✔ The OUAC circulates *INFO* magazine to your school in mid-September. Your counsellor will provide you with a copy that you can use to begin your formal university application planning.

October: Application forms go out to schools

✔ The OUAC begins distributing *OUAC 101 application forms* and instruction booklets to secondary schools. Your counsellor will distribute them to you soon after that.

November: Early completed application forms are sent back to the OUAC

✔ Some schools send in the completed application forms earlier than the December 1 deadline. As your applications are received and processed by the OUAC, the *verification/amendment forms* are sent out to you and your school.

December: Deadline for completed application forms to be sent back to the OUAC

✔ December 1 is the deadline for your high school to submit your completed application form and fees to the OUAC.

✔ Applications received after December 1 will still be processed by the OUAC and distributed to the universities. However, Ontario universities have specific application deadlines for some programs. If you are applying for admission after December, you should check with the universities you have selected to find out if the deadline has passed.

January: The OUAC verifies application forms and processes changes

✔ The OUAC continues to process the application forms. Your verification/amendment form is mailed to you and your school as soon as your application is processed. The universities receive your application by February 1.

February: Last-minute changes to application forms must be received by the OUAC

✔ February 23 is the *recommended* last date for you to submit all information to the OUAC, including university and program changes as well as additional university/program choices, in order for you to be eligible for consideration for early admission. Changes received after this date will continue to be accepted and processed by the OUAC. However, some universities begin their admission decision process based on information received by the February 23 date.

✔ By late February, your high school will have sent your grades to the OUAC. (If your high school is semestered, it will send the grades from your first-semester courses; if it's not, it will send your mid-term grades from your full-year courses.) The OUAC transmits those grades to the universities by March 26.

Late March/early April: Early (conditional) offers of admissions are sent out from the universities

✔ Once they have received the required academic information, the universities may make *conditional offers of admission* to you. These offers are based on a combination of your final grades from your first OAC semester, or your mid-term OAC grades, and your marks in grade 11 and 12 courses. Refer to the *INFO* magazine for more details.

✔ If you receive a conditional offer of admission, you have until June 13 to decide whether or not you wish to accept it.

April: More grades are reported from your high school

✔ In late April, your high school provides the OUAC with either your second-semester mid-term grades or an update of your mid-term full-year course grades. This second reporting tells the universities whether you have kept your marks up in the second half of the year.

May: More conditional offers are sent out from the universities

✔ The grades received by the OUAC in April are transmitted to the universities by mid-May. Some universities may make further conditional offers of admission at this point.

June: You will hear the news this month, for sure

✔ By June 6, all Ontario universities must respond to your application for admission. There are three possible responses:

1. An offer of admission

2. A refusal

3. A deferral, pending receipt of specific additional information. This is called the Waiting List

✔ June 13 is the earliest date that Ontario universities require you to respond to (accept or decline) their conditional offers of admission.

July: Your final grades are sent to the OUAC

✔ Your high school sends your final current-year course grades to the OUAC by mid-July. The OUAC transmits your final standing to the universities by late July. If you've kept your marks up, you have nothing to worry about. If you haven't, you have some explaining to do to the appropriate university admissions officers.

✔ If you've been sick, get a doctor's note. If you've had domestic problems, get a note from your high school counsellor or other informed individual. Don't run from any problems: face up to them! The university wants you. It just wants to know you can handle the workload and the pressure. Convince them that you can!

August: Final university acceptances are sent out

✔ When the universities receive your final grades, they determine whether your final standing meets the conditions of the offer of admission they gave you earlier in the year. This finalizes your admission to university.

September: You start your university adventure

✔ Congratulations! You begin university this month — and the folks that run the OUAC repeat the cycle for another year.

University admissions officers meet regularly during the admissions process to discuss all the students in the *maybe* pile. You should have already sent in a letter explaining why your final term's marks were so bad. Point to your great marks in previous years, or the fact that you simply *have* to get into the program you've selected at Top-choice because you want to go on to medical school at the university — and the reason your marks aren't higher is because you got caught up with volunteering at the local hospital (as proven by a glowing letter of recommendation from the hospital's chief resident).

Now is the time to call and ask for an appointment. If Top-choice's admissions office doesn't work that way, offer to fax in some paperwork supporting your admission from your counsellor, teacher, principal (or boss at the hospital). Anything that will give you a second chance.

You get the idea. As long as you have a *real, legitimate* excuse (not the usual, "my dog ate the application form, that's why I couldn't get it in on time…"), you may have a chance at Top-choice.

On the other hand, the fact that you didn't get into Top-choice U may be a blessing in disguise. You might have been miserable at Top-choice, despite all your research. Sometimes, fate has a way of telling you things that you can't see for yourself. You never know: One of the other schools that accepted you may become your *new* Top-choice U!

What If You Didn't Get In, Period?

This is a problem facing an increasing number of students every year. Either they didn't pick their *safety net* university properly, or competition was really heavy that year, or their marks simply weren't good enough to get into university.

Our guess is that these students probably didn't pick a safety net university properly. The whole point of a safety net is to ensure a student doesn't get left high and dry without a school to attend in September.

Another possibility is that the students didn't choose *enough* universities. In effect, they have put all their eggs in one or two (or three) baskets. It's possible that all three choices were extremely competitive this year. Since they didn't have a realistic view of the university market, they now have to scramble.

However, if the unthinkable does occur, what should you do? You have several options:

✔ **Try to get into another university.** Ignoring your bruised ego for a moment, can you see yourself in another university this September? Another university may not have made it onto your original list because it was too far away, didn't have the exact program you were looking for, or some other reason. If you want to give it a try, contact the admissions office of the university *now* (not tomorrow, not next week) to see if you can apply or be wait-listed there. Don't worry about what your friends will say. Your friends are not you. It's possible that none of them was offered admission, either.

✔ **Try to get into a college or technical institute.** It's possible that you can get where you're going with a college education. Investigate whether you can take your desired courses at the college level. You may love it, or you may be able to transfer to university next year after getting some valuable practical instruction. Your counsellor should be able to help. Check out Chapter 22 for additional details about why college might be a good alternative for you.

✔ **Take a year off and take a course or two to upgrade your overall average.** Check with your counsellor to see how this might work in your situation. If you work part-time during this period, you may be able to accumulate enough money to make a serious dent in next year's tuition.

✔ **Try part-time studies and transfer into full-time later.** Check with your counsellor or with the admissions office at the university about the options available to you.

Putting It All Together

You've been accepted by Favourite University, Threebie Tech, Fourmost U, and U Safety. You were not accepted at Long-reach, and Top-choice finally sends you the letter indicating you're off the Waiting List and not getting an offer of admission. That's okay, at least you know your options. Speaking of which, let's look at your four university options and figure out where you should go:

✔ Favourite University is in your hometown, so you can live with your family while attending. It hasn't offered you any money, but you believe you can get a student loan to cover your expenses.

✔ Threebie Tech offers you some money, but not all that you need. However, when combined with the money you have set aside in your RESPs it will be enough to cover all your educational costs. Threebie Tech is located in the city where your grandparents live, so you can live with them while going to university. Or you can take out a student loan to cover the cost of residence.

✔ Fourmost U offers you enough money to cover tuition and all other university fees. However, it is located across the country, so you will have the expenses of room and board along with transportation costs. Still, you should be able to get a student loan to cover these additional expenses.

✔ U Safety offers you some money — but again, not all you need. Just like Threebie, when combined with the money you have set aside in your RESPs it will be enough to cover all your educational costs. Besides, U Safety is located in your hometown, so you can live with your family while attending university.

Many scholarship offers are divided among your four years of university. But in order to keep seeing that scholarship money year after year, you have to keep your marks up. That's the catch. Now, you have to consider your options. It looks like you can emerge from university debt-free by going to either Threebie Tech or U Safety, but maybe you really have your heart set on Favourite University. Think again about how much you might value living in residence. Consider whether you will be happy living in a different environment in a city across the country. Figure out if you can really stand living with your grandparents for four (or more!) years.

Most importantly, consider the quality of education you will get at each university. There's usually a reason why one university is your favourite!

Chapter 20

Before You Go

*T*his chapter sums up a lot of the things we've been talking about throughout the entire book. It's probably been a long time since you first picked up this book and started reading. But that's okay. None of us thought you'd read the whole thing cover to cover in one sitting. *War and Peace* this isn't. Lucky you.

For most students, choosing a university or college is the biggest life decision they've ever made (so far). This chapter provides a framework so that you can look at the big picture, see what's what, and rethink any decision before it's too late. Ready? Okay, let's go!

Step Back and Rethink Everything

Buying a university or college education — which is essentially what we've been talking about throughout this book — is clearly one of the most expensive decisions you will ever make in your life. Sure, you may go on to buy a car (or your parents may donate that old clunker to you soon). Later on, you may be lucky enough to own your own home or even a cottage up north. But for the sheer enormousness of the decision, nothing can beat making huge life choices when you're 17, 18, or 19 years old.

In fact, if you start your planning in grade 4, as we suggest, your post-secondary education decision process really starts when you're about nine or ten years old. Obviously, no child or young adult can make a final life decision such as this without a few bouts of second-guessing. In fact, if you were one of those people who knew exactly what you wanted to be when you were only nine or ten years of age, you were in a very small minority!

But no matter how old you are, it's important to gather all the facts you can, talk with your parents, relatives, and friends, as well as your school counsellors and other academic contacts. In the end, though, it's all about *you*. Yes, you need to listen to everyone's advice, but it's your life. *You* are the one investing two, three, four, or more years in university or college. The final decision is yours to make.

Breathe in, breathe out, repeat

Now that we've put all this pressure on you to decide your entire life in the next few months (or years, if you're reading this in grade 9 or 10), take a few deep breaths and just relax. Compared to those students who haven't read this book, you're at the top of the class when it comes to understanding what it takes to survive (and thrive) when going for a higher education.

Even if you make a few horrendous mistakes choosing a university or college and end up having a miserable time, it won't ruin your life. Trust us.

Lots of people who have gone on to bigger and much better things have made mistakes in university and college, ranging from picking the wrong one, picking the wrong program, not bothering to study and thus failing out, and other assorted tragedies.

Chances are that none of these horrors will befall you — because you've done the necessary research, read all the materials, and made some informed decisions. But it may be comforting to know that despite all of the pressures, you can still screw up, turn yourself around, and survive quite well. In other words, don't wear yourself out with worry. Enjoy the *journey* of university or college.

Re-evaluating the schools

The first thing you might think about doing is re-evaluating your choice (and prioritization) of schools. Are you still comfortable with the choices you made so long ago concerning what things are important to you and thus what schools have the highest priority for you? Try to answer the question of school choice by considering both academic and non-academic factors.

On the academic side, ask yourself these all-important questions: Does the university or college have the program you need? Does it have adequate library and computer services? Are the professors and other instructors approachable, as evidenced by your campus visits? Are the classes the right size for you? (Remember, some students thrive in large classes while others thrive in smaller ones.) The trick here is to figure out which type of student you are and see if that type matches your choice of school.

Other academic factors include whether you plan to go on to graduate school and whether you can afford the university or college (or specific program!). We talk a bit more about money later in this chapter.

Non-academic factors are also very important in your choice of school. In fact, we venture that non-academic factors are just as important as academic ones. As we emphasize throughout this book, not only do you have to survive and learn at university or college, but also you have to *thrive* there as well. Going off to university or college to learn new things isn't just about stuffing more factual knowledge into your head. It's about growing in other ways: learning about yourself, learning about others, learning about what you like, and learning about what you dislike. Bottom line: how can each school on your list facilitate this process?

It's a tall order, but we know you're up to the task. It's possible that your priorities have remained the same since you were 14 or 15 years old in grade 9. It's just as possible, however, that your priorities have changed and thus your choice of school may also have changed in the last four or five years. It's better to know this now than to spend two or three years at a school studying a subject or following a program that you can't stand, just because you feel you've painted yourself into the proverbial corner.

Re-evaluating the program

Another consideration for you, besides the school itself, is your program of study. Sometimes the program of study you want is taught at only a few schools. Here, your choices are easy: choosing one of three or four options is obviously easier than choosing one of, say, 50 or 100.

Other times, the choice of program will be very difficult because you haven't made up your mind about what type of career you'd like. This is why many universities don't make you declare a major or specialty until the end of your first year at university. This doesn't mean that certain choices will still be open to you after you take your first-year courses; it just means there are more choices open to you than if you were forced to declare a major at the beginning of your academic career.

For instance, if you want to go into law but wish to specialize in patent law, perhaps you should become an engineer first and then a lawyer. Obviously, with this type of academic background, you would need to keep a lot of options open in subjects such as math, English, and some science courses. If you want to go into medicine, you will most likely embark on a science program so that you will be concentrating your efforts on such courses as calculus, chemistry, biology, and possibly physics.

Take the harder courses, take the harder programs, take the harder degrees. At the beginning of this book, you may have asked yourself why we were being so harsh. By now you probably already know our philosophy: to get more out of life, you have to put more into it. Yeah, we know this sounds pretty trite, but it's true. We know this because we've been through what you're about to go through.

Before you decide on your major, talk to your counsellor, your favourite professor, your faculty advisor, and other trusted advisors. Study the course calendar and ask a lot of questions. Get the names of the people you talk to — be a bit of a pest, if you must.

Re-evaluating the money offers

A related, but separate part of your decision process relates to money. We know we tried to shield you from the money decisions at the beginning of the book. You might also remember that we spent the entire fourth part of the book talking about your different financial options.

In Chapter 12, we helped you figure out the actual cost of university or college, and in Chapter 13 we discussed various long-term financial planning strategies. In Chapter 14, we discussed how to get financial aid and in Chapter 15 we talked about the various scholarships available. Chapter 16 outlined various work-study options, including co-op programs — even joining the military. You got a few ideas about keeping your debt low, or at least manageable, in Chapter 18.

Deciding where you are going to go to school for the next few years of your life often comes down to dollars and sense. On the one hand, it's important to get the education you need to achieve your life's goals. On the other hand, only people who live in a fantasy world can ignore the financial aspects of paying several thousands of dollars for an education.

Thus, the dilemma that faces many students: If savings aren't enough to cover the complete cost of education (including tuition, incidental fees, books, materials, and a whole host of other items), you must get money from other sources. These sources might include government loans, scholarships, bursaries, and other options. But if one university offers you an entrance scholarship while another doesn't, this could be the deciding factor between the two of them. Seek out as much information as you can about financing your university or college education. As surveys and studies have continually proven, a university degree helps people earn a better living, more money, and, yes, even achieve a greater level of satisfaction.

Spend some quality time comparing the various financial aid packages each university is offering you. If you can't decide between two equally viable educational options, the level of financial aid each school is offering you may tip the balance in favour of one school.

Your Options

It may not seem so now, but the time after high school can be one of the best times of your life, especially if you understand all of your options. For the college-bound, it can mean learning a technical trade that will (hopefully) provide employment for the rest of your life. More so, it can catapult you ahead both in terms of life experiences and opportunities. Programs at the high-end niche colleges can provide a framework for incredible growth and money-making potential, not to mention happiness.

Whether you learn how to become an emergency medical technician, a Web designer, an actuary, or a respiratory technologist, going to college can open doors throughout the rest of your life. There are some colleges that are held in such high esteem that members of the entire graduating class are offered jobs while they're still in school.

University, on the other hand, doesn't teach specific skills. Rather, a bachelor's degree from university provides the big picture through which future study, development, and application can be accomplished. Universities teach critical thinking skills, research skills, and the ability to reason out problems no matter what the size or scope.

Deciding not to go

By now, you've read most (if not all) of this book, so you have a good feel for the admissions process. You've also done some research about which options are best for you. You may feel that university isn't for you. At least not right now.

Perhaps you don't relish another four years of school. Maybe you skipped a grade and now's the time to gain a bit of general life experience. At the risk of upsetting your hardworking (and ever-hopeful) parents, you have to do what's best for you. One of us took a year off after high school before proceeding to university and survived quite well, thank you.

Deferring your acceptance

Some universities or colleges will allow you to defer your acceptance; others won't. Find out if deferring is an option at your schools of choice. If one of your top choices offers a deferral while another does not, the final selection process may have just become easier for you.

Transferring credits

Most colleges and universities allow you to transfer the credits that you've earned in one school to another — assuming the other school has a similar or equivalent course. This reciprocity is important in the world of academia because it ensures that one diploma in a particular subject is roughly equivalent to a similar diploma from another school. Likewise, an engineering degree from one university is recognized by another university.

Since you can transfer credits from one school to another, it's not the end of the world if you decide you're miserable at one school and wish to try an alternative. If you do the best you can and achieve good marks, odds are you can apply your credits to another similar program. That said, there is no obligation for the new school to accept the credits of your old school. Find out how your particular school handles the transferring of credits.

Some colleges offer a *university equivalency* in some of their programs and courses. This means that, in some cases, your college credits may also be counted as university courses — provided your marks are high enough. Not all universities accept college credits, and those that do place stringent requirements on college students hoping to upgrade their diploma program to that of a degree program.

Feeling Good about Your Final Choice

If you've read this far and done all the thinking, researching, and soul-searching, you know that our number-one priority is to help you feel good about your final academic choice. By good, we don't mean that you've selected your university or college because you think it's the easiest one or because all of your friends are going there, or for some other frivolous reason. We hope that you've selected a school based on the *toughest* and *strongest* criteria you could construct, knowing that the harder you work, the more you'll look back on your years at school saying, "Wow, I really *did* learn a lot during those years."

Part VI
The Part of Tens

The 5th Wave   By Rich Tennant

"Our curriculum is based on the latest manufacturing processes. Our liberal arts assembly line is completely automated. Let's go onto the shop floor and I'll show you how we retool incoming freshmen."

In this part . . .

Here come the lists. This part is called the Part of Tens because the lists are composed of ten things. Smart, eh? This list-filled part has become a tradition in . . . *For Dummies* books, and we certainly don't want to buck tradition, do we?

These lists give you a bunch of important information about the university planning process, all wrapped up in four neat little packages. There are four chapters in this part; hence, four lists. Some of the things in the lists are mentioned in the rest of the book and some aren't. You might want to use the list in Chapter 23 as a checklist when you are gathering information about universities. Chapter 24 has a list of things *not* to do when you're planning your university career. We hope having this information pulled together in one place will give you a helping hand.

We also hope these lists are fun to read — you might even crack a smile or three. So, enjoy!

Chapter 21

Ten Reasons to Go to University

Part of the decision-making process we take you through in this book is deciding whether or not university is for you. It's certainly not for everyone. With all the other options available — going to reputable colleges and institutes, along with working on your own through distance learning — some people are starting to wonder if university is useful at all. Add to this the importance the public — and, we're guessing, probably your parents — place on preparing for an actual job instead of just getting an education, and you've got quite a bit to ponder.

Well, despite all that, there's still *immense* value in getting a university education. We've taken the liberty of listing a few of the benefits for you, but we're sure you can come up with lots more on your own.

Qualifying for Graduate or Professional Studies

It may sound obvious, but you can't get into graduate school until you graduate with your bachelor's (or undergraduate) degree. Similarly, you can't apply to law school, medical school, or other professional programs without at least a few years of university under your belt.

Some students find they like learning so much that they decide to make it their life's work. After earning their bachelor's degree, they move on to a master's degree, and then even to a *Doctor of Philosophy* (Ph.D.), the highest post-graduate degree you can attain. A Ph.D. is usually the minimum qualification in most Canadian universities to become a full professor on the *tenure track*, a system that guarantees long-time employment at the particular school.

An added benefit of the Ph.D. is that you get to call yourself "doctor." And won't that make your parents proud?

Landing a Job

A university education makes it easier to get a job. Hands down. Here's what Statistics Canada says on the subject: "When it comes to success in the labour market, it pays to stay in school. With each increased level of education attained, employment rates rise and unemployment rates fall."

Just because you've won an admission place at the university of your choice doesn't mean you can slack off. Nosireebob. You know how we feel about *that* subject. Getting into university is just the beginning. It's really important to keep your grades up throughout university. Many employers, especially those large, prestigious firms, actually look at your university marks to figure out whether you should come to work for them. And, if you want to go on to professional programs such as medicine, law, education, or a host of others, you can bet these faculties will look at your undergraduate marks as well.

The director of software giant Adobe Systems Canada Inc. told Caryn and David flat out that a degree is required for any position at that company. In fact, he indicated that there is only one person currently working at Adobe Canada who does not have a university degree. Adobe is hardly the exception, it's the rule — in the high-tech sector and beyond. The chances of dropping out of school, inventing some nifty new gadget, and becoming a multi-millionaire are so slight they can't be considered an option.

Earning a Higher Salary

People with a university education earn more than people without one. Statistics Canada is here again to back us up: "Data on recent post-secondary graduates show their earnings increase progressively with more advanced post-secondary qualifications." Translation: The more education you get, the more money you are likely to make.

A university degree is especially important if you're a woman who wants to earn more money. In 1997 (the last year for which figures are available), females with a university degree earned almost *twice* as much as females with only a high-school diploma or some post-secondary education. In contrast, males with a university degree earned only 60 percent more than males with high-school or some post-secondary education. Although at first glance it seems that males get the short end of the university-education stick, when you factor in that males earn significantly more than females overall, you see why it's vital that females attend university.

Landing That Senior Position

Compared to other developed countries, the Canadian labour force has the highest proportion of people with post-secondary education. By any standards, there are a lot of educated people in Canada. If you want to compete in the job market, a university education is a serious advantage.

Most people who do the hiring in companies are busy, so they cut down on their workload by pre-screening job applicants based on certain criteria. Yes, this means they weed out applicants before they ask you to come in for an interview. If you look through the want ads of any newspaper, or in the careers section of any Web site, you'll find that almost every executive position advertised requires a university degree.

The Prestige Factor

Don't knock it. In a world where everyone is trying to sell you something, it pays to have credibility. A university degree identifies you as part of the elite group of educated people in Canada and the world.

When people are trying to establish a relationship in business, one of the first things they discuss is where they went to school — not high school, university. Comparing professors, courses, fraternities, and associations can help you build an instant rapport with a colleague. If both of you went to the same university, there is a feeling of bonding. If you went to rival universities, that feeling of friendly competition may grow into something more.

The prestige of a university degree also helps if you are trying to get a loan for your business, or even for a home.

And, how could we forget Mom and Dad? It'll make them very proud!

Changing Careers

While we've described the many benefits of a college diploma or certificate, the fact remains that they prepare you for a specific job in a specific industry. The more generalized, well-rounded education you get from university makes it easier to adapt to changes in the job market. You're more flexible. You're more fluid. You're less hemmed in when and if you decide to make a career change. (And statistics show, by the way, that you will likely change careers — not just jobs — several times in your life.) A university degree gives you a solid foundation on which to build more advanced knowledge and experiences.

Say your friend has gone to college or a technical institute and qualified as a mechanic. One day, she decides she wants to work in the high-tech industry. Chances are she'll have to go back to school before she can make this career change a reality. But let's say you earned a bachelor's degree in the social sciences and are now working in a senior position in the automotive industry. One day you too decide you'd like to make a career change to the high-tech industry (you sense it's about time for a change, since we're supposed to go through so many). Chances are this jump will be easier for you than your college-trained counterpart, because the skills you learned at university are more generalized and transferable. You probably won't have to go back to school. In fact, you can likely head straight to the interview.

University Degrees Travel

A university degree is a universal recognition of achievement (we didn't mean that play on words, really). Wherever you go — whether it be across the country or across the world — people will take notice of your degree. It's not quite the same thing as having a certificate from your local technical institute.

People with university degrees tend to be more mobile. They find it easier to move to other countries. Getting a work visa or immigrating to most industrialized nations can be a challenge, even for Canadians. A university degree makes the process much easier. Canadian university graduates with a job offer in the United States, for example, can be fast-tracked through the American Immigration and Naturalization Service visa program, whereas those without a degree go through a much more rigorous scrutiny process.

Having a university degree usually means you can work in the United States. Not having a university degree usually means you can't, all other things being equal. This may not be fair, but it's reality.

Learning to Think

Remember that great scene in the movie *The Paper Chase,* where Professor Kingsfield explains the ins and outs of Harvard Law School to his first-year law students?

"You come in here with a skull full of mush, and you leave thinking like a lawyer."

Well, you don't have to go to law school for that stirring experience. In fact, that's the whole point of going to university — you learn to think. Trade schools may teach you how to do a particular task well, but universities teach you how to *adapt*: how to look at a problem from many sides and find a number of possible solutions. You learn to formulate arguments and how to articulate them convincingly. This skill is valuable in any walk of life.

Having Fun

University is more than just a place to study. It's a lifestyle and a community. Many people look back on their university years as one of the best times of their lives. Most meet a few lifelong friends. Some meet the person they eventually marry. Hey, it's not *all* hard work and studying until 2 a.m., you know!

You'll do things at university that you will never forget. Whether they are related to your studies (that moment when quantum physics truly came alive for you), or completely unrelated (painting the dome in the quadrangle with your sorority sisters — or fraternity brothers — on the coldest night of the year), these experiences shape who you are and what you'll become.

In fact, you may like university so much that you decide to stay. We know graduate students who go back for their third, fourth, even fifth degrees, usually teaching there to sustain their academic existence. They become part of the university and the university becomes part of them.

Even after you've moved on, your university won't forget you. You remain an alumnus of the university, and are welcome there anytime. No, your university won't forget you, and it won't let you forget it, either. For the rest of your life, your university will pester you for donations.

Being Happier

We thought we'd save our most convincing argument for last.

We think that going to university will make you happier. Sure, university teaches you how to think and how to learn. But it also teaches you how to live. In many cases, university teaches you how to work with other people and cope with adversity. It teaches you the value of hard work — sometimes breathtakingly hard work. And it also empowers you to overcome challenges, do the things you love, and become a better person.

Chapter 22

Ten Reasons Why Colleges and Institutes Are Worth a Look

. . . .

In This Chapter

▶ Taking more specialized courses

▶ Spending less time learning

▶ Excelling in smaller classes

▶ Benefiting from a hands-on learning approach

▶ Choosing from a larger number of schools

. . . .

Going to university may be the only option you've considered for life after high school. Or maybe you have been working for a few years and realize you would be far better able to move your career ahead if you had some more education. But before you jump straight into the university application process, take a few minutes to consider your other educational options.

Some people may tell you that the type of education you get at university is so different from what you get at a college or institute that comparing the two is like comparing apples and oranges. Well, we say, what's wrong with that? If you're hungry, you can decide whether you would prefer an apple or an orange. If you want an education, you have a bunch of different options. Colleges and institutes have changed dramatically over the years. Not only have they grown in numbers, they have also grown in popularity, areas of instruction, and acceptance in society. Colleges and institutes seem to be everywhere nowadays. Some of these schools are the best places in the world to study a particular subject. How about them apples — or oranges?

When considering colleges, you should be aware of the vast differences between colleges of applied arts and sciences and private colleges. *Colleges of applied arts and sciences* are publicly funded and regulated by the same government bodies that watch over universities. Their instructors must meet certain standards, and many of them have agreements set up with specific universities that allow college credits to count toward university degrees.

Private colleges must pass far less stringent regulatory requirements, and they run the gamut from the top schools in their discipline to shady operations that might not exist the next day. The warnings we give in this chapter apply primarily to private colleges, not colleges of applied arts and sciences.

This chapter lists reasons why you may want to consider attending a college or institute.

Employment

Here's an interesting statistic: Within two years of graduating with a bachelor's degree from a Canadian university, about 5 percent of 1995's graduating class re-entered the school system through a college program! What's more, the statisticians that collected this data predict that this number is likely to be rising. Why are these university graduates turning to colleges? The quick answer is, to get a job.

Sometimes the demand in the labour market is for people who have specific skills. And specific skills (technical, vocational, and others) are usually taught at colleges, not universities.

Specialized Curriculum

As we just mentioned, the specific skills some employers want aren't taught at university. They're not part of the "ivory tower" curriculum of universities. Skills such as how to use a particular software program, operate a certain piece of machinery, or use a specialized set of business tools *are* on the curricula of colleges and institutes, however.

Although you should certainly be able to use Microsoft Word by the time you finish a four-year degree in computer engineering at university, will you know the actual operations of a word-processing centre? Likewise, your English literature degree might have trained you to discuss the subtleties of language used in Jane Austen's novels, but can you write a press release to promote the next Steven Spielberg blockbuster? Sure, you learned how to construct dynamic graphics arrays in C++ when you got your computer science degree, but do you know how to project manage production of a CD-ROM-based game in time for the important holiday sales period? You get the idea.

As a general rule, universities teach you how to understand a particular subject and learn about the big picture. Colleges and institutes, on the other hand, give you practical training about a specific topic.

It Takes Less Time

Courses of study at colleges or institutes generally take less time to complete. Most diplomas require only two years of study, and certificates can be obtained in a few months. Sometimes, one college credit course can be completed over a weekend!

This is not always the case, however, especially in the top colleges and institutes. Almost half of the programs at Oakville's Sheridan College, for example — from architectural technology to illustration to sports injury management — take three years to complete — as much time as a typical degree at a major university.

It's the Top School in Your Field

The computer animation program at Sheridan College, in Oakville, Ontario, is one of the toughest programs to get into in the country, beating out all other colleges — and universities — offering similar programs. Top animation companies around the world compete to hire Sheridan animation graduates. Why? Because it's the best program out there. Bar none.

Sheridan College isn't the only college in Canada with an outstanding reputation in animation and other high-tech fields. The boom in the high-tech market over the past decade has translated into a soaring demand for people with technical and design skills. A number of Canadian colleges and institutes have responded with innovative, challenging programs. There are a wealth of renowned Canadian facilities where you can get high-tech and other types of training.

For every college or institute that provides top-quality education, there is another that provides virtually no education. There are lots of fly-by-night private operations out there, so make sure you investigate the school thoroughly before you hand over your tuition cheque. The same things we talk about in Chapter 9 regarding checking out university campuses also apply to colleges and institutes. While that shiny brochure looks great sitting on your desk, it's only by visiting the school that you'll see it's in fact located over a busy hardware store in a seedy part of town.

Hands-on Learning Style

One of us went to law school after getting an undergraduate degree. Just like all other law schools, it was often theoretical to the point of failing to give its students enough practical, hands-on experience. You know, the kind you need in a job. For example, in a course on contracts law, students never got their hands on a single contract. Sure, they were taught important principles about different types of contracts, as well as the case law relating to each. But they never actually *held* a sample contract between their fingers and dissected it piece by piece (or paragraph by paragraph). In practice, lawyers have to deal with contracts all the time. Why, then, doesn't university law school use contracts to teach the course? A good question!

It's typical of the philosophy of university. You are there to learn *concepts*, not practical stuff. You don't attend university to learn how to do a specific job or to learn a particular skill.

Well, at colleges and institutes, that's exactly what you are there to do. And you learn the skills by actually doing them, usually from an instructor who has actually done (or is doing) what you want to do. Students learn massage therapy from a registered massage therapist, and by actually massaging people. Students learn PC programming by actually working on personal computers. Go figure. A practical approach to education!

While some of the learning-by-doing concept is creeping into universities, it is still a far cry from the hands-on style of most colleges and institutes.

Faculty

Who can teach you what to do in a particular job better than someone who already does that job every day? Many colleges and institutes hire their instructors directly from the relevant industry. There are a lot of advantages to being taught by someone actively working where you want to work. You get to know someone in the industry — often on a first-name basis. Your instructor might be able to help you get a job in the field after graduation. Most are on the lookout for the best and brightest to invite them to join their company. And, even if there are no openings for you with your instructor's company, a good relationship could result in a great letter of recommendation.

Teachers who also work in the industry are often difficult to reach except during class hours. They don't have an office on campus where you can visit them to discuss your assignment or marks. As well, most have never been trained at teaching, so some may be unable to get their point across clearly. As always, the best solution is preventive: Research your teacher before you take the course!

Smaller Classes

Because of their hands-on learning style, colleges and institutes — particularly the private ones — tend to limit class size to a small, workable number. Some technical classes allow a maximum of only 12 students. You'll rarely find classes with more than 40. What a far cry from universities, where lecture halls are sometimes filled with several hundred students — especially in first-year courses.

The smaller classes in colleges and institutes give you more direct contact with your instructor, and more opportunity to be heard and to ask questions. Most people learn better with a lower student–teacher ratio and more direct feedback.

Individual Attention

It's hard to be anonymous in a class of 12 students, especially when the instructor is calling on you for your comments and answers. Most colleges and institutes even take attendance and may give you a participation mark.

At university, you have to be self-motivated. Oftentimes, no one even notices if you don't show up for class. The attitude at university is that you are an adult and capable of taking care of yourself. Colleges and institutes work well for those people who prefer to have someone actively motivating them.

Getting In Is (Often) Easier

While colleges of applied arts and sciences are administered by the govern-ment, other colleges and almost all institutes are private facilities. That means they are in the business of providing education. That also means that they want you to enrol, and many of them don't care what your marks were in high school. This is in marked contrast to university admission.

Because they want you to enrol, some colleges and almost all institutes will also help you get financing. Now, we're not saying they will *provide* financing. These schools are businesses, and they rarely give scholarships just because you are smart or for any other reason. However, the process of administering a student loan is made extremely easy at the hands of a typical institute's admissions official. The forms are ready; you are told what to put where; and they will even send them in for you. This is not the norm at university.

While it may appear easy to get financing with the help of the institute's staff, you're on your own when it comes to *paying back* your loan. And most institutes are much more costly than universities, because they do not get government subsidies. For example, a nine-month program at a typical computer college can set you back $10,000.

Greater Selection

There are 51 universities listed in Appendix A, "Directory of Universities and Colleges." We have chosen to profile the more specialized, often high-tech colleges in the second part of the directory only (if we'd listed the many colleges of applied arts and technology and career colleges that populate our fair country, this would have been a two-volume book!). Nonetheless, colleges and technical institutes greatly outnumber universities in Canada. So, there are more schools for you to choose from.

Look in your telephone book. There are institutes that teach everything from business and computers to hairdressing to homeopathy to bartending to massage. They're everywhere, which means there is probably one close to where you live. This is convenient because it allows you to stay at home while you get your education, even if you live far away from a major city.

Chapter 23

Ten Questions to Ask about a University

. . . .

In This Chapter

▶ Figuring out whether you fit in

▶ Making decisions about class size and professors

▶ Finding a place to hang your hat — and dump your books

▶ Gauging campus safety

. . . .

*Y*ou probably already know what we're going to say here: To make your right decision about which university to attend, you need to make some choices that only you can make. It sounds obvious, but only you know what's important to *you*. Sure, we can guide you and let you know a bunch of things to consider and what to watch out for — and we can help you make lists and pare down your choices. But the emphasis you place on each factor is up to you. Going to university may be your first real step into adulthood, so make sure you consider it long and hard before taking it.

But, as we said, we're here to help. We've put together ten important questions to ask when considering each university on your list. It's stuff we've talked about in the rest of the book, but it's nice to have it all together in one place. You can run these pages through a photocopier and keep a copy in the section on each university in your University Applications File.

Bring these pages along with you on your campus visits to remind yourself of questions you should ask and things you need to find out. Some are questions you will ask of other people. Some are questions you will ask of *yourself*. When all the questions are answered, you will be well on your way to knowing which universities are the best ones for you.

Does My Personality Match the University's?

Are you a computer geek or a party animal? Or both? Are you a neat freak or a bit of a slob? Right wing or left wing? Or do you not care about politics? Do you like your music measured in megadecibels or soft and gentle? Is a campus dominated by fraternities and sororities appealing or a turn-off?

Whether you are capable of answering yes or no, or whether your responses fall somewhere in between all those extremes, it's important to get the feel of the campus before you apply. Each university campus and student body has its own personality. The reputation of a university is sometimes born of tradition and no longer applies, but sometimes the reputation is right on the money!

After all, some types of students truly are more prevalent on some campuses than others. This is because of the types of courses offered, the activities of the more vocal members of the faculty — even the general attitudes of the people in the region or province. The only way you can know whether you fit in with the students is to visit the campus and spend some time with them. An overnight stay in residence is an ideal way to find out who these students really are and whether your lifestyles mesh.

University is a commitment of several years, so make sure you do all the research you can before you send in that application.

Can I Really Get In, Or Am I a Long Shot?

Sure, the university's published minimum average for acceptance is 65 percent, but no one got into your preferred program last year with less than an 80 percent average. There's absolutely nothing stopping you from applying to one of the highly competitive programs at schools that boast extremely high entrance averages, but you do need to be realistic.

If you've got only the minimum average for a program you know is highly competitive, and there is nothing else in your application to distinguish you from all the other students applying, you probably won't get in. Sorry. Again, there's nothing wrong with applying — all they can say is no. However, if money is tight, you might not want to apply to too many long-shot universities, because each charges an application fee. In Ontario, the OUAC (Ontario Universities' Application Centre) charges Ontario high-school students a flat fee of $80 for the first three universities you apply to, and then $25 for each additional school. Out-of-province students pay $85 for the first three choices, and the same $25 for each choice after that. Outside Ontario, you have to deal with each university, and its application fee, separately.

If you find yourself in this position, you should seriously consider other options — there are lots of them! Investigate which schools don't always fill all their spaces. Find out if what makes you unique will be appreciated at some of the other universities out there. Consider staying on for another year of high school or taking a summer school course to raise your overall average. Think about going to a college or institute instead — maybe just for a year — to learn something practical. You may find that pursuing one or more of these options really increases your chances of getting into your preferred program, at your preferred university.

Is This the Right Place for What I Want to Study?

This question has three parts. First, *does this university teach what I want to study?* The answer to this is fairly easy to discover: Check the list of majors and courses in the university calendar.

Second, *does this university teach well what I want to study?* To find out the answer to this one, you need to do a bit more research. Ask around — your teachers and counsellors, students on campus — anyone you know who has attended that university in the past. Ask people working in the field about the reputation of the university. Research the professors to find out if any are particularly renowned. Get a feel for the relative importance of your chosen field at the university.

Just because a university has a good reputation doesn't mean it is particularly good at the field you want to study.

Third, *am I going to the right college or campus of the university for my particular field of study?* Many of the larger universities have a variety of campuses that may be far away from each other. For example, Université du Québec has campuses in Québec City, Abitibi-Témiscamingue, Chicoutimi, Hull, Montréal, Rimouski, and Trois-Rivières. Typically, each campus of a given university has a few areas of study in which it is known to specialize.

If you are going to the University of Toronto and you want to specialize in forensic pathology, you should go to the Erindale campus, out in Mississauga, instead of the St. George campus in downtown Toronto. If you want to study computer engineering, then the downtown campus is probably where you want to be. The fact that different programs may be taught at different locations may also affect your residence application. You need to investigate your *program of study* before you decide where you're going to live.

Can I Live on Campus? If Not, Where?

If you look forward to life in residence as part of your university experience, you'll want to know your chances of getting into one. What percentage of the first-year class does the student residences handle? How likely is it that there will be a place in residence for you if you get accepted at the university? How — and when — do you apply to get into residence? How much does it cost? How much money must you put down to hold a place? Any university residence official can answer all of these questions for you.

If you can't get into residence, what are your options? Does the university have a list of off-campus housing? If so, is any kind of approval required to get on a list? Does the university help first-year students locate housing?

If a university official shrugs off these questions or says she doesn't know the answers, ask for the name of a person who does. You're entitled to this information. If you can't get satisfactory answers, perhaps it's not the right university for you.

How Large (or Small) Are Classes?

Are first-year students required to take large introductory courses where a professor lectures from a stage and students are identified by number? Or are all classes small enough that professors know students and can give them some individual attention? Ask this question of admissions officers, professors, and students. See if the answers are the same.

Better yet, drop in to a class or two and see for yourself. Be sure to sit in on a required introductory course for your field of study. Typically, these *feeder* courses (courses that are intended to weed out those students who are not sufficiently capable or dedicated in the particular major) are usually the ones that have the worst student–professor ratios.

Believe it or not, there are some students who thrive in really big classes and don't do too well in smaller classes. Typically, these students like to fit into the crowd and concentrate on the information, not on the class interactions. In a small classroom setting, you probably have to speak up and contribute. This can intimidate some students not accustomed to having the spotlight on them. The only way you can know what you're getting into is to visit the classes.

Who Teaches the Classes?

You might think professors teach all classes at universities. Professors *do* teach a lot of them, but on many campuses some courses — especially first-year introductory courses — are turned over to part-time instructors or teaching assistants. This is not necessarily a bad thing.

Part-time instructors are usually people who work in the particular field of study who can give students a clear perspective on what happens in the real world. Teaching assistants may be graduate students working on a Ph.D. in the field. Professors, meanwhile, are concentrating on upper-level courses — and their research.

You may find this disappointing or even galling. Here you've been looking forward to soaking up the wisdom of a learned professor, and a professor is nowhere in sight. Having been there, we can tell you that the most important thing is not the teacher's status but whether or not he can teach.

Find out who will be teaching your courses and how well the teacher can teach by asking the present students and by reading the *course evaluations*. These are like report cards on courses and professors, with ratings and comments from students who have taken the course before. Course evaluations are a great resource if you want the real scoop on a course, from the people who actually had to go to the lectures and write the exam. Course evaluations will help you determine if this university is for you.

You also have to find out if you have any control over which *section* you get placed in for a given course. (A section is a smaller group of students in a given course usually managed by a single teaching assistant.) At most universities, you apply for the course and get assigned a professor and a section. Unless you have a compelling reason to make a change (such as a conflict or a religious preclusion against, for instance, Friday-night courses), you are stuck with what you get.

Is There an Effective Advisor Program?

Advisor programs vary considerably from university to university. At some schools, professors or instructors are assigned to advise a particular number of first-year students. They actually meet with the students, discuss their goals, and help them devise a study schedule to meet those goals. Sometimes, first-year students meet with senior students, who give them a solid understanding of how the university operates. On other campuses, students are matched up with alumni who work in the area that the students are studying. On some campuses, you're simply on your own.

The best way to find out what kind of advisor program is available is to ask at the admissions office. The best way to find out if the advisor program is *effective* is to ask other students at the university.

How Often Can I Get Home?

How often do you want to go home? That's a question you should ask yourself early in the planning process. Do you need to be home every other weekend to see what the crowd is up to? Is once a month enough? Or can you tolerate returning to the nest only at the December holiday break and maybe *reading week* (a week-long break, usually in February)? Do you care one way or the other?

Your answers to this question may cause you to eliminate a lot of universities from your list because of their location. However, try to think *beyond* your immediate feelings right now. Maybe your friends at home are incredibly important to you, but you know what? You'll be making a bunch of new friends at university. Think back in your life. When you moved from public school to high school, did you keep all the same friends, or did you make some new ones? What about your dependence on your family? When you go to university, you're going out into the world and taking that first step toward adulthood. It's important to have a strong connection to your family, but it's also important to be independent.

University requires a lot of hard work. Even if your school is only a couple hundred kilometres from your home, you probably won't be able to return every weekend. You will be researching in the library, doing labs, or meeting with your study groups. And, in case you're wondering, every university residence across Canada has laundry facilities. You don't have to use Mom's (or Dad's) Washing Service anymore. (Of course, you don't have to tell them that when you bring home eight duffle bags full of dirty clothes at Thanksgiving, right?)

How Safe Is the Campus?

Crime statistics are something every university student (present and prospective) should investigate and consider. Most universities are very aware of crime and take active measures to protect their students. *Walk safer* programs (programs that offer students a safe person or two to walk them to and from classes and residence in the evenings) are available at most universities across Canada.

Some universities will give safety reports to any student who is interested, so make sure you ask about them at the admissions office. In some universities, crime stats are posted in high-traffic areas such as cafeterias and libraries.

Campus crime statistics can be misleading, however. The surrounding area is probably covered by a different police force than the university's police or security force on campus. So the statistics posted in the cafeteria might reflect only the situation on campus — not in the rest of the area. You can call the municipal police to find out the crime statistics in the area surrounding the university. Many police officers are very willing to tell you which areas are known to be unsafe so that you can avoid them. They can tell you where crimes have occurred and how frequently.

Perhaps the best people to ask are the students themselves. Ask the people who live on campus how safe they feel. Ask about crime in the area. Ask about security in the residences. Are residence doors left open? Are smart cards used to track when people come and go? There may be someone sitting at the security desk at all times, but does he check the IDs of everyone who enters? Security should be important to you, so make sure you find out all you can before you apply.

What Are My Prospects after University?

Does the university offer any help in obtaining a job after you graduate? Does it have a *career centre*, both for summer employment (to help pay for next year's courses) and for permanent placements? Does the school have a faculty of graduate studies? Once you graduate, does the university offer anything other than a stream of letters asking for alumni donations?

Sometimes, just the reputation of the university is enough to open doors for you after graduation, but it helps to know in advance what that reputation is. Ask around. Find out what sort of research the university is known for. Visit the career centre and find out if they help graduates or soon-to-be graduates. They may have statistics showing how many of their graduates got jobs within a few months of graduating. If they don't have such information, that may be a clue that, once you graduate, you'll be all on your own.

Chapter 24

Ten Big Mistakes in University Planning

*N*obody's perfect. Everyone makes mistakes now and then. But one of the reasons you're reading this book is to reduce the number of mistakes you'll make in planning for university. Right? This chapter reminds you of some mistakes that many of your friends may make but that you'll now know how to avoid.

Some mistakes grow out of myths. A friend says one particular section of the application form is all university admissions officers look at, so you don't bother filling out the whole application. You see a TV show about getting into university and believe what the "experts" say — forgetting that the show is American and the process is very different here in Canada. Some mistakes happen because people can't be bothered to spend the time or energy to avoid them. Those people are . . . well . . . let's just say those people will not be joining you in your first year at university.

We've mentioned many of these mistakes elsewhere in this book. Here, you get them all together in one handy list.

Believing You Have to Go to University — and That You Have to Go There Right Away

It's your last year in high school and you haven't had much life experience. Your counsellor starts telling you and your friends that it's time to apply to universities. Your friends are doing it. Your parents want you to do it. So, you figure, okay, why not?

Well, if "why not?" is the only reason you can come up with, you should not apply. Simple as that. People who go to university without giving it any thought tend to do poorly in their first year. And you know what? They tend to *keep* doing poorly; that is, if they stay at all. We've seen too many people head off to university when they weren't ready, bottom out, and come home. It's a big waste of time, money — and really, a big waste of yourself. There are other options.

First of all, think about what you want to do with your life. Do some research. Think about what you want to study. If you have no real desire to study *anything*, you may be better off delaying university for a year. Get out into the workforce and learn the value of an education when trying to get a job or trying to get ahead. Travel or volunteer with a foreign-aid organization — open yourself up to experiences in another part of the world.

Look at other education options. Check out colleges and institutes (and our top ten list about these alternatives in Chapter 22) that may lead you into the career you really want. Look at universities in other countries. The Internet and your local library have a wealth of information about these options. Don't go to university by default. This is *your* life — make sure you are actively involved in your own decisions!

Applying to a University You Haven't Seen Up Close and Personal

When you apply to a university, you're investing a portion of your life. Would you agree to go into business with someone you've never met? How about buying a car without taking it for a test drive?

You can find out a lot about a university by reading catalogues and brochures, looking at its Web site, and talking to people who have been there. But you can't find out *everything* about a university this way. Some things you just have to experience in person.

Every university is a community where students learn from each other as well as from professors and other faculty members. Visiting a campus, talking to students, and observing how they live gives you a realistic feel for that particular community. After you get a sense of the place, you, and only you, will be able to decide whether it's the kind of place where you would be comfortable. (Don't forget, there's much more advice on campus visits in Chapter 9.)

It happens all the time. Bright students with outstanding high school records become so unhappy at university that they transfer after their first year — or even *during* their first year. The common mistake among them was not checking out the campus before they applied. Transferring isn't the worst thing in the world but it can be pretty traumatic and discouraging. Don't let it happen to you!

If you are visiting at the end of your grade 11 year or at the beginning of your grade 12 year, you'll want to make appointments to meet with people before you show up. The most important person to see on a campus visit is an admissions officer. He's the expert at dealing with — and providing information to — potential applicants such as yourself. You want to leave a favourable impression at the admissions office, in case you apply. So it's best to call at least two weeks before you arrive to schedule an appointment at the admissions office. Then, build the rest of your visit around that appointment.

You should also consider making an appointment at the financial aid office and, if you are leaning toward a certain major, with a professor or *undergraduate secretary* in that area. An undergraduate secretary isn't a secretary at all. He or she is usually a full professor who deals with undergraduate matters (such as course conflicts, schedules, staffing, and other important administrative concerns). In many large schools, there is an undergraduate secretary for each department and professional faculty, and it is his or her job to provide academic counselling services for students.

You have to do most of this work yourself. Now is not the time to pull the blankets over your head and hope everything will just work out. While it's true that Mom or Dad can call for your appointment, it's better if you do it yourself. The people you visit will have a better impression of you if you do the work yourself instead of relying on parental backup.

Thinking That Canadian Schools Are Just Like American Schools

We look alike. We talk alike. We even watch the same TV shows. But Americans and Canadians are not alike — and neither are their universities. Of course, American universities are usually called *colleges,* but it goes far beyond this difference in semantics.

The application process for American universities is very different. American universities require SAT scores and a personal essay — and look at all sorts of other information about you. Canadian universities focus on your high school transcripts and *may* look at other factors, but generally only if you are a borderline applicant.

Tuition fees are drastically different, as well. An American college may charge more than $30,000 per year just for tuition — and that's in American currency! State colleges charge less, certainly, but they are still far more expensive than Canadian universities, which average closer to $3,500 per year — in Canadian currency.

Financial aid is also processed differently. The exorbitant tuition fees that American students pay make it almost a necessity for students to get aid packages in order to attend college. Most first-year students at American colleges get some sort of financial aid. In Canada, the lower prices tend to make it easier to pay the whole sticker price. Still, lots of Canadian students get financial aid anyway — but more often than not it is in the form of a loan rather than aid you don't have to pay back.

There are many other ways in which our universities differ from American colleges. Sports scholarships are only starting to make inroads in Canada. Unlike American colleges, fraternities and sororities don't tend to dominate Canadian campuses. Canada offers French-speaking universities. And there are more differences — many more.

Recognize that you have to do independent research on Canadian universities and follow the guidelines that are set out instead of relying on anything you may have heard about applying to American schools.

Ruling Out Going to University Because You Can't Afford It

Most students know that financial aid is out there somewhere, but they don't think that they can get it. These students operate under the misconceptions that financial aid is:

- ✔ Only for the poor.
- ✔ Unavailable to families making more than $50,000 in combined income.
- ✔ Limited to families living in public housing.

Yes, some financial aid is designed to help the poor. At the other end of the spectrum are scholarships — financial aid that goes only to very *smart* students, regardless of how much money their parents make. Scholarships are usually given to students the universities really want.

Between those two extremes, however, are millions of dollars given away each year to average, ordinary students who are neither very poor nor exceedingly brilliant. And you can trigger the process of getting some of that aid by filling out a simple form and putting it in the mail — or sending it online. Some universities include a financial aid application when you receive your acceptance letter. Sometimes, you must ask for this paperwork separately. Just ask, okay?

Perhaps the best part about the Canadian financial aid process is that aid can be made available to anyone who needs it. This means that if you don't have the money to attend university and you don't have the marks for a scholarship, you are still entitled to a *Canada Student Loan*, a government-backed student loan.

As you read this book, keep in mind that more than half the students attending a university in Canada have a student loan, and many others are getting other types of financial aid. You probably can too.

Lying on Your Application

Don't make up information! Don't even think about doing it. Not even on a simple little question on an application form that seems meaningless. Resist any temptation to embellish your record with a few colourful but inaccurate items. Universities are built on a foundation of honesty and trust. If the admissions office discovers that you have been less than truthful about any part of your application, you'll be dead in the water. Your application will almost assuredly be denied. If you have received an offer of admission and the truth comes out later, the offer could be revoked. And if the truth comes out when you have already started classes, you could be expelled immediately.

Just don't do it!

Missing Deadlines

This seems obvious, but some people — yes, even those really smart high school students — sometimes let deadlines slip away and go unmet. Then they have to plead with whoever set the deadline to give them a break. You have better things to do than plead for a break because you forgot a deadline. And the university admissions officer has better things to do than listen to your pleading.

Meanwhile, you are competing with those thousands of other applicants who didn't miss the deadline. Get the picture?

If a university wants your application by January 15, for example, get it in by the end of December at the *latest*. Mail sometimes gets lost around the December holidays because there's so much of it, so give your application extra time to get there.

Don't forget to call to make sure your package got there if you do not receive confirmation. You'll not only make sure the application is on time, but also you'll beat the last-minute rush and get more attention in a less-busy admissions office.

Submitting a Messy or Incomplete Application

Hey, we're not here to judge you. If you've chosen a messy lifestyle, that's fine with us. If you're not a "details" kind of person, preferring to look at the big picture, you should be who you want to be. But sometimes you must adjust your lifestyle to get what you want. And if you want to get into university, messy and incomplete won't make it at the admissions office.

It's a well-known fact that 943 of every 1,000 university applicants are meticulous neat freaks. Okay, we made up the numbers — but all the admissions officers we talked with told us that most applications they receive are neatly typed or word-processed, with *every* applicable field completed. They also told us that they get really aggravated when they have to track down students to fill in parts that were forgotten or that they can't decipher. Do you want to aggravate the people deciding whether or not to let you into university? Probably not.

The bottom line is this: Keep your work neat. Don't use that goopy white stuff to correct errors. And don't cross things out. If you make a mistake, get another form and start over.

Messiness in a university application sticks out like a weed in a flower garden. And such messy work creates a negative impression on the people who have to read the messy stuff. The last thing you need is a negative impression of you at the admissions office.

Sending Just the Application

If you have maintained a 95 percent average throughout your high school career, you can almost assuredly get into any university you apply to without any supplementary materials. But if you are borderline, if you want to get into a particularly competitive program, or if you have erratic marks, the university will usually want to know more about you before it makes its decision.

By providing that extra information along with your application, you do more than answer the admissions officer's questions. You also show yourself to be proactive and responsible — exactly the kind of student every university wants!

Send doctors' notes or explanations written by your principal, counsellor, or a teacher to explain any erratic marks. If you have had a personal trauma that caused you to miss a year of school, let the admissions officer know. If you have won awards, received commendations, or built a business while in high school, toot your own horn. Let teachers who know you well toot your horn too. This tooting can come in the form of recommendation letters explaining how very exceptional you are.

Choosing a University for Its Reputation Alone

A university has a good reputation for one reason: A lot of people like it. But you're not a lot of other people. And what other people like may not be the same as what makes a university right for you. It's important to find out why people like the university or think well of it. Perhaps your cousin really enjoyed the school because it was party central and he had a really good time. Perhaps your grandmother loved her university because of her professors — the ones who retired from teaching there 40 years ago.

We would never suggest that you ignore other people's opinions. Seek out opinions and carefully listen to them, especially from people you respect. Give them serious consideration. But the final decision on where to spend those four years of your life must be yours.

Do your own research and get the feel of the university before you decide to apply. If you select a university solely on its reputation, without considering all the other important factors, you may just find yourself desperate to transfer out after the first few weeks!

Putting Parents in Charge

In selecting the right university, your parents are your advisors. They undoubtedly are wise advisors. Their advice should be accepted graciously and considered seriously. But your parents cannot, and should not, make the decision for you.

When you go to university, your parents stay home. It's your life on the line. You're the one who must become part of a university community.

If your parents seem like they want to take control of your university search, show them this book. They'll be hurting you more than helping if they insist on running your university life. When you arrive for a campus interview, an admissions officer wants to see you bring your parents along — not the other way around. Face the fact, Mom and Dad, your baby's a big boy or girl now.

Part VII
Appendixes

The 5th Wave   By Rich Tennant

"and here's our returning champion, spinning for her 3rd & 4th year university tuition..."

In this part . . .

Didn't we just have a bunch of lists? Do we really need more? In a word: Yes!

Listed in the following pages are some resources to help you research Canadian universities, colleges, and technical institutes, gather information about costs, financial aid, and scholarships, and catalogue the general feelings you get out of the various schools. Appendix A, "Directory of Universities and Colleges," gives you the basic information you need to begin assessing your educational options.

But that's not all! Appendix D, "The Mull List," brings together the top issues from all the other lists we've provided throughout the book — and gets you thinking about these issues before you apply. Since many students will start their research using the Internet, we've also put together a great list of the top online resources (besides the official university and college Web sites). Finally, we provide a handy list of financial planning resources. Now that you've come to the end of the book, it's definitely time to think about the monetary aspects of attending university or college.

As you'll learn throughout your post-secondary education, resources are invaluable in any publication. They allow you to take the message you've just read and move forward. That's what we hope you'll do with these listings. Check each of them out. Let each of them lead you to even more resources and information. Education is a never-ending process, but with the right tools you're off to a great start. Good travels!

Appendix A

Directory of Universities and Colleges

· ·

*B*efore we get started, we'd like to explain some of the criteria we use in this directory, and offer you a few pointers on how to get the most out of the information in these bright yellow pages.

Size of Institution

The size of a given university is an important determining factor for many students and we have included this information in the following pages. For the purposes of this directory, we have classified universities that have 1 to 5,000 students as "small"; universities that have 5,001 to 20,000 students as "mid-size"; and those schools that have over 20,000 students as "large." When we refer to a school as located in a "university town," this indicates a place where the university is relevant and noticeable due to the size of the town and the impact of thousands of students attending every year. Provincial capital cities are not considered university towns because they have a diverse range of activities and cultural offerings beyond the university whereas some towns double their population because university students have joined their ranks.

Remember that *bigger* is not necessarily *better*. In fact, in some cases, *bigger* might actually be *not better*. It depends on you, your expectations, and your educational goals. If you're from a small town, you may feel overwhelmed by the sheer size of major metropolitan areas such as Toronto, Vancouver, Calgary, Montréal, or Edmonton. If you're from a large city, will you grow quickly bored of a small-town university?

Some students thrive in big cities (just as some students thrive in big universities and big classrooms). Of course, there are many students who do better in the opposite situation, avoiding *big* as much as they can. It depends on what you want out of the school — and out of life.

Admissions

When looking at the admission dates, remember these are the *last possible* dates by which you must apply. Also remember that many universities use a rolling admission, meaning they accept or reject students as the applications are processed. If you send your application to arrive on the last possible day, chances are the university will already have filled its available spaces with students that were a little faster on the draw.

Tuition Fees

We've provided an average rate for full-time, first-year studies in arts or sciences, but you must check your program to figure out your particular rate. Many universities charge fees per course, others charge per semester, and others charge per year. Some include the incidental university fees as mandatory and others allow you to opt in or out of some. You'll notice that the majority of Canadian universities do not discriminate against out-of-province students except for universities in the province of Québec, where in-province students are treated to a substantially discounted university tuition. Québec's out-of-province tuition fees aren't *more* than they are in other provinces, it's just that the in-province fees are *substantially less*. All fees in this section have been rounded to the nearest dollar.

Residence Costs

These vary widely across the Canadian universities, mostly based on size of city, whether you get a meal plan, if you opt for a single, double, triple, or even quadruple room, and if you get an apartment-style dwelling instead of a more traditional residence room. All other things being equal, the cost of residence is directly proportional to the size of the city in which a given university is located. We've used the average rates for residence, usually in a double room, with a full meal plan.

Some universities allow students to completely *opt out of* (decide not to use) the standard residence meal plan. Other schools let you purchase meals à la carte, meaning that you deduct the cost of the occasional meal from your university-supplied (and charged) smart card. Some other schools let you decide to have breakfast at school ("the most important meal of the day") and buy food out for the remainder of the day.

If you decide to opt out of your college or university meal plan, try to eat nutritionally balanced meals. There's little sense in having yummy junk food every day if you gain weight, have no energy, and start breaking out — and can't get a date on Saturday because you don't look your best. Remember, the athletic complex isn't just a building you walk past on your way to the nearest fast-food place!

Things Change

The information we've listed is the latest we could gather, but remember that things change, prices go up, and universities alter their courses and programs. Check everything before you commit yourself and the next four years of your life.

Canadian Universities

Read on to find useful information about Canada's 51 major universities.

Acadia University

Based in Wolfville, Nova Scotia, in the Annapolis region, Acadia University offers an intimate learning environment in a university town. Its "Acadia Advantage" program requires that students pay a lot more in tuition but get use of an IBM notebook computer. These computers link easily into all information systems at the university for a more "wired" education. Some students are dismayed at the extra cost but many enjoy the easier access to information. The program has been inducted into the Smithsonian Institute. The university has been ranked number one in *Maclean's* magazine's annual survey in the *Best Overall*, *Most Innovative*, and *Leaders of Tomorrow* categories for primarily undergraduate universities in Canada. Acadia prides itself on a reputation for academic excellence and, overall, seems to try harder than many other universities.

Contact

- Address: Acadia University, Wolfville, Nova Scotia B0P 1X0
- Phone: (902) 542-2201
- Fax: (902) 585-1072
- Web site: www.acadiau.ca
- E-mail: ask.acadia@acadiau.ca

Admissions

- Total student population: 3,877 (full time: 3,435; part time: 442)
- Tuition in-province: $5,805
- Tuition out-of-province: $5,805 (same as in-province)
- Tuition international students: $10,331
- 2001/2002 application deadline: March 15, 2001
- Application fee: $25
- Average cost of residence: $5,130

Key details

Students must have completed the admission application process by February 1 for early consideration or March 1 at the latest for normal admission. Students must have overall averages of at least 85 percent in both grade 11 and grade 12 or their equivalents. After March 15, applications are reviewed as space permits on a rolling admission basis. Acadia University begins its scholarship consideration process in mid-February. In 2001, this process began on February 15. Acadia University has more than 200 degree combinations from the faculties of arts, pure and applied science, professional studies, and theology. The school also boasts a diverse international community, with students from more than 50 countries. There are over 1,000 part-time jobs on campus and a wide range of co-operative education and internship opportunities.

University of Alberta

Located in Edmonton, the capital of Alberta, the University of Alberta (the "U of A," as it is known to students and faculty alike), sports a student base of over 30,000 undergraduates and graduates. One of the two large schools in the province (the other being the University of Calgary), the University of Alberta has a diverse variety of programs and courses. Edmonton itself has a well-established artistic population, with one of the best fringe theatre festivals in the world. This diversity lends itself to the fascinating mix of student groups around campus. If you expect nothing but hockey, snow, and cowboys in Edmonton, you've got another think coming. However, let's not diminish the winter weather — it gets cold, *really* cold, in Edmonton.

Contact

- Address: 114 St. and 89 Ave., Edmonton, Alberta T6G 2M7

- Phone: (780) 492-3111

- Toll-free: (888) 929-8632

- Fax: (780) 492-7172

- Web site: www.ualberta.ca

- E-mail: info@ualberta.ca

Admissions

- Total population: 30,922 (full time: 26,874; part time: 4,048)

- Tuition in-province: $3,983

- Tuition out-of-province: $3,983 (same as in-province)

- Tuition international students: $10,425

- 2001/2002 application deadline: May 1

- Application fee: $60

- Average cost of residence: $3,500

Key details

The University of Alberta is one of the largest schools west of Ontario and ideal for students who enjoy a large student community in a large Canadian city. The university's 2000/2001 admissions totalled 30,922 students, with $29.62 million dollars in scholarships and bursaries awarded. A total of $12.5 million in scholarship money was awarded in the 2000/2001 session for 7,397 undergraduate scholarships, with a dollar average of $1,690 each.

Bishop's University

Located approximately 160 km east of Montréal, Bishop's University is a small university in the small town of Lennoxville, just outside of Sherbrooke, Québec. Although a proud Québec university, Bishop's language of instruction and administration is predominately English (except for specific French-language courses and programs). Since it is small, Bishop's attracts students who enjoy a cozy liberal arts environment in which students know each other and professors actually know your name. The folks at admissions boast that no class has more than 75 students (including the first-year "feeder courses"), in part because the largest classroom in the school seats 75 people! It gets very cold in Lennoxville but there is terrific skiing in the area so students are encouraged to be active.

Contact

- Address: PO Box 5000, Lennoxville, Québec J1M 1Z7

- Phone: (819) 822-9600

- Fax: (819) 822-9661

- Toll-free: (800) 567-2792

- Web site: www.ubishops.ca

- E-mail: liaison@ubishops.ca

Admissions

- Total population: 2,494 (full time: 1,914; part time: 580)

- Tuition in-province: $2,390

- Tuition out-of-province: $4,430

- Tuition international students: $9,890

- 2001/2002 application deadline: March 1

- Application fee: $55

- Average cost of residence: $5,500

Key details

All CEGEP students (Québec only) with an 80 percent average on academic courses are guaranteed entrance scholarships of at least $2,000 from Bishop's University. Ontario and western Canadian high school students with academic averages of 85 percent are also guaranteed scholarships of at least $2,000. Students from Atlantic Canada with academic averages of 88 percent are guaranteed scholarships of at least $2,000. To be eligible for a scholarship, an application form along with a current transcript must be received by March 1. Only those marks submitted will be used to determine scholarship eligibility. Renewable scholarships range from $2,000 to $4,000.

Brandon University

One of three universities in Manitoba (the others being the University of Manitoba and the University of Winnipeg), Brandon University is located in the small town of Brandon. The university is a major focus of this university town and provides a large source of income for the community. A comparatively large percentage — fully one-third — of Brandon's student population attend on a part-time basis, attesting to the fact that many mature and non-traditional students are earning their degrees from Brandon. The university is particularly suited to students who enjoy small classes at a small school in a rural setting. Manitoba's capital, Winnipeg, is approximately 200 km away. Alberta's capital, Edmonton is farther north, but Brandon may be the coldest place in Canada to get an education! Of course, if you don't get out much, you'll have more time to study.

Contact

- Address: 270 18th St., Brandon, Manitoba R7A 6A9

- Phone: (204) 728-9520

- Fax: (204) 726-4573

- Web site: www.brandonu.ca

- E-mail: discover@brandonu.ca

Admissions

- Total population: 2,800 (full time: 1,848; part time: 952)

- Tuition in-province: $3,033

- Tuition out-of-province: $3,033 (same as in-province)

- Tuition international students: $6,000

✔ 2001/2002 application deadline: May 1

✔ Application fee: $35

✔ Average cost of residence: $2,500

Key details

Brandon awards loyalty and drive. Graduates of accredited Canadian high schools who choose Brandon University as their first choice of post-secondary institution will receive an entrance scholarship. Students who achieve an overall average of 85 to 89.9 percent will receive a scholarship of $800, going up to $1,400 for averages of 90 to 94.9 percent and $2,000 for 95 or higher. Brandon offers a world-renowned music program and an excellent program in native studies.

The University of British Columbia

The largest, and arguably the most prestigious, university in western Canada, the University of British Columbia is one of four general universities in the province including Simon Fraser University, the University of Northern British Columbia, and the University of Victoria. Located near downtown Vancouver close to the trendy Kitsilano area, the UBC campus is large, beautiful, and popular with students for both academic and non-academic activities. UBC (and Vancouver) boasts one of the most multicultural populations in western Canada and many of the faculty are internationally renowned in their fields. Vancouver itself has an immense diversity of cultural, sporting, and entertainment offerings with a population that tends to be active. The climate is temperate but those gorgeous Rockies have the unfortunate effect of bringing in a lot (we mean *a lot*) of rain.

Contact

✔ Address: (Registrar's Office) Room 2016, 1874 East Mall, Vancouver, British Columbia V6T 1Z1

✔ Phone: (604) 822-2211

✔ Fax: (604) 822-3599

✔ Web site: www.ubc.ca

✔ E-mail: student.information @ubc.ca

Admissions

✔ Total population: 34,938 (full time: 25,274; part time: 9,664)

✔ Tuition in-province: $2,669

✔ Tuition out-of-province: $2,669 (same as in-province)

✔ Tuition international students: $13,830

✔ 2001/2002 application deadline: March 31

✔ Application fee: $54

✔ Average cost of residence: $7,000

Key details

There are over 75 major entrance scholarships for students entering UBC from high school. These range in value from $1,750 one-time awards to "full" scholarships of $26,000, payable in $6,500 annual instalments for four years. UBC's $601.8-million endowment fund endows chairs and scholarships at the university and ranks as one of the largest endowment funds among Canadian universities. UBC's 2001/2002 under-graduate scholarships were awarded to 4,600 students for a total value of $9 million, for an average award of approximately $1,957 per student.

Brock University

Located in picturesque St. Catharines (less than 30 km from Niagara Falls), Brock University is a mid-sized university with a small-town feel. Brock's part-time student base is higher than many other universities, at approximately 40 percent of its total enrollment. The Niagara escarpment offers excellent trails and scenery, and the nearby Shaw Festival (running from April to October) has some of the best theatre in Canada.

Contact

- Address: 500 Glenridge Avenue, St. Catharines, Ontario L2S 3A1
- Phone: (905) 688-5550
- Fax: (905) 688-2789
- Web site: www.brocku.ca
- E-mail: admissns@brocku.ca

Admissions

- Total population: 10,984 (full time: 6,846; part time: 4,138)
- Tuition in-province: $4,256
- Tuition out-of-province: $4,256 (same as in-province)
- Tuition international students: $9,817
- 2001/2002 application deadline: Standard OUAC application deadline
- Application fee: Standard OUAC fee payable
- Average cost of residence: $5,700

Key details

Brock offers admission scholarships based on a student's overall high school marks. For students who have achieved an overall average between 80 to 89.9 percent, Brock awards admission scholarships of $1,000. For students who have achieved overall averages of 90 to 93.9 percent, Brock awards $1,500. For exceptional students who achieve an overall average of 94 percent or more, Brock awards entrance scholarships of $2,500. Students entering Brock with at least a 90 percent average from high school (and who maintain at least an 85 percent average over at least four university credits) will be eligible to renew these entrance scholarships in subsequent years. Residence in one of the four excellent buildings is guaranteed to first-year students who have at least a 75 percent average, on a first-come, first-served basis.

University of Calgary

Nestled near the foothills of the Rocky Mountains, the University of Calgary is the second-largest general admission university in Alberta (smaller than Edmonton's University of Alberta yet larger than the University of Lethbridge). The city of Calgary has an interesting mix of rural/cowboy, oil-boom worker, and environmentalist demographics. The student body is highly active — in terms of politics, sports, and spirit. Any student who wants to get a point across can spray-paint it on The Rock — a big boulder located in the middle of campus. The weather is highly changeable — during a visit to Calgary one summer, Caryn and David joked that they had experienced all four seasons in a few hours with snow, rain, wind, and blistering heat in rapid succession.

Contact

- Address: 2500 University Drive NW, Calgary, Alberta T2N 1N4
- Phone: (403) 220-5110
- Toll-free: (866) 220-4992
- Fax: (403) 282-7298
- Web site: www.ucalgary.ca
- E-mail: applinfo@ucalgary.ca

Admissions

- Total population: 25,367 (full time: 21,106; part time: 4,261)
- Tuition in-province: $4,260
- Tuition out-of-province: $4,260 (same as in-province)
- Tuition international students: $8,094
- 2001/2002 application deadline: June 1
- Application fee: $65
- Average cost of residence: $5,500

Key details

The University of Calgary increased its tuition and other fees earlier than the other Alberta universities, so there is less protest activity about the relatively smaller incremental increases these days. A variety of scholarships and bursaries are available, although the university has a lower endowment than some of the longer- established universities. The University of Calgary was founded in only 1967, an offshoot of the University of Alberta. The rivalry continues to this day!

University College of Cape Breton

A small university located at the eastern tip of Cape Breton Island, this school mainly caters to local folks wishing to get a solid university education while still staying in the area. The school has fewer than 3,500 students enrolled (including approximately 470 part-timers). This intimate environment allows students a lot of interaction with their professors. One representative described UCCB as "A family university where you get to know everyone on a first-name basis." The local environment is convivial, with the sort of friendly "come on over and lift a pint" attitude that Cape Breton is known for.

Contact

- Address: PO Box 5300 Stn A, Sydney, Nova Scotia B1P 6L2
- Phone: (902) 539-5300
- Toll-free: (888) 959-9995
- Fax: (902) 562-0119
- Web site: www.uccb.ns.ca
- E-mail: registrar@uccb.ca

Admissions

- Total population: 3,433 (full time: 2,961; part time: 472)
- Tuition in-province: $4,282
- Tuition out-of-province: $4,282 (same as in-province)
- Tuition international students: $7,532
- 2001/2002 application deadline: Mar 15
- Application fee: $20
- Average cost of residence: $2,500

Key details

Recipients are determined primarily on the basis of academic standing. However, in certain cases, other conditions come into play. For example, the Rita MacNeil *Working Man Scholarship* requires the applicant to be the son, daughter, or spouse of a coal miner in Nova Scotia. Although 75 percent is the minimum grade average, with no failures, most scholarships are offered to students with an 80 percent grade point average or higher.

Carleton University

Carleton University is justly famous for its top-notch journalism program and its emerging focus in high-tech courses, but this large school offers a wide variety of programs across many disciplines. Due to its closeness to the political centre of Canada, political science, economics, and related programs also are very popular at the school. Students themselves tend to become active in the political scene as well — debates and rallies are a frequent occurrence and it is hard to avoid getting caught up in the fervour of one cause or another. Trying to escape from its reputation as "Last-Chance U," Carleton has upped its admission standards in recent years.

Contact

- Address: 1125 Colonel By Drive, Ottawa, Ontario K1S 5B6
- Phone: (613) 520-7400
- Fax: (613) 520-3847
- Web site: www.carleton.ca
- E-mail: liaison@carleton.ca

Admissions

- Total population: 15,305 (full time: 12,780; part time: 2,525)
- Tuition in-province: $4,421
- Tuition out-of-province: $4,421 (same as in-province)
- Tuition international students: $9,511
- 2001/2002 application deadline: Standard OUAC application deadline
- Application fee: Standard OUAC fee payable
- Average cost of residence: $6,000

Key details

Like many universities, Carleton has a multi-tiered scholarship consideration system based on final high school grades. For students graduating with an average of 80 to 81.9 percent, the university offers $600. For averages of 82 to 83.9 percent, the university gives $4,000 in scholarship money over the course of four years ($1,000 per year). For students graduating high school with an average of 84 to 87.9 percent, Carleton awards a total scholarship of $8,000 over four years ($2,000 per year). For students who score better in the final year of high school, Carleton sweetens the scholarship pot even further. Students averaging 88 to 94.9 percent are awarded $10,000 over four years ($2,500 per year). For the stellar students (those scoring from 95 to 100 percent), Carleton gives $14,000 over four years ($3,500 per year).

Concordia University

Based in the heart of Montréal, Concordia University is a mid-sized university offering a wide variety of programs and courses. Concordia is the largest university in Québec whose primary language of instruction and administration is English (just beating out McGill University).

Contact

✔ Address: 1455 de Maisonneuve Blvd West, Montréal, Québec H3G 1M8

✔ Phone: (514) 848-2424

✔ Fax: (514) 848-2621

✔ Web site: www.concordia.ca

✔ E-mail: admreq@alcor.concordia.ca

Admissions

✔ Total population: 25,825 (full time: 13,243; part time: 12,582)

✔ Tuition in-province: $1,668

✔ Tuition out-of-province: $3,708

✔ Tuition international students: $8,268

✔ 2001/2002 application deadline: March 1

✔ Application fee: $50

✔ Average cost of residence: $5,000

Key details

You need not submit a separate entrance scholarship application unless otherwise notified. All students submitting an application to Concordia University by March 1 for the fall term, and November 1 for the winter term, will automatically be considered for an entrance scholarship. Only those students offered an entrance scholarship will be notified.

Concordia distinguishes between entrance bursaries, entrance scholarships, and other types of student financial aid such as government student loans. In addition, Concordia also has several scholarships open to mature students.

Dalhousie University

One of four universities located in Halifax (the others being the University of King's College, Mount Saint Vincent University, and Saint Mary's University), Dalhousie is the largest university in the city and boasts a wide variety of programs and courses, including professional programs in nursing and law. Halifax is known for its bitter winters and beautiful summers. However, Dalhousie has a convivial atmosphere as befits a Maritime university. It has the most culturally diverse student population of the Atlantic universities, with a wide range of students from outside the province and even outside the country.

Contact

✔ Address: 1236 Henry Street, Halifax, Nova Scotia B3H 3J5

✔ Phone: (902) 494-2450

✔ Fax: (902) 494-2319

✔ Web site: www.dal.ca

✔ E-mail: admissions@dal.ca

Admissions

✔ Total population: 12,798 (full time: 10,782; part time: 2,016)

✔ Tuition in-province: $4,744

✔ Tuition out-of-province: $4,744 (same as in-province)

- Tuition international students: $7,094
- 2001/2002 application deadline: June 1
- Application fee: $40
- Average cost of residence: $5,450

Key details

Dalhousie offers a variety of entrance scholarships valued at $500 to $7,000, which must be applied for by April 15 with an indication of class rank from your high school counsellor. Admissions staff are particularly helpful and willing to go the extra mile to get students the information they need.

University of Guelph

Known around the world for its veterinarian school and crop genetics expertise, Guelph is much more than just an agricultural university. A wide variety of science, social science, and arts courses are taught at Guelph. The campus is located somewhat out of the actual city of Guelph and has a modern (although very rural) look and feel. The city of Guelph is about a one-hour drive from Toronto. Guelph attracts not only local students but also those from Toronto who want a less hectic campus life. Only slightly more than 13 percent of Guelph's entire student population are part-time learners.

Contact

- Address: 50 Stone Rd. East, Suite 158, Guelph, Ontario N1G 2W1
- Phone: (519) 824-4120
- Fax: (519) 763-6809
- Web site: www.uoguelph.ca
- E-mail: info@registrar.uoguelph.ca

Admissions

- Total population: 14,519 (full time: 12,621; part time: 1,898)
- Tuition in-province: $3,950
- Tuition out-of-province: $3,950 (same as in-province)
- Tuition international students: $18,000
- 2001/2002 application deadline: Standard OUAC application deadline
- Application fee: Standard OUAC fee payable
- Average cost of residence: $6,000

Key details

The University of Guelph says it will offer more than $10 million in student financial aid this year. Most students live in residence for the first year and then move off to one of the student ghettos for the next few years. It's important to search out a place early, as the best locations get snapped up quickly.

University of King's College

This tiny university is associated with Dalhousie University, upon whose campus it sits. This proximity leads to a constant rivalry between the two venerable institutions; however, both benefit from the other's facilities. King's boasts a highly academic environment and has an excellent reputation, especially for its extremely competitive journalism program and its focus on classics. Despite its pretentious reputation, the students and faculty are a close-knit bunch. The head of admissions could not recall a year when all first-year positions in the university were not filled.

Contact

- Address: 6350 Coburg Road, Halifax, Nova Scotia B3H 2A1

- Phone: (902) 422-1271

- Toll-free: (877) 361-2829

- Fax: (902) 423-3357

- Web site: www.ukings.ns.ca

- E-mail: admissions@ukings.ns.ca

Admissions

- Total population: 800 (full time)

- Tuition in-province: $4,550

- Tuition out-of-province: $4,550 (same as in-province)

- Tuition international students: $6,900

- 2001/2002 application deadline: March 1

- Application fee: $35

- Average cost of residence: $5,000

Key details

Scholarships of various levels are available based on submission of an essay, class ranking, and, of course, marks. Many of the professors are world-renowned and you get to pick their brains at your leisure. Despite the university's excellent reputation, there are virtually no international students on campus.

Lakehead University

The Thunder Bay location has a serious impact on the university — it's situated several hours of driving away from everything in a place that gets *mighty* cold in the wintertime. The stark wilderness just outside of town may be glorious to some and truly frightening to others.

However, the jovial atmosphere and spirited raucousness of the student body makes anyone open to a little friendly joshing feel right at home. The university's history as a technical institute is shown in its concentration on engineering — and qualifying college engineering graduates can do a summer session and final two years at Lakehead to wind up with a B.Eng. degree. You'll find a wide range of program offerings, but along with engineering the university is best known for forestry, education, and native studies.

Contact

- Address: 955 Oliver Road, Thunder Bay, Ontario P7B 5E1

- Phone: (807) 343-8110

- Fax: (807) 343-8023

- Web site: www.lakeheadu.ca

- E-mail: admissions@lakeheadu.ca

Admissions

- Total population: 6,336 (full time: 5,052; part time: 1,284)

- Tuition in-province: $4,150

- Tuition out-of-province: $4,150 (same as in-province)

- Tuition international students: $8,500

- 2001/2002 application deadline: Standard OUAC application deadline

- Application fee: Standard OUAC fee payable

- Average cost of residence: $5,500

Key details

Lakehead University offers a comprehensive scholarship program available to qualified undergraduate entrants and in-course students. Every student with at least an 80 percent overall average automatically receives a minimum of scholarship or other award funds from Lakehead. You must specifically apply for Lakehead's entrance scholarships by printing out and completing a copy of the scholarship application that's available on the university's Web site. The form is also available from your high school counsellor's office. Completed applications must be returned to Lakehead's financial aid office by mid-April (specific dates vary slightly by year). In-course and transfer scholarships are also available for students continuing their studies at Lakehead University.

Laurentian University of Sudbury

Similar to Lakehead, Laurentian is a northern school surrounded by all the stark and stunning beauty of the Canadian Shield — and all of its excitement. One of the few fully bilingual universities in Canada, most of the student body comes from the surrounding area. It has a well-earned reputation as a party school, but this also reflects a solidarity and camaraderie that makes all willing students feel at home. You will likely know your professors on a first-name basis. Laurentian is best known for its sports programs, sports administration and physical education — along with anything to do with mining.

Contact

- Address: 935 Ramsey Lake Road, Sudbury, Ontario P3E 2C6
- Phone: (705) 675-1151
- Fax: (705) 675-4891

- Web site: www.laurentian.ca
- E-mail: admission@nickel.laurentian.ca

Admissions

- Total population: 5,659 (full time: 3,707; part time: 1,952)
- Tuition in-province: $3,951
- Tuition out-of-province: $3,951 (same as in-province)
- Tuition international students: $8,750
- 2001/2002 application deadline: Standard OUAC application deadline
- Application fee: Standard OUAC fee payable
- Average cost of residence: $4,500

Key details

Laurentian offers over 1,000 part-time jobs on campus, and a wide range of co-operative education and internship opportunities. The university awards over $1 million annually in bursaries and has an extensive work-study program. The school guarantees a room to all first-year students, with an optional meal plan. The B.F. Avery Physical Education Centre is a good example of Laurentian's focus on sports and the outdoors. The Centre offers an Olympic pool, gymnasium, weight and training room, a rock-climbing room, and an outdoor stadium with an eight-lane 400-metre track.

Université Laval

Université Laval is located close to historic Old Québec, the only walled city left in North America. Québec is so beautiful, it was declared a UNESCO World Heritage site in 1985. Université Laval's primary language of instruction and administration is French, and over the last few years Université Laval, along with Montréal's McGill University, has recorded the highest graduation rate among Québec universities. Every year, about 1,800 international students from some 86 different countries choose to study at Université Laval.

Contact

✔ Address: Cité Universitaire, CP 2208 Succ Terminus, Québec G1K 7P4

✔ Phone: (418) 656-2131

✔ Toll-free: (800) 561-0478

✔ Fax: (418) 656-2809

✔ Web site: www.ulaval.ca

✔ E-mail: scom@scom.ulaval.ca

Admissions

✔ Total population: 33,231 (full time: 21,140; part time: 12,091)

✔ Tuition in-province: $1,668

✔ Tuition out-of-province: $3,708

✔ Tuition international students: $8,268

✔ 2001/2002 application deadline: March 1

✔ Application fee: $30

✔ Average cost of residence: $1,664 (residence only; no meal plans offered)

Key details

Since January 1998, the Université Laval has offered a work-study program that provides undergraduate students the opportunity to acquire hands-on work experience in a teaching environment or university department. This remunerated work experience offers a direct link to the student's field of study. The program is managed by the university placement service. Another interesting benefit to attending the Université Laval is that all students enjoy free Internet access. E-mail, Web, Telnet, FTP, and newsgroup access — both on-campus and off — is available free to all registered students. Finally, three on-campus daycare centres make it easier for parents to study.

The University of Lethbridge

If you want to study at a university in Alberta and you prefer a small to mid-sized school, Lethbridge is the place to be. Management and education studies have been a traditional focus of the school, but you can get a degree in almost all traditional subjects as well. Native studies is a key specialty, which makes sense considering the university's location in the Blackfoot Confederacy. U Lethbridge also offers excellent co-op programs in a wide variety of studies — mostly sciences and business specialties, but you can also take co-ops in English or philosophy.

Contact

✔ Address: 4401 University Drive West, Lethbridge, Alberta T1K 3M4

✔ Phone: (403) 329-2201

✔ Toll-free: (800) 666-3503

✔ Fax: (403) 329-2097

✔ Web site: www.uleth.ca

✔ E-mail: inquiries@uleth.ca

Admissions

✔ Total population: 6,026 (full time: 5169; part time: 857)

✔ Tuition in-province: $3,964

✔ Tuition out-of-province: $3,964 (same as in-province)

✔ Tuition international students: $7,928

✔ 2001/2002 application deadline: June 1

✔ Application fee: $50

✔ Average cost of residence: $3,731

Key details

If you are entering the university from high school, there are a number of financial award options available. The university's Board of Governors' Admission Scholarship has a one-time value of $1,000 each, and 150 scholarships will be granted to the highest achieving applicants from geographic regions in Alberta, southern British Columbia, and southern Saskatchewan. To be eligible for this award, you must apply for admission to the U of L by January 4 or sooner.

Early-entrance awards valued from $1,000 to $5,000 are also available. Over 20 individual scholarships are available on the basis of student academic achievement as well as other criteria, such as leadership ability, volunteer experience, and artistic ability. A separate scholarship application is required by April 1. Automatic high school entrance awards, with a value of up to $2,000, are awarded to all high school

applicants with an overall admission average of 80 percent or greater. Almost 40 percent of incoming high school applicants were offered a University of Lethbridge administered scholarship in 1999, with the average disbursement being $1,100.

University of Manitoba

U of M is a large university located in a capital city, so students are fairly diverse and there is more independence than school spirit. All the standard programs are available, but the university is best known for its agrarian courses with both a scientific and management focus, along with its excellent program in nursing. The university offers a unique program for all first-year students, called Introduction to University, where students learn about the university experience, how to study, and all the other crucial things that most university students have to pick up on their own. Winnipeg gets *seriously* cold, so most students move around campus using the excellent tunnel system once the outside world dips below zero. It's so extensive that residents brag they can stay in shorts all year round. Much of the information on the Web site is from 1999, so make sure you get an admissions package by mail. Admissions staff are terrific — as befits a province where the car licence plates proclaim, "Friendly Manitoba"!

Contact

✔ Address: 66 Chancellors Circle, Winnipeg, Manitoba R3T 2N2

✔ Phone: (204) 474-8880

✔ Toll-free: (800) 224-7713

✔ Fax: (204) 474-7536

✔ Web site: www.umanitoba.ca

✔ E-mail: admissions@umanitoba.ca

Admissions

✔ Total population: 21,069 (full time: 16,026; part time: 5,043)

✔ Tuition in-province: $2,847

✔ Tuition out-of-province: $2,847 (same as in-province)

✔ Tuition international students: $6,000

✔ 2001/2002 application deadline: May 1

✔ Application fee: $35

✔ Average cost of residence: $3,500

Key details

Approximately a total of $165,000 is awarded annually to new and continuing university students who qualify for membership on any CIAU-recognized university team. The amount of the award for individual students is recommended by the individual coaches, with a usual range of $500 to $1,500.

The university subsidizes a bursary program for new and continuing full-time and part-time students with good academic marks who demonstrate a significant level of financial need. Bursaries are usually issued in amounts ranging from $100 to $1,000, with approximately $700,000 awarded annually.

McGill University

The second-largest university in Québec whose primary language of instruction and administration is English (it's just slightly smaller than Concordia), McGill is where the "old money" students of English-speaking Montréal go. The university has a diverse range of programs and courses (and students!) and is one of most respected schools in Canada and around the world. The university's prestige is bolstered by its entrance requirements — some of the more competitive programs didn't accept anyone with less than 90 percent in recent years. And, of course, you get to live in glorious Montréal, with its nightlife and activities and some of the best food in the country!

Contact

✔ Address: 845 Sherbrooke St. West, Montréal, Québec H3A 2T5

✔ Phone: (514) 398-3594

✔ Fax: (514) 398-4455

✔ Web site: www.mcgill.ca

✔ E-mail: welcome@aro.lan.mcgill.ca

Admissions

✔ Total population: 24,418 (full time: 20,720; part time: 3,698)

✔ Tuition in-province: $1,668

✔ Tuition out-of-province: $3,438

✔ Tuition international students: $8,268

✔ 2001/2002 application deadline: February 1

✔ Application fee: $60

✔ Average cost of residence: $6,000

Key details

McGill has an extensive program of entrance awards to recognize and honour scholarship. Awards range in value from $2,000 to $15,000, are renewable, and are based on outstanding academic achievement and leadership qualities. Scholarships are offered to Canadian and international students alike.

McMaster University

Located an hour west of Toronto, in Hamilton, McMaster gets most of its students from the surrounding Golden Horseshoe. The school is best known for its science faculty, where researchers in biology, chemistry, and physics have made quite a name for themselves and "Mac." Supplementary information is not only welcome but also usually *required* when applying. The McMaster Web site is a challenge to navigate, and it's difficult to reach anyone on the telephone, but admissions staff are helpful once you find them.

Contact

- Address: 1280 Main Street West, Suite 20, Hamilton, Ontario L8S 4L8

- Phone: (905) 525-9140

- Toll-free: (800) 463-6223 (continuing education department)

- Fax: (905) 521-1504

- Web site: www.mcmaster.ca

- E-mail: madadmit@mcmaster.ca (admissions)

Admissions

- Total population: 16,942 (full time: 13,910; part time: 3,032)

- Tuition in-province: $3,830

- Tuition out-of-province: $3,830 (same as in-province)

- Tuition international students: $9,000

- 2001/2002 application deadline: Standard OUAC application deadline

- Application fee: Standard OUAC fee payable

- Average cost of residence: $4,700

Key details

It can be very difficult to reach many administrative departments at McMaster, especially the financial aid folks, either using the Web or by telephone. Prospective students should set aside more than the usual time allotment to research the scholarship situation at this school. Entrance scholarships are usually awarded to those students coming directly from high school. There are quite a few awards open to students, of which McMaster Scholar Awards are the most prestigious (and the most lucrative).

The school awards five university-wide Scholar Awards valued at $25,000 (payable over four years); seven faculty- or program-specific awards valued at $15,000 (payable over four years); 15 university-wide awards valued at $12,000 (payable over four years); and 50 faculty- or program-specific awards valued at $3,000 (payable for one year).

The McMaster Scholar Awards require a special application. All-around out-standing students, who have made contributions in extracurricular or community activities and who have a final-year average in the 90s, are encouraged to apply. The application deadline is mid-February. There are many other awards, including the McMaster Honour Awards (arts and science) and the Nortel Networks Entrance Scholarships (awarded to engineering students).

Memorial University of Newfoundland

Bigger even than Dalhousie, Memorial has the largest student body of any university in the Atlantic provinces. There are campuses in St. John's and Cornerbrook, and its location is not lost on its focus — you'll find excellent programs in marine studies at the school. Of course, there is a wide range of traditional programs as well. Make sure you get a printed application package and contact admissions directly, as some parts of the Web site have not been updated since 1997! While Memorial is a large university, the classes are generally kept small so you get to know your professors pretty well. Besides, it's in Newfoundland, where we're pretty sure it's against the law to be unfriendly. As befits its reputation, Newfoundlanders — especially those at Memorial — go out of their way to be helpful and make you feel welcome.

Contact

- Address: PO Box 4200 Stn C, St. John's, Newfoundland A1C 5S7
- Phone: (709) 737-8000
- Fax: (709) 737-8611
- Web site: www.mun.ca
- E-mail: new.students@mun.ca

Admissions

- Total population: 15,660 (full time: 12,894; part time: 2,766)
- Tuition in-province: $3,300
- Tuition out-of-province: $3,300 (same as in-province)
- Tuition international students: $7,600
- 2001/2002 application deadline: March 1
- Application fee: $40
- Average cost of residence: $4,750

Key details

There is a wide variety of entrance and special scholarships and bursaries available. Some are in-kind awards, such as the Air Labrador Award offered to assist Labrador residents to attend the university by providing airfare to the island, where the campuses are located.

Université de Moncton

The Université de Moncton is a small university in which instruction and administration is offered in French. The university is actually distributed over three separate campuses: Moncton (go figure), Edmundston, and Shippagan. As you might guess, the largest campus is in Moncton and has the widest selection of courses and programs, ranging from engineering to nutrition to education to arts to sciences — and more. The smaller campuses in Edmundston and Shippagan offer degrees in business administration, humanities, forestry, and other subjects. The admissions staff are fully bilingual and ever so helpful.

Contact

- Address: 165 avenue Massey, Moncton, Nouveau Brunswick E1A 3E9
- Phone: (506) 858-4000
- Fax: (506) 858-4379
- Web site: www.umoncton.ca
- E-mail: registrariat@umoncton.ca

Admissions

- Total population: 5,608 (full time: 4,397; part time: 1,211)
- Tuition in-province: $3,245

- Tuition out-of-province: $3,245 (same as in-province)

- Tuition international students: $5,555

- 2001/2002 application deadline: June 1

- Application fee: $30

- Average cost of residence: $4,600

Key details

Any applicant with an 85 percent average or over in grade 11 and the first term of grade 12 is guaranteed a $1,000 entrance scholarship, and up to $2,000 may be available for those with higher marks. For those students applying from colleges, the school calculates the average based on the last two years of study. The different campuses administer their scholarships separately, and Edmundston and Shippagan also offer entrance scholarships to students with averages of 80 to 85 percent. In addition, Moncton offers one excellence scholarship to every francophone high school in the Atlantic provinces (31 in all) at $3,000 renewable for four to five years. Students need not apply for these scholarships, as they will be automatically considered with application to the university.

Students do have to apply for extracurricular scholarships ($1,000 each) and bursaries (up to $2,000). For each, applicants must send a résumé and a recommendation letter from their high school counsellor. Bursary applicants must also establish their financial need.

Université de Montréal

The largest university in Québec whose primary language of instruction and administration is French, the Université de Montréal is a wide multidisciplinary school serving the post-secondary education needs of the metropolitan area of Montréal, the largest city in the province of Québec. The university has an unusually large number of affiliated colleges throughout the province, including Abitibi-Témiscamingue, Ahuntsic, André-Grasset, Beauce-Appalaches, Bois-de-Boulogne, Chibougamau, Chicoutimi, Drummondville, Édouard-Montpetit, François-Xavier-Garneau, Jean-de-Brébeuf, Jonquière, Laflèche, Lionel-Groulx, Maisonneuve, Marie de France, Marie-Victorin, Outaouais, Petit Séminaire de Québec, Rimouski, Rivière du Loup, Rosemont, Saint-Félicien, Saint-Hyacinthe, Saint-Jean-sur-Richelieu, Saint-Jérôme, Sainte-Foy, Sherbrooke, Stanislas, Trois-Rivières, Valleyfield, Vanier, and Vieux-Montréal.

Contact

- Address: CP 6128 succ Centre ville, Montréal, Québec H3C 3J7

- Phone: (514) 343-6111

- Toll-free: (877) 620-4777

- Fax: (514) 343-2098

- Web site: www.umontreal.ca

- E-mail: fraisscol@fin.umontreal.ca

Admissions

- Total population: 45,978 (full time: 30,139; part time: 15,839)

- Tuition in-province: $1,668

- Tuition out-of-province: $3,708

- Tuition international students: $8,268

- 2001/2002 application deadline: March 1

- Average cost of residence: $6,000

Key details

Like many universities across Canada, the Université de Montréal has a tiered entrance scholarship system based on final year high school (out-of-province) or CEGEP (in-province) marks. Unlike other universities across Canada, all Québec-based universities have higher tuition fees for out-of-province students.

Mount Allison University

Mount Allison is a fascinating enclave tucked away in the university town of Sackville — there are as many Mount A. students in the town as there are town residents not attending university. With high academic standards and a flourishing arts community, this is a place for people who want to go away and be intellectual. Cutbacks have, well, cut back the number of courses taught at Mount Allison, so students should figure out their entire university career when choosing their courses for first year — otherwise, they may get to fourth year and not be able to complete their program unless they stay on longer. The vast majority of first-year students live in residence, the social centre of campus life.

Contact

- Address: 65 York Street, Sackville, New Brunswick E4L 1E4
- Phone: (506) 364-2269
- Fax: (506) 364-2216
- Web site: www.mta.ca
- E-mail: admissions@mta.ca

Admissions

- Total population: 3,000 (full time: 2,250; part time: 750)
- Tuition in-province: $4,390
- Tuition out-of-province: $4,390 (same as in-province)
- Tuition international students: $8,780
- 2001/2002 application deadline: April 1
- Application fee: $40
- Average cost of residence: $5,850

Key details

Scholarships range from $500 to approximately $5,000 fully renewable for four years. Most Mount Allison scholarships are renewable at varying rates, and are based on academic standing or a combination of academic standing and financial need. Students who have an admissions average of 90 percent or above are guaranteed a minimum $1,000 award.

Mount Saint Vincent University

A women's university until men were finally allowed to apply in the 1970s, males make up only about 15 percent of the student body. There's a nunnery on the grounds but the Sisters of Charity — the order that founded the institution — doesn't get involved in day-to-day activities anymore. In fact, with the majority of students being mature, there are fewer than normal student activities at the Mount at all. The university is located outside the downtown core in a less-than-trendy area, but the hill (hardly a mountain) does offer a pretty view across the bridge. The traditional courses and programs are offered at the university, but the Mount specializes in unique programs such as tourism, hospitality management, and public relations.

Contact

- ✔ Address: 166 Bedford Hwy, Suite 1, Halifax, Nova Scotia B3M 2J6

- ✔ Phone: (902) 457-6788

- ✔ Fax: (902) 457-6455

- ✔ Web site: www.msvu.ca

- ✔ E-mail: admissions@msvu.ca

Admissions

- ✔ Total population: 3,992 (full time: 2,156; part time: 1,836)

- ✔ Tuition in-province: $4,110

- ✔ Tuition out-of-province: $4,110 (same as in-province)

- ✔ Tuition international students: $7,110

- ✔ 2001/2002 application deadline: August 17

- ✔ Application fee: $30

- ✔ Average cost of residence: $5,000

Key details

Despite its relative small size, there are a wide variety of entrance and in-course scholarships available from Mount Saint Vincent (we lost track at 70!). Entrance awards are made to students entering Mount Saint Vincent directly from high school, except where specifically noted otherwise. Students entering from high school do not require a separate scholarship application form, but may want to include a résumé of experience or letter of explanation to further indicate

their suitability. Entrance awards are made for one year only and are not automatically renewable. Students are evaluated annually and scholarship decisions are made according to their most recent academic results.

High school entrants with a minimum 80 percent average and high ranking within their class will be considered. The Committee on Admissions and Scholarships may request additional information from students or from high school counsellors before making an award. Only students applying for admission prior to March 15 will be considered for entrance awards, which are offered in May.

University of New Brunswick

When Anne of Green Gables went "off-Island" to study, she went to King's College — the venerable institution that started life as the College of New Brunswick back in 1785 and later became the University of New Brunswick. Today, the university offers a wide range of courses for a diverse and international student body. Student politics are reputedly rather right wing, but no one will notice if you choose not to get involved.

Contact

- ✔ Address: PO Box 4400, Station A, Fredericton, New Brunswick E3B 5A3

- ✔ Phone: (506) 453-4666

- ✔ Fax: (506) 453-4599

- ✔ Web site: www.unb.ca

- ✔ E-mail: unbfacts@unb.ca

Admissions

- Total population: 11,274 (full time: 9,386; part time: 1,888)

- Tuition in-province: $3,635

- Tuition out-of-province: $3,635 (same as in-province)

- Tuition international students: $6,435

- 2001/2002 application deadline: March 31

- Application fee: $35

- Average cost of residence: $5,000

Key details

Students must have been accepted for admission before applying (yes, you have to *apply*) for an entrance scholarship, and you must have at least an 80 percent average. Any student with a scholarship admission average of 95 percent or higher will now be considered for a renewable scholarship worth up to $20,000 ($5,000 per year for four years). This new scholarship replaces the President's Leadership Awards, which were not renewable.

Nipissing University

A small university located in the heart of northern Ontario, Nipissing University caters mainly to local students who want a good-quality education and are unwilling (or unable) to move to the big city to get one. Nip U is best known for its excellent program in education, although it offers a number of other programs in arts and sciences. Located in North Bay, it may not be as exciting as universities in some of the big cities, but the place is populous enough to provide a certain amount of activity. Besides,

Nipissing University has all the benefits of a small university — small class size, school spirit, and close relations with professors and other students.

Contact

- Address: Box 5002, Stn Main, North Bay, Ontario P1B 8L7

- Phone: (705) 474-3450

- Fax: (705) 474-1947

- Web site: www.unipissing.ca

- E-mail: nipureg@unippissing.ca

Admissions

- Total population: 3,398 (full time: 1,832; part time: 1,566)

- Tuition in-province: $3,800

- Tuition out-of-province: $3,800 (same as in-province)

- Tuition international students: $6,500 (including a $630 fee for incidentals)

- 2001/2002 application deadline: Standard OUAC application deadline

- Application fee: Standard OUAC fee payable

- Average cost of residence: $5,500

Key details

All students will automatically be considered for the $12,000 President's Scholarships and the $500 to $2,000 Carl Sanders Scholarships — it's not necessary to apply. A student may not receive both scholarships in the same academic year; however, there are many other forms of financial aid available. Out-of-province applicants are also eligible for these scholarships based on OAC/final year equivalent marks.

University of Northern British Columbia

UNBC is the little university that tries harder. Opened in 1994, it's the youngest of the universities in our directory. Prince George is a rather isolated location, which is perhaps why most students are from northern BC and Alberta — they are already accustomed to the way of life. As befits its location (and its endowment sources), the curriculum is best known for its programs in forestry, natural resources, and northern studies. Hands-on learning is offered in the form of a wide variety of co-op programs and practicums. The scenery is spectacular and there's good skiing nearby, but there's very little to do in terms of culture and nightlife in Prince George.

Contact

- Address: 3333 University Way, Prince George, British Columbia V2N 4Z9
- Phone: (250) 960-5555
- Toll-free: (888) 419-5588
- Fax: (250) 960-5791
- Web site: www.unbc.ca
- E-mail: registrar-info@unbc.ca

Admissions

- Total population: 3,394 (full time: 2,217; part time: 1,177)
- Tuition in-province: $2,258
- Tuition out-of-province: $2,258 (same as in-province)
- Tuition international students: $5,079
- 2001/2002 application deadline: July 16
- Application fee: $10
- Average cost of residence: $4,000

Key details

UNBC gives a number of awards aimed specifically at those students who are just leaving high school and attending a post-secondary institution for the first time. These include awards such as the President's Scholarships ($5,000, renewable at $3,000 per annum for up to three years); Raven Scholarships ($3,700); UNBC Achievement Awards ($1,500); and the UNBC Scholars (full tuition fees, renewable to a maximum of 120 credit hours). Most scholarships are based on academic excellence, but some use a community or student leadership component to assist the awards committee. In most cases, students have to specifically apply for scholarships, although UNBC does automatically put forward students for other awards. Forms are available from the school or your high school counsellor.

University of Ottawa / Université d'Ottawa

While the university is fully bilingual, you can get along quite well if you speak only one of Canada's official languages. Located in the nation's capital, it draws a lot of international students, so you are likely to hear anything from Urdu to Spanish to Mandarin on campus. Attempting to rid itself of its unfortunate nickname, "U of Zero," the U of O has been quietly building its academic credentials over the past decade. The result is higher overall standards and, in particular, excellent programs in political science (go figure!), criminology, and certain graduate programs. There is a fair bit of interaction between U of O and Carleton, and students often take transferable credits at the other university when one specific course might not be available at their own.

Contact

- Address: PO Box 450 Stn A / CP 450 succ A, Ottawa, Ontario K1N 6N5
- Phone: (613) 562-5800
- Toll-free: (877) 221-2637 (lots of options, but we've never been able to connect with a real, live person)
- Fax: (613) 562-5323
- Web site: www.uottawa.ca
- E-mail: infoserv@uottawa.ca

Admissions

- Total population: 24,477 (full time: 17,891; part time: 6,586)
- Tuition in-province: $3,892
- Tuition out-of-province: $3,892 (same as in-province)
- Tuition international students: $5,000
- 2001/2002 application deadline: Standard OUAC application deadline
- Application fee: Standard OUAC fee payable
- Average cost of residence: $5,500

Key details

Lots of entrance scholarships are available, and students are considered in various ranges depending on their high school average. A student with an overall average of 95 to 100 percent will typically be awarded a $3,500 scholarship. Students with overall averages ranging from 88 percent to 94.9 percent receive

$2,500. If you've managed an average of 84 percent to 87.9 percent, you can expect a $2,000 award. Students with averages of 82 percent to 83.9 percent get $1,000; while an overall average of 80 percent to 81.9 percent will yield $500 in scholarship money.

University of Prince Edward Island

"It's a great small university!" its admissions staff told us enthusiastically. As you would imagine in a small, intimate locale, professors get to know your name and are willing to chat, hang out, and even play sports with you. Don't try to call yourself an Islander unless your family has been there for at least three generations, but locals are among the warmest and gentlest Canadians you are likely to meet. That's a good thing, as about 20 percent of the student population comes from "away" — meaning off-Island. While UPEI covers all the undergraduate basics, it is best known for its programs in veterinary medicine, biology, and other health-related fields. Charlottetown is not terribly exciting, but the whole island is wonderfully picturesque.

Contact

- Address: 550 University Avenue, Charlottetown, Prince Edward Island C1A 4P3
- Phone: (902) 566-0439
- Toll-free: (800) 606-UPEI (8734)
- Fax: (902) 566-0420
- Web site: www.upei.ca
- E-mail: liaison@upei.ca

Admissions

- ✔ Total population: 3,107 (full time: 2,609; part time: 498)

- ✔ Tuition in-province: $3,480

- ✔ Tuition out-of-province: $3,480 (same as in-province)

- ✔ Tuition international students: $6,880

- ✔ 2001/2002 application deadline: August 13

- ✔ Application fee: $35

- ✔ Average cost of residence: $6,000

Key details

UPEI scholarships are awarded on the basis of the high school record, extracurricular activities, and in some cases, an interview. Most scholarships are for first-year entrance only. Some of the scholarships are renewable on the condition that scholarship holders maintain a satisfactory standard of work, which means obtaining an average of at least 75 percent on the combined work of the first and second semesters in the first year, and 80 percent in the remaining years, providing the student carries a minimum of 30 semester hours of credit or 10 credits, to a maximum of 40 credits.

Université du Québec

One of two French-speaking universities in Québec (the other being the Université Laval), this large university has campuses in Montréal, Trois-Rivières, Chicoutimi, Rimouski , Hull, and Abitibi-Témiscamingue. It also runs a distance learning program called Télé-université.

Université du Québec is located close to historical Old Québec, the only walled city left in North America. Québec is so beautiful, it was declared a UNESCO World Heritage site in 1985. Université du Québec's primary language of instruction and administration is French.

Contact

- ✔ Address: 475, rue de l'Église, Québec, Québec G1K 9H7

- ✔ Phone: (418) 657-3551

- ✔ Toll-free: (800) 567-1283

- ✔ Fax: (418) 657-2132

- ✔ Web site: www.uquebec.ca

- ✔ E-mail: registraire@uqah.uquebec.ca

Admissions

- ✔ Total population: 6,000 on the main campus

- ✔ Tuition in-province: $1,668

- ✔ Tuition out-of-province: $3,708

- ✔ Tuition international students: $9,168

- ✔ 2001/2002 application deadline: March 1

- ✔ Application fee: $30

- ✔ Average cost of residence: $325 per month per person. Students live in three- or four-bedroom apartments and cook their own meals.

Key details

Like many universities across Canada, the Université du Québec has a tiered entrance scholarship system based on final-year high school (out of province) or CEGEP (in-province) marks. Unlike other universities across Canada, all Québec-based universities have higher tuition fees for out-of-province students.

Queen's University

Queen's is one of the best-reputed universities in Canada. This big university in a relatively small town has plenty of school spirit. Entrance standards are extremely high — some programs accept only applicants with 90 percent or higher. The university offers all the traditional undergraduate courses, but is best known for commerce and engineering. Most students live in residence first year and then move to the well-established student ghetto for the rest of their university career. It's known for its parties, but for other cultural activities many students take a weekend off in Montréal, Ottawa, or Toronto.

Contact

✔ Address: 99 University Avenue, Kingston, Ontario K7L 3N6

✔ Phone: (613) 533-2000

✔ Fax: (613) 533-6300

✔ Web site: www.queensu.ca

✔ E-mail: admissn@post.queensu.ca

Admissions

✔ Total population: 16,001 (full time: 14,013; part time: 1,988)

✔ Tuition in-province: $4,030

✔ Tuition out-of-province: $4,030 (same as in-province)

✔ Tuition international students: $11,220

✔ 2001/2002 application deadline: Standard OUAC application deadline

✔ Application fee: Standard OUAC fee payable

✔ Average cost of residence: Set annually depending on the local rental market. Being a university town, Queen's uses this and other policies to integrate itself into the neighbourhood.

Key details

There are a number of entrance scholarships that will interest students. For example, the Marie Mottashed Entrance Scholarship (established by Marie Mottashed in 1941) awards funds on the basis of academic excellence to a female student entering the first year of a bachelor of science (honours) program. Two scholarships are available every academic year and the value of each award is $2,500. Another example is the 12 Nortel Networks National Entrance Scholarships. Established by Nortel Networks and Queen's University to recognize students entering the faculty of applied science and the faculty of arts and science who have superior academic ability and who have indicated an initial interest in pursuing studies in an eligible program. Ten scholarships of $5,000 each are available in applied science and two $4,000 awards are available in arts and science.

University of Regina

This mid-sized university in the middle of the Prairies in a province known for its level-headedness is pretty much as normal a university as you can find. It offers the traditional undergraduate programs with a few co-ops thrown in for good measure. There are some international students and there is some campus activity, but nothing out of the ordinary. It's simply a solid liberal arts and sciences university.

Contact

- ✔ Address: 3737 Wascana Parkway, Suite 100, Regina, Saskatchewan S4S 0A2

- ✔ Phone: (306) 585-4111

- ✔ Toll-free: (800) 588-4378

- ✔ Fax: (306) 585-5203

- ✔ Web site: www.uregina.ca

- ✔ E-mail: admissions.office @uregina.ca

Admissions

- ✔ Total population: 11,697 (full time: 8,424; part time: 3,273)

- ✔ Tuition in-province: $2,813

- ✔ Tuition out-of-province: $2,813 (same as in-province)

- ✔ Tuition international students: $4,831.

- ✔ 2001/2002 application deadline: July 31

- ✔ Application fee: $50

- ✔ Average cost of residence: $4,500

Key details

The University of Regina offers a number of specialized entrance scholarships such as the Cameco Corporation Northern Scholarship, awarded to local students who have "demonstrated career interest related to some aspect of the mining industry." Our favourite is the Casino Regina Scholarship, of which one is preferably awarded to a student of aboriginal ancestry who is enrolled in a program related to "recreational and leisure studies, business administration, hospitality management, electronic or computer technology and or communications." U Regina also offers sports scholarships based on basketball, rugby, and hockey performance, as well as various locally funded scholarships for local students. There are also industry-specific scholarships, such as the Husky Oil Educational Awards Program for Native People and the Petro-Canada Education Awards for Native Students.

Royal Military College of Canada

Kingston, Ontario-based RMC is a fully bilingual institution and Canada's only military university. A Royal Military College education consists of academics, military training, physical fitness, and second-language training (French or English, depending on your native language). As an officer cadet you will earn a salary while you study. Upon graduation you will embark on (at least) a five-year career in the Canadian Forces.

Although programs of study are somewhat restricted when compared to a traditional university, RMC students can follow programs in arts and humanities (such as English, history, or French), social science (politics and economics), military and strategic studies, and business administration.

You can also follow an honours science program in subjects such as chemistry, mathematics, and information science, or physics, space science, and general science. As you might imagine, RMC also places heavy emphasis on engineering, and several programs are available in the specialties of chemical and materials, civil, computer, electrical, and mechanical engineering.

Contact

- ✔ Address: PO Box 17000 Stn Forces, Kingston, ON K7K 7B4
- ✔ Phone: (613) 541-6000
- ✔ Fax: (613) 542-3565
- ✔ Web site: www.rmc.ca
- ✔ E-mail: registrar@rmc.ca

Admissions

- ✔ Total population: 1,500 (full time: 1,500; part time: 0)
- ✔ Tuition in-province: $0, provided you commit five, seven, or nine years of after-school service
- ✔ Tuition out-of-province: $0 (same as in-province)
- ✔ Tuition international students: Not applicable
- ✔ 2001/2001 application deadline: March 1
- ✔ Application fee: No fee
- ✔ Average cost of residence: No charge

Key details

Under the Regular Officer Training Plan (ROTP), the costs of tuition, uniform, books, instruments, and other essential fees are borne by the Department of National Defence; in addition, the officer cadet is paid a monthly salary. Medical and dental care are also provided.

Applications should be made as early as possible, and all forms should be submitted without necessarily waiting for the results of the first set of examinations in the final year of high school. It is strongly recommended that students apply to several universities in addition to their application to RMC so that they are not denied the opportunity of attending other schools in the event they are not selected for the Royal Military College.

Ryerson Polytechnic University

The expanding demand for qualified technical people in the workforce helped change Ryerson's reputation (Ry High) into one of the most in-demand institutions of higher education in the country. Best known for its programs in multimedia, journalism, hospitality, and fine arts, Ryerson offers a wide range of courses. Instruction focuses on hands-on learning, which is one reason why graduates are so likely to quickly land a job. Located in downtown Toronto, a lot of students are commuters, many are mature students, and part-time students just beat out full-time students in terms of numbers. As you might imagine, you won't find a lot of people cheering on the teams at sporting events.

Contact

- ✔ Address: 350 Victoria Street, Toronto, Ontario M5B 2K3
- ✔ Phone: (416) 979-5000
- ✔ Fax: (416) 979-5221
- ✔ Web site: www.ryerson.ca
- ✔ E-mail: inquire@ryerson.ca

Admissions

- ✔ Total population: 21,198 (full time: 10,373; part time: 10,825)
- ✔ Tuition in-province: $4,509
- ✔ Tuition out-of-province: $4,509 (same as in-province)

✔ Tuition international students: $12,234

✔ 2001/2002 application deadline: Standard OUAC application deadline

✔ Application fee: Standard OUAC fee payable

✔ Average cost of residence: $7,300

Key details

There are various entrance scholarships ranging from $500 to the full cost of tuition, but most scholarships are for later years. These are awarded for combined academic excellence and contribution to your field of study through internships or extracurricular activities. You are expected to be active in your chosen field when you attend Ryerson.

Université Sainte-Anne

A tiny university catering primarily to the large French Acadian population in the area, the Université Sainte-Anne is located in the small, picturesque town of Baie Sainte-Marie, Nova Scotia. This small university's language of instruction and administration is predominantly French, although other languages are heard at the school. Due to its small size, students and faculty know each other very well. The school's administration likes to say that at Université Sainte-Anne you get a private-school education for a public-school price!

Contact

✔ Address: Pointe-de-l'Église, Baie Sainte-Marie, Nouvelle-Écosse B0W 1M0

✔ Phone: (902) 769-2114

✔ Toll-free: (888) 338-8337

✔ Fax: (902) 769-2930

✔ Web site: www.ustanne.ednet.ns.ca

✔ E-mail: admission@ustanne.ednet.ca

Admissions

✔ Total population: 363 (full time: 318; part time: 45)

✔ Tuition in-province: $3,750

✔ Tuition out-of-province: $3,750 (same as in-province)

✔ Tuition international students: $5,901

✔ 2001/2002 application deadline: Rolling deadline, until fall

✔ Application fee: $30

✔ Average cost of residence: $2,600 (meal plan: $2,566 in standard rooms; optional for those students with kitchenettes)

Key details

Like many universities across Canada, the Université Sainte-Anne has a tiered entrance scholarship system based on final-year high school or CEGEP marks. The deadline for bursary and scholarship applications is March 25, and awards are based on all grade 11 and grade 12 marks (or grade 12 and OAC marks for Ontario students). In the 2001/2002 academic year, about 50 students (approximately 15 percent of all students) received a financial award. The average award was $1,000.

Saint Francis Xavier University

SaintFX is a small but vocal university, with an excellent reputation for its arts and sciences programs. A lot of politicians seem to come from the school, so if you love to debate you'll be in good company. Antigonish is gorgeous in the summer when no one is there, but there are a lot of cultural (read: Celtic) activities all year round. A large percentage of the student body comes from elsewhere, so most students in first year live in a raucous residence.

Contact

✔ Address: PO Box 5000 Stn Main, Antigonish, Nova Scotia B2G 2W5

✔ Phone: (902) 863-3300

✔ Toll-free: (877) 867- StFX (7839)

✔ Fax: (902) 867-5153

✔ Web site: www.stfx.ca

✔ E-mail: admit@stfx.ca

Admissions

✔ Total population: 4,502 (full time: 3,537; part time: 965)

✔ Tuition in-province: $4,300

✔ Tuition out-of-province: $4,300 (same as in-province)

✔ Tuition international students: $7,300

✔ 2001/2002 application deadline: March 1

✔ Application fee: $30

✔ Average cost of residence: $5,500

Key details

Entrance scholarships range in value from $1,000 to $5,000, and are, with few exceptions, for the first year of university study only. At the end of their first year, students with a high grade average and rank are considered for university *in-course* scholarships. No special application is needed for scholarships, with the exception of Philip W. Oland Scholarships and J.P. McCarthy Scholarships.

Saint Mary's University

Halifax has a lot of universities and each one has a distinct reputation. For Saint Mary's, it's sports. SMU is an easygoing university where students learn how to function in the real world instead of an ivory tower — and everyone enjoys a good football game. Considering this salt-of-the-earth attitude it's surprising (and welcome!) to see a lot of international students on campus. Best known for programs in business, Atlantic studies, and Irish studies, Saint Mary's is a solid undergraduate university with terrific spirit.

Contact

✔ Address: 923 Robie St., Halifax, Nova Scotia B3H 3C3

✔ Phone: (902) 420-5400

✔ Fax: (902) 420-5566

✔ Web site: www.stmarys.ca

✔ E-mail: admissions@stmarys.ca

Admissions

- Total population: 7,300 (full time: 5,300; part time: 2,000)
- Tuition in-province: $4,210
- Tuition out-of-province: $4,210 (same as in-province)
- Tuition international students: $9,531
- 2001/2002 application deadline: July 1
- Application fee: $35
- Average cost of residence: $5,700

Key details

All high school students who achieved an overall average of 80 percent or above as calculated by the university's admissions office will be eligible for an entrance scholarship ranging from $500 to $3,000. Entrance scholarships are non-renewable. Presidential scholarships are valued at $6,000 and are renewable for a total of $24,000 (over a four-year period of study). Students must be ranked number one or the first in their class to be considered and must provide a résumé along with a letter of recommendation from their school.

Saint Thomas University

Known for its focus on liberal arts, Saint Thomas is a small but serious university. Classes are small and everybody knows everybody else. Saint Thomas shares some facilities with the nearby University of New Brunswick, and there's the inevitable friendly rivalry between the two local universities. There's a high proportion of women on campus — about two-thirds. Getting into residence is fairly easy, with a variety of single-sex and coed options to choose from.

Contact

- Address: PO Box 4569, Station A, Fredericton, New Brunswick E3B 5G3
- Phone: (506) 452-0640
- Toll-free: (800) 367-9006
- Fax: (506) 450-9615
- Web site: www.stthomasu.ca
- E-mail: admissions@stthomasu.ca

Admissions

- Total population: 2,445 (full time: 2,213; part time: 232)
- Tuition in-province: $3,060
- Tuition out-of-province: $3,060 (same as in-province)
- Tuition international students: $6,120
- 2001/2002 application deadline: July 31
- Application fee: $30
- Average cost of residence: $4,770

Key details

Recognized as Eastern Canada's scholarship leader, Saint Thomas University devotes more of its operating budget to scholarships and bursaries than any other university in the region. The school annually commits in excess of $1 million in scholarships to entering students. In fact, one in every two first-year students wins an entrance scholarship, and one in every 11 holds a renewable award ranging in value from $2,000 to $37,000 over four years. Many other entering students hold non-renewable, annual scholarships valued from $500 to $3,000. More than 150 scholarships-in-course with values up to $4,000 per annum are awarded.

University of Saskatchewan

The University of Saskatchewan offers 58 degrees, diplomas, and certificates in over 100 areas and disciplines. Best known for agricultural and health-related studies, the University of Saskatchewan offers a wide array of courses and programs. Saskatchewan is the birthplace of the New Democratic Party and almost everyone has a political opinion, so it's no wonder that political science is also a specialty. The campus has a number of public facilities ranging from antiques, galleries, and agricultural farms to an observatory. As befits a cold Prairie institution, the U of S has an excellent tunnel and skywalk system, so students hardly need to go outside all winter.

Contact

✔ Address: 105 Administration Place, Saskatoon, Saskatchewan S7N 5A2

✔ Phone: (306) 966-4343

✔ Fax: (306) 966-8670

✔ Web site: www.usask.ca

✔ E-mail: admissions@usask.ca

Admissions

✔ Total population: 17,749 (full time: 14,842; part time: 2,907)

✔ Tuition in-province: $3,240

✔ Tuition out-of-province: $3,240 (same as in-province)

✔ Tuition international students: $8,000

✔ 2001/2002 application deadline: May 15

✔ Application fee: $50

✔ Average cost of residence: $4,400

Key details

There are a variety of entrance and other excellence scholarships as well as bursaries at the University of Saskatchewan. Top awards include the George and Marsha Ivany President's Scholarships (worth up to $17,000), the Louis Riel Scholarships (for Métis students), and the University of Saskatchewan Alumni Association Scholarships (open to anyone). Many scholarships are specific to a particular college (division of the university) or program and there are several scholarships and bursaries available to specific minority groups, so investigate all aspects of eligibility with a financial aid officer. As a general rule, any student may be granted only one award administered by the university. Students must apply for entrance scholarships by February 15 to be eligible for consideration.

Université de Sherbrooke

Best known for its engineering, business, and medicine degrees, Sherbrooke has a wide variety of programs, most of which are offered as co-ops. There's a stunning view of the nearby mountains and lakes from the university's mountain peak, and students can take a break for some excellent skiing. Most students live in the student ghettos in town, but about 1,000 can be found in residence. The students come from all over Québec and the other provinces as well as Europe and more distant locales. Everything is available on this campus, which is a city within a city. Generally, all your classes will be in the same complex. You don't get classes in huge lecture halls — generally there are between 30 and 60 students per class in first year and fewer as the years progress. Sherbrooke's medicine program has been named the best in Canada for two years running, and you can apply to get in after only one year of university. Admissions staff are particularly helpful and enthusiastic, even if you don't speak French.

Contact

✔ Address: 2500 boul de l'Université, Sherbrooke, Québec J1K 2R1

✔ Phone: (819) 821-7000

✔ Toll-free: (800) 267-8337

✔ Fax: (819) 821-6900

✔ Web site: www.usherb.ca

✔ E-mail: information@courrier. usherb.ca

Admissions

✔ Total population: 15,821 (full time: 9,941; part time: 5,880)

✔ Tuition in-province: $1,708

✔ Tuition out-of-province: $3,690

✔ Tuition international students: $8,567

✔ 2001/2002 application deadline: March 1

✔ Application fee: $30

✔ Average cost of residence: $3,040

Key details

About 170 entrance scholarships are available, 150 of which are for $1,000. There are five scholarships of $2,000 each, three scholarships of $5,000 each, and two $10,000 scholarships. All are awarded strictly on the basis of academic excellence. These are not renewable; you can apply separately every year for further scholarships. About 200 to 250 are available for later years.

The FORCE student foundation offers bursaries for students in need. From an endowment of about $1 million it provides students with awards of $500 to $2,000.

Simon Fraser University

SFU is considered a commuter university because there are very few residence spaces available. However, you will find a diverse mix of students on campus, including many from out of province. Burnaby is a suburb of Vancouver, and the university sits atop Burnaby Mountain, with a stunning view of the Rockies and Vancouver harbour. Students can enjoy quick access to lots of activities — both indoor and outdoor.

Contact

✔ Address: 8888 University Drive, Burnaby, British Columbia V5A 1S6

✔ Phone: (604) 291-3111

✔ Fax: (604) 291-4969

✔ Web site: www.sfu.ca

✔ E-mail: undergraduate-admissions @sfu.ca

Admissions

✔ Total population: 18,620 (full time: 10,191; part time: 8,429)

✔ Tuition in-province: $2,310

✔ Tuition out-of-province: $2,310 (same as in-province)

✔ Tuition international students: $9,240

✔ 2001/2002 application deadline: April 30

✔ Application fee: $25; $65 for out-of-province students

✔ Average cost of residence: $5,500

Key details

Even before the recent relaxation of policy allowing Canadian universities to offer limited sports scholarships, SFU was offering them as a member of the American University Sports Association. Lots of other scholarships and awards are also available, so investigate with the bursar what might be available for you. Once you have received all of your disbursements from an entrance scholarship, or if you do not receive an entrance scholarship, you may qualify for an open undergraduate scholarship while studying at SFU as well.

University of Toronto

U of T is the biggest university in Canada, with a vastly diverse student body and courses in almost anything you can imagine. To make it feel more homey, the immense faculty of arts and sciences is broken into several "colleges" — each with a distinct environment, focus, and reputation. The downtown St. George campus is the largest, but the Erindale (Mississauga) and Scarborough campuses offer much the same range of courses — although each has its own specialties.

First-year classes at U of T are generally big (some are actually *immense*), but they get smaller and smaller as you specialize and get into higher levels. With an excellent international reputation, many of the top professors in Canada can be found at the U of T. Residence is guaranteed to all first-year students, but lots of students are commuters or live in nearby neighbourhoods.

Contact

✔ Address: 27 King's College Circle, Toronto, Ontario M5S 1A1

✔ Phone: (416) 978-2011

✔ Toll-free: (888) 550-8055

✔ Fax: (416) 978-8182

✔ Web site: www.utoronto.ca

✔ E-mail: info@utoronto.ca

Admissions

✔ Total population: 54,613 (full time: 41,166; part time: 13,447)

✔ Tuition in-province: $4,029

✔ Tuition out-of-province: $4,029 (same as in-province)

✔ Tuition international students: $9,000

✔ 2001/2002 application deadline: Standard OUAC application deadline

✔ Application fee: Standard OUAC fee payable

✔ Average cost of residence: $6,000

Key details

Not only is the University of Toronto Canada's largest university, it is located in the country's largest city. The U of T, through its colleges and faculties, offers approximately 2,400 admission scholarships and over 2,000 in-course scholarships every year. Competition is *very* intense at the University of Toronto, as it is arguably the top university in the country. Admission scholarships are awarded on the basis of academic standing in your final year of high school, performance in open competitions such as the University of Toronto's National Scholarship program, and academic standing in previous senior high school courses.

No application is required for the U of T admission scholarships. In-course scholarships are awarded to recognize students who excel in their university-level studies. Most do not require applications.

Trent University

If you want to get a degree in environmental studies in Canada, you go to Trent. This relatively small liberal-arts university gives students a lot of individual attention in a tolerant environment. As one person in the liaison office said, "we allow students complete freedom of thought." Affiliated with the Ontario Ministry of Natural Resources, Trent offers top-quality programs in environmental research, geography, cultural studies, anthropology, and more. Its unique water-quality centre induces lots of experts and professors from other universities to visit Trent. Graduate programs in such topics as watershed ecosystems are world-renowned. To top it off, the staff are very helpful.

Contact

- ✔ Address: PO Box 4800, Peterborough, Ontario K9J 7B8
- ✔ Phone: (705) 748-1011
- ✔ Toll-free: (888) 739-8885
- ✔ Fax: (705) 748-1246
- ✔ Web site: www.trentu.ca
- ✔ E-mail: registrar@trentu.ca

Admissions

- ✔ Total population: 5,129 (full time: 3,929; part time: 1,200)
- ✔ Tuition in-province: $4,827

- ✔ Tuition out-of-province: $4,827 (same as in-province)
- ✔ Tuition international students: $10,500
- ✔ 2001/2002 application deadline: Standard OUAC application deadline
- ✔ Application fee: Standard OUAC fee payable
- ✔ Average cost of residence: $5,530

Key details

Most Trent University scholarships are entrance scholarships for those with a minimum average of 80 percent. If you have 80 percent or better, you will automatically be considered for the entrance scholarships and information will be sent to you about the three larger scholarships available from Trent. All Trent University scholarships may be held in conjunction with scholarships awarded by outside agencies when the conditions of the latter permit. However, a university student may not receive funds from more than one major Trent University scholarship in an academic year. Holders of renewable scholarships must maintain a minimum average of 80 percent in a sequence of five full courses in order for their scholarship to be renewed. The university endeavours to provide all scholarship holders, including those from the Peterborough area, with places in residence if they wish them.

University of Victoria

Caryn fully admits having a bias toward her law school alma mater — but who better to tell you about a school than one of its students? UVic offers a friendly atmosphere in a lovely setting. Many students live on or near the many beaches in Victoria, and there is a lot of outdoor activity on the island. There's not a huge amount of entertainment considering this is a capital city, but that means there is more time to study. A relatively new university, it boasts an unusually high proportion of top-notch professors. Often this is because they have moved to the warm location (there's a golf tournament on Boxing Day!) and less competitive, more collegial environment to enjoy life more. Lucky students gain the advantage of being able to hang out with the professors who wrote the definitive textbooks in their field.

Contact

- Address: PO Box 1700 STN CSC, Victoria, British Columbia V8W 2Y2
- Phone: (250) 721-7211
- Fax: (250) 721-7212
- Web site: www.uvic.ca
- E-mail: srsad13@uvvm.uvic.ca

Admissions

- Total population: 16,996 (full time: 11,280; part time: 5,716)
- Tuition in-province: $2,265
- Tuition out-of-province: $2,265 (same as in-province)
- Tuition international students: $6,795
- 2001/2002 application deadline: February 28
- Application fee: $25; $65 for out-of-province applicants
- Average cost of residence: $4,600

Key details

Eligibility for entrance scholarships is determined based on grades in nine academic grade 11 and 12 courses, which must include English 12 and three additional approved academic grade 12 courses (or provincial equivalents for those students applying from provinces outside of British Columbia). There are ten renewable entrance scholarships at $3,500 per year over four years, 30 scholarships at $3,000 for one year, and 30 scholarships at $2,500 for one year.

University of Waterloo

Well known for its excellent computer co-op program, Waterloo also offers a wide variety of other programs with a modern attitude. Waterloo provides what is arguably the best co-op program in the country, and many students are offered jobs in their field before they have graduated. The students are a diverse and interesting mix — but, yes, there is a high percentage of the computer geek population at this school.

Contact

- Address: 200 University Avenue West, Waterloo, Ontario N2L 3G1
- Phone: (519) 885-1211
- Fax: (519) 884-8009
- Web site: www.uwaterloo.ca
- E-mail: registrar@uwaterloo.ca

Admissions

- Total population: 22,677 (full time: 18,031; part time: 4,646)
- Tuition in-province: $4,477

✔ Tuition out-of-province: $4,477 (same as in-province)

✔ Tuition international students: $13,628

✔ 2001/2002 application deadline: Standard OUAC application deadline

✔ Application fee: Standard OUAC fee payable

✔ Average cost of residence: $5,750

Key details

Close to 1,000 entrance bursaries, valued at approximately $500 to $3,000, are available for students entering first-year programs at the University of Waterloo, Renison College, and St. Jerome's University. Many of the awards are offered by companies that provide employment for students in the many co-op programs.

University of Western Ontario

There's a lot more than just sports, parties, and attitude at the University of Western Ontario, but these factors do have a huge impact on campus life. This is a big school with a lot of spirit. While best known for its business programs, you can be accepted into them only after first year. Those who don't get in continue in the other programs — of which there is a wide and diverse assortment.

Contact

✔ Address: 1151 Richmond Street, London, Ontario N6A 3K7

✔ Phone: (519) 661-2111

✔ Fax: (519) 661-3710

✔ Web site: www.uwo.ca

✔ E-mail: reg-records@julian.uwo.ca

Admissions

✔ Total population: 27,080 (full time: 22,914; part time: 4,166)

✔ Tuition in-province: $3,920

✔ Tuition out-of-province: $3,920 (same as in-province)

✔ Tuition international students: $9,000

✔ 2001/2002 application deadline: Standard OUAC application deadline

✔ Application fee: Standard OUAC fee payable

✔ Average cost of residence: $5,960

Key details

The University of Western Ontario's reputation of having well-heeled alumni shines through in the school's various scholarship programs. For example, each of Western's President's Entrance Scholarships is worth $6,000 per year for four years plus first-year room and board — and 11 were handed out last year. Fully 21 Faculty Entrance Scholarships (amounting to $4,000 per year for four years plus first-year room only) were also awarded. Lesser awards are quite common, as well. There were 88 four-year scholarships ($2,000 per year) awarded as well as 325 one-year scholarships (each amounting to $2,000 per student). There were 588 one-year scholarships in the amount of $1,000. Finally, 1,158 Western Scholarship Awards were distributed, each in the amount of $750. In addition, UWO handed out a total of 3,632 bursaries, for a total of $3,872,651.

Wilfrid Laurier University

Specializing in business courses, there are also a variety of programs in other topics where classes will be smaller and more intimate. The entire campus is pretty intimate, located on one square block. Residence is guaranteed to first-year students as long as you apply early, and most first-year students choose to live in one of the many residences on campus. Some of the facilities are set aside for business students, much to the chagrin of students in other programs. However, a spirited and collegial atmosphere reigns.

Contact

✔ Address: 75 University Avenue West, Waterloo, Ontario N2L 3C5

✔ Phone: (519) 884-1970

✔ Fax: (519) 886-9351

✔ Web site: www.wlu.ca

✔ E-mail: admissions@wlu.ca

Admissions

✔ Total population: 9,015 (full time: 6,982; part time: 2,033)

✔ Tuition in-province: $3,951

✔ Tuition out-of-province: $3,951 (same as in-province)

✔ Tuition international students: $8,840

✔ 2001/2002 application deadline: Standard OUAC application deadline

✔ Application fee: Standard OUAC fee payable

✔ Average cost of residence: $5,300

Key details

A variety of entrance scholarships are available, but a student may not hold more than one entrance scholarship. Laurier offers many performance-based entrance scholarships specifically to Brant County students but all other students, including international exchange students, may be eligible to receive a scholarship.

University of Windsor

The University of Windsor has worked hard to lose its reputation as "Last-Chance U" (there are a few universities that had to overcome that moniker) and entrance standards have risen steadily over the past decade. Located in a border town, right near the American city of Detroit, it offers co-ops with both Canadian and American companies. U of W has a diverse student body and a wide range of courses, specializing in business and health-related programs.

Contact

✔ Address: 401 Sunset Avenue, Windsor, Ontario N9B 3P4

✔ Phone: (519) 253-3000

✔ Fax: (519) 973-7050

✔ Web site: www.uwindsor.ca

✔ E-mail: liaison@uwindsor.ca

Admissions

✔ Total population: 12,649 (full time: 9,402; part time: 3,247)

✔ Tuition in-province: $4,116

✔ Tuition out-of-province: $4,116 (same as in-province)

✔ Tuition international students: $4,100 for students from countries that are members of NAFTA (North American Free Trade Agreement); $9,688 for students from non-NAFTA countries

✔ 2001/2002 application deadline: Standard OUAC application deadline

✔ Application fee: Standard OUAC fee payable

✔ Average cost of residence: $6,000

Key details

Awards range in value from $500 to $12,000, depending on the qualifications of the applicant. Major awards are renewable for up to three additional years, providing first-class standing is maintained. Lesser awards are of one year's duration.

University of Winnipeg

The other U of W is an easygoing place to study any of the traditional university programs. Best regarded for its science courses, there are a few co-op programs offered as well.

Contact

✔ Address: 515 Portage Avenue, Winnipeg, Manitoba R3B 2E9

✔ Phone: (204) 786-7811

✔ Toll-free: (888) 393-1830

✔ Fax: (204) 786-8983

✔ Web site: www.uwinnipeg.ca

✔ E-mail: adm@uwinnipeg.ca

Admissions

✔ Total population: 6,208 (full time: 4,237; part time: 1,971)

✔ Tuition in-province: $3,150

✔ Tuition out-of-province: $3,150 (same as in-province)

✔ Tuition international students: $6,380

✔ 2001/2002 application deadline: August 3

✔ Application fee: $35

✔ Average cost of residence: $3,500 (operated through a housing registry system, so meals are not included)

Key details

Financial support is available to University of Winnipeg students in many different forms, from scholarships and awards to loans and bursaries. For the 1999/2000 academic year, the university awarded more than $655,000 in entrance and undergraduate scholarships. In the 2000/2001 year, approximately 300 high school graduates received entrance scholarships to the university, ranging in value from $200 to $4,000.

There are many different types of awards, including the Alumni Entrance Scholarships (six to ten scholarships of $4,000 each available annually to graduates of Manitoba high schools); the Marsha P. Hanen Entrance Scholarship (one scholarship of $10,000 — $4,000 for Year 1 and renewable at $2,000 per year for up to three additional years); the Walter Leatherdale Entrance Scholarship (full tuition costs for 30 credit hours will be offered annually to an outstanding student from rural Manitoba, preferably from a farming community); and special entrance scholarships ($3,000 for the two students with the highest averages,

$2,250 for students with averages of 95 percent and higher, $1,750 for students with averages of 90 to 94 percent, $1,100 for students with averages of 86 to 89.9 percent, $800 for students with averages of 80 to 85.9 percent), and others.

York University

The huge Keele campus and relatively smaller bilingual Glendon campus combine to make one of the largest universities in Canada, third only to the University of Toronto and Université de Montréal. As befits a large, mostly commuter university, there is a vast diversity among the student body and not a lot of school spirit. Academic standards are high, and many universities have copied York's innovative teaching methods over the years — you'll find a fair bit of hands-on learning at this school.

Contact

- Address: 4700 Keele Street, North York, Ontario M3J 1P3

- Phone: (416) 736-2100 (if your call is long distance, you will be given priority)

- Fax: (416) 736-5700

- Web site: www.yorku.ca

- E-mail: info@yorku.ca

Admissions

- Total population: 36,347 (full time: 28,466; part time: 7,881)

- Tuition in-province: $3,951 ($4,440 with mandatory ancillary fees)

- Tuition out-of-province: $3,951 to $4,440 (same as in-province)

- Tuition international students: $10,381

- 2001/2002 application deadline: Standard OUAC application deadline

- Application fee: Standard OUAC fee payable

- Average cost of residence: $4,693

Key details

Like many large universities in Canada, York has a large number of scholarships and awards available for students. York's Awards of Distinction, for example, amount to $32,000 ($8,000 for four years), plus the cost of residence for first year (at least $4,000). These awards are based on the student's outstanding academic record and accomplishments in community service, leadership, the arts, or sports. The deadline for this award is mid-February of every year.

There are also 18 President's Scholarships amounting to $21,600 ($5,400 over four years). These are awarded to students who present the highest entrance average. No application is required. There are also eight Awards of Achievement ($16,000 — $4,000 over four years) for students with a minimum average of 85 percent who have made a contribution to school or community, are Canadian citizens or permanent residents, and can demonstrate achievement and financial need. There are other, privately donated entrance awards as well, each valued between $750 and $3,600.

Canadian Colleges and Technical Institutions

There are hundreds of colleges and institutes across Canada (and thousands in the United States and abroad). In this part of the directory, we list some of the very best ones in Canada. This list is by no means exhaustive — be sure to investigate your local options, especially for career colleges and skills-training institutes.

Just as we did for the universities, tuition rates listed are *averages,* as most college programs vary depending on the particular course of study. In colleges, they may vary even more widely.

Alberta College of Art and Design

This long-established college offers various degree and diploma programs running in length from two to four years.

Contact

- Address: 1407-14th Avenue NW, Calgary, Alberta T2N 4R3
- Phone: (403) 284-7678
- Toll-free: (800) 251-8290
- Fax: (403) 289-6682
- Web site: www.acad.ab.ca
- E-mail: admissions@acad.ab.ca

Key details

Tuition is approximately $3,500 per year, but books and supplies can easily cost $2,000 as well. Courses range from traditional painting to digital technologies to such artisan fields as ceramics and jewellery-making. Portfolios must be submitted along with application forms.

Algonquin College

Algonquin College, in the Ottawa Valley, offers a wide range of courses including business; commercial pilot and aviation management; computer programming; cooking; early childhood education; electronics engineering; forestry; general arts and science; gerontology; hospitality and tourism; motive power technician; nursing; office administration; palliative care; police and public safety; marketing; media and design; microcomputing; and more.

Contact

- Address: 1385 Woodroffe Avenue, Nepean, Ontario K2G 1V8
- Telephone: (613) 727-0002
- Toll-free: (800) 565-4723
- Fax: (613) 727-7632
- Web site: www.algonquinc.on.ca
- E-mail: registrar@algonquin college.com

Key details

Distance education is available for certain courses. Most tuition rates for full-time studies are about $1,800 per term for Canadian students and about $10,000 for international students.

Banff Centre for the Arts

Courses at the Banff Centre for the Arts focus on an all-encompassing definition of artistry and include aboriginal arts, music and sound, dance, media, and more.

Contact

- Address: Box 1020, Banff, Alberta T0L 0C0
- Phone: (403) 762-6180
- Toll-free: (800) 565-9989
- Fax: (403) 762-6345
- Web site: www.banffcentre.ab.ca
- E-mail: arts_info@banffcentre.ca

Key details

Programs at the Banff Centre run for a few days or a few months and costs are variable. A term program in music, for example, can cost anywhere from $600 to $3,400. A particular writing workshop requires a fee of $1,400 but returns a "commission" of $1,000 to $3,000 upon completion and submission of a particular work on time.

British Columbia Institute of Technology (BCIT)

BCIT offers a full range of learning opportunities in full-time and part-time studies through eight program areas, including business, construction, electrical, health, manufacturing, preparatory, processing, and transportation programs.

Contact

- Address: 3700 Willingdon Avenue, Burnaby, British Columbia V5G 3H2
- BCIT Directory: (604) 434-5734
- Admissions: (604) 432-8419
- Fax: (604) 430-1331
- Web site: www.bcit.ca
- E-mail: admissions@bcit.ca

Key details

The college also offers advanced training, distance, and online learning, and industry training. Tuition rates average from $2,000 to $10,000 for a full-time course load.

Canadian Film Centre

This institute focuses on practical, hands-on training with industry professionals in the fields of film, television, and new media.

Contact

- Address: 2489 Bayview Avenue, Toronto, Ontario M2L 1A8
- Phone: (416) 445-1446
- Fax: (416) 445-9481
- Web site: www.cdnfilmcentre.com

Key details

Workshops run for about four months and cost approximately $3,500, but these details may vary widely from course to course and program to program

Canadore College

The college in North Bay offers a wide variety of studies from business to hospitality to nursing, but is best known for its specialties in aviation-related studies and ecotourism.

Contact

- Address: 100 College Drive, PO Box 5001, North Bay, Ontario P1B 8K9
- Phone: (705) 474-7600
- Fax: (705) 495-2862
- Web site: www.canadorec.on.ca
- E-mail: info@canadorec.on.ca

Key details

Programs cost about $2,100 per year and are held in a regular classroom setting as well as in the field during practical training sessions.

Centennial College

Established in 1966, Centennial College is Ontario's first community college, primarily serving the Toronto communities of Scarborough and East York through four campuses and two satellite locations. Centennial has been the fastest-growing Ontario college during the past decade. The school offers, on a full- and part-time basis, more than 80 diploma and certificate programs in business, communication arts, community and consumer services, engineering technology, and health and transportation. Centennial's award-winning Bell Centre for Creative Communications is Canada's largest interactive multimedia training facility. Ashtonbee Campus is home to Centennial's School of Transportation — the largest automotive and aircraft technology training centre in Canada.

Contact

- Mailing address: PO Box 631, Station A, Scarborough, Ontario M1K 5E9
- Main Campus: 651 Warden Avenue, Scarborough, Ontario M1L 3Z5
- Phone: (416) 289-5000
- Fax: (416) 289-5352
- Web site: www.centennial college.ca
- E-mail: success@centennial college.ca

Key details

Tuition ranges widely at Centennial, depending on whether students wish to follow a single course (upward of $300) to a sophisticated program such as the school's digital animation program. A full year's tuition (including incidental fees) in one of the standard programs is about $2,000 for Canadian students and almost $10,000 for international students.

College of the North Atlantic

The largest skills and career college in the Atlantic provinces, the College of the North Atlantic offers its programs at several campuses around the province. The college has a wide variety of programs offering a combined class-based and hands-on training style.

Contact

- Address: PO Box 5400, Stephenville, Newfoundland A2N 2Z6
- Phone: (709) 643-7730
- Toll-free: (888) 982-2268 (within Newfoundland and Labrador); (709) 758-7037 (outside Newfoundland and Labrador)
- Fax: (709) 643-7734
- Web site: www.northatlantic.nf.ca
- E-mail: info@northatlantic.nf.ca

Key details

Tuition is quite low, at about $1,500 for Canadian students and $3,300 for international students.

Durham College

The local career college in Oshawa, Durham offers over 50 certificate and diploma programs focusing on real-world utility.

Contact

- Mailing address: PO Box 385, Oshawa, Ontario L1H 7L7
- Campus address: 2000 Simcoe Street North, Oshawa Ontario
- Phone: (905) 721-2000
- Fax: (905) 721-3113
- Web site: www.durhamc.on.ca
- E-mail: info@durhamc.ca

Key details

Through special programs, students can take full-time courses from Trent and York universities at Durham. Canadian students pay annual tuition of $2,165 for most programs, while international students pay $9,687.

Emily Carr Institute of Art and Design

This small and intimate school is located on the trendy island in the middle of Vancouver, home to artists and artisans and some really terrific views. It has a cutting-edge gallery where up and coming artists (traditional, photographic, and new media) display their pieces.

Contact

- Address: 1399 Johnston Street, Granville Island, Vancouver, British Columbia V6H 3R9
- Phone: (604) 844-3800
- Toll-free: (800) 832-7788
- Fax: (604) 844-3801
- Web site: www.eciad.bc.ca
- E-mail: admissions@eciad.bc.ca

Key details

Canadian students pay tuition of $2,587 for two semesters while international students pay tuition of $9,300.

George Brown College

One of the many general career colleges in Toronto, George Brown is well known for its hospitality and tourism program and exceptional cooking courses. It also offers programs in fashion, technology, general arts and sciences, business, graphics, performing arts, community services, health sciences, and languages.

Contact

- Address: PO Box 1015, Postal Station "B" Toronto, Ontario M5T 2T9
- Phone: (416) 415-2000
- Toll-free: (800) 265-2002
- Web site: www.gbrownc.on.ca
- E-mail: info@gbrownc.on.ca

Key details

Known as the City College, George Brown has several locations around the city. Courses may take a few weeks or a full year and programs may take a few years. Full-year tuition is an average of about $2,500.

Georgian College

Georgian offers a wide range of career studies at its many campuses in Barrie, Orillia, Owen Sound, Collingwood, Midland, Muskoka, Orangeville, and Parry Sound, covering the Ontario heartland.

Contact

- Address: One Georgian Drive, Barrie, Ontario L4M 3X9
- Phone: (705) 728-1951
- Fax: (705) 722-5123
- Web site: www.georgianc.on.ca
- E-mail: inquire@georgianc.on.ca

Key details

Tuition varies depending on your course choices; most individual courses run from $250 to $450.

Glenn Gould Professional School of the Royal Conservatory of Music

With only 200 students, this special part of the Royal Conservatory of Music is devoted to the genius of Glenn Gould and seeks to develop gifted students to become the new musical talent of our time. While many students focus on piano, all orchestra instruments plus voice and guitar are also offered.

Contact

- Address: 273 Bloor Street West, Toronto, Ontario M5S 1W2
- Phone: (416) 408-2824
- Toll-free: (800) 462-3815
- Fax: (416) 408-3096
- Web site: www.rcmusic.ca/ggps
- E-mail: professional_school@rcmusic.ca

Key details

The two-year programs cost $6,500 to $7,500 per year for Canadian students and $10,000 to $11,500 per year for international students.

Grant MacEwan College

This is a huge college with a wide variety of career and academic programs, ranging from digital arts to social work to massage therapy.

Contact

- Address: PO Box 1796, Edmonton, Alberta T5J 2P2
- Phone: (780) 497-5040
- Toll-free: (888) 497-4622
- Fax: (780) 497-4622
- Web site: www.gmcc.ab.ca
- E-mail: info@admin.gmcc.ab.ca

Key details

Tuition is approximately $1,400 a year for Canadian students and $10,000 for international students.

Langara College

This college offers a wide variety of courses and programs including some interesting offerings in ecology studies and aboriginal studies.

Contact

- Address: 100 West 49th Avenue, Vancouver, British Columbia V5Y 2Z6
- Phone: (604) 323-5511
- Fax: (604) 323-5555
- Web site: www.langara.bc.ca
- E-mail: geninfo@langara.bc.ca

Key details

Tuition is approximately $1,400 per year for Canadian students or $7,500 for international students.

The Michener Institute for Applied Health Sciences

This medical technical institute has an excellent reputation in its field, offering programs from acupuncture to vascular technology. The teaching methodology is combined classroom and hands-on learning, and an incredible 96 percent of graduates gain employment in their fields within three months of graduation.

Contact

- Address: 222 St. Patrick Street, Toronto, Ontario M5T 1V4
- Phone: (416) 596-3177
- Toll-free: (800) 387-9066
- Fax: (416) 596-3180
- Web site: www.michener.on.ca
- E-mail: info@michener.on.ca

Key details

Program fees vary widely, from $2,000 to over $9,000 a year for Canadian students, with international students paying $10,600 to $16,000 per year.

Mount Royal College

This long-established career college offers a wide variety of programs, from business to gerontology to freelance writing. The college also offers a respected series of programs at its Conservatory of Music.

Contact

- ✔ Address: 4825 Richard Road, Calgary, Alberta T3E 6K6
- ✔ Phone: (403) 240-6111
- ✔ Fax: (403) 240-5938
- ✔ Web site: www.mtroyal.ab.ca
- ✔ E-mail: admissions@mtroyal.ab.ca

Key details

Tuition averages about $3,600 for Canadian students and about $7,000 for international students.

Northern Alberta Institute of Technology (NAIT)

NAIT is well known as a leader in hands-on training of technological studies. The institute confers certificates, diplomas, and applied degrees in 195 programs including 32 apprenticeship offerings and 1,300 continuing education courses. Its areas of expertise are academic foundations and bridging; applied building science; applied media and information technology; business; electrical and electronics technology; health sciences; hospitality; mechanical and manufacturing technology; and resources and environmental management.

Contact

- ✔ Address: 11762–106 Street NW, Edmonton, Alberta T5G 3H1
- ✔ Phone: (780) 471-7400
- ✔ Toll-free: (800) 661-4077
- ✔ Fax: (780) 471-4077

- ✔ Web site: www.nait.ab.ca
- ✔ E-mail: registrar@nait.ab.ca

Key details

Diploma programs generally take two years and costs are about $1,600 to $3,000.

Ontario College of Art & Design (OCAD)

The only college that is part of the OUAC admissions process, OCAD is renowned for its cutting-edge art and design programs and its even more cutting-edge students. Admissions are mainly based on the results of a portfolio submission and classes are hands-on.

Contact

- ✔ Address: 100 McCaul Street, Toronto, Ontario M5T 1W1
- ✔ Phone: (416) 977-6000
- ✔ Fax: (416) 977-6006
- ✔ Web site: www.ocad.on.ca
- ✔ E-mail: jsage@ocad.on.ca

Key details

Standard fees and expenses are $4,293 for Canadian students and $11,100 for international students.

Red Deer College

This is the local career college for central Alberta, offering a variety of programs but best recognized for business, music and theatre, and kinesiology and sport studies.

Contact

- Address: PO Box 5005, Red Deer, Alberta T4N 4H5
- Phone: (403) 342-3148
- Toll-free: (888) 340-8940
- Fax: (403) 340-8940
- Web site: www.rdc.ab.ca
- E-mail: inquire@rdc.ab.ca

Key details

Diploma programs run for two years and cost about $2,500 to $4,000 for Canadian students. The college offers several university transfer programs and some degree-completion programs.

Royal Roads University

This relatively new university combines an eclectic mix of short-term programs (in management, peace and conflict studies, and organizational leadership), master's degrees, and two bachelor's degrees (in commerce and a new offering, environmental studies).

Contact

- Address: 2005 Sooke Road, Victoria, British Columbia V9B 5Y2
- Phone: (250) 391-2511
- Toll-free: (800) 788-8028
- Fax: (250) 391-2522
- Web site: www.royalroads.ca
- E-mail: rruregistrar@royalroads.ca

Key details

While Royal Roads can certainly call itself a "university," it does not have the broad scope of all the universities in our Directory of Universities so we have included it in this grouping instead. The bachelor's degrees can be done as "completers," so you must provide transcripts from universities or colleges where you studied the first two years of the degree so that you can complete it at Royal Roads in an accelerated manner. The school also offers distance education. Tuition for Canadians for the B.Comm. is $2,900; it's $2,500 for the B.Sc. in environmental studies, and double the fees for international students.

Seneca College

Seneca has an excellent reputation for its digital technology and media courses, but also offers a wide variety of other disciplines including business and office administration, golf course technology, fashion arts, and various types of engineering technician programs.

Contact

- Address: 1750 Finch Avenue East, Toronto, Ontario M2J 2X5
- Main telephone: (416) 491-5050
- General admission inquiries: (416) 493-4144
- Web site: www.senecac.on.ca
- E-mail: admissions@senecac.on.ca

Key details

Tuition fees are generally $1,718 per year for Canadian students, or $9,755 for international students (including the required insurance). Some programs, however, such as the hot and in-demand 3-D animation programs, can be many times the basic tuition price.

Sheridan College

Sheridan is the best-known Canadian college for digital technology and media. Students in its famous digital animation program (and several other programs) are typically recruited by top Canadian, American, and international companies well before they graduate. Sheridan also offers a variety of programs of study in business, community and liberal studies, computing and information management, and science and technology.

Contact

✔ Address: 1430 Trafalgar Road, Oakville, Ontario L6H 2L1

✔ Phone: (905) 845-9430

✔ Fax: (905) 815-4027

✔ Web site: www.sheridanc.on.ca

✔ E-mail: infosheridan@sheridanc. on.ca

Key details

Basic tuition costs $1,720 for Canadian students and $9,000 for international students, but some of the special programs may be much more — $7,000 for the animation program and topping the list at nearly $17,000 for the information technologies professional internship. Portfolios are required when applying to any of the design courses.

Southern Alberta Institute of Technology (SAIT)

This school is aiming with an aggressive attitude to be Canada's premier technical institute by 2010. It offers programs in business and tourism; construction; energy; health and public safety; information and communications technologies; manufacturing and automation; and transportation.

Contact

✔ Address: 1301–16th Avenue NW, Calgary, Alberta T2M 0L4

✔ Phone: (403) 284-7062

✔ Toll-free: (877) 284-SAIT (7248)

✔ Fax: (403) 284-7112

✔ Web site: www.sait.ab.ca

✔ E-mail: registrar@sait.ab.ca

Key details

There are courses taught at SAIT that are hard to find elsewhere, such as applied petroleum engineering technology. The fee schedule is all over the map, so you'll have to ask about your particular program.

University College of the Cariboo

Set in a lovely location in the Rockies, Cariboo offers a wide variety of general college courses but is best known for specialties such as the degree program in natural resource science and diplomas in adventure travel guiding, animal health, and respiratory therapy.

Contact

- ✔ Address: 900 McGill Road, PO Box 3010 Stn Terminal MPP, Kamloops, British Columbia V2C 5N3
- ✔ Phone: (250) 828-5000
- ✔ Fax: (250) 371-5960
- ✔ Web site: www.cariboo.bc.ca
- ✔ E-mail: admissions@cariboo.bc.ca

Key details

Tuition runs approximately $1,300 per year but varies depending on whether you are taking the upper- or lower-level courses.

Vancouver Film School

This small and selective college is well known in the new-media world. It offers programs in film, acting, writing, 2-D animation, 3-D animation, and new media, with frequent visits from industry insiders.

Contact

- ✔ Address: 420 Homer Street, Vancouver, British Columbia V6B 2V5
- ✔ Phone: (604) 685-5808
- ✔ Toll-free: (800) 661-4101
- ✔ Fax: (604) 685-6389
- ✔ Web site: www.multimedia.edu
- ✔ E-mail: registrar@vfs.com

Key details

Tuition rates vary by program. The film program, for example, costs $18,725 for a 40-week regular program, and $23,250 for a 48-week diploma program.

Appendix B

Money Sources

• •

*T*his appendix contains a wealth of financial information (yes, the pun is fully intended) to help you pay for your post-secondary education. We include information about and URLs for government programs and loans, bank loans, and scholarships, as well as foundations and granting councils.

Government Programs and Loans

In addition to its federal student loan program (Canada Student Loans), the Canadian government has several programs to encourage students and their parents to save ahead of time for university. We also list information about provincial and territorial student loan programs.

CanLearn: You'll find some terrific information and tools to help you plan the financial aspects of getting a post-secondary education. Included are publications such as "The Debt-Free Guide" and "Long-Term Planner." Tools include the "Student Financial Planner," which has a cost calculator and resource estimator; and the "Debt Management Planner," which includes a loan repayment scheduler. Web site: www.canlearn.ca.

Registered Education Savings Plans (RESPs): These plans allow you to save money for the benefit of a child's education without having to pay taxes on the interest and investment income. They are administered by the Canada Customs and Revenue Agency. Web site: www.ccra-adrc.gc.ca.

The Canada Education Savings Grant program (CESG): These grants are given as an incentive for people to set up RESPs. Free money is paid into the RESP account as a percentage of contributions annually up to a lifetime maximum of $7,200. The program is administered by Human Resources Development Canada. Toll free: (888) 276-3624; Web site: www.hrdc-drhc. gc.ca/cesg.

Canada Student Loans Program: Address: National Student Loans Service Centre, Public Educational Institutions Division, PO Box 4030, Mississauga, Ontario, L5A 4M4; Toll free: (888) 815-4514 (within North America); (800) 225-2501 (outside North America; requires appropriate country code); (905) 306-2950 (if the two numbers above don't work, you can call this number *collect*); Web site: www.hrdc-drhc.gc.ca/student_loans.

If you want to know if you qualify for a Canada Student Loan and find out how much financial aid you can likely obtain, try the Student Need Assessment Software (SNAS) at the CanLearn/Canada Student Loans Web site: www.canlearn.ca/english/csl/hrdcsnas/snasen.shtml.

Provincial student loans programs: Québec, Nunavut, and the Northwest Territories operate their own student assistance plans separate from the Canada Student Loans program. Residents should contact the appropriate provincial or territorial student assistance office to find out about applying for financial assistance.

- **Newfoundland:** Student Financial Assistance, Department of Education; Web site: www.edu.gov.nf.ca/studentaid.
- **Prince Edward Island:** Student Aid Division, Department of Education; Web site: www2.gov.pe.ca/educ/resources/stu_aid/index.asp.
- **Nova Scotia:** Student Assistance Office, Department of Education; Web site: www.ednet.ns.ca/educ/student.
- **New Brunswick:** Student Financial Services, Department of Advanced Education and Labour; Web site: www.studentaid.gnb.ca.
- **Québec:** Direction générale de l'aide financière aux étudiants, Ministère de l'éducation; Web site: www.afe.gouv.qc.ca.
- **Ontario:** Student Affairs Branch, Ministry of Education and Training; Web site: http://osap.gov.on.ca.
- **Manitoba:** Manitoba Student Financial Assistance Program, Department of Education and Training; Web site: http://direct.gov.mb.ca.
- **Saskatchewan:** SaskNetWork Student Financial Assistance, Post-Secondary Education and Skills Training; Web site: www.sasknetwork.gov.sk.ca.
- **Alberta:** Alberta Learning Information Service, Advanced Education and Career Development; Web site: www.alis.gov.ab.ca/learning/FinancialAssistance.
- **British Columbia:** Student Services Branch, Advanced Education, Training and Technology; Web site: www.aett.gov.bc.ca/studentservices.
- **Yukon:** Student Financial Assistance Unit, Department of Education; Web site: www.yesnet.yk.ca/sites/sfa. **Note:** The Web site is currently under construction, so call: (867) 667-5929 or (800) 661-0408 local 5929, toll-free within Yukon

> ✔ **Northwest Territories:** Student Financial Assistance Program, Department
> of Education, Culture and Employment; Web site: www.nwtsfa.gov.nt.ca.
>
> ✔ **Nunavut:** Web site: www.gov.nu.ca/education.htm.

Group RESP Foundations

These are some of the better-known foundations, organizations, and trust
companies that offer group RESPs. Check them out at their Web sites,
listed here.

Canadian Scholarship Trust Foundation: Go to www.cstplan.com.

Children's Education Trust of Canada: Go to www.educationtrust.ca.

Heritage Scholarship Trust Foundation: Go to www.heritageresp.com.

Universitas Foundation of Canada: Go to www.universitas.qc.ca.

USC Education Savings Plans: Go to www.resp-usc.com.

Banks

Many of the large Canadian banks have established programs to help students
and their parents plan for the financial part of getting an education.

Bank of Canada: This organization has all sorts of resources to help you
understand inflation rates and investment. Check out the Web site, at
www.bankofcanada.ca, for the weekly, monthly, and annual Bank of Canada
Commodities Price Index (BCPI) and other indices, along with an inflation
calculator and an investment calculator to show you the effects of each
over time.

Canadian Bankers Association: The Canadian Bankers Association Web site
is at www.cba.ca. You can also check out the YourMoney Network, created to
provide a resource for young Canadians who wish to talk about financial
matters. Web site: www.yourmoney.cba.ca.

Bank of Montreal Brain Money: Go to www.bmo.com/BrainMoney.

CIBC SmartStart Parents: Go to www.cibc.com/smartstart/parent.

TD Student Budget Planner: Go to www.tdbank.ca/student/stbud.

Scotia Student Budgeting Tips: Go to www.scotiabank.com/cda/content.

Scholarships

You might want to check out these sites — for both locating scholarships you are eligible for and applying for them.

Student Awards: A free search engine that helps you find scholarships. Web site: `http://studentawards.com`.

National Aboriginal Achievement Foundation: Provides merit-based scholarships for First Nations people. Web site: `www.naaf.ca`.

Millennium Scholarships: Scholarships for students already attending university. Web site: `www.millenniumscholarships.ca/en/main`.

Foundations and Granting Councils

There are many more sources for scholarships and grants other than the universities themselves. These are just a few of them.

Canadian Foundation for Economic Education (CFEE): Go to `www.cfee.org`.

Natural Sciences and Engineering Research Council of Canada (NSERC): Go to `www.nserc.ca`.

Social Sciences Humanities Research Council of Canada (SSHRC): Go to `www.sshrc.ca`.

Canadian Institutes of Health Research (CIHR): Go to `www.cihr.ca`.

Appendix C

Useful Web Sites

• •

*W*e mention most of these Web sites at various points in the book. But save yourself the trouble of flipping back as you rack your brain trying to remember where, oh where, you saw the URL for the Association of Universities and Colleges of Canada, or the College Board. In this appendix, you'll find a selection of Web sites devoted to the many aspects of post-secondary education, all in one place. Just point, click, and go!

General Information

These sites cover the basics, but in a comprehensive way. They are a good place to start your search.

Association of Universities and Colleges of Canada (AUCC): The AUCC provides a considerable amount of information and statistics about universities, professors, students, and everything to do with university life. It also has links to all the universities across Canada. Check it out at www.aucc.ca.

Canadian Education on the Web: This *huge* portal site is run by the University of Toronto, but provides links to all universities and colleges across Canada, as well as over 100 educational organizations across the country (from the ABC Canada Literacy Foundation to the Youth Science Foundation Canada). Other links include education journals, libraries and boards of education, private schools, and various student and teacher organizations. Start your search at www.oise.utoronto.ca/~mpress/eduweb.html.

CanLearn: This site provides a wide variety of materials to help students plan ahead for post-secondary education. Go to www.canlearn.ca.

Council of Ontario Universities (COU): This organization administers the collective activities of the universities in Ontario and also provides statistics, documents, and other information about Canadian universities in general. Go to www.cou.on.ca.

SchoolNet: This federal government site connects Canada's public schools and libraries at every level. Go to www.schoolnet.ca.

Colleges

These Web sites are dedicated to colleges in Canada.

Association of Canadian Community Colleges: Go to www.accc.ca.

National Association of Career Colleges: Go to www.nacc.ca.

Ontario College Program Locator: Go to www.ocas.on.ca/locator/index.html.

Open-Admission Universities

As long as you have a high school diploma or the equivalent, these universities are open for business — and for you.

Athabasca University: Go to www.athabascau.ca.

British Columbia Open University: Go to www.ola.bc.ca.

Applications

These sites provide the forms and guidelines for applying to a university or college in Ontario and British Columbia. They also probably tell you some stuff you don't want to know, such as the minimum mark you need to get into that commerce program you have your eye on. Oh well. Keep studying!

Ontario College Application Service (OCAS): A one-stop shop for students headed for Ontario colleges. This site provides information and forms for the standardized college application in the province. Go to www.ocas.on.ca.

Ontario Universities' Application Centre (OUAC): The OUAC issues the standard application form for all Ontario universities. Applicants can apply online, but copies are sent each year to every Ontario high school — as well as to many schools outside the province. Go to www.ouac.on.ca.

Post-secondary Application Service of British Columbia (PASBC): British Columbia has something similar to Ontario in that you can apply to all BC universities, colleges, and technical institutes online. However, each university maintains a separate application form, and you must submit separate application fees for each university to which you apply. Go to www.pas.bc.ca.

First Nations Students

Check out these sites for programs and services for First Nations students.

The Department of Indian and Northern Affairs Canada: This site can help you figure out if you qualify as a Status Indian under the *Indian Act*. If so, you qualify for the Post-Secondary Student Support Program (PSSSP), which provides financial support for tuition, travel, and living expenses for First Nations people attending a post-secondary institution. Go to www.inac.gc.ca.

Financial information: There are a wide variety of scholarships and grants open only to First Nations students. You can find listings of these offerings in a downloadable document called, "Scholarships, Bursaries and Awards for Aboriginal Students." Go to www.ainc-inac.gc.ca/ps/ys/pdf/sbaas_e.pdf.

International Students

Turn to these informative sites if you are contemplating heading abroad — or coming to Canada — for the university experience.

College Board: The College Board administers the SAT I test, plus other tests. Go to www.collegeboard.org.

FastWeb: You can create a personalized student profile, which is then matched against FastWeb's database of over 4,000 American colleges and 600,000 scholarships, to let you see what schools and scholarships for which you qualify. It's a free service, but be warned: There's lots of advertising to help pay for everything you see. Still, it's pretty neat. Check it out at www.fastweb.com.

FinAid: Billing itself as "The SmartStudent Guide to Financial Aid," this Web site takes students headed for American colleges through the often-arcane process of finding scholarships and other financial aid. Go to http://finaid.org.

U.S. Department of Education Student Guide: A comprehensive guide for financial aid including information on grants, loans, and work-study programs. Go to www.ed.gov/prog_info/SFA/StudentGuide/.

U.K. Department for Education and Employment: This is the official portal site of the British educational and employment system, with some good links to other related organizations. Go to www.dfee.gov.uk.

Embassy Web: This site provides a list of links to embassies around the world. Go to www.embassyweb.com.

Immigration Canada: This site lists what is required to study in Canada if you are from another country. Go to www.cic.gc.ca.

English-Language Proficiency Tests

If English is not your first language, or you are not completely fluent in it, you need to show the universities that you are proficient enough to understand what the professor is saying in class, take proper notes, write your exams — in short, that you can earn a degree taught in English. Here are some organizations that administer English proficiency tests.

Certificate of Proficiency in English (COPE): Go to www.copetest.com.

International English Language Testing System (IELTS): Go to www.ielts.org.

Michigan English Language Assessment Battery (MELAB): Go to www.lsa.umich.edu/eli/melab.htm.

Test of English as a Foreign Language (TOEFL): Go to www.toefl.org.

Student Organizations

These are the sites to surf to if you're interested in getting involved in student activities — besides studying — on campus.

Canadian Alliance of Student Associations: Go to www.casa.ca.

Canadian Federation of Students: Go to www.cfs-fcee.ca.

F.E.U.Q. (Fédération étudiante universitaire du Québec): Go to www.feuq.qc.ca.

Appendix D

The Mull List

Questions to Ask Before Applying to a University

1. **Do I really want to go to university?**
   You may not. Or maybe you don't want to attend right away. Consider your reasons for attending university and make sure you are doing it because it is the best decision for you.

2. **Do I want to go to this university just because other people want me to go there?**
   Remember, it's you who will spend the three or four (or more!) years at this school. You should listen to what your parents, friends, counsellors, and others have to say — but ultimately, the choice of university has to be yours.

3. **Where is this university?**
   Do you like life in small towns or big cities? Or in the suburbs? Or way out in idyllic rural environments? There are Canadian universities in each of these settings. You have a choice.

4. **How large (or small) is this university?**
   Can you thrive on a giant campus with 50,000 (or more) students and lots of social and cultural opportunities? Or would you feel better at a smaller school where everyone knows everyone else?

5. **Do you want to leave home?**
   Do you look forward to university as a chance to cut your family ties and flee the nest? Or do you want to keep the security of your home and your family? Can you afford the added cost of living in residence or in an apartment off campus?

6. **How far away do you want to go?**
   If you plan to leave home, do you need to get home every weekend? Or can you tolerate returning home only for major holidays, reading week, and perhaps over the summer?

7. **Can you get in?**

   Do you have a reasonable shot at meeting this university's minimum academic criteria? Are your marks in the range that it considers acceptable? Are there any special circumstances that will give you a better chance at getting accepted?

8. **Does this university teach what you want to learn?**

   How strong are the courses in your field of study? What kind of vibes do you get from the professors who teach those courses? Go there and find out.

9. **Can you live with these people?**

   Does your personality mesh with the university's personality? Are the students the kind of people you'll be comfortable living with for four years (or longer)? Does the campus have your kind of social life? Check out the university in person to find out the real story.

10. **Can you live on campus?**

    Do all first-year students get a room in a residence? If not, what are your chances of getting one? Will you live in residence only if you can get a single room? How realistic is this expectation? And if you can't get into residence or get the kind of accommodations you need, what other living accommodations are available?

11. **How safe is this campus?**

    Do some research on campus crime statistics and campus security measures. When you visit the campus, talk with students and ask them how safe they feel. Large universities often have campus police; other schools have security guards. Ask about both minor crime (such as thefts) and major crime (such as sexual assaults) on campus.

12. **How large (or small) are the classes?**

    Are first-year students required to take large courses where a professor lectures from a stage and students are identified by number? Or are all classes small enough that teachers know students and you can get individual attention?

13. **Do professors teach?**

    In some first-year introductory courses, most of the teaching is done by graduate students not much older (or wiser) than you. Ask professors and students. See if they give you the same answer.

14. **What interesting programs are available?**

    Does the university have an exchange program with a university in another country allowing you the opportunity to study elsewhere for a while? Does the university operate a co-op program that can help you pay for university while attending — and provide you with valuable work experience by the time you graduate? Find out what makes this university unique.

15. **How much will you have to pay?**
    Start with the published sticker price and work it out from there. How much more will the final price be, factoring in residence, books, and other costs?

16. **Can you get financial aid?**
    Over half of the students in Canadian universities get a student loan and about two-thirds of all Canadian university students get some form of financial aid, including scholarships, bursaries, and grants. Do you qualify? How much financial aid can you reasonably expect?

17. **Are scholarships available?**
    Does this university give financial aid based on a student's academic ability? If so, how much is available and how high do your marks have to be to earn a scholarship? Are there other awards available based on special talent, ethnic origin, or other factors?

18. **Are you ready to borrow?**
    You'd probably take out a loan to buy a car or a house. Is a university degree just as important to you? If you're a typical student, you'll have to borrow to pay at least part of your bills. Are you ready?

19. **What kind of feel did you get?**
    Don't underestimate your gut reaction. If you feel uncomfortable on campus, if you hate the food in residence, if you find the students snobby — it's not going to get any better when you actually attend this university. Don't let the prestige of a university, its convenience, or the attitudes of other people override your better judgment. If a university is not for you, it's just not for you!

20. **Will you change your mind by the time you get to university?**
    Probably yes! You may be reading this book in grade 4, grade 9, or even grade 11, but your opinions will likely change by the time you submit your applications. Make a list of what's important to you in a university. This list will change over time as you grow and mature. You may have thought you didn't want to go away to school in grade 9, but by the time grade 12 rolls around and you look again at your list, you may be just *itching* to leave home. You may change your mind about other aspects of attending university, too. That's okay. Changing your mind shows that you're using it.

Glossary

As you search for a university and the money to pay for a university, you'll read and hear some words that people just assume you know. Maybe you do know them. Maybe you know them in other contexts, but not how they're used at university. So here's a list to help you understand the words you should know.

Anti-calendar: An annual publication, written and published by the students' union of some Canadian universities, which rates courses — and even specific sections of courses — giving the opinions of the students who took the course in the past year. In smaller schools, you have to look at individual course evaluations for this information.

Application fee: The money a university charges to consider your application. In Ontario, you can apply to three universities for $80, while universities outside Ontario charge anywhere from $10 to $65.

Borderline: An application that fulfills the minimum requirements for admission but is not quite good enough to get an immediate *yes*. University applications officials keep these borderline applications separate until they have weeded out all of the *no* and *yes* applications. If there are spaces still available, they turn to the borderline applications and rate them. Supplementary information can go a long way to pushing your application into the *yes* pile if your application starts off as borderline. At times in the book, we say that borderline applications are found in the *maybe* pile.

Bursaries: An endowment given to a student who demonstrates financial need. Sometimes the term is applied to scholarships and grants, but in this book we use it to refer to gifts of money to students in financial need. Financial aid offices in universities are sometimes still referred to as *bursar's offices*, and the people who run them as *bursars*.

Calendar: An official document published annually by a university, containing the descriptions of all the courses the university offers for that calendar year. Often, selected text from the calendar is put on a university's Web site, but this source is usually considered less official than the printed calendars. American colleges sometimes use the term *catalogue* (or *catalog*) to mean the same publication.

Certificate: An award signifying successful completion of a course of study at certain colleges and institutes.

Coed: Serving both sexes, as in, "I'm living in a *coed* residence." This term is used less frequently in its old, politically incorrect context to describe female students on a two-gender campus.

College: (1) In the United States, the generic word for *university*; (2) In Canada, a post-secondary school (a school you go to after high school) that offers diplomas or certificates in a given subject. Diplomas typically require a two-year study commitment, while certificates can be achieved in as little as a few weeks; (3) Also in Canada, the smaller units into which certain large faculties are divided.

Core courses: The courses that carry the most weight on a high school transcript. They are English, math, science, social studies, and foreign languages.

Degree: An award signifying successful completion of a course of study at university. A bachelor's degree takes three or four years, or sometimes even five years. Degrees that require four or five years of study are called *specialist* or *honours* degrees. *Master's* and *doctoral* degrees are earned after the bachelor's degree. *Professional* degrees may require a bachelor's degree first, or may simply require one, two, or three years of university prior to entry.

Diploma: An award signifying successful completion of a course of study at a Canadian college, or a "two-year college" in the United States.

Discipline: (1) A field of academic study, such as history, psychology, chemistry, or math; (2) An academic penalty imposed for violation of a university rule or regulation.

Double cohort: Ontario's class of 2003, which will include both the final OAC class (what used to be known as grade 13) and the grade 12 graduating class. This one-time event is expected to leave thousands of "extra" Ontario students competing for the same university places.

Environment: (1) A university's location, as in "We offer you an idyllic rural *environment*"; (2) The student body, as in "We pride ourselves on a diverse *environment*."

Faculty: (1) The division of your university discipline, such as the faculty of arts and sciences, the faculty of medicine, or the faculty of engineering; (2) The professors and instructors at a university. *Faculty* refers to the professors; *staff* refers to the administrative, technical, and other personnel that keep the university humming along.

Gap: (1) A clothing store; (2) The difference between your parents' expectations and your grade point average; (3) The difference between your financial *need* and your financial *aid*.

GMAT: Graduate Management Aptitude Test. Required by almost every graduate school of business in Canada, the United States, and some parts of Europe. It is a standardized exam that is designed to test your aptitude for management (i.e., M.B.A.) school.

GRE: Graduate Record Examination. The all-day exam you have to write to get into almost every graduate school. Your mark is considered along with your university marks, although other factors may also be considered, including a personal interview.

Incomplete: A university application that is missing information. If your application is incomplete, it could result in a long delay in processing — which may seriously damage your chances for admission, since other applicants will be snapping up the spots while your application sits in the incomplete pile.

Institute: A school where you learn a specific skill — including technical, clerical, or service-oriented skills such as bartending, hairdressing, or computer programming. Students obtain a certificate upon completion of a course, which can run anywhere from a few days to two years.

Institution: A university, college, or institute. Of course, it is also used to describe a prison and an insane asylum, but we're sure that's just a coincidence. The term is often used by a university to describe itself, as in, "This *institution* meets every student's financial need, until our money runs out."

Interdisciplinary: An academic major that takes courses from several subject areas, such as English, history, sociology, and math.

Legacy: (1) A student related to a graduate of the university (usually the student is a son or daughter). This term is typically used in connection with American colleges. (2) Also used in a similar connection with fraternities and sororities. If your father or mother were members of a fraternity or a sorority when they were going to university, odds are the organization will take you, too, as a *legacy*.

Liberal arts/liberal studies: Other names for a broad arts academic program at a university. (Note: It has *nothing* to do with the Canadian political party.)

Major: A university student's chosen field of study. It may change — sometimes several times — over the course of a university career.

Mature student: Anyone entering university who did not come directly from high school. Some universities consider a student mature if he is entering university at age 21 or older, while others place the cut-off mark at age 25. Most universities have slightly different entry requirements for mature students.

Merit: (1) An adjective identifying an excellent high school student, as in Merit Scholar; (2) The reason financial aid is awarded without regard to need, as in *merit money*.

Need: The difference between the cost of your university and the amount that a computer determines you are able to pay.

Need-based: Refers to money you get because of your need, as in, "These grants are 100 percent *need-based*."

Open-admission university: A university that accepts anyone with a high school diploma. This sort of university is generally operated virtually, with students required to submit all classwork over the Internet. In Canada, Athabasca University and British Columbia Open University are the best-known open universities.

Package: (1) Food (other than Kraft Dinner) from home; (2) The total financial aid you are offered from each university's financial aid office.

Post-graduate: Refers to courses taken after a bachelor's degree is earned.

Private university: A university that relies solely on tuition fees for its operational costs and intended profit. The newly announced private universities are being created specifically for the profit motive, but other private universities offer education with a particular slant — such as private religious degree-granting institutions.

Public university: A university that is operated and subsidized by the province where it's located. The costs associated with teaching are covered by both the provincial government and by tuition fees.

Residence: Also known as a "dorm," this is the university-operated housing facility where many students live while attending university.

RESP: Registered Education Savings Plan. A federal government initiative that allows people to shield some of their investment income from taxation as long as it remains in a fund that will be used for their child's (or someone else's child's) education.

SAT: Scholastic Aptitude Test. A three-hour test used in the United States to measure a student's potential for doing university (or college) work. The modern version is the SAT I, and there is also the SAT II, which measures a student's ability in specific subjects. SAT I test results are not usually considered (or requested) for admission to Canadian universities.

Scholarship: Money you get for being exceptional at school. The only catch is that this money must be put toward your university education.

Student loan: Money you get so that you can attend university. The only catch is that you have to pay it back after you stop attending university.

Term: A period during which courses are offered, as in "I'll wait to take zoology in the spring *term*."

TOEFL: Test of English as a Foreign Language. This test (there are others that go by different names) must be taken and passed by most people applying to an English-speaking Canadian university if English is not the applicant's first language and the applicant has not spent a few years studying at an English-speaking high school.

TOFFL: Test of French as a Foreign Language. The French version of the TOEFL.

Undergraduate: A student trying to get a bachelor's degree.

University: A post-secondary school (a school you go to after high school) that awards undergraduate and sometimes post-graduate degrees.

University Applications File: The file you should start in grade 9 to track your high school career, your ideas about university, and all the materials you will collect about universities prior to sending in your applications.

Yield: The percentage of accepted students who enrol at a university.

Index

• N •

• T •

Notes

Notes

Notes

Notes